Library of New Testament Studies

616

Formerly the Journal for the Study of the New Testament Supplement series

Editor
Chris Keith

Editorial Board
Dale C. Allison, John M.G. Barclay, Lynn H. Cohick, R. Alan Culpepper,
Craig A. Evans, Robert Fowler, Simon J. Gathercole, Juan Hernandez Jr.,
John S. Kloppenborg, Michael Labahn, Love L. Sechrest, Robert Wall,
Catrin H. Williams, Britanny Wilson

The Lord's Prayer and Sermon on the Mount in Matthew's Gospel

Charles Nathan Ridlehoover

LONDON • NEW YORK • OXFORD • NEW DELHI • SYDNEY

T&T CLARK
Bloomsbury Publishing Plc
50 Bedford Square, London, WC1B 3DP, UK
1385 Broadway, New York, NY 10018, USA
29 Earlsfort Terrace, Dublin 2, Ireland

BLOOMSBURY, T&T CLARK and the T&T Clark logo are trademarks of Bloomsbury Publishing Plc

First published in Great Britain 2020
Paperback edition first published 2021

Copyright © Charles Nathan Ridlehoover, 2020

Charles Nathan Ridlehoover has asserted his right under the Copyright, Designs and Patents Act, 1988, to be identified as Author of this work.

For legal purposes the Acknowledgements on p. vii constitute an extension of this copyright page.

All rights reserved. No part of this publication may be reproduced or transmitted in any form or by any means, electronic or mechanical, including photocopying, recording, or any information storage or retrieval system, without prior permission in writing from the publishers.

Bloomsbury Publishing Plc does not have any control over, or responsibility for, any third-party websites referred to or in this book. All internet addresses given in this book were correct at the time of going to press. The author and publisher regret any inconvenience caused if addresses have changed or sites have ceased to exist, but can accept no responsibility for any such changes.

A catalogue record for this book is available from the British Library.

A catalog record for this book is available from the Library of Congress.

ISBN: HB: 978-0-5676-9232-0
PB: 978-0-5677-0208-1
ePDF: 978-0-5676-9233-7
eBook: 978-0-5676-9235-1

Series: Library of New Testament Studies, 2513–8790, volume 616

Typeset by Newgen KnowledgeWorks Pvt. Ltd., Chennai, India

To find out more about our authors and books visit www.bloomsbury.com and sign up for our newsletters.

Contents

List of Tables		vi
Acknowledgments		vii
List of Abbreviations		viii
1	Introduction and Survey of Scholarship	1
2	Methodology and Plan of Book	15
3	The Structure of the Sermon on the Mount and the Lord's Prayer: Survey of Structures and a Proposal	29
4	The Matthean Petitions: An Examination of the Father, Will, and Evil Petitions	65
5	Matthew's "Slightly" Different Petitions: An Examination of the Kingdom, Bread, and Forgiveness Petitions	123
6	The Remaining Petitions: An Examination of the Name and Temptation Petitions	175
7	Conclusion: The Sermon's Prayer, Word and Deed/Hearers and Doers, and Points for Further Research	203
Appendices		209
Bibliography		217
Index of Primary Sources		227
Index of Authors		239

Tables

1.1 Scholars who have noted the centrality of the Lord's Prayer 6
3.1 Diagram of Grundmann, Bornkamm, and Guelich's Lord's Prayer as Structuring Agent 44
3.2 Word similarities in the Sermon's central section (Mt. 6:2-18) 61
3.3 The Sermon's prayer 63
4.1 The distribution of the invocation's wording 71
4.2 "Father" parallels in the Sermon on the Mount/Plain 80
4.3 The distribution of the third petition 89
4.4 The distribution of the seventh petition 110
4.5 Jewish parallels to the seventh petition according to similar wording 113
5.1 "Kingdom" in Matthew's Gospel 127
5.2 Daniel's contrasts of "kingdoms" 135

Acknowledgments

The present book is a revision of my doctoral work at the University of Bristol, Trinity College, finished in the summer of 2018. This project would not have been possible without my *Doktorvater* David Wenham, who offered an opportunity to pursue my life's dream, a study of the life of Jesus Christ and his teachings, at the highest academic level. His characteristic and unassuming academic advice, humility, room and board, history lessons, political banter, and last, but certainly not least, devotion to the gospel of Jesus Christ have encouraged not only my education but also my desire to live faithfully to the teaching contained in the following volume. In addition to David, I owe immense thanks to my second supervisor Charles Quarles. His attention to detail and patient guidance allowed me to overcome my largest hurdle during the writing process.

The faculty and staff at Trinity College Bristol also deserve gratitude. Timely comments have come along the way through the wise scholarship of Justin Stratis, John Nolland, Jon Coutts, and Jamie Davies. I would also like to express my gratitude to my co-laborers—Katy Smith, Peter Turnill, Benjamin Quinn, Graham Michael, Timothy Harmon, Brian LePort, Marc Groenbech-Dam, and Michael Spalione. The theology and pub have been worth every walk.

I would like to thank Scott Kellum, my mentor, pastor, and friend, for his advice about every facet of life. I am appreciative of my friends Joshua Tyler Walthall, Andrew Scott Beaver, and Robert Lee Dean III. Bobby, my lifelong friend, has listened to hours of "thinking-out-loud" over the course of six years. Additional insights and help have come from Matt Kimak, Emily Parker, K. Leigh Forell, and the Zurawel and Parker families.

I am thankful for my family, who have seen this project to its end. Mom, Devin, Tom, Brenda, Mike, and Angie have endured to varying degrees the financial, emotional, and stress-filled pains of doctoral studies. I would also add my NRCA family for giving me a place to teach and test ideas.

I cannot adequately thank my wife Erin for her constant anchoring of my storm-wrenched heart and mind. She has faithfully taken on the roles of mother and "father" at times when I have been mentally absent. Erin has continually called me back to the joy of being a husband and father to my wonderful children, Jonah and Millie.

The following volume is dedicated to the "Nathan's" in our family, specifically my late father, Joseph Nathan Ridlehoover. The PhD tenure has been one of great loss as my father, grandfather, and father-in-law passed onto heavenly light. With the loss of these men, it quickly became apparent that the "Father in heaven" would take on whole new meanings.

Abbreviations

AASF	Annales Academiae Scientiarum Fennicae
AB	Anchor Bible (Commentary)
BBR	*Bulletin for Biblical Research*
BDAG	A Greek-English Lexicon of the New Testament and Other Early Christian Literature, 3rd ed.
BETL	Bibliotheca ephemeridum theologicarum lovaniensium
Bib	*Biblica*
BibInt	*Biblical Interpretation*
BibInt	Biblical Interpretation Series
BJRL	*Bulletin of the John Rylands University Library of Manchester*
BTB	*Biblical Theology Bulletin*
BZNW	Beihefte zur *Zeitschrift für die neutestamentliche Wissenschaft*
CBC	Cambridge Bible Commentary
CBR	*Current in Biblical Research*
CBQ	*Catholic Biblical Quarterly*
COQG	Christian Origins and the Questions of God Series
CTJ	*Calvin Theological Journal*
DJG	*Dictionary of Jesus and the Gospels*. 1st ed. Edited by Joel B. Green, Scot McKnight, and I. Howard Marshall. Downers Grove, IL: InterVarsity Press, 1992
DJG	*Dictionary of Jesus and the Gospels*. 2nd ed. Edited by Joel B. Green, Jeannine K. Brown, and Nicholas Perrin. Downers Grove, IL: InterVarsity Press, 2013
EBC	F. E. Gaebelein, ed., *Expositor's Bible Commentary*
EGGNT	Exegetical Guide to the Greek New Testament
ESV	English Standard Version
ExpTim	*Expository Times*
GNS	Good News Studies
HBT	*Horizons in Biblical Theology*
HTR	*Harvard Theological Review*
HTS	*Harvard Theological Studies*
IBS	*Irish Biblical Studies*
ICC	International Critical Commentary
IEJ	*Israel Exploration Journal*
Int	*Interpretation*
JBL	*Journal of Biblical Literature*
JBQ	*Jewish Bible Quarterly*
JEC	*Jewish-Christian Relations*

JETS	Journal of the Evangelical Theological Society
JSHJ	Journal for the Study of the Historical Jesus
JSNT	Journal for the Study of the New Testament
JSNTSupp	Journal for the Study of the New Testament, Supplement Series
JSOT	Journal for the Study of the Old Testament
JSOTSupp	Journal for the Study of the Old Testament, Supplement Series
JTS	Journal of Theological Studies
LNTS	Library of New Testament Studies
NASB	New American Standard Bible
NCBC	New Century Bible Commentary
Neot	Neotestamentica
NICNT	New International Commentary on the New Testament
NIGTC	New International Greek Testament Commentary
NovT	Novum Testamentum
NRSV	New Revised Standard Version
NTM	New Testament Message
NTS	New Testament Studies
NTTS	New Testament Tools and Studies
PAAJR	Proceedings of the American Academy of Jewish Research
PNTC	Pelican New Testament Commentaries
RelStTh	Religious Studies and Theology
RevExp	Review and Expositor
RevQ	Revue de Qumran
RTR	The Reformed Theological Review
SBFA	Studium Biblicum Franciscanum Analecta
SBT	Studies in Biblical Theology
SCE	Studies in Christian Ethics
SEÅ	Svensk exegetisk årsbok
Semeia	Semeia
TBei	Theologische Beiträge
TDNT	Theological Dictionary of the New Testament
THNT	Theologischer Handkommentar zum Neuen Testament
TRE	Theologische Realenzyklopädie
TRENT	Traditions of the Rabbis from the Era of the New Testament
TS	Theological Studies
VC	Vigiliae christianae
WBC	Word Biblical Commentary
WTJ	Westminster Theological Journal
WUNT	Wissenschaftliche Untersuchungen zum Neuen Testament
WW	Word and World

Pseudepigrapha/Apocrypha

Apoc. Bar.	Apocalypse of Baruch
Add. Est.	Additions to Esther

As. Mos.	*Assumption of Moses*
1 En.	*1 Enoch*
1 Macc.	*1 Maccabees*
3 Macc.	*3 Maccabees*
PsSol.	*Psalms of Solomon*
Sir.	*Sirach*
Tob.	*Tobit*
Wis.	*Wisdom of Solomon*

Other Early Jewish and Christian Literature

Gen. Rab.	*Genesis Rabbah*
Ex. Rab.	*Exodus Rabbah*
Pesiq. R.	*Pesiqta Rabbati*
Tg. Isa.	*Targum Isaiah*
Tg. Mic.	*Targum of Micah*
Tg. Neof. Ex.	*Targum Neofiti Exodus*
Tg. Onk.	*Targum Onkelos*
Tg. OnkE.	*Targum Onkelos of Exodus*
Tg. Zech.	*Targum Zechariah*
B. Bat.	*Baba Batra*
y. Ber.	*Jerusalem Berakot*
b. 'Abod. Zar.	*'Abodah Zarah*
b. Ber.	*Babylonian Berakot*
b. Hag.	*Babylonian Hagigah*
b. Menah.	*Babylonian Menahot*
b. Ned.	*Babylonian Nedarim*
b. Sanh.	*Babylonian Sanhedrin*
b. Ta'an.	*Babylonian Ta'anit*
b. Yebam.	*Babylonian Yebamot*
t. Ned.	*Tosefta Nedarim*
m. 'Abot	*Mishnah 'Abot*
m. Ber.	*Mishnah Berakot*
m. Cant. R.	*Mishnah Canticles Rabbah*
m. Kil.	*Mishnah Kil'ayim*
m. Ned.	*Mishnah Nedarim*
m. Sanh.	*Mishnah Sanhedrin*
m. Šebu	*Mishnah Šebu'ot*
m. Sotah.	*Mishnah Sotah*
m. Ta'an.	*Mishnah Ta'anit*
m. Yoma.	*Mishnah Yoma*
Josephus Ant.	*Jewish Antiquities*
Did.	*Didache*
Gos. Thom.	*Gospel of Thomas*

Dead Sea Scrolls

1QH	*Hodayot*
4Q 'Amram B	*Visions of Amram*
4QLevi^b	*The Prayer and Ablutions of Levi*
4Q280	*Curses*
4Q372	*Apocryphon of Joseph^b*
4Q544	*Visions of Amram*
11QMelchizedek	*Melchizedek*
11QPs	*Psalms*
CD	*Damascus Document*

1

Introduction and Survey of Scholarship

Matthew 6:9a: Οὕτως οὖν προσεύχεσθε ὑμεῖς

The Lord's Prayer and the Sermon on the Mount continue to be among the most discussed texts within Christian scriptures, particularly in their Matthean versions. Because of their rich literary and theological import, it is no wonder that students of Matthew continue to bring out "treasures new and old" (Mt. 13:51-52) from these texts. The Lord's Prayer and the Sermon on the Mount are found in two places in the Gospels. Matthew's Gospel has the Lord's Prayer (Mt. 6:9-13) in the center of the Sermon on the Mount (Matthew 5–7), while Luke's Gospel presents a shortened sermon ("on the plain") in ch. 6 (vv. 20-49) followed by a shortened Lord's Prayer in ch. 11 (vv. 2-4).[1]

Luke's recording of the Lord's Prayer has Jesus responding to a disciple's inquiry on how to pray (Lk. 11:1). This question (Κύριε, δίδαξον ἡμᾶς προσεύχεσθαι, καθὼς καὶ Ἰωάννης ἐδίδαξεν τοὺς μαθητὰς αὐτοῦ) and response (i.e., the Lord's Prayer) forms the first part of an extended section on prayer (Lk. 11:1-13). Matthew, on the other hand, appears to have the Lord's Prayer "out-of-place" in the Sermon on the Mount. Consider the comments of Matthean scholar Donald Hagner:

> The Evangelist has here inserted further traditional material stemming from Jesus on the subject of prayer, thereby breaking the smooth sequence of the three parallel sections on the practice of righteousness (vv. 2-4; 5-6; 16-18). This entire pericope would hardly be missed if it were omitted from the present context. Vv. 9-15 (Lord's Prayer) in particular *do not fit well* their present context.[2]

Graham Stanton agrees: "The Lord's Prayer and two related sayings (6:9–15) *partly 'spoil'* the very impressive symmetry of this part of the Sermon."[3] France goes even further,

---

[1] For the sake of convention, I will refer to the authors of the Gospels as Matthew, Mark, Luke, and John as they have been traditionally recognized. The question of authorship has no bearing on the method or results of the following analysis.
[2] Donald Hagner, *Matthew 1–13*, WBC (Dallas: Word, 1993), 145. Emphasis mine.
[3] Graham Stanton, *Gospel for a New People: Studies in Matthew* (Edinburgh: T&T Clark, 1992), 297–8. "This part of the Sermon" is referring to chs 5–6. Emphasis mine.

calling the insertion of the Lord's Prayer a "literary digression."[4] Each commentator has implied the insertion of something that does not seem to fit. Unfortunately, their assessments assert that the Lord's Prayer is intrusive instead of a careful placement. Through the failure to recognize the centrality of the Lord's Prayer in the Sermon on the Mount, the interpretation of both texts has been impoverished. In the church and the academy, the tendency is to study these texts in isolation from one another.[5]

Central to this study are the following questions: What is the relationship between the Lord's Prayer and the Sermon on the Mount in Matthew's Gospel? What role does the Sermon on the Mount have in properly understanding the Lord's Prayer? And, what role does the Lord's Prayer have in properly understanding the Sermon on the Mount? We will argue that the Lord's Prayer is placed in the center of the Sermon on the Mount structurally and becomes a focal point for lexical and thematic parallels with the surrounding material in the Sermon. As we shall see, the Prayer's centrality is not a new concept but, nonetheless, a concept that has lacked specificity and clarity. The aim of this book is not only to argue for the centrality of the Lord's Prayer within the Sermon on the Mount but also to give definition and purpose to the Prayer's central position. It is likely that Matthew noted similarities between the Lord's Prayer and Sermon on the Mount from the traditions he received, leading him to establish the connection between the two texts. Matthew edited parts of the Sermon, and the Prayer itself, with a desire to increase the parallelism between the two texts, making prayer central. Matthew's desire to make prayer a central feature of the Sermon on the Mount also includes his editing and placement of the instruction to "ask, seek, and knock" at the end of the Sermon's body (Mt. 7:7-11). As we shall argue, the Sermon on the Mount was not built and ordered around the Lord's Prayer, but Matthew has seen and enhanced lexical and thematic parallels with the petitions, bringing out continuity between the two texts. No single petition parallels all the material in the Sermon on the Mount, but rather, each petition, through its parallels to the Sermon, makes a case for its integrated position (structurally, lexically, and thematically) as the "centerpiece" of the Sermon.[6]

The purpose, or "why," of this centrality for Matthew is to clarify what the answer to the petitions of the Lord's Prayer might look like in the life of the disciple of Jesus. The results are as follows: (1) a prayer in which the petitions are grounded in the passages of the Sermon, sharing lexical and thematic parallels; (2) the Sermon on the Mount describes what happens when the Lord's Prayer is answered in the disciple's life; and (3) this prayer to the Father is key to committing to and living by the Sermon's kingdom righteousness.

As we will show, little detailed historical and exegetical work has been done on the relationship between the Lord's Prayer and the Sermon on the Mount. Although the

---

[4] R. T. France, *The Gospel of Matthew*, NICNT (Grand Rapids: Eerdmans, 2007), 233.
[5] By analogy, the tendency is to study the Sermon and Prayer as separate as Luke records them. This comment is not meant to convey that the Matthean versions of both texts is better or should be preferred because they are together. Additionally, we want to avoid the implication that Matthew has it "right" and Luke "messed things up."
[6] Throughout the following book, we will primarily refer to each petition by its main subject (i.e., "Father" petition, "Name" petition, etc.) except for stylistic reasons or when noting that its numerical placement in the Prayer is relevant to the overall argument.

two sets of texts can be understood apart from one another, the following study will argue that in Matthew's Gospel, the best reading is one in which they are read together with consideration of their structural, lexical, and thematic relationship.

Why Is This Book Worth Writing?

This book is worth writing to contend for a fresh understanding of the Lord's Prayer. Admittedly, to propose a fresh understanding of the Lord's Prayer is a risky endeavor. Yet at an academic level, studies of the Lord's Prayer have hit a stalemate. New treatments of the Lord's Prayer typically reproduce the emphases of previous studies and little new understanding emerges. These previous studies have concentrated on the following: (1) the "form" in which the Lord's Prayer was transmitted; (2) the sources which gave rise to the Lord's Prayer; (3) a reconstruction of the communities that received their respective versions of the Lord's Prayer; (4) the original language of the Lord's Prayer; or (5) the various redactions in Matthew, Luke, and the *Didache's* version. While these issues are important for understanding the history behind the Lord's Prayer, they often become the sole means for understanding the Prayer.[7] The following book will argue for an understanding of the Lord's Prayer that takes into consideration the final or transmitted form of the text and its intentional placement by Matthew into the Sermon on the Mount. It will also seek to establish why Matthew has intentionally centered the Prayer within the Sermon.

The second benefit of writing this book is to establish an ignored angle of the Sermon on the Mount, notably the thrust of its central text. It is widely agreed that the Sermon on the Mount is the greatest collection of Jesus's ethical teachings. If the Sermon on the Mount's shape and themes connect with the Lord's Prayer, it is reasonable to assume that the Lord's Prayer gives vital clues as to how to fulfill the Sermon's ethic. The standard themes of the Sermon on the Mount are generally agreed to be righteousness and kingdom living. By placing the Lord's Prayer at the center of the Sermon on the Mount, Matthew indicates that prayer is a prominent theme along with righteousness and the kingdom. As we will seek to argue, the Lord's Prayer is placed at the center of the Sermon on the Mount to serve as the interpretive key to living out the kingdom righteousness prescribed in the Sermon on the Mount.

---

[7] More recently, studies of the Lord's Prayer have moved into the study of reception history. See Dale C. Allison, *The Sermon on the Mount: Inspiring the Moral Imagination* (New York: Herder & Herder, 1999); Simon J. Kistemaker, "The Lord's Prayer in the First Century," *JETS* 21.4 (1978): 323–8; Ulrich Luz, *Matthew 1–7: A Commentary*, Hermeneia (Minneapolis: Fortress, 2007); Daniel L. Migliore, ed., *The Lord's Prayer: Perspectives for Reclaiming Christian Prayer* (Grand Rapids: Eerdmans, 1993); Kenneth Stevenson, *The Lord's Prayer: A Text in Transition* (Philadelphia: Fortress, 2004). More recently, David Clark, *On Earth as in Heaven: The Lord's Prayer from Jewish Prayer to Christian Ritual* (Philadelphia: Fortress, 2017). On the interpretive history of the Sermon on the Mount, see Clarence Bauman, *The Sermon on the Mount: The Modern Quest for Its Meaning* (Macon: Mercer, 1991); Jeffrey P. Greenman, Timothy Larsen, and Stephen R. Spencer, eds., *The Sermon on the Mount through the Centuries: From the Early Church to John Paul II* (Grand Rapids: Brazos, 2007); Harvey K. McArthur, *Understanding the Sermon on the Mount* (London: Epworth, 1960).

The third benefit arising from this book is the advance of compositional criticism and intratextuality in Matthean studies, as well as the Synoptic Gospels. The canonical writings of the Gospels were not created in a vacuum. Each writer used a variety of sources, both canonical and noncanonical. These written sources were a part of a shared cultural memory among the Jewish people. Studying the relationship between old and new texts/ideas and how they are shaped into new contexts is an exercise in intratextuality and part of the ongoing literary study of the New Testament. The present study will analyze how the Lord's Prayer works intratextually within the Sermon on the Mount.[8] If the relationship between these texts can be established by way of parallels, a fourth benefit arises.

By situating the Lord's Prayer in the Sermon on the Mount and asserting that the Sermon on the Mount helps to explain the petitions of the Lord's Prayer, a new aspect of New Testament prayer emerges. This aspect is the marrying of word and deed, prayer and praxis. Unfortunately, prayer is often seen only for its communicative aspects or as a mantra to be repeated. A petitioner comes to God offering thanks, lament, praise, and petition. Yet, Mt. 6:33 ("But strive first for the kingdom of God and his righteousness, and all these things will be given to you as well"[9]) uses prayer language ("strive") alongside a call to discipleship (i.e., "the kingdom and righteousness"). The Lord's Prayer as the "centerpiece" of the Sermon on the Mount would evidence an extended example of the combining of prayer and day-to-day discipleship. Conversely, the Lord's Prayer is then properly understood when the petitioner follows the demands of the Sermon on the Mount.

The Lord's Prayer and Sermon on the Mount in Recent Research

The literature examining the relationship of the Sermon on the Mount and Lord's Prayer is noticeably smaller than the individual treatments of these texts. Because the texts are studied in isolation from one another, only the occasional observation about their relationship is found in scholarly work.[10] In fact, Günther Bornkamm,

---

[8] A recent study that also explores the intertextual links of the Sermon on the Mount/Lord's Prayer and Matthew's "cultural encyclopedia" is Jonathan Pennington, *The Sermon on the Mount and Human Flourishing: A Theological Commentary* (Grand Rapids: Baker, 2017). The present book has significant overlaps with Pennington's work but is more focused on the Lord's Prayer and its relationship with the Sermon on the Mount. Pennington's commentary is focused on the Sermon's message of human flourishing and intertextual links with the Greek and Jewish traditions.

[9] All translations are from the NRSV unless otherwise stated.

[10] Scholarly treatments on the Lord's Prayer include: Craig A. Evans, *Matthew*, NCBC (Cambridge: Cambridge University, 2012), 141–9; Birger Gerhardsson, "The Matthean Version of the Lord's Prayer (Matt. 6:9b–13): Some Observations," in *The New Testament Age: Essays in Honour of Bo Reicke*, vol. 1. (Mercer: Mercer University, 1984); M. D. Goulder, "The Composition of the Lord's Prayer," *JTS* 14 (1963): 32–45; Robert H. Gundry, *Matthew: A Commentary on His Handbook for a Mixed Church under Persecution*, 2nd ed. (Grand Rapids: Eerdmans, 1982), 104–8; Joseph Heinemann, "The Background of Jesus' Prayer in the Jewish Liturgical Tradition," in *The Lord's Prayer and Jewish Liturgy*, ed. J. J. Petuchowski and M. Brocke (New York: Seabury, 1978), 81–9; Joachim Jeremias, *The Prayers of Jesus*, SBT 6 (London: SCM, 1967); Craig Keener, *A Commentary on the Gospel of Matthew: A Socio-Rhetorical Commentary* (Grand Rapids: Eerdmans, 1999), 214–26;

Mark Kiley, and Mary Hinkle are perhaps the only scholars in modern biblical studies who have devoted specific publications to the relationship between the Sermon on the Mount and the Lord's Prayer, even if in article form.[11] This section will provide an examination of Bornkamm, Kiley, and Hinkle along with some of the others who have noted the relationship between the Lord's Prayer and Sermon on the Mount in broader works. Those who have commented on the relationship between the Sermon on the Mount and the Lord's Prayer fall generally into four categories. These categories are the following: (1) no-consequence, (2) thematic, (3) expositional/structurally centric, and (4) combination. In the sections that follow, we will define each category along with examining the work of representatives of each position. We will argue that while these studies have made a notable observation concerning the relationship of the Sermon on the Mount and the Lord's Prayer, they miss the entirety of Matthew's intentional "centering" and reading strategy for these two texts (Table 1.1).

No-Consequence

The "no-consequence" category of scholars are those who note the centrality of the Lord's Prayer within the Sermon on the Mount but do not elaborate on this centrality. The centrality of the Lord's Prayer does not have any effect on the interpretation of the Prayer or the Sermon. Scholars who have noted the central position of the Lord's Prayer include Dale Allison, Jack Kingsbury,[12] and Charles Quarles.[13] We will consider the work of Dale Allison as exemplary of this approach.[14]

Dale C. Allison

Among modern Matthean scholars, few have written as much concerning the Sermon on the Mount as Dale C. Allison.[15] Allison's contribution to ongoing studies of the

---

Jan Milič Lochman, *The Lord's Prayer*, trans. Geoffrey W. Bromiley (Grand Rapids: Eerdmans, 1990); Ernst Lohmeyer, *The Lord's Prayer* (London: Collins, 2005); T. W. Manson, "The Lord's Prayer," *BJRL* 38 (1955/56): 436–88; John Nolland, *The Gospel of Matthew: A Commentary on the Greek Text*, NIGTC (Grand Rapids: Eerdmans, 2005), 279–93; Sjef Van Tilborg, "A Form-Criticism of the Lord's Prayer," *NovT* 14 (1972): 94–105. The standard view is that the Lord's Prayer is an interpolation into the Sermon on the Mount and primarily serves as an addendum or exemplar of the type of prayer instructed in Mt. 6:5-6.

[11] Günther Bornkamm, "Der Aufbau der Bergpredigt," *NTS* 24 (1978), 419–32; Mary E. Hinkle, "The Lord's Prayer: Empowerment for Living the Sermon on the Mount," *WW* 22.1 (2002), 9–17; Mark Kiley, "The Lord's Prayer and Matthean Theology," in *The Lord's Prayer and Other Texts from the Greco-Roman Era*, ed. James H. Charlesworth, Mark Harding, and Mark Kiley (Valley Forge: Trinity International, 1994), 15–27. Outside of Biblical studies, Oliver O'Donovan, "Prayer and Morality in the Sermon on the Mount," *SCE* 22.1 (2009): 21–33, has analyzed the relationship of the Sermon on the Mount and the Lord's Prayer from an ethical perspective. Also, William C. Mattison, *The Sermon on the Mount and Moral Theology: A Virtue Perspective* (Cambridge: Cambridge University, 2017), 9, 238–69.

[12] Jack Kingsbury, "The Place, Structure, and Meaning of the Sermon on the Mount within Matthew," *Int* 41 (1987): 141.

[13] Charles Quarles, *Sermon on the Mount: Inspiring Christ's Message to the Modern Church*, NAC Studies in Bible and Theology (Nashville: B&H Academic, 2011), 16.

[14] We will consider the implications of Allison's structural proposal separately in Chapter 3.

[15] Dale Allison's work includes: "The Configuration of the Sermon on the Mount and Its Meaning" in *Studies in Matthew: Interpretation Past and Present* (Grand Rapids: Baker, 2005); "The Sermon on the

Table 1.1 Scholars Who Have Noted the Centrality of the Lord's Prayer

Approaches	No-Consequence	Thematic	Expositional/ Structurally Centric	Combination
Key Figures	D. C. Allison J. Kingsbury C. Quarles	H. D. Betz O. O'Donovan D. Garland M. Hinkle W. Mattison	W. Grundmann G. Bornkamm R. Guelich A. Schweizer J. Lambrecht R. Schnackenburg J. Meier M. Kiley	U. Luz J. Pennington

structure of the Sermon has been especially helpful, as he has noted the repetition of triads throughout the Sermon on the Mount. The main body of the Sermon on the Mount consists of the triad of 5:21-48, 6:1-18, and 6:19–7:11. The central section, 6:1-18, is split into a further triad of 6:2-4, 5-15, and 16-18. Following this pattern, one encounters the uneven middle section on prayer (6:5-15). Within this section, Allison notes the triad of 6:5-6, 7-13, and 14-15. Verses 5-6 contrast righteous and hypocritical prayer generally, while vv. 14-15 address the topic of forgiveness. Regarding vv. 7-13, Allison notes, "Even Matthew's version of the Lord's Prayer (unlike Luke's version) contains three 'your' petitions ('hallowed be your name, your kingdom come, your will be done') and three 'us' petitions ('give us this day our daily bread, and forgive us our debts . . . do not bring us to the time of trial but deliver us from the evil one')."[16]

Allison concludes, "On this analysis, the Lord's Prayer, which is at the centre of the section on prayer, is at the very centre of the Sermon on the Mount as a whole. One wonders whether Matthew did not design it to be so."[17] He comments elsewhere, "The neat scheme is interrupted by 6:7-15, the section on the Lord's Prayer, which, like the irregular last beatitude, therefore calls attention to itself."[18] Although acknowledging the irregularity of the section on prayer, Allison does not elaborate on Matthew's purposes.

Allison's careful examination of the Sermon on the Mount and its structure is a careful balance of historical and literary concerns. His structural proposal illustrates the composition of the Sermon on the Mount as a unified whole and argues for the Prayer's integrated position. According to Allison, Matthew has inserted the Lord's Prayer into the middle section carefully. Yet, to Allison's rhetorical comment, "One wonders whether Matthew did not design it to be so," his implied answer seems to be no based on his treatment of the Lord's Prayer. He neither alludes to the Sermon in

---

Mount: A Commentary on the Sermon on the Mount, Including the Sermon on the Plain: Matthew 5:3–7:27 and Luke 6:20–49: A Review," *JBL* 117 (1998): 136–8; *The Sermon on the Mount: Inspiring the Moral Imagination* (New York: Herder & Herder, 1999); "The Structure of the Sermon on the Mount," *JBL* 106 (1987): 423–45.

[16] Allison, *Sermon on the Mount*, 36. See also Allison, *Studies in Matthew*, 187.
[17] Allison, *Sermon on the Mount*, 36.
[18] Allison, *Sermon on the Mount*, 108.

his explanations of the Prayer's petitions nor uses the Prayer in a significant way when dealing with sections of the Sermon. In other words, the centrality of the Lord's Prayer is noted, but of "no consequence."

Thematic

The "thematic" category refers to those scholars who emphasize the thematic connections between the Lord's Prayer and the Sermon on the Mount. Structural elements between the Lord's Prayer and Sermon on the Mount are mentioned but only serve as introductions to the "deeper" and more important thematic connections. Scholars who have noted thematic connections between the Lord's Prayer and the Sermon on the Mount include Oliver O'Donovan,[19] David Garland,[20] Mary Hinkle, and Hans Dieter Betz. We will consider the work of Hans Dieter Betz and Mary Hinkle because of their specific focus on the thematic parallels between the Lord's Prayer and Sermon on the Mount.[21]

Hans Dieter Betz

Hans Dieter Betz is known primarily for his scholarship on the book of Galatians and exhaustive commentary on the Sermon on the Mount, both in the *Hermeneia* series. Betz's acknowledgment of the Prayer's centrality is stated in his discussion of Matthew's redaction. He states,

> If, as I assume, the author/redactor took over the two instructions of 6:1–6, 16–18, and 6:7–15, and merged them, it is not difficult to see why he did so. These sections provided the ideal building blocks for the second main part of the SM dealing with worship. As the composition of the SM now stands, the Lord's Prayer is found in the centre not only of the cultic teaching in 6:1–18 but of the SM as a whole.[22]

Betz does not elaborate on his structural proposal but nonetheless notes the Prayer's centrality. Unlike the no-consequence category, Betz sees exegetical significance to the Prayer's centrality. He states, "The centrepiece within the central subsection is the Lord's Prayer (6:9b–13). This architecture points to the central importance of prayer for the SM (prayer is mentioned also in the first subsection [5:44], and in the following subsection [7:7–11])." Betz's argument is that prayer is featured within the Sermon and

---

[19] O'Donovan, "Prayer and Morality in the Sermon on the Mount," 21–33.
[20] David Garland, "The Lord's Prayer in the Gospel of Matthew," *RevExp* 89 (1992): 215–28.
[21] O'Donovan's argument is more concerned with the connection of prayer and ethics and thus uses the Sermon on the Mount and the Lord's Prayer as examples of this connection in his article. David Garland's work is focused on the Lord's Prayer and its connection with Matthew's Gospel. Garland mentions several Sermon parallels to the Lord's Prayer but has a wider focus.
[22] Hans Dieter Betz, *Sermon on the Mount: A Commentary on the Sermon on the Mount, Including the Sermon on the Plain: Matthew 5:3–7:27 and Luke 6:20–49*, Hermeneia (Philadelphia: Fortress, 1995), 351.

even at its center. Prayer is therefore thematically significant to the Sermon's rhetorical patterns.[23] He states later,

> In one sense, the Beatitudes form the beginning of the Two Ways pattern, using the image of the ways of life. In another sense, the eschatological goals (7:13–23) determine the construction of the SM; even its beginning Beatitudes (5:3–12) contain eschatological promises. In yet another sense, the centrepiece of the Lord's Prayer calls attention to the centrality of approaching God in prayer; it also reminds us that this prayer is the oldest part of the tradition, going back, for all we know, to the historical Jesus. Thus, the SM begins historically in the centre as well.[24]

Betz's conclusion is an exciting prospect in understanding the Lord's Prayer and the Sermon on the Mount. Although acknowledging the centrality of the Lord's Prayer, Betz fails to show any detailed exegetical consequences within his exposition of the Sermon on the Mount. This omission is even after asserting that the Lord's Prayer is a "building block." Betz does make a step forward with his conclusion that prayer is thematically significant to the Sermon on the Mount, but he fails to note any direct connections with the individual petitions. We will argue that each petition is thematically related to differing portions of the Sermon on the Mount and these connections function reciprocally. The Sermon on the Mount describes what happens when the Lord's Prayer is answered in the disciple's life, and the praying of this prayer is a commitment to the kingdom righteousness as described in the Sermon on the Mount.

Mary Hinkle

In writing on the Lord's Prayer, Mary Hinkle seeks to advance an insight noted in Allison's *The Sermon on the Mount: Inspiring the Moral Imagination*. In response to the suggestion that the Sermon is an impossible ideal, Allison offers three means that a hearer of the Sermon on the Mount can perform the ethic prescribed.[25] Hinkle's proposal seeks to add a fourth, namely prayer. She states, "In the midst of a seemingly relentless barrage of imperatives addressed to disciples is a small collection of imperatives addressed to God. At the heart of the intricately structured Sermon on the Mount is the Lord's Prayer."[26] She continues, "In this prayer, the community of Jesus'

---

[23] In his structural proposal of the Sermon on the Mount, Betz, *Sermon on the Mount*, 50–8, esp. 51–7, shows how the rhetoric of the Sermon on the Mount is patterned on the Greco-Roman *epitome*. Betz argues that the rhetorical effect of the Sermon is to persuade one to adopt a "way of life" that mimics Jesus. For further discussion on the Sermon as paraenesis, see James G. Williams, "Paraenesis, Excess, and Ethics: Matthew's Rhetoric in the Sermon on the Mount," *Semeia* 50 (1990): 163–87. For a counter argument, see Stanton, *Gospel for a New People*, 307–25, who argues that the Sermon is not an *epitome* but shaped and reinterpreted in ways that are consistent with the rest of the Gospel.

[24] Betz, *Sermon on the Mount*, 64–5.

[25] Allison, *Sermon on the Mount*, 28–30. The three sources of empowerment are as follows: (1) Jesus's healing ministry, (2) the rewards/hope of the future, and (3) God's promise to care for his children.

[26] Hinkle, "Lord's Prayer," 11.

followers ask for what it needs to live the sermon. As God answers this prayer, God is empowering a community to live the sermon as a whole."[27] In what follows, Hinkle addresses the connections between each petition and the material in the Sermon.

In her exposition, Hinkle explains the meaning of each petition before moving to thematic parallels in the Sermon on the Mount. For example, Hinkle focuses on the name of God in the first petition as the opposite of falsehood. This allows her to parallel the first petition to the teachings on vows in Mt. 5:34-37. She asks, "How does one let his word be 'Yes, Yes,' or 'No, No'?" God's people should pray the first petition. Hinkle similarly addresses the rest of the petitions, showing how each petition is thematically linked to various portions of the Sermon. "Your kingdom come" relates to Mt. 5:17-19 in which the law and prophets are fulfilled as people keep God's commandments. The kingdom is where moth, rust, and thieves do not corrupt the heavenly treasure (Mt. 6:19-21) and the king gives good gifts to those who ask (Mt. 7:11). The will petition is thematically connected with Mt. 7:21 in which the "will" is explicitly mentioned. Additionally, Hinkle connects the will petition to Mt. 5:16 (the disciples' work bringing glory to the Father) and Mt. 5:44 (love your enemies).

The focus changes in the second half of the Sermon. Whereas the first half is specifically addressed to God, the latter half addresses the needs of those praying. Hinkle states, "In these petitions, as in the others, those who pray the prayer ask for what they need to live in the kingdom Jesus describes."[28] In the fourth petition, Hinkle draws attention to the discussion of worry in which bread is explicitly mentioned (Mt. 6:25-34).[29] The petition allows the hearer to avoid the anxiety of even the barest of necessities, food, and clothing. Hinkle interestingly also connects the fourth petition to Jesus's teaching in Mt. 5:42. In 5:42, Jesus instructs his followers to give to everyone who begs from you, whether coat or cloak.

In the fifth petition, the vertical (God and people) and horizontal (interpersonal) relationships intersect.[30] Hinkle highlights the places in the Sermon that address strained relationships. She connects the petition to Mt. 5:22-24 and 5:48. What is the empowerment for reconciliation? She states, "Those who pray the Lord's Prayer ask for forgiveness from God; forgiveness of the brother and sister follows from the forgiveness that God offers." Hinkle finishes with an analysis of the last two petitions, dealing with them together. She points out two passages in which hearers of the Sermon are instructed to endure persecution (5:11-12, 39). She asks, "Does the Sermon on the Mount urge followers of Jesus toward their own self-defeating surrender to evil?"[31] Without the last two petitions, one might succumb to evil. Instead, they appeal to God for deliverance from the evil one.

Hinkle's analysis of the thematic connections between the Sermon on the Mount and the Lord's Prayer furthers the observations of Betz. She sees the Lord's Prayer as a focal point of the Sermon and basis for connections between prayer and discipleship.

---

[27] Hinkle, "Lord's Prayer," 11.
[28] Hinkle, "Lord's Prayer," 14.
[29] Hinkle, "Lord's Prayer," 15.
[30] Hinkle, "Lord's Prayer," 15.
[31] Hinkle, "Lord's Prayer," 16.

Unfortunately, Hinkle's analysis misses several insights. First, Hinkle conflates the structural proposals of Allison, Kingsbury, and Luz.[32] As we have partially argued above and will argue more extensively in Chapter 3, each of these proposals has different implications. The structural consequences of noting the centrality of the Lord's Prayer do not lead to a de facto interpretation. Second, and more importantly, Hinkle neglects several parallels that are signaled by lexical and thematic clues. For the sake of brevity, we will only note a few examples. In Hinkle's analysis of the Name petition, she mentions the connection of speaking God's name and truthfulness. This connection leads to Hinkle's association of the first petition with taking vows (Mt. 5:33-37).[33] While truthfulness is inherent in the Name petition, Hinkle misses the connection of the Name petition with Mt. 7:21 in which a specific name of God is mentioned ("Lord, Lord"). Also, Mt. 7:21 addresses "doing the will of the Father" and contrasts those who truly know the name of God and those who do not. Arguably, this reference to doing God's will is the definition of "hallowing." Therefore, Mt. 7:21 appears to be a substantial parallel to the Name petition, but Hinkle ignores its lexical and thematic parallels. In Hinkle's dealing with the evil petition, she mentions connections with Mt. 5:11-12 and 5:39. Hinkle's recognition of these two instances misses the other seven examples of "evil" being mentioned (Mt. 5:37, 45; 6:23; 7:11, 17-18, and 23). As we will argue in Chapter 4, these instances of evil are not only lexically parallel but also share parallel themes.

Expositional/Structurally Centric

The "expositional/structurally centric" category refers to those scholars who believe that the Lord's Prayer controls the ordering of the Sermon on the Mount.[34] In other words, the Lord's Prayer is central, as the petitions dictate the order of the material around it. The Sermon does not point to the Prayer's centrality; instead, the Prayer is central because it orders sections of the Sermon and the sections function as an exposition of their respective petition. Scholars who have noted the structuring significance of the Lord's Prayer include Walter Grundmann, Günther Bornkamm, Robert Guelich,[35] Eduard Schweizer,[36] Jan Lambrecht,[37] Rudolf Schnackenburg,[38] John Meier,[39] and Mark Kiley.[40] Because of their influence on later scholarship, we will

---

[32] See Hinkle, "Lord's Prayer," 11, fn.8. She states that most commentators see the Lord's Prayer as the heart of the Sermon on the Mount. This assertion is just not true. Outside of the scholars mentioned in the following survey of scholarship, few people see this relationship.

[33] Hinkle, "Lord's Prayer," 12–13. Hinkle mistakes the numerical reference for taking vows on p. 12. She notes the leading verse of 5:33-37 as "6:33."

[34] The following section will only serve as a brief summary. We will survey structural proposals more extensively in Chapter 3.

[35] Robert Guelich, *The Sermon on the Mount: A Foundation of Understanding* (Waco: Word, 1982), 36–7.

[36] Eduard Schweizer, *The Good News According to Matthew* (Atlanta: John Knox, 1975), 202–3.

[37] Jan Lambrecht, *The Sermon on the Mount: Proclamation and Exhortation*, GNS 14 (Wilmington: Glazier, 1985), 155–64.

[38] Rudolf Schnackenburg, *All Things Are Possible to Believers: Reflections on the Lord's Prayer and the Sermon on the Mount*, trans. James S. Currie (Louisville: Westminster, 1995), 27–8.

[39] J. P. Meier, *Matthew*, NTM 3 (Collegeville: Liturgical, 1980), 59.

[40] Kiley, "Lord's Prayer and Matthean Theology," 15–27.

consider the work of Grundmann and Bornkamm specifically. Bornkamm's proposal influenced the work of Guelich, Schweizer, Lambrecht, Schnackenburg, Meier, and Kiley with little revision.[41]

Walter Grundmann and Günther Bornkamm

Walter Grundmann[42] and Günther Bornkamm[43] were among the first to note a structuring purpose to the Lord's Prayer. Both scholars have argued that the centrality of the Lord's Prayer is used to structure major sections of the Sermon (Mt. 5:3–7:12). Grundmann contended that each petition of the Lord's Prayer is assigned a different portion of the Sermon. The first half of the Sermon (Mt. 5:1-48) corresponds to the first half of petitions (Mt. 6:9-10) collectively, while the latter half of the Sermon (Mt. 6:19–7:23) corresponds to the latter half of the Prayer (Mt. 5:1-2 and 7:7-12 to Petition 1; 5:3-16 to Petition 2; 5:17-48 to Petition 3; 6:19-34 to Petition 4; 7:1-6 to Petition 5; and 7:13-23 to Petitions 6 and 7).

Bornkamm amended the argument of Grundmann by reducing the Prayer's structuring to the second half of the Sermon (Mt. 6:19–7:11).[44] He reasoned that the teachings on prayer found in the Sermon (Mt. 6:9-13; 7:7-11) are combined in Lk. 11:1-13. Bornkamm argued that Matthew has split the teaching on prayer (Mt. 6:7-15; 7:7-11) to form an *inclusio* around 6:19–7:6. Within this *inclusio*, Mt. 6:19-24 connects to the first three petitions, Mt. 6:25-34 connects to the fourth petition, Mt. 7:1-5 connects to the fifth petition, and Mt. 7:6 connects with the last two petitions. To establish these connections between the Sermon and Prayer, Bornkamm points out the similar vocabulary and shared thematic elements.

Grundmann and Bornkamm both have noted an important point concerning the Sermon on the Mount and the Lord's Prayer. The structure between the two texts is indicative of Matthew's reading strategy. We will argue that the centrality of the Lord's Prayer is significant for how the Sermon is understood, but the Lord's Prayer does not structure the Sermon in which it is found. While this exegesis is intriguing, it is plagued with two major problems. First, many of the exegetical parallels between the Sermon and the respective petition are stretched. Examples include: (1) the connection of Mt. 7:6 in Grundmann's proposal to the forgiveness petition,[45] (2) in Bornkamm, connecting Mt. 6:19-24 to God's will being accomplished,[46] and (3) in both proposals,

---

[41] Kiley, "Lord's Prayer and Matthean Theology," 15–16, has recently argued that the connections between the Sermon on the Mount and the Lord's Prayer extend beyond 7:7-11.
[42] Walter Grundmann, *Das Evangelium nach Matthäus*, THNT (Berlin: Evangelische Verlagsanstalt, 1981), 204–6.
[43] Bornkamm, "Der Aufbau der Bergpredigt," 419–32.
[44] See also Lambrecht, *Sermon on the Mount*, 155–64. Schnackenburg, *All Things Are Possible to Believers*, 27–8, is sympathetic to this view, although he doubts that it can be proven with certainty.
[45] The aphoristic nature of the phrase does easily lend itself to being about forgiveness. The phrase explains that one should not give "what is holy" to the unholy, but the prayer petition commands that forgiveness be given without condition. As we will argue, a clearer connection can be made between Mt. 7:6 and the temptation petition. See Bornkamm, "Der Aufbau der Bergpredigt," 427–30.
[46] Bornkamm's connection here is problematic in two ways: (1) He splits 6:19-24 and 25-34. Taken as a whole (6:19-34), the section speaks to material needs and God's provision for even the "least of

the connection of Mt. 7:1-5 to the forgiveness proposal.[47] The second major issue is the disproportionate arrangement that occurs when each scholar assigns the Sermon's content to its respective petition. Two examples will suffice: (1) In both proposals, the bread petition governs fifteen or more verses, and the temptation and evil petition govern one verse; (2) In Bornkamm's proposal, Mt. 6:19-24 governs the first three petitions collectively, while the rest of the Sermon is split among the remaining petitions. These critiques will be explored more heavily in Chapter 3.

Combination

The "combination" approach refers to scholarship that considers both the structural and thematic clues concerning the Prayer's centrality. The Sermon's structure is indicative of the importance of the Prayer's "centrality." The Prayer is also thematically linked to the material found in the Sermon on the Mount. In this approach, the structure of the Sermon on the Mount indicates how it should be understood, with the Lord's Prayer being central. The thematic connections strengthen the marrying of the Lord's Prayer and the Sermon on the Mount. Ulrich Luz and Jonathan Pennington's work is representative of the "combination" approach. Because of his pioneering work in this approach, we will specifically consider the work of Ulrich Luz.

Ulrich Luz

In his *Hermeneia* commentary on the Gospel of Matthew, Ulrich Luz presents a concentric proposal for the Sermon.[48] Luz couples his structural proposal with his understanding of the dynamics of oral compositions. An attribute of oral compositions is the use of the *inclusio*. Luz argues that Matthew uses six such *inclusios* (5:1-2//7:28–8:1a; 5:3-16//7:13-27; 5:17-20//7:12; 5:21-48//6:19–7:11; 6:1-6//6:16-18; 6:7-8//6:14-15) around the Lord's Prayer, making it the centerpiece of the Sermon on the Mount.

In terms of his structural proposal, Luz has created a sensible proposal that attempts to do justice to the structural markers, major themes, and redactional clues in the Sermon. Luz highlights the role of prayer as a major thrust in the Sermon based on its centrality. This emphasis is evident in his summation of the structure of the Sermon, when he states,

---

these." (2) The emphasis in the Prayer's petition is on earth but also clearly in heaven. The emphasis in 6:19-24 focuses more on the earthly aspect, pointing out that man should not be subservient to wealth while on earth.

[47] The problem with this connection is not the connection itself but the way the connection is described. Each respective phrase has differing emphases. The forgiveness petition prefaces man's forgiveness with God's forgiveness. Matthew 7:1-5 emphasizes judgment among men. See Allison, "Structure of the Sermon on the Mount," 426; and Lambrecht, *Sermon on the Mount*, 164. We will argue that the forgiveness petition parallels Mt. 7:1-5 based on their shared emphasis on debt language and their triangular shape. This will be explained in more depth in Chapter 5.

[48] Luz, *Matthew 1–7*, 172. Luz's proposal is based on the work of two earlier studies: Josef Kürzinger, "Zur Komposition der Bergpredigt nach Matthäus," *Bib* 40 (1959): 569–89; and Rainer Riesner, "Der Aufbau der Reden im Matthäus-Evangelium," *TBei* 9 (1978): 173–6.

Introduction and Survey of Scholarship   13

The Lord's Prayer is its central text. Thus, the Sermon on the Mount takes its readers along a way that leads them from God's radical demands into the "interior" of faith where they experience the Father's nearness in prayer. Then it leads them back into the praxis of renouncing possessions and of love.[49]

A major strength of Luz's proposal is his connection between the literary structure and the theology of the Sermon. In each case, the one helps the other.

Luz's work on the relationship between the Lord's Prayer and Sermon on the Mount has not received a great deal of scholarly attention.[50] Luz neglects three aspects of the textual connection between the Lord's Prayer and Sermon on the Mount. First, Luz's explanation of the second half of the Sermon on the Mount misses a thematic thread that runs through Mt. 6:19–7:12. The section addresses social issues, as Luz notes, but also centers on the theme of heaven and earth. We will seek to demonstrate this theme further in Chapter 4.

Second, Luz's connections between petitions and Sermon parallels are underdeveloped in the latter half of the Lord's Prayer. A comparison of Luz's analysis of the invocation and the evil petition serve as evidence. Luz notes each instance of "Father" throughout the Sermon and parallels these instances to the invocation.[51] In Luz's treatment of the evil petition, he does not mention any of the other references to "evil" in the Sermon. This omission is puzzling due to the high number of references to "evil."[52]

Third, Luz's proposal leaves the centrality of the Lord's Prayer ambiguous. He does not clearly define what "centrality" means. In his structural proposal, the Lord's Prayer appears as a hinge between the demands in 5:21-28 and 6:19–7:12, drawing the reader into the "interior" of faith. This statement would appear to signal a major theme for the Sermon on the Mount, but Luz does not address prayer in his "Sermon themes" section.[53] In fact, the centrality of the Lord's Prayer is not mentioned again until Luz summarizes his findings on the Sermon on the Mount. In his explanation of the interplay between deeds and grace within the Sermon (point 2 of 7), Luz gives three examples. In his second example, Luz states, "In its centre (6:9–13), the Sermon on the Mount wants to bring the acting person to prayer to the Father. An interpretation that overlooks the reality that in the Sermon on the Mount praxis is at its core prayer misunderstands the evangelist."[54] Although Luz's wording (i.e., "centre," "core") appears to reemphasize his initial statements in the exegetical sections, his overly brief summary has the effect of softening his argument for centrality. The Lord's Prayer is not a hinge to move readers "up" one side of the Sermon and "down" the other. Rather, the Lord's Prayer "stands" atop the mountain of the Sermon.[55] The structure and textual connections signal a

---

[49] Luz, *Matthew 1–7*, 172.
[50] This omission is hinted by France, *Gospel of Matthew*, 155, fn.8, who is sceptical of this approach.
[51] See Luz, *Matthew 1–7*, 295; see also 208.
[52] See Chapter 4.
[53] Luz, *Matthew 1–7*, 176–7.
[54] Luz, *Matthew 1–7*, 391.
[55] The metaphor of a "mountain" was helpfully suggested by Francis Watson at the 2014 Trinity College Bristol Postgraduate Conference. After we argued for differing structuring levels throughout the Sermon in the following paper, "The Sermon's Prayer: Seeing the Lord's Prayer in Context," Watson commented that the proposed structure builds upward "almost like a mountain." Recently,

defined centrality, making the Lord's Prayer the interpretive lens through which the Sermon on the Mount is understood.

Conclusion

The dialogue with the major figures who have seen a relationship between the Sermon on the Mount and the Lord's Prayer should not be viewed as an attempt at a thorough critique. However, those who have attempted to posit a structuring relationship of the Lord's Prayer to the Sermon on the Mount have mostly neglected the lexical and thematic connections between the Lord's Prayer and the Sermon on the Mount. Those who have seen lexical and thematic connections between the petitions of the Lord's Prayer and sections of the Sermon on the Mount have mostly not observed the structural arguments. The exception to this rule is Ulrich Luz and, more recently, Jonathan Pennington.

Yet, this project has at least four distinctives from Luz's work. First, this study seeks to take seriously the context that Matthew provides for the Lord's Prayer. A thorough review of the literature has led to the discovery that the Sermon on the Mount has not been analyzed from the perspective of the Lord's Prayer, nor the Lord's Prayer within the context of the Sermon on the Mount. Such an analysis will be accomplished by observing the details of Matthew's redaction/composition and noting the parallels between these two important texts. Matthew's centering is not happenstance but rather more precise than has been previously argued. Second, we will argue that Matthew's centering is not an "either/or" concerning structure and lexical/thematic, but a "both/and." Matthew uses structural, lexical, and thematic clues to indicate the ways in which the Sermon and Prayer should be understood. Third, this study seeks to analyze the Lord's Prayer as a part of Jewish prayer for its most basic meaning. By locating the Lord's Prayer in its cultural milieu, a basis for parallels with the Sermon on the Mount is established. Fourth, this study seeks to answer why the Prayer is central to the Sermon on the Mount.

Pennington, *Sermon and Human Flourishing*, 133–4, has described his own structural proposal for the Sermon as a "mountain."

2

Methodology and Plan of Book

Before laying out the plan of the present book, a word is in order on basic presuppositions, scope, and methodology. In this chapter, we will address these presuppositions regarding Matthew's Gospel and its interpretation, along with explaining the limitations and scope of the present study. Next, we will describe the methodology employed throughout the book, including its implications. Our method is eclectic, incorporating insights from historical and literary methods of exegesis, specifically redaction criticism and rhetorical criticism. Finally, we will give an outline of each chapter, detailing its purpose for the present argument.

Presuppositions and Scope

In the reading of any ancient text and especially Scriptural texts, interpreters come with presuppositions. Presuppositions are unavoidable and form a basis for methodology. They also provide a means of avoiding distracting, and sometimes only tangentially important, discussions. Given the restraints of time, space, and certainty, we will note three working presuppositions, which in turn, limit the scope of the present book. We will address the issue of source criticism, the historical Jesus, and Jesus's understanding of eschatology. The first two are not directly relevant to the present investigation, while the third will be stated to avoid repetition throughout the book.

First, we will assume the majority view that the Gospel of Mark is the earliest of the four canonical Gospels. Since Mark does not have a version of the Lord's Prayer, this observation is only indirectly relevant. We will equally assume that Matthew and Luke drew upon Mark, particularly for the narrative portions of their respective texts.[1] Certainty beyond this point concerning sources is difficult. The common approach among scholars is to argue that Matthew and Luke have used a source designated as "Q" to explain the similarities in content and independent sources ("M" and "L," respectively) to explain variances within their respective Gospels. This view has recently

---

[1] To clarify, Matthew has a structure which places five discourses throughout the narrative portions of his Gospel. This fivefold discourse structuring differentiates the flow of Matthew's Gospel from Mark's Gospel.

been questioned with vigor, particularly the case for "Q."[2] Since "Q" is nonextant and remains unmentioned within documents of church history, some scholars remain hesitant to accept the two (or four)-source theory.[3] A possible way forward may be the recent renewal of interest in oral tradition.[4] Working within this paradigm, one is not predisposed to assume the originality of a story or saying based on Markan priority or literary "Q." Matthew and Luke may have had a source in front of them when recording the Sermon on the Mount/Plain and the Lord's Prayer (i.e., perhaps a "Q"), but they were not limited to copying its every word. If Matthew is writing as an eyewitness, it is likely he knew of an oral tradition that predated his written sources.[5] The acceptance of oral transmission seems appropriate in the present subject matter, given the nature of the Lord's Prayer as a Jewish prayer.[6] Scholars have long noted that the norm for Jewish prayers was to avoid a fixed form, preferring oral tradition instead.[7] This preference for orality allowed spontaneity and expression in one's own performance. The differences in Matthew and Luke's versions of the Lord's Prayer may partially be explained by this Jewish tendency.

What is more certain than the search for sources is that the two Sermons/Prayers have a significant overlap in material. Both Sermons follow the same basic ordering, beginning with a similar introduction (Mt. 5:1-2/Lk. 6:20a), followed by the *macarisms* (Mt. 5:3-12/Lk. 6:20b-23),[8] teaching on "loving your enemy" (Mt. 5:38-48/Lk. 6:27-36),

---

[2] Recent alternatives to the two-source hypothesis are well documented in Stanley E. Porter and Bryan R. Dyer, eds., *The Synoptic Problem: Four Views* (Grand Rapids: Baker, 2016). Specific arguments against "Q" as the source of the Sermon on the Mount can be found in Mark A. Matson, "Luke's Rewriting of the Sermon on the Mount," in *Questioning Q: A Multidimensional Critique*, ed. Mark Goodacre and Nicholas Perrin (Downers Grove: IVP, 2004), 43–70.

[3] See particularly Mark Goodacre, *The Synoptic Problem: A Way through the Maze*, Understanding the Bible and Its World (London: T&T Clark, 2004). Most recently, Francis Watson, *Gospel Writing: A Canonical Perspective* (Grand Rapids: Eerdmans, 2013), 158–67.

[4] See David Wenham, *From Good News to Gospels: What Did the First Christians Say about Jesus?* (Grand Rapids: Eerdmans, 2018). Also, Rainer Riesner, "The Orality and Memory Hypothesis," in *The Synoptic Problem: Four Views*, ed. Stanley E. Porter and Bryan R. Dyer (Grand Rapids: Baker, 2016), 89–111.

[5] On Matthew as an eyewitness, see Richard Bauckham, *Jesus and the Eyewitnesses: The Gospels as Eyewitness Testimony* (Grand Rapids: Eerdmans, 2008), 202–39. This text is now in its second edition.

[6] For a helpful explanation of the Lord's Prayer in the Jewish liturgical tradition, see Asher Finkel, "The Prayer of Jesus in Matthew," in *Standing Before God: Studies on Prayer in Scriptures and in Tradition with Essays in Honor of John M. Oesterreicher*, ed. A. Finkel and L. Frizzell (New York: KTAV Publishing, 1981), 131–69; Heinemann, "The Background of Jesus' Prayer," 81–9.

[7] See David Crump, *Knocking on Heaven's Door: A New Testament Theology of Petitionary Prayer* (Grand Rapids: Baker, 2006), 109–12; also, James D. G. Dunn, *Jesus Remembered*, Christianity in the Making, vol. 1 (Grand Rapids: Eerdmans, 2003), 226–8. Dunn, *Jesus Remembered*, 231–3, offers the same explanation for the Sermon on the Mount/Plain. Betz, *The Sermon on the Mount*, 370, states, "The three recensions [i.e., Matthew, Luke, *Didache*], therefore, represent variations of the prayer in the oral tradition . . . there was never only one original written Lord's Prayer . . . the oral tradition continued to exert an influence on the written text of the New Testament well into later times."

[8] One may notice the preference for *macarism* instead of "Beatitude." *Macarism* refers to the transliteration of the Greek term which begins each isocolon within Mt. 5:3-12. Because "Beatitude" is often translated as "happy" or simply as "blessed," we have retained the transliterated term. As we will discuss below, the meaning of the *macarisms* certainly includes happiness and God's blessings but is chiefly concerned with human flourishing. In cases where the author under consideration uses "Beatitudes," we will use their language in our analysis. In all other cases, we will use the transliterated term.

judging (Mt. 7:1-5/Lk. 6:37-42), Golden Rule (Mt. 7:12/Lk. 6:31), fruits (Mt. 7:16-20/ Lk. 6:43-45), those who say "Lord, Lord" (Mt. 7:21/Lk. 6:46), the two builders (Mt. 7:24-27/Lk. 6:47-49), and finally, Jesus concluding his teaching (Mt. 7:28/Lk. 7:1).[9] In the case of Mt. 6:24/Lk. 16:13, twenty-seven of the twenty-eight words are shared.[10] The Prayers are in the same ordering and share the same petitions except for Matthew's three added phrases (i.e., "Our Father in heaven," "your will be done, on earth as in heaven," and "deliver us from the evil one"). For this reason, the present book seeks to examine the literary shape of the Lord's Prayer and the Sermon on the Mount in their final form, without identifying the specific literary and oral sources of each composition. We will compare the *content* of the two versions as they are preserved in Matthew and Luke's Gospels, searching for each text's distinctive elements.[11] We are not as concerned with the *process* of how we received the two versions but rather what the differences may tell us about Matthew's version. My argument is that Matthew recognized, recorded, and enhanced the traditions, whether literary or oral, to establish parallels between the Lord's Prayer and the Sermon on the Mount.

Second, and closely related to the question of sources, is the discussion of the historical Jesus. Matthew is a compiler of Jesus's words, and oftentimes the "shape" and wording of the texts in his Gospel complicate the task of identifying the author of the sayings (i.e., the written Gospel). In other words, it is difficult to know what might go back to Jesus himself. It is also likely that Matthew's community helped shape the reception of some of the texts under examination, particularly one like the Lord's Prayer, as it was likely used within the community's worship.[12] Because the focus of our study is the final form of the text and the purpose and function of the prayer as it stands, these historical issues are irrelevant to our book. The present book will only examine the differing voices of Jesus, Matthew, and the community to the extent that the voices focus attention on distinctive elements in Matthew's Gospel.[13] For the sake of convenience, we will use the name "Jesus" to refer to those sayings that are attributed to Jesus (i.e., "then Jesus said ...," etc.) and use "Matthew" to refer to the shaping, parallelism, repetition, word count, and compositional techniques throughout Chapters 5–7. We are not going to discuss how the community may have shaped the traditions before Matthew received them, but only how Matthew has the community and its needs in mind.[14] We will avoid historical and tradition critical discussions concerned with the historical Jesus, Matthew, and Matthean community, and instead focus on the rhetoric of the texts under examination.

Third, we will assume that Jesus's understanding of eschatology is, in the words of Jeremias, eschatology "in the process of realization."[15] As Ladd noted, Jesus's teaching

---

[9] See Guelich, *Sermon on the Mount*, 33–5.
[10] For a further analysis of shared vocabulary and Synoptic comparison, see Appendix B–C.
[11] A further explanation of "distinctive elements" is addressed below.
[12] Jeremias, *Prayers of Jesus*, 87–9.
[13] This statement will be explained in more depth below.
[14] See Warren Carter, *Matthew: Storyteller, Interpreter, Evangelist*, rev. ed. (Peabody: Hendrickson, 2004), 231–41. Also, Richard Lischer, "The Sermon on the Mount as Radical Pastoral Care," *Int* 41 (1987): 157–69; Mattison, *Sermon and Moral Theology*, 238–69; Mathias Nygaard, *Prayer in the Gospels: A Theological Exegesis of the Ideal Pray-er*, BibInt 114 (Leiden: Brill, 2012).
[15] Joachim Jeremias, *The Parables of Jesus* (London: SCM, 1954), 18. Jeremias is referring specifically to the parables of Jesus, but Jeremias's assessment would include Jesus's other teachings.

on the kingdom is that it is *already* inaugurated in his ministry and actions, but the kingdom has *not yet* fully come.[16] This broad understanding of eschatology has not been accepted by all. Common among modern interpreters is a narrower definition of eschatology in which the emphasis is entirely on the future.[17] Raymond Brown is the most noted proponent of this understanding of eschatology as it relates to the Lord's Prayer. In his words, the petitions of the Lord's Prayer do not refer to "daily circumstances, but to the final times."[18] Brown summarizes,

> The Christian community of the first century, anxiously expecting the Second Coming, prays that God will completely glorify His name by establishing His kingdom, which represents the fulfilment of the plan He has willed for both earth and heaven. For its portion in this consummation of time, the community asks a place at the heavenly banquet table to break bread with Christ, and a forgiveness of its sins. A titanic struggle with Satan stands between the community and the realization of its prayer, and from this it asks to be delivered.[19]

Brown's arguments focus on (1) Jewish parallels that point to the future, (2) the use of the aorist tense in each petition signalling finality, and (3) the general assumption that if most of the petitions are eschatological future, then all the petitions are eschatological future.[20]

Brown's arguments are commendable for their inclusion of Jewish parallels and desire for consistency in method but are not without their faults. Briefly considered, Brown neglects the full range of Jewish parallels to the various petitions. In many cases, Brown's selection of parallels only focuses on the future when equally convincing parallels argue for an eschatological "now." Examples include his omission of Mt. 12:28

---

[16] George E. Ladd, *The Gospel of the Kingdom: Popular Expositions on the Kingdom of God* (Grand Rapids: Eerdmans, 1959). Contra the recent interpretation of David Aune, "Apocalyptic and the Lord's Prayer," in *Jesus, Gospel Tradition and Paul in the Context of Jewish and Greco-Roman Antiquity*, WUNT 303 (Tübingen: Mohr Siebeck, 2013), 75–93, who reads the Lord's Prayer as apocalyptic eschatology.

[17] At the other end of the spectrum is the recent defence of the non-eschatological interpretation of the Lord's Prayer by Jeffrey B. Gibson, *The Disciples' Prayer: The Prayer Jesus Taught in its Historical Setting* (Minneapolis: Fortress, 2005).

[18] Raymond Brown, "The Pater Noster as an Eschatological Prayer," *TS* 22.2 (1961): 175. Similar treatments include: G. R. Beasley-Murray, *Jesus and the Kingdom of God* (Grand Rapids: Eerdmans, 1986), 147–57; Jeremias, *Prayers of Jesus*, 94–107; John P. Meier, *A Marginal Jew: Rethinking the Historical Jesus*, vol. 2 (New York: Doubleday, 1994), 291–302. More tentatively, W. D. Davies and Dale Allison, *Matthew 1–7*, ICC (Edinburgh: T&T Clark, 1988), 590–615. More recently, Brant Pitre, "The Lord's Prayer and the New Exodus," *Letter & Spirit* 2 (2006): 69–96, has argued that the eschatology of the Lord's Prayer is "typological." Building on the thesis of N. T. Wright, "The Lord's Prayer as a Paradigm for Christian Prayer," in *Into God's Presence: Prayer in the New Testament*, ed. Richard N. Longenecker (Grand Rapids: Eerdmans, 2001), 132–54, Pitre argues that the Old Testament parallels are not only future but also a prayer for a new Exodus for God's people, recapitulating Israel's deliverance from Egypt.

[19] Brown, "Pater Noster as an Eschatological Prayer," 208.

[20] Similarly, Davies and Allison, *Matthew 1–7*, 594, state, "For the eschatological interpretation gives the text a pleasing thematic unity, and the objections raised against that interpretation are far from decisive."

and its importance for the kingdom petition,[21] his downplaying of Mt. 6:25-34 and its parallels to the bread petition,[22] and his misreading of the evidence for the temptation petition. Both Mt. 12:28 and 6:25-34 clearly point to the present. Concerning the temptation petition, Luz states, "Almost everything speaks against the [eschatological future view]. Neither in Jewish apocalypticism nor in the New Testament is πειρασμός an apocalyptic technical term."[23] The futuristic understanding of πειρασμός is provided by the context of Rev. 3:10 but is lacking in the context of the Lord's Prayer. Conclusively then, Brown's argument illuminates the importance of the futuristic aspects of the Lord's Prayer but overextends its application and excludes parallels to the petitions which argue for the present.

In our argument, the Lord's Prayer focuses on not only the future consummation of Jesus's kingdom (most notably, "your kingdom come") but also day-to-day discipleship. Jesus's prayer contains an eschatological "future" and eschatological "now" dualism. Arguments for the eschatological future aspect of the Lord's Prayer include (1) its close parallelism with other Jewish prayers for the future, notably the *Kaddish* and *Tefillah*;[24] (2) the Old Testament parallels (Isa. 63:10-17; Ezekiel 36; Mic. 4:8); and (3) the use of passive verbs in the initial petitions, signaling requests to God that he will accomplish (i.e., "hallowing his Name," "bringing about his kingdom," and "accomplishing his will" in the consummation of the world).[25] The eschatological "now" aspects of the Lord's Prayer, as we will argue, are evident in the prayers for daily bread, the obligation to forgive others (see also Mt. 6:14-15), and the avoidance of temptation and evil. One might note that the first and second halves evidence a change in focus. Petitions 1–3 emphasize the eschatological future, but not at the expense of day-to-day living. Petitions 4–7 emphasize day-to-day discipleship (i.e., the present), but as a means of preparing for the coming kingdom and future battles of discipleship. Crump helpfully summarizes this dual focus/dimension within the Lord's Prayer:

> Jesus *first* teaches disciples to yearn for the Father's ultimate, eternal glorification in the return of Christ and the establishment of the new heavens and the new earth. We are emphatically reminded of our total dependence on God to perform his own work in his own timing, something the early church reinforced each time it cried out in worship, "Maranatha—Come, O Lord" (1 Cor. 16:22). Then and

---

[21] Matthew 12:28 states, "But if it is by the Spirit of God that I cast out demons, then the kingdom of God has come to you." For a discussion of "has come" (ἔφθασεν), see C. C. Caragounis, "Kingdom of God/Kingdom of Heaven," in *DJG*, IVP Bible Dictionary Series, 1st ed., ed. Joel B. Green, Scot McKnight, and I. Howard Marshall (Downers Grove: IVP, 1992), 420-4. We agree with those scholars who believe Mt. 12:28 refers to imminence. See Gundry, *Matthew*, 235; Keener, *Gospel of Matthew*, 363-4; Nolland, *Gospel of Matthew*, 501.

[22] We will argue for this parallel extensively in Chapter 5.

[23] Luz, *Matthew 1–7*, 322. Luz's only exception is Rev. 3:10, in which the context clearly dictates a future interpretation. This explicit emphasis on the future is missing in the context of the Lord's Prayer.

[24] Also, Davies and Allison, *Matthew 1–7*, 594.

[25] The use of the passive verb tense in which God is the implied subject is often called the "divine passive." We will discuss the agency of God in the first three petitions in the chapters that follow. As we will argue, the "divine passive" does not negate human responsibility, even if God is the "accomplisher."

only then are we free to consider an important secondary dimension: that Jesus disciples must meanwhile walk a daily path of preparation for his coming in joyful surrender and the consequent obedience proving our devotion true.[26]

In summary, the following book is *not* an exercise in source criticism, tradition and historical inquiries, or properly defining Jesus's understanding of eschatology. Rather, this book is an exercise in intratextual reading. We will read two passages, the Lord's Prayer and Sermon on the Mount, as they are presented together within Matthew's Gospel.

Methodology

In the following book, we will use a version of composition criticism commonly called rhetorical criticism. Two recent studies on the Gospel of Matthew have used this approach. Joel Willitts has analyzed the phrase, "the lost sheep of Israel" and its role in Matthew's depiction of Jesus as the Shepherd-king.[27] More recently, Jason Hood has analyzed the genealogy of Jesus in Matthew's Gospel as a summary of Israel's story and examined its inclusion of four Gentile women.[28] Both studies have produced substantive results by examining the final form of the text rather than "its antecedent aspects (Mark, Q, Aramaic Matthew)."[29] This approach does not imply that the antecedent aspects are without consequence, but only function as background to the composition itself. In the following section, we will discuss the interplay of redaction criticism, a discipline that examines the antecedents, and rhetorical criticism, a discipline which examines the final form.[30] We will argue that a bridge between these disciplines is relevant to the study of the Lord's Prayer within the Sermon on the Mount.[31]

Redaction Criticism

At the turn of the Second World War, Günther Bornkamm produced an article entitled "The Stilling of the Storm in Matthew" and began the quest for Matthew's redactional

---

[26] Crump, *Knocking on Heaven's Door*, 120.
[27] Joel Willitts, *Matthew's Messianic Shepherd-King: In Search of 'The Lost Sheep of the House of Israel,'* Beiherfte Zur Zeitschrift Für Die Neutestamentliche Wissenschaft (Berlin: De Gruyter, 2007).
[28] Jason B. Hood, *The Messiah, His Brothers, and the Nations: Matthew 1:1–17*, LNTS 441 (London: T&T Clark, 2011). See also the earlier study, Michael Knowles, *Jeremiah in Matthew's Gospel: The Rejected Profit Motif in Matthean Redaction*, JSNTSupp Series 68 (Sheffield: Sheffield Academic, 1993).
[29] The words of Hood, *Messiah, His Brother, and the Nations*, 3.
[30] See Grant Osborne, "Redaction Criticism," in *DJG*, IVP Bible Dictionary Series, 1st ed., ed. Joel B. Green, Scot McKnight, and I. Howard Marshall (Downers Grove: IVP, 1992), 662, describes four "schools" of Biblical criticisms: (1) Form criticism, (2) Tradition criticism (also known as Source criticism), (3) Redaction criticism, and (4) Literary criticism. The following book will implement the methods described in Osborne's third and fourth schools.
[31] Contra Thomas R. Hatina, "Intertextuality and Historical Criticism in New Testament Studies: Is There a Relationship?" *BI* 7.1 (1999), 28–43. For a helpful overview of how redaction criticism and compositional criticism are similar, see Randall K. J. Tan, "Recent Developments in Redaction Criticism: From Investigation of Textual Prehistory Back to Historical-Grammatical Exegesis?" *JETS* 44.4 (2001): 599–614.

hand. This essay would later be published alongside a series of articles by his students, G. Barth and H. J. Held, under the title of *Tradition and Interpretation in Matthew*.[32] Although not the first example of redaction criticism in the Synoptics, *Tradition and Interpretation* became a standard for later studies of redaction criticism in Matthew's Gospel. The method of redaction criticism has developed considerably since its incipient stages, but it has remained consistent with its emphasis on repeated features, key structuring elements, and use of sources.[33] Redaction critics use these elements to "discover" the theology of the respective author.

As we noted above, taking stock of sources is a difficult task. In the present book, more attention will be given to repeated features and structuring elements. These areas of attention have become known as Mattheanisms.[34] We will define Mattheanisms under the following headings: dissonance, repetition, prominence, consistency, and internal structuring. (1) "Dissonance" refers to those words or phrases that appear in Matthew's Gospel that do not appear in Mark and Luke. For example, "our Father in heaven" is exclusively found in Matthew and for this reason, is considered a Mattheanism.[35] (2) "Repetition" refers to a phrase used throughout Matthew's writing. This criterion is assessed through word statistics. If a writer uses a phrase not found in another's work and uses the phrase often, the chances of it being distinctive to the writer's work increase. Thus, "Father in heaven" is used on twenty different occasions in Matthew's Gospel, making it common within the Gospel itself. (3) "Prominence" is closely related to repetition but focuses on the location of the repetition within the Gospel. Of the twenty references to the "Father in heaven," ten of those instances are found in the Sermon on the Mount (chs 5–7) without any significant concentration elsewhere. This clustering signals a greater likelihood that the hand of the Evangelist is present, and the references should be read together. (4) "Consistency" refers to a writer's tendency to use a phrase throughout their work with similar functionality. So, if "our Father in heaven" is found only in Matthew, does Matthew use the phrase in a consistent way? The answer is yes. The "Father in heaven" is almost exclusively used in a contrasting manner, as a foil to earthly kingdoms and a term for defining the relationship between God and his disciples. (5) "Internal structuring" refers to passages with a structure absent in the Markan and Lukan parallels. Matthew uses structuring devices throughout his Gospel, but parallelism and *inclusios* are especially of note in the Sermon on the Mount. For example, the teaching on salt and light are in synonymous parallelism (Mt. 5:13-16) in Matthew's Gospel. This parallelism is signaled by the similar wording of these teachings and the added phrases, "of the earth" and "of the world," to the respective metaphors.

---

[32] Günther Bornkamm, G. Barth, and H. J. Held, *Tradition and Interpretation in Matthew* (Philadelphia: Westminster, 1963).

[33] Mark Goodacre, "Redaction Criticism," in *DJG*, IVP Bible Dictionary Series, 2nd ed., ed. Joel B. Green, Jeannine K. Brown, and Nicholas Perrin (Downers Grove: IVP, 2013), 662–8.

[34] See Gundry, *Matthew*, 1–5. Gundry provides a thorough discussion of Mattheanism, but at a basic level it refers to Matthew's favourite diction.

[35] Some argue that Lk. 11:13 is an example of the "Father in heaven" outside of Matthew's Gospel. We will argue that is not a proper usage and therefore not a parallel to Matthew's references.

You are the **salt** *of the earth* (5:13)
You are the **light** *of the world* (5:14)

The parallelism is furthered by the addition of contrasts to each metaphor (i.e., useless salt/light under a basket). In the Markan and Lukan parallels, the teaching on salt and light are not found together. The teaching on salt is found in Mk. 9:49-50 and Lk. 14:34-35, while the teaching on the light/lamp is found in Mk. 4:21 (vv. 22-23) and Lk. 8:16 (vv. 17-18) and 11:33. Matthew appears to bring these teachings together and strengthens their parallelism with the use of modifiers. In addition to parallelism, Matthew is also fond of *inclusios*.[36] We will argue that the Lord's Prayer and the Sermon on the Mount are structured differently from their Lukan counterparts, with both texts shaped by a series of *inclusios* to form a concentric structure.

A word of caution is in order with the defining of Mattheanism. An interpreter must be careful not to assume that significance is only found in "distinctive" words or phrases. We agree with Stanton who writes,

> The formation of Matthew's gospel may have been the result of a much longer and a much more complex process than the "one-stage" redaction commonly envisaged. Even though it is very difficult indeed to isolate with confidence changes made to Mark, Q, or "M" traditions by redactors other than Matthew, there are good grounds for urging caution: not every difference between Matthew and the sources which he drew represents a modification introduced by the evangelist Matthew himself.[37]

Stanton's careful remarks argue that distinctive units do not always necessitate the hand of the Evangelist at work. The retention of shared phrases between the Synoptics can be as intentional as differing material. For example, the name and temptation petitions in both the Matthean and Lukan versions of the Lord's Prayer are unchanged and remain important to the Prayer's message. For this reason, our study of redaction will consider the Markan and Lukan parallels, but for the sake of comparison and not necessarily contrast. In the cases of contrast, we will note the defining characteristics of Mattheanism.[38]

Rhetorical Criticism

In 1969, James Muilenburg delivered the presidential address to the annual *Society of Biblical Literature*, offering a corrective to the form criticism of his day. Muilenburg

---

[36] See Luz, *Matthew 1–7*, 7–8; Nolland, *Gospel of Matthew*, 23–6.
[37] Stanton, *Gospel for a New People*, 41. Also, Willitts, "Presuppositions and Procedures in the Study of the 'Historical Jesus': Or, Why I Decided Not to be a 'Historical Jesus' Scholar," *JSHJ* 3.1 (2005): 106–7.
[38] A similar methodology is found in R. T. France's *Matthew: Evangelist and Teacher* (Downers Grove: IVP, 1998), 49, in which he calls for a neutral redaction criticism. He states, "I believe, then, that an open verdict on the literary relationships of the synoptics is not a barrier to fruitful study of the distinctive methods and message of each of them."

argued that more attention should be paid to the rhetorical features of a pericope. In form criticism, generalization is preferred because it "is concerned with what is common to all the representatives of a genre."[39] Muilenburg offers that this approach to the text does not pay attention to what is unique and unrepeatable in each formulation. It is for this reason that redaction criticism was a necessary corrective to form criticism, with its attention to the unique or distinctive elements to the text. Yet, Muilenburg goes further than redaction criticism. He states, "It is the creative synthesis of the particular formulation of the pericope with the content that makes it the distinctive composition that it is."[40] Muilenburg urges attention to the literary features of a text, particularly as they appear in their final forms.[41]

Muilenburg's observation offers relevance for the following study of the Lord's Prayer and Sermon on the Mount. In Muilenburg's first suggestion for a rhetorical critic, he draws attention to the limits and scope of a literary unit. He states, "The literary unit is in any event an indissoluble whole, an artistic and creative unity, a unique formulation."[42] Our study will focus on Mt. 5:1–8:1 as a unique and artistic unity. Second, a rhetorical critic is to recognize the structure of a composition.[43] We will argue that Matthew has structured the Sermon on the Mount to draw attention to the Lord's Prayer as its centerpiece (Chapter 3). Attention to structure inevitably leads to the question of functionality. If Matthew has structured the Sermon on the Mount to reflect the centrality of the Lord's Prayer, what effect does this text have on our understanding of the Sermon? And, is structure the only clue of centrality? We will argue that the Lord's Prayer is not only structurally central to the Sermon on the Mount but also shares wording and themes with the surrounding Sermon. Collectively, the structure and lexical/thematic parallels suggest that the Lord's Prayer is the centerpiece of the Sermon on the Mount. In concert with Muilenburg's final observation, we agree that "form and content are inextricably related. They form an integral whole."[44]

Methodological Implications

The examination of redaction and rhetorical criticism has numerous consequences[45] for the present study. In the following section, we will show how each of these consequences affects the shape of the book. The current approach focuses on the final

---

[39] James Muilenburg, "Form Criticism and Beyond," *JBL* 88.1 (1969): 5.
[40] Muilenburg, "Form Criticism and Beyond," 5.
[41] This appeal to rhetorical function is different than the approach of many readers of the Sermon on the Mount. "Rhetoric" does not necessarily indicate an appeal to Greek categories of persuasion. Examples of those who use Greek categories include: Betz, *Sermon on the Mount*; George A. Kennedy, *New Testament Interpretation through Rhetorical Criticism*, Studies in Religion (Chapel Hill: University of North Carolina, 1984).
[42] Muilenburg, "Form Criticism and Beyond," 9. Interestingly, Muilenburg notes that an indicator of the beginning and end of a unit is repetition of wording. This repetition forms a "ring composition" or *inclusio*. This use of *inclusios* is precisely what we will argue concerning the structure of the Sermon on the Mount.
[43] Muilenburg, "Form Criticism and Beyond," 10.
[44] Muilenburg, "Form Criticism and Beyond," 5.
[45] Hood's study, *Messiah, His Brothers, and the Nations*, 5–7, helpfully lays out the following categories.

form (rhetorical criticism) of the texts, the distinctive features (redaction criticism) of the text, and related compositions (rhetorical/redaction criticism) of the text.

Final Form Focus

The following book will analyze the final form of Matthew 5–7. The inclusion of the Lord's Prayer appears to be part of this organization. The beginning and ending of the Sermon on the Mount are defined by Jesus ascending (Mt. 5:1-2) and descending a mountain (Mt. 7:28–8:1) as well as mention of those gathered to hear the Sermon (i.e., disciples [Mt. 5:1] and crowds [Mt. 7:28]). In conjunction with Muilenburg's insights, we will examine the structure of the Sermon on the Mount as it is delineated by these dual inclusions. We will argue that the structure of the Sermon on the Mount has a concentric shape that draws attention to the Lord's Prayer as its center. The Prayer's centrality then becomes the foundation for subsequent parallels, both lexical and thematic, with the Sermon on the Mount.

Focus on Distinctive Features

Crucial to the present project is not only the structurally central position of the Lord's Prayer but also its distinctive features. Rhetorical criticism, while examining the final form, does not ignore Synoptic comparisons. Synoptic comparisons show that each text has features that are distinctive to its composition (i.e., Mattheanisms). The distinctives of the Matthean Lord's Prayer will be gleaned from a comparison with the other Synoptics, with special reference to the Lukan Lord's Prayer. We will argue that the additional petitions and distinctive wording are indicative of Matthew's intentional centering. Not only is the wording itself indicative of Matthew's intentions but also the clustering of the phrases within the Sermon on the Mount, in comparison with chs 8–28.

Focus on Related Compositions

Compositional criticism differentiates itself from other literary criticisms in its inclusion of historical texts that serve as parallels. As Willitts states, "Concerns with the issues of historical background, the real author and *referentiality* in the extra-textual world where that author lives and breathes remain in the foreground."[46] This material allows Matthew and Jesus to be understood in the world in which they occupy.[47]

Richard Hays provides a helpful analogy from the study of Renaissance poetry, stating that "to hear and understand the poet's allusions we need to know not only

---

[46] Willitts, *Matthew's Messianic Shepherd-King*, 39. Emphasis mine.
[47] See Ulrich Luz, "Intertexts in the Gospel of Matthew," *HTR* 97.2 (2004): 119–37. Also, Luz, *Matthew 1–7*, 314, fn.55, states, the Lord's Prayer is an ideal text for studying reception. As D. C. Allison, *The New Moses: A Matthean Typology* (Minneapolis: Fortress, 1993), 289, argues, "If it is true that Jesus was, for Matthew, the hermeneutical key to unlocking the religious meaning of the Jewish Bible, it is also true that the Jewish Bible was for him the hermeneutical key to unlocking the religious meaning of Jesus."

the tradition to which the allusion points but also the way in which that tradition was understood in the poet's time and the contemporary historical experience or situation with which the poet links the tradition."[48] The import of this argument is the necessity of looking at similar phrases and prayers within Matthew's cultural milieu that give us insights into the meaning of the Lord's Prayer.[49] Specifically, we will search for parallels in not only the Hebrew Scriptures[50] but also Second Temple Literature[51] and relevant Rabbinic literature.[52] By most accounts, the Lord's Prayer was inspired by Jewish prayer, given by a Jewish man,[53] recorded by a Jewish author, and received by Jewish hearers.[54] Therefore, an examination of Jewish parallels seems appropriate for a thorough examination of each petition.

In terms of examination, a search for textual connections creates an issue for the interpreter. Whereas some textual connections are more explicit, some parallels can refer to a variety of things.[55] For clarification, we will establish some indicators to assist

---

[48] Richard B. Hays, *Echoes of Scripture in the Letters of Paul* (New Haven: Yale University, 1989), 18.

[49] "Cultural milieu" is also commonly called "cultural encyclopedia." Leroy A. Huizenga, "The Old Testament in the New, Intertextuality, and Allegory," *JSNT* 38.1 (2015): 28, helpfully notes, "The world of the text is not immanent, but exists and can only be perceived coherently in relationship to the wider materials from which it is constructed, its cultural encyclopaedia." He continues, "Interpretation, then, is both dynamic and constrained: constrained, because interpreting a particular text involves examining its particular relations to the appropriate encyclopaedia from which it was produced, but also dynamic, because texts have infinite potential connections to other texts and cultures, even those which do not yet exist." We will argue that the cultural encyclopedia of the Lord's Prayer helps us to understand its meaning, but then Matthew has connected this Prayer to its context, the Sermon on the Mount.

[50] Mark J. Boda, "Poethics? The Use of Biblical Hebrew Poetry in Ethical Reflection on the Old Testament," *CBR* 14.1 (2015): 45–61, has recently shown how Old Testament poetry has become a centerpiece for studies of Old Testament ethics. See also Ulrich Luz, "Vaterunser I. Neues Testament," *TRE* 34 (2002): 504–12.

[51] For a helpful overview of prayer in Second Temple literature, see David Flusser, "Psalms, Hymns, and Prayers," in *Jewish Writings of the Second Temple Period*, vol. 2, ed. Michael E. Stone (Philadelphia: Fortress, 1984), 551–77.

[52] M. J. J. Menken, *Matthew's Bible: The Old Testament Text of the Evangelist*, BETL 173 (Leuven: Leuven University, 2004), argues persuasively that Matthew most often quotes from the LXX. For this reason, we will note the Greek parallels to the petition under consideration with only occasional reference to the Hebrew and Aramaic. Additionally, the search for "relevant" Rabbinic parallels can be a slippery slope. As most of the material postdates the writing of the canonical documents, finding contemporary parallels is difficult. Yet, postdated material may contain ideas consistent with the earlier traditions. We will generally examine texts that are thought to originate in the first century. For a helpful overview of the issues and their relevance to the Lord's Prayer, see David Instone-Brewer, *Prayer and Agriculture*, vol. 1, TRENT (Grand Rapids: Eerdmans, 2004); Craig A. Evans, *Jesus and His Contemporaries: Comparative Studies* (Leiden: Brill, 2001), 276–97. For a helpful starting point to Rabbinic parallels to the Lord's Prayer, cf. Hermann L. Strack and Paul Billerbeck, *Kommentar Zum Neuen Testament: aus Talmud und Midrasch*, vol. 1: *Das Evangelium Nach Matthäus* (München: C.H. Beck'sche Verlagsbuchhandlung, 1922), 402–24; and C. G. Montefiore, *Rabbinic Literature and Gospel Teachings* (London: Macmillan, 1930), 125–34.

[53] For an examination of prayer during the time of Jesus, see James H. Charlesworth, "Jewish Prayers in the Time of Jesus," in *The Lord's Prayer: Perspectives for Reclaiming Christian Prayer*, ed. Daniel Migliore (Grand Rapids: Eerdmans, 1993), 36–55. Also, Nijay K. Gupta, *The Lord's Prayer*, Smyth & Helwys Bible Commentary Supp Series (Macon: Smyth & Helwys, 2017), 1–12.

[54] For the sake of argument, we will assume that the Lord's Prayer was created by Jesus and recorded by Matthew. For a fuller discussion of the *ipsissima vox Jesu*, see Jeremias, *Prayers of Jesus*, 108–15.

[55] Several terms are used in the process of identifying inner-biblical allusions. Among those terms are quotations, allusions, echoes, metaphors, exegesis, and even plagiarism. For the sake of convenience, we will narrow our nomenclature to allusions and echoes. Allusions are clear connections between

in differentiating the types of textual connections we will refer to in the following chapters. The following list will work from the clearest parallels to less obvious.

The first category consists of instances with verbal and formal similarity between traditions. We will refer to these connections as allusions. The following category describes those passages or links that share similar wording, word order, and/or function within respective contexts. Leonard summarizes,

> (1) Shared language is the single most important factor in establishing a textual connection. (2) Shared language is more important than non-shared language. (3) Shared language that is rare or distinctive suggests a stronger connection than does language that is widely used. (4) Shared phrases suggest a stronger connection than do individual shared terms. (5) The accumulation of shared language suggests a stronger connection than does a single shared term or phrase. (6) Shared language in similar contexts suggests a stronger connection than does shared language alone. (7) Shared language need not be accompanied by shared ideology to establish a connection. (8) Shared language need not be accompanied by shared form to establish a connection.[56]

Leonard's observations draw attention to shared wording. While these connections may seem plain, the interpreter might heed the warning of David Wenham, who argues that shared/similar wording does not necessitate a parallel, especially if the subject was a common source or well-known saying.[57] Also, similarities between passages do not necessitate direct literary borrowing. Clearer connections are established with the higher amount of verbal links or unique words that are shared between separate sources.[58]

The second category contains parallels between similar thoughts. This category represents the most difficult connections to establish because of the lack of explicit verbal agreements. While the verbal agreement may be lacking or absent, agreements in thought and outlook are still possible. It is important to emphasize the degree of probability in these cases and not the degree of certainty. In his now classic treatment of intertextuality in Paul's writings, *Echoes of Scripture in the Letters of Paul*, Richard Hays provides seven criteria for discerning similarity of thought.[59] The seven criteria are availability, volume, recurrence, thematic coherence, historical plausibility, history

---

texts, while echoes are loosely connected to earlier texts. Allusions will have several shared words and signals to intentional borrowing. Echoes may share the same ideas/themes but lack clear lexical parallels. While each connection has degrees of proximity, we will attempt to avoid thematic connections that were simply part of Jewish consciousness and lack clear lexical catchwords. See Hays, *Echoes of Scripture in Paul*, 14–33.

[56] Jeffrey Leonard, "Identifying Inner-Biblical Allusions: Psalms 78 as a Test Case," *JBL* 127.2 (2008), 246.

[57] David Wenham, *Paul: Follower of Jesus or Founder of Christianity?* (Grand Rapids: Eerdmans, 1995), 27–8, states, "Similar wording in itself does not necessarily prove a significant connection between two traditions. The similarity could be coincidental, especially if the general topic under discussion is the same or if the two authors concerned could be drawing directly or indirectly on a common source, for example, a well-known proverb."

[58] Wenham, *Paul*, 27–8.

[59] Hays, *Echoes of Scripture in Paul*, 29–32.

of interpretation, and satisfaction. Hays's criterion of thematic coherence is especially helpful for identifying proposed echoes. Hays expounds the criterion with a series of questions.[60] The questions are as follows, but with reference to Matthew:

1. How well does the alleged echo fit into the line of argument that Matthew is developing?
2. Is its meaning effect consonant with other quotations in Matthew's Gospel?
3. Do the images and ideas of the proposed precursor text illuminate Matthew's argument?

In what follows, we will point out these "looser" parallels as we attempt to answer Hays's questions.

Structure of this Book

To attend to the final form, distinctive features, and related compositions, we will investigate three aspects of the centrality of the Lord's Prayer in the Sermon on the Mount. In the first part of the research (Chapter 3), we will argue that the Sermon on the Mount is structured in such a way to draw the readers' attention to its center. This structural arrangement, built on *inclusios*, highlights the Lord's Prayer as the focal point of the Sermon on the Mount. We will additionally argue that the Lord's Prayer is similarly structured with seven petitions arranged in a concentric fashion (1st/2nd with 6th/7th; 3rd with 5th; 4th as center). This chapter provides a foundation for the remaining chapters as it examines the shape of the Sermon on the Mount and argues for the Lord's Prayer as the structural centerpiece.

In the remaining chapters, we will examine the textual connections between the Prayer's petitions and the surrounding Sermon on the Mount. In accordance with Muilenburg's observations, we will note distinctive features of each petition and examine its related compositions (i.e., Jewish parallels). Chapters 4 through 6 will be similarly ordered. In the first section of each chapter, we will show the distinctive wording of the petition under examination as a foundation for lexical parallels. The Matthean Lord's Prayer is distinctive from the Lukan version in its inclusion of added petitions (i.e., Father, will, and evil) and different wording.[61] These added petitions are prominent not only in Matthew's Gospel but also clustered together in Chapters 5–7. We will argue that this prominence strengthens the argument for distinctiveness and reinforces the Prayer's centrality within the Sermon on the Mount. This pattern is repeated to a lesser degree in the Matthean petitions which have "slightly" different wording (i.e., bread, forgiveness) than their Lukan parallel (Chapter 5).

---

[60] Hays, *Echoes of Scripture of Paul*, 30
[61] An exception to this statement is the Name and temptation petitions. Although the kingdom petition is verbatim in Matthew and Luke, we will argue that the addition of the will petition explains Matthew's understanding of the kingdom petition.

The second section will examine the meaning of each petition as a basis for thematic parallels. To establish the meaning of each petition and subsequent thematic parallels, we will ground the petitions in Matthew's "world" by examining related compositions, particularly in Jewish literature. Research into Matthew's cultural milieu assists in defining how each petition may have been heard, understood, and used. This second section, along with the previous section, will provide a basis for identifying textual connections, both lexical and thematic, between the Lord's Prayer and the Sermon on the Mount.

The third section of Chapters 4 through 6 will examine the lexical and thematic parallels between each petition and the Sermon. Having established each petition's distinctive wording (Section 1) and meaning (Section 2), we will examine how each petition parallels the various sections of the Sermon on the Mount, thus making a case for its integrated position as the "centerpiece" of the Sermon. After examining the strongest parallels, we will note plausible echoes.

Chapter 7 will summarize the above findings concerning the relationship between the Lord's Prayer and the Sermon on the Mount. Dale Allison is persuasive when he comments, "It is my conviction that the discussion [concerning the Sermon on the Mount] has not yet run its course, that some interesting and important observations have been missed."[62] As we hope to demonstrate, the cumulative evidence of Chapters 3 through 6 extends Allison's conviction to a reading of the Sermon on the Mount that considers the importance of the Lord's Prayer as its structural, lexical, and thematic centerpiece.

---

[62] Allison, *Studies in Matthew*, 173.

3

The Structure of the Sermon on the Mount and the Lord's Prayer

Survey of Structures and a Proposal

This chapter will address the structure of the Sermon on the Mount and argue that the Lord's Prayer is its significant center. Most commentators have shied away from this view, seeing the Lord's Prayer as included by Matthew to serve as an explanation of proper prayer (see Mt. 6:5-8) with little added significance. This chapter will come to a very different conclusion, interacting with several proposals concerning the Sermon on the Mount's structure before arguing the case for a particular view of the centrality of the Lord's Prayer. It is important to acknowledge at the outset that determining the structure of a particular passage can be a daunting task, fraught with dangers. It is easy in seeking to discern the mind of the author to see structuring where structuring is not intended.[1] This is easily done with the Sermon on the Mount, as we will see. The conclusions of this chapter will establish the Prayer as the foundation for subsequent parallels, both lexical and thematic, with the Sermon on the Mount.

Major Structural Proposals of the Sermon on the Mount

In assessing the various proposals, we may identify five major categories: (1) Thematic/Theological, (2) Triadic, (3) Chiastic, (4) Expositional/Structurally Centric, and (5) Concentric.[2] These headings attempt to describe the final proposal as it is outlined

---

[1] The presupposition is that the structuring of the passage is from the hand of the author (Matthew from this point forward). Postmodern critics have sought to validate the idea that the audience is the determiner of meaning and related issues such as structure. Although there is considerable debate revolving around these issues, it is beyond the scope of this chapter.

[2] Although not dealt with in depth in the following analysis, there are some who would fall into the "simple outline" category. These proposals do not have one major theme or structural "key." These proposals simply follow the text and outline each major topic. The major sections are usually 5:3-20, 5:21-48, 6:1-18, 6:19-7:12, and 7:13-27. Different exegetes split the sections in various ways but invariably to reflect topical/thematic changes. Common examples of this approach would be: W. F. Albright and C. S. Mann, *Matthew: Introduction, Translation, and Notes*, AB (Garden City: Doubleday, 1971), 45-89; Willoughby C. Allen, *A Critical and Exegetical Commentary on the Gospel According to St. Matthew*, 3rd ed., ICC (Edinburgh: T&T Clark, 1993), 37-8; A. W. Argyle, *The Gospel According*

in each respective author's work. Within these proposals, different methodologies are employed, which will be addressed in each section.

Because of the multiplicity of structural proposals, it is difficult to narrow down a who's who of proposals. Interestingly, the concern for structure is a relatively modern phenomenon. The early commentators on the Sermon were more concerned with the theology of the Sermon rather than structure. In the modern era, commentators have noted how structure actually reflects and may be the key to the theology of a piece of writing. While several exegetes have proposed outlines for the Sermon in books on other subjects, the following survey seeks to engage those who have published major monographs on the subject of the Sermon's structure or written major Matthean commentaries that address the subject at length. The survey will cover theological/thematic structures before moving to more formal/rhetorical structures.

Thematic/Theological Structure

We begin by examining proposals that have identified major themes or theological emphases as the structural guide. The most popular theme noted by scholars is "righteousness."[3] The following analyses will consider the literary methods of Jack Kingsbury and the work of the redaction critic Robert Guelich.[4]

Jack Kingsbury

Jack Kingsbury is perhaps most noted for his work on the structure of Matthew's Gospel and his analysis of Jesus as the Son of God in Matthew's narrative. Beginning his career as a redaction critic, Kingsbury eventually turned to a literary approach of reading the Gospels as stories.[5] In this shift of methodology, Kingsbury brings a different set of presuppositions and questions to the Sermon. In his approach, he addresses the

---

to Matthew, CBC (Cambridge: University, 1963), 43–64; F. W. Beare, The Gospel According to Matthew: A Commentary (Oxford: Basil Blackwell, 1981), 123; J. Dupont, Les Béatitudes, vol. 1 (Paris: Gabalda, 1969), 175–83; Craig A. Evans, Matthew, NCBC (Cambridge: University, 2012), 96–183; France, Gospel of Matthew, viii–ix, 153–6; David E. Garland, Reading Matthew: A Literary and Theological Commentary (Macon: Smyth & Helwys, 2001), 51–2; Douglas R. A. Hare, Matthew, Interpretation (Louisville: Westminster John Knox, 2009), 33–87; Daniel J. Harrington, The Gospel of Matthew, Sacra Pagina (Collegeville: Liturgical, 2007), 76–111; Herman Hendrickx, The Sermon on the Mount, Studies in the Synoptic Gospels (London: Geoffrey Chapman, 1984), v–vii; Meier, Matthew, 76; Nolland, Gospel of Matthew, vii–viii; Alfred Plummer, An Exegetical Commentary on the Gospel According to Matthew (London: Robert Scott, 1915), 57; Georg Strecker, The Sermon on the Mount: An Exegetical Commentary, trans. O. C. Dean (Nashville: Abingdon, 1989), 11–5.

[3] Lesser known examples include: David Hill, "The Meaning of the Sermon on the Mount in Matthew's Gospel," IBS 6 (1984): 122–3, 128–9; and partially, Neil J. McEleney, "The Principles of the Sermon on the Mount," CBQ 41 (1979): 552–70.

[4] Although not dealt with here, other examples include: Wisdom, see Gary Tuttle, "Sermon on the Mount: Its Wisdom Affinities and their Relation to its Structure," JETS 20.3 (1977): 213–30, the Disciples' calling, see F. D. Bruner, Matthew: A Commentary, vol. 1 (Grand Rapids: Eerdmans, 2004), 150–1; and "a way of life," see Betz, Sermon on the Mount, 50–8. Those sympathetic to aspects of Betz's approach include: Keener, Gospel of Matthew, 162–3; and Kennedy, New Testament Interpretation through Rhetorical Criticism, 39–72.

[5] Compare Parables of Jesus in Matthew 13: A Study in Redaction Criticism (London: SPCK, 1977) and Matthew as Story, 2nd ed. (Minneapolis: Fortress, 1988).

issues relevant to reading the entirety of Matthew as a story with a beginning, climax, and end. Instead of comparing Matthew's Sermon with Luke's Sermon or focusing on the Sermon as a "piece" of Matthew, Kingsbury deals with how the Sermon fits into the overall flow of Matthew. He reads Matthew as a completed text with little regard for the various criticisms of source, form, and redaction.

Before turning to the Sermon's structure, Kingsbury lays out some of his interpretive presuppositions. First, Kingsbury argues that the story in Matthew culminates in the crucifixion.[6] So, the Sermon is an important piece, but it does not set the tone for the remaining Gospel.[7] Second, Kingsbury places the Sermon in the narrative block of Mt. 4:17–11:1. Here in these eight chapters, Jesus's ministry of teaching, preaching, and healing is highlighted. The Sermon becomes the example *par excellence* of Jesus's teaching and points beyond itself to Jesus's passion in Matthew's storyline.

For Kingsbury, not only is the narrative flow important for understanding the Sermon's structure but also the intended audience, referred to as "the implied reader." Kingsbury argues that the two groups ("disciples" and "crowds") mentioned by Matthew do not fit the message and purpose of the Sermon. In both cases, Jesus's message sets forth an ideal set of teachings that each group is incapable of keeping. Kingsbury thus reasons that Jesus is speaking beyond the audience that Matthew describes and, instead, is speaking to the readers who may find themselves in persecution and trials before Jesus's second coming.

These issues form the backdrop for Kingsbury's literary approach to understanding the Sermon's message. The Sermon is part of the narrative of Matthew. It is but one section working toward the climactic moment of the Passion. The Sermon's intended audience is a disciple of Jesus living between the two advents and experiencing persecution. In this advent, Jesus is the identified Son of God. These literary concerns are foundational for the Sermon's major theme: righteousness.

In describing the Sermon's structure, Kingsbury notes the *inclusio* of ascending (Mt. 5:1-2) and descending the mountain (Mt. 7:28–8:1). Beyond these observations, the key to the Sermon's structure is found in Mt. 5:20: "For I tell you, unless *your righteousness exceeds* that of the scribes and Pharisees, you will never enter the kingdom of heaven."[8] Kingsbury argues that this key verse sets the theme for the entire Sermon. His structure is as follows:

1. Introduction: On Those Who Practice the Greater Righteousness (5:3-16)
2. On Practicing the Greater Righteousness toward the Neighbor (5:17-45)
3. On Practicing the Greater Righteousness before God (6:1-18)
4. On Practicing the Greater Righteousness in Other Areas of Life (6:19–7:12)
5. Conclusion: Injunctions on Practicing the Greater Righteousness (7:13-27)

---

[6] Kingsbury argues that the idea of the Sermon on the Mount being the primary speech in Matthew's Gospel originated in the work of Benjamin Bacon, *Studies in Matthew* (London: Constable, 1930).
[7] Kingsbury, "Place, Structure, and Meaning," 133, states, "Although Matthew's story of Jesus culminates in the passion, it is nonetheless testimony to the great store that Matthew sets by Jesus' teaching that the Sermon on the Mount is the imposing composition it is."
[8] Emphasis and translation his.

The Sermon according to Kingsbury's outline begins with an introduction explaining who the implied reader should be. It is followed with four major blocks on how the implied reader should act. Each of the four blocks highlights a different group of people through which "greater righteousness" is to be practiced.[9] In summary, Kingsbury reasons that the ethic of the Sermon and its theme of greater righteousness call the disciple into the "sphere of God's eschatological kingdom, the sphere in which God rules as Father."[10]

Kingsbury's Thematic Approach Critiqued

Kingsbury's proposal is attractive. His reading of the Sermon and Matthew's Gospel involves a finished text that has a beginning and an end. This type of approach helps to see the integration of each paragraph as part of the overall narrative. So far as the Sermon as a whole is concerned, Kingsbury highlights its presence as an integral part of revealing Jesus's identity as the Son of God and shows how it fits into Matthew's Christology and climactic Passion.

Although Kingsbury's proposal has definite advantages, it also has some questionable aspects. First, Kingsbury's conclusions rely heavily on his literary approach to reading Matthew.[11] Much of Kingsbury's work on the Sermon depends on his view of the audience, of how the Sermon fits into the overall flow of Matthew, and of how it is moving toward a perceived climax. Because of Kingsbury's strictly literary approach, his insights tend to be limited. Only seeing the Sermon as a part of Matthew's narrative misses out on important insights that are gained when comparing the Sermon on the Mount with Luke's Sermon on the Plain. By comparing the two differing accounts, one can see the distinctive elements in each version of the Sermon. If one considers these features in Matthew, the reader gains insight into the tendencies of Matthew as a writer with his varying theological aims.

Second, even outside of the Sermon's composition, there is the question of Matthew structuring his Gospel around five major discourses. Although Kingsbury argues that noting the structural markers is an inaccurate reading of Matthew, it is hard to ignore the "fulfillment" quotations that end each discourse. These quotations and other factors help to illustrate the compositional aspects of Matthew's Gospel and give insights into individual sections as they begin and end.

Third, in Kingsbury's assignment of passages to an outline, he uses some questionable nomenclature. Kingsbury notes that point one defines the *identity* of those of "greater righteousness," while the rest of the points define the *practices* of those of "greater righteousness." Upon closer inspection, the Sermon does not fit neatly into the mold of "identity" and "practice" as outlined by Kingsbury's five points.

---

[9] See also Charles H. Talbert, *Reading the Sermon on the Mount: Character Formation and Decision Making in Matthew 5–7* (Grand Rapids: Baker Academic, 2006), 10–26.

[10] Kingsbury, "Sermon on Mount," 143. After Mt. 5:16 (5:3-16: "The Setting"), Talbert splits the remainder of the Sermon into six subunits (5:17-48; 6:1-18; 6:19-34; 7:1-12; and 7:13-27). He titles the entire section the "Higher Righteousness."

[11] Others have come to the same conclusions as Kingsbury regarding his "righteousness" structure but have used different methodologies to get there. See below Robert Guelich and his redactional approach to the Sermon.

Examples include: (1) The *macarisms* are a mix of "identity" themes (poor in spirit, mourners, meek, etc.) and "practices" ("peace-making"); (2) The metaphors of salt and light most likely describe the identity of a disciple ("salty") along with their influence among others ("being a light"); (3) The teaching on the law is closed by a word on being "perfect." The word itself follows on the heels of performing the Mosaic law well. By practicing the Mosaic law well, one is "identified" as perfect. This mix of identity and practice continues throughout the Sermon. Although this mixing does not detract from Kingsbury's major case, it does call for greater clarity among his finer points.

Fourth, smaller nuances throughout Kingsbury's construction cause hesitation in accepting parts of his proposal.

1. There is a noticeable gap between points two and three ("On Practicing the Greater Righteousness toward the Neighbor [5:17-45]" and "On Practicing the Greater Righteousness before God [6:1-18]"). Kingsbury does not assign Mt. 5:46-48 to either outline point.
2. There is no clear explanation why Mt. 5:13-16 is considered part of point one as opposed to point two. As mentioned above, the metaphors of salt and light describe people who practice righteousness, but they could also be considered part of practicing righteousness toward neighbors ("salty/being a light").

Conclusion

Kingsbury's proposal highlights an important aspect of the Sermon, namely the theme of righteousness. Undoubtedly, Matthew's view of righteousness finds some of its fullest expression in the Sermon on the Mount. Kingsbury's observation of this central theme in the Sermon fits nicely into the overall theology of Matthew. Kingsbury's literary approach is a welcome addition to the various criticisms and helps the reader to see how the Sermon connects to other parts of Matthew's narrative. Kingsbury's structural proposal is not without its weaknesses though. In terms of methodology, Kingsbury's approach is best when combined with other approaches. A comparison with Luke's version of the Sermon yields many valuable insights. Overall, the recognition of righteousness is key to the Sermon's message, but by supplementing his argument with other approaches, the structural proposal is strengthened.

Robert Guelich

In *The Sermon on the Mount: A Foundation for Understanding*, Robert Guelich presents an important contribution to the continuing research on the Sermon on the Mount. In terms of the Sermon's structure, Guelich is clear: "One must look for the pivotal concepts and phrases, the thematically related material, and the underlying framework of the Sermon tradition."[12] Guelich approaches the text as a redaction critic, noting the various traditions behind the Sermon's structure. In drawing together his insights, he proposes that Matthew has followed a basic tradition that underlies both the Sermon

---
[12] Guelich, *Sermon on the Mount*, 36–7.

on the Mount and Luke's Sermon on the Plain. The basic outline underlying both Sermons is the Beatitudes (Mt. 5:3-12; Lk. 6:20-23), Admonitions (Mt. 5:21–7:12; Lk. 6:27-42), and Warnings (Mt. 7:13-27; Lk. 6:[43-45] 46-49).

Within this tradition, Guelich notes that Matthew puts summarizing verses along with groupings of verses that reflect the evangelist's theological shaping of the Sermon.[13] Besides the Beatitudes (Mt. 5:3-12),[14] Matthew introduces the "Antitheses" of Mt. 5:21-48 with the "greater righteousness" of 5:20. "Doing righteousness" in 6:1 functions as a *kelal* to 6:1-18. The Golden Rule of Mt. 7:12 acts as a concluding remark to the section Guelich calls the "Admonitions." Lastly, Guelich notes that the parable of Mt. 7:24-27 connects with the warnings of 7:13-23, forming a lengthy conclusion to the entire Sermon.[15] This outline and the additional groupings give theological shape to the Sermon. Guelich's outline is as follows:

A. The Blessing of the Kingdom: 5:3-16
   1. The Beatitudes: 5:3-12
   2. Discipleship: 5:13-16
B. The Greater Righteousness: 5:17–7:12
   1. Jesus and the Law: 5:17-20
   2. Righteousness with Reference to Others: 5:21-48
   3. Righteousness with Reference to God: 6:1–7:11
      a. Worship: 6:1-18
      b. A Life of Prayer: 6:19–7:11
   4. Conclusion: The Golden Rule: 7:12
C. The Alternatives: 7:13-27
   1. The Two Ways: 7:13-14
   2. False Prophets: 7:15-23
   3. The Two Builders: 7:24-27

In noting this theological shaping by the Evangelist, Guelich begins with a treatment of the Beatitudes.[16] Here, Guelich notes that the Evangelist has worked within the tradition to heighten the Christological and eschatological focus by connecting the Beatitudes with Isaiah 61. This Christological and eschatological focus of the Beatitudes is heightened by an ecclesiological element as described in Mt. 5:13-16. Together, these two sections of verses form an introduction to the body of the Sermon. The introduction thus combines the eschatological, Christological, and ecclesiological in describing the blessings of the kingdom.

The main section of the Sermon is dominated by the theme of "greater righteousness" (see Mt. 5:20). In this section, Guelich notes Jesus's interaction with the Mosaic law (Mt. 5:17-20) and how one can express righteousness toward others (Mt. 5:21-48).[17]

---

[13] Guelich, *Sermon on the Mount*, 37.
[14] Guelich prefers the traditional nomenclature for Mt. 5:3-12.
[15] Guelich, *Sermon on the Mount*, 37.
[16] Guelich, *Sermon on the Mount*, 37.
[17] Guelich, *Sermon on the Mount*, 39.

Guelich's divisions follow the standard markers noted by most commentators in handling ch. 5.[18] In his treatment of ch. 6, Guelich sets v. 1 aside as a thematic marker covering the three marks of Jewish piety (Mt. 6:2-18). The theme of this section is proper "worship" as it relates back to the theme of greater righteousness.

Guelich's proposal for the remainder of the Sermon body is an elaboration of the Lord's Prayer (Mt. 6:9-15).[19] Each section of the remaining Sermon body (excluding Mt. 7:12) connects to one of the petitions. Guelich titles the section a "life of prayer" under the heading "righteousness with reference to God." Guelich's outline owes many of its cues to the work of Günther Bornkamm.[20] Like Bornkamm, Guelich connects Mt. 6:19-24 with the first three petitions. In these passages, there are several verbal and thematic links regarding "God's honour and sovereign will in one's life in terms of one's ultimate priorities."[21] Guelich also suggests that there is a probable connection between "treasures in heaven and earth" (Mt. 6:19-20) with the reference to "heaven and earth" in Mt. 6:10. Matthew 6:25-34 speaks to the issue of anxiety over material needs. This teaching on anxiety connects with the bread petition.

Matthew 7 begins with a teaching on judging others (Mt. 7:1-5). This teaching sensibly connects with the Prayer's fifth petition concerning forgiveness. Judging others is deterred when forgivingness is a priority. The next section concerns throwing holy things to dogs and pigs (Mt. 7:6). Guelich agrees with Bornkamm that this verse is most likely referring to apostasy. If this interpretation is valid, it takes on added significance as it connects to the sixth and seventh petitions.[22] The last petitions of the Lord's Prayer refer to deliverance from evil and perseverance in times of temptation. In order to resist apostasy, one would cry out for deliverance and perseverance, as the Lord's Prayer illustrates.

The last set of verses in the Sermon body speaks of persistent prayer ("asking, seeking, and knocking" [Mt. 7:7-11]). These verses form an *inclusio* with the Lord's Prayer and act as a conclusion. Whereas the Lord's Prayer begins with a word on God's knowledge of things "before you ask" (Mt. 6:8), this last section on prayer ends with assurance to "those who ask" (Mt. 7:11).[23] Matthew uses this last section on prayer to bring the reader back full circle to the remaining Sermon body's organizing principle, namely the Lord's Prayer.

In Guelich's final section, he notes the Sermon's "alternatives" of living. The emphasis is on those who heed the Sermon's teachings versus those who go against its teachings. Guelich's exposition highlights the Sermon's warning against false prophets and apostasy.[24] He concludes that the Sermon sets forth a gospel for kingdom living that has radical implications.[25]

---

[18] See fn.2.
[19] Guelich, *Sermon on the Mount*, 324–5.
[20] We will examine Bornkamm's approach below.
[21] Guelich, *Sermon on the Mount*, 324.
[22] Guelich, *Sermon on the Mount*, 324.
[23] Guelich, *Sermon on the Mount*, 325.
[24] Guelich, *Sermon on the Mount*, 39.
[25] Guelich, *Sermon on the Mount*, 39.

Overall, Guelich's outline is a hybrid of structural proposals. His proposal attempts to look for the transitional units in the Sermon's organization as well as highlight the importance of the Lord's Prayer as a structuring guide for the second half of the Sermon. Guelich's proposal also attempts to deal with the redactional changes in Matthew's presentation of the Q tradition. These emphases give a theological shape to the Sermon's traditional material. Guelich shows the importance of "righteousness" as the overall message of the Sermon and relates this theological emphasis to the Sermon's structure.

Guelich's Thematic Approach Critiqued

Guelich's approach to the Sermon's structure is really an expansion of Kingsbury's work. He only differs from Kingsbury in his methodology, preferring redaction criticism. As with Kingsbury, Guelich highlights a very important part of the Sermon's emphases, namely righteousness, but he goes further in bringing forth prayer as a dominant theme. Guelich relies heavily upon Bornkamm's structural outline for the second half of the Sermon (Mt. 6:19–7:11), and this dependence creates problems for his structural proposal. We will examine these problems below.

Triadic Structure

In the following proposal, Dale Allison notes the use of triads in the Sermon. The triad was a common Jewish literary device. Although different commentators see differing types of triads, the following proposal argues that the Sermon on the Mount is a series of triadic thought units.[26]

Dale Allison

In several articles and chapters, Dale Allison has defended a triadic structure in the Sermon on the Mount.[27] Although the idea of triads is not a new concept, Allison makes the most thorough examination of their presence in the Sermon. Allison points out that the Sermon is filled with various triads from beginning to end. The Sermon body is couched between an introduction (Mt. 5:1-2) and conclusion (Mt. 7:28–8:1), which is a triad. This Sermon body (Mt. 5:2–7:27) breaks down to a further set of triads: nine blessings/Beatitudes (Mt. 5:3-12), the main body (Mt. 5:13–7:12), and three warnings (Mt. 7:13-27).

After Jesus's nine blessings, there is a transitional unit (Mt. 5:13-16) before Jesus gives his teaching on the Mosaic law. This unit consists of Jesus's twin metaphors of salt and light. Allison treats this passage as a general heading for the main body and a bridge between the eschatological emphasis of the Beatitudes and the present-day emphasis of what follows. The explanation of "salt and light" living begins with Jesus's

---

[26] For an alternative triadic structure, see Glen H. Stassen, "The Fourteen Triads of the Sermon on the Mount (5:21–7:12)" *JBL* 122.2 (2003): 267–308.

[27] See "Structure of the Sermon on the Mount," *JBL* 106 (1987): 423–45; *Sermon on the Mount*, 27–57; and "Configuration of the Sermon on the Mount and its Meaning," 173–215.

handling of the Mosaic law (Mt. 5:17-48). This section begins with another general introduction (Mt. 5:17-20), which, as Allison states, gives "what sort of attitude and behaviour Jesus requires and how his demands surpass those of the *Torah* without contradicting the *Torah*."[28] Jesus takes up six Old Testament teachings/interpretations, thus producing two major triads. Each command starts with an introductory formula "You have heard that it was said" followed by "But I say to you."

The next major section in Allison's proposal looks at the three marks of Jewish piety in Mt. 6:1-18. This section breaks down to a simple triad covering the subjects of almsgiving, prayer, and fasting. Within the section on prayer, there is the inclusion of the Lord's Prayer in which Allison sees three "your" clauses followed by three "us" clauses. Jesus follows up this section on Jewish piety (Mt. 6:1-18) with a section on social issues. Much like the two triads in Mt. 5:17-48, 6:19–7:11 contains two triads. Each of the two sections in Mt. 6:19–7:11 begins with an exhortation (Mt. 6:19-21/7:1-2), followed by a parable concerning the eye (Mt. 6:22-23/7:3-5), and a conclusion wrapped in a second parable (Mt. 6:24/7:6).[29] The only exception is the inclusion of Mt. 6:25-33 and 7:7-11 as "encouragements" to carry out the demands of the previous exhortations. This final teaching completes the main body of the Sermon. As mentioned above, the rest of ch. 7 contains three warnings and a conclusion. The conclusion (Mt. 7:28–8:1) is the reaction of the crowds to Jesus's teaching, and this section forms an *inclusio* with the introduction (Mt. 5:1-2).

Additionally, Allison notes some interesting historical parallels between first-century Judaism and Matthew's Gospel.[30] He illustrates how the Jewish practice of orality favored certain numbers, in this case three. Given the Sermon's triadic orientation, Allison argues that there is a connection between this Jewish practice and the context of Matthew's writing of the Sermon. Following W. D. Davies, Allison finds evidence for his proposal in the teachings of Simeon the Just. Simeon describes three core values to the Jewish faith to which Allison argues that Jesus's triadic Sermon on the Mount is countering.

Allison's Triadic Structure Critiqued

Combining historical insight and literary sensitivity, Allison's structural proposal focuses the interpreter's eye to Matthew's use of triads. Although the triad is an

---

[28] Allison, "Structure of the Sermon on the Mount," 33.
[29] Allison, "Structure of the Sermon on the Mount," 35.
[30] In cataloging Allison's structure, Warren Carter posits Allison's historical arguments as the guiding factor for his structural arrangement. See *What Are They Saying about Matthew's Sermon on the Mount?* (New York: Paulist, 1994), 45. Another proposal that works from historical concerns is the work of Joachim Jeremias. Interestingly, he comes to a completely different conclusion in terms of structuring. Jeremias, *The Sermon on the Mount* (London: Athlone, 1961), 23, states,

> After the introduction (5:3-19) and the thematic sentence 5:20, the first part of the Sermon deals with the controversy concerning the interpretation of scripture between Jesus and the theologians (Matt. 5:21-48). As the second part there follows his controversy with the righteousness of the Pharisees, for almsgiving, the keeping of the three hours of prayer, and representative fasting on behalf of Israel, are characteristics of these pious groups of laymen (6:1-18). The concluding section (6:19–7:27) develops the new righteousness of the disciples of Jesus.

important organizing principle in the Sermon, it is not as prominent as Allison contends.

In ch. 5, Allison argues that the first appearance of triads is in the "Blessings" (5:3-12) section. Allison sees here three sets of three, although there is sufficient reason to believe there are two sets of four with an expanded word on "persecution."[31] This interpretation would create an *inclusio* between the first and the eighth *macarism* connected by the words "for theirs is the kingdom of heaven." The eightfold structure also acknowledges the use of third person in the first eight *macarisms* as opposed to the second person present in the "ninth" *macarism*.

The next major section in Allison's treatment starts in Mt. 5:13. Jesus gives two images of things that the disciples are to emulate: salt and light (Mt. 5:13-16). Allison makes this section and Mt. 5:17-20 general introductions, but they are obvious breaks from the triadic pattern he is proposing. In ch. 6, the structure of the Lord's Prayer also argues against Allison's use of triads. Recently, David Wenham has pointed out that the historical understanding of the Prayer's structure has been seven petitions as opposed to six.[32] He gives several convincing arguments to support his book based on grammatical concerns, specifically noting the use of conjunctions in the latter half of the Prayer.[33]

There are also some less plausible elements in Allison's understanding of the structure. From the start of the Sermon until Mt. 6:19, Allison has pointed out a consistent thread of triads, but in the last sections of the main body, he starts to deviate from his prior consistency. As mentioned earlier, Mt. 6:25-33 and 7:7-11 are "encouragement" sections. They follow on the heels of proposed triads but stand alone in their structural connection. Carter notes, "While there is no dispute that these sections offer encouragement, that function may have more to do with the content and imperatival style than with the absence of a triadic pattern."[34] The point is that there is a break from the triadic consistency evidenced in other parts of the Sermon. Additionally, Glen Stassen has shown that Allison's naming of the particular elements of Mt. 6:24–7:11 is tenuous. They do not clearly illustrate what the text says and seem contrived in order to maintain the triadic scheme.[35] One is also left wondering how Mt. 6:34 fits into Allison's triadic structure. In his diagrams, Allison completely omits the verse from his explanations.

Apart from Allison's numbering, there is a question regarding his connecting of Matthew with Jewish tradition. Allison agrees with W. D. Davies that the Sermon on

---

[31] See H. Benedict Green, *Matthew, Poet of the Beatitudes*, JSNTSupp Series 203 (Sheffield: Sheffield Academic, 2001), 176–261. Green argues that the first four Beatitudes are in parallel structure to the next set of four. Also, David Wenham, "How do the Beatitudes Work? Some Observations on the Structure of the Beatitudes in Matthew," in *The Earliest Perceptions of Jesus in Context: Essays in Honour of John Nolland*, LNTS, ed. Aaron White, David Wenham, and Craig A. Evans (London: Bloomsbury, 2018), 203.

[32] David Wenham, "The Sevenfold Form of the Lord's Prayer in Matthew's Gospel," *ExpTim* 121 (2010): 379–82.

[33] Similar arguments will be made below.

[34] Carter, *What Are They Saying?*, 47.

[35] Stassen, "Fourteen Triads," 297–8. Based on his own triadic proposal, Stassen argues that there are four sets of teaching in Mt. 6:19–7:12 instead of three. See Stassen's chart on p. 299.

the Mount is a response to the events of Jamnia.[36] He notes the words of Simeon the Just after the events of Jamnia: "Upon three things the world standeth: upon Torah, upon Temple service and upon deeds of loving-kindness (*m. 'Abot* 1.2)."[37] In Allison's triadic structure, ch. 5 depicts Jesus's teaching on the Mosaic law; Mt. 6:1-18 refers to the Jewish cult; and Mt. 6:19–7:12 refers to social behavior. Allison states, "The first evangelist, one is tempted to conclude, arranged his discourse so as to create a Christian interpretation of the three classical pillars."[38] He contends, the religious leaders of the time were discussing how to pick up the pieces of Judaism, and Matthew was simply offering a commentary on the three rabbinic pillars in light of the Jesus tradition.

This interpretation has some appealing elements, notably its connection with the historical situation of Matthew, but it rests on some unresolved historical issues. The connection of Matthew with the situation in Jamnia is simply conjectural. Without an explicit referent, it is difficult to prove with certainty the connection between these two events. Undoubtedly, one can agree that Matthew may have been referring to the developments in Judaism, but Matthew could have been addressing any number of issues. The results of Jamnia are also quite difficult to pinpoint. There is an array of opinions regarding what the council accomplished, making strong connections with Matthew's Gospel an even more difficult task.[39] The parallels with Simeon the Just is another difficult matter. As with Jamnia, Matthew and Simeon the Just may just reflect a common theme among first-century Jews without any specific correlation. Luz has pointed out that even Allison's attribution of the last two sections of the Sermon to the Temple and loving-kindness is unclear.[40] This critique would cause further harm to Allison's historical parallels. As we will argue in later chapters, Mt. 6:19–7:12 has a strong financial theme, an emphasis on rightly placed priorities, and an interest in the contrast between heaven and earth.

The final argument against Allison's proposal concerns the splitting of Mt. 6:18 and 6:19. This finer point is a less strong argument than the previous arguments but still worth mentioning. In Mt. 6:1-18, Allison's arrangement of the marks of Jewish piety into a triad is a natural progression that flows from the text. Each section begins with a teaching on the motivation or virtue associated with practicing righteousness and ends with the proper action to be performed. Couched in each section is an admonition against outward displays of righteousness that draws attention to the worshipper. Allison divides vv. 19-21 from this section because of its different subject matter and insistence that it heads a triad parallel to Mt. 7:1-2. It is reasonable to argue that

---

[36] Allison, "Structure of the Sermon on the Mount," 442–5. Davies, *The Setting of the Sermon on the Mount*, 305–7. See especially fn.44 in Allison, "Structure of the Sermon on the Mount," 444–5.
[37] The reference to "deeds of loving-kindness" is a translation decision by Allison based on the work of J. Goldin, "The Three Pillars of Simeon the Righteous," *PAAJR* 27 (1958), 43–56. Goldin summarizes that the three areas that matter most are the law, the cult, and the social acts of benevolence.
[38] Allison, "Structure of the Sermon on the Mount," 443.
[39] Christopher Rowland, *Christian Origins: An Account of the Setting and Character of the Most Important Messianic Sect of Judaism* (London: SPCK, 1985), 299–301, comments, "The disentanglement of the relationship between the Christians and the rabbis of Jamnia is a task which still awaits completion, though, of course, the paucity of information at our disposal makes the completion of it a very difficult enterprise."
[40] Luz, *Matthew 1–7*, 172–3.

Mt. 6:19-21 is a conclusion to the thematic material referenced in Mt. 6:1 rather than a parallel to Mt. 7:1-2. If this understanding of 6:19-21 holds up to scrutiny, it would throw off the triadic symmetry of Allison's final section. While the triad of alms, prayer, and fasting remains intact, the subsequent triad would be missing its first component, namely vv. 19-21.

Conclusion

In conclusion, Allison's proposal sheds light on many of the significant structuring elements present in the Sermon. Undoubtedly, triads are a major literary element in Matthew generally and the Sermon specifically. But, only to highlight triads in the structuring nature of the Sermon does not do justice to the full range of creativity Matthew is employing. Allison's historical connections between Matthew and rabbinic Judaism are also appealing in that it tries to ground Jesus's teaching in Matthew's *Sitz im Leben*. While his historical account is difficult to validate, Allison is careful to preserve the Sermon on the Mount's radical teachings in a historically tumultuous time.

Chiastic

The following proposal identifies a chiastic structure in the Sermon on the Mount.[41] A useful definition is suggested by James Bailey and Lyle Vander Broek: a chiasm is a "reverse parallelism. Two or more terms, phrases or ideas are stated and then repeated in reverse order."[42] Oftentimes, this ordering draws attention to its central verses. Daniel Patte argues from his chiastic proposal that the Sermon on the Mount is centered on disciple-making.

Daniel Patte

In *The Gospel According to Matthew: A Structural Commentary on Matthew's Faith*, Daniel Patte offers a fresh rendering of the Sermon's structure, noting its symmetrical patterning.[43] Patte argues that the Sermon is constructed in the following chiastic pattern:

A1 5:3–10. Beatitudes. Who the disciples are.
    B1 5:11–16. The disciples' vocation.
        C1 5:17–19. Conditions for implementing the vocation.
            D1 5:20. Introduction of antitheses (framing material).

---

[41] Other attempts at chiastic proposals include Nils W. Lund, *Chiasmus in the New Testament: A Study in the Form and Function of Chiastic Structures* (Peabody: Hendrickson, 1992), 240–61; John Breck, *The Shape of Biblical Language: Chiasmus in the Scriptures and Beyond* (Crestwood: St. Vladimir's Seminary, 1994), 123–43; John Welch, ed., *Chiasmus in Antiquity: Structures, Analyses, Exegesis* (Hildesheim: Gerstenberg Verlag, 1981), 235–237.

[42] James L. Bailey and Lyle Vander Broek, *Literary Forms in the New Testament: A Handbook* (Louisville: Westminster, 1992), 49.

[43] Daniel Patte, *The Gospel According to Matthew: A Structural Commentary on Matthew's Faith* (Valley Forge: Trinity, 1987).

> E1 5:21–47. Antitheses. The overabundant righteousness.
> D2 5:47–48. Conclusion of antitheses (framing material).
> D3 6:1. Introduction to next unit (framing material).
> E2 6:2–18. The overabundant righteousness.
> D4 6:19–21. Conclusion of preceding unit (framing material).
> C2 6:22–7:12. Conditions for implementing the vocation.
> B2 7:13–20. The disciples' vocation.
> A2 7:21–27. Who the disciples are.

Patte begins his proposal with an explanation of Mt. 5:1-2 and 7:28-29. In Patte's construction, these verses serve as a narrative framework for the Sermon on the Mount. In these verses, Matthew mentions the hearers of the Sermon and the effect of the Sermon upon their lives. This transformation of the hearers is the main theme of chs 5–7 according to Patte.[44] Also, in these framework passages, Jesus establishes himself as an authoritative teacher whose teaching demands obedience.

In Patte's A section, Jesus's teaching establishes an "I-you" relationship between speaker and hearer. The goal is that the reader identifies the "I" (the speaker) and the "you" (potential disciples). These two sections (Mt. 5:3-10; 7:21-27) prepare the reader for the rest of the discourse and describe the reasons that someone would want to become a disciple.[45] In the B section, Patte lays out the disciple's vocation. The disciple is one who is persecuted, "salt of the earth," a "light of the world," finds the "narrow gate," and bears "good fruit" (Mt. 5:11-16; 7:13-20).

The next section in Patte's construction describes the conditions for becoming a disciple. The first C section expresses negatively that a disciple must never think that Jesus has abolished the Mosaic law. The second C section states positively that disciples understand that a correct interpretation of Scripture entails observance of the Golden Rule.[46] The next section (D) forms the central part of the Sermon. These sections form a frame around the E material. Matthew 5:20 connects with 5:47-48, while 6:1 connects with 6:19-21. The E sections describe "overabundant righteousness." Patte comments, "Whereas the first section (Mt. 5:21-47) deals with the attitude that disciples need to have toward other people in order to have such a righteousness, the second section (Mt. 6:2-18) focuses on the disciple's 'relationship with God.'"[47]

Patte's Chiastic Structure Critiqued

Patte's structural proposal makes some notable contributions to the examination of the Sermon. His structural assessment takes seriously the theme of "righteousness" that is prevalent throughout the Sermon and constitutes a major challenge to the reader who is called to follow the mandates of righteousness in Jesus's Sermon. Patte is very careful to identify framing material and verbal cues throughout the Sermon's structure.

---

[44] Patte, *Matthew*, 60.
[45] Patte, *Matthew*, 63.
[46] Patte, *Matthew*, 64.
[47] Patte, *Matthew*, 64. These sections are explained in more detail in Patte's commentary, pp. 75–90.

Although the identifying of the twin emphases on righteousness and discipleship is commendable in Patte's construction, there are other thematic conclusions and structural assignments that are forced. In Patte's A1 material, he splits vv. 11-12 from Mt. 5:3-10. Because he labels A1, "Who the disciples are," this separation seems unwise. Verses 11-12 reiterate the same message and mimic partially the same form of vv. 3-10. It seems much more likely that vv. 11-12 are an expansion of the last *macarism* (v. 10). Although there is a connection between vv. 11-12 and 13-16, this latter section sets itself apart with its use of the twin metaphors of salt and light. Arguably, the twin metaphors of "salt" and "light" would also fit the description of "who the disciples are," rendering Patte's titles imprecise. In Patte's A2 and B2 sections, he splits the conclusion, labeling them as "who the disciples are" (A2) and the "disciples' vocation" (B2). Reading the two sections together creates a more comprehensive conclusion that presents a series of contrasts. Each of these contrasts serves to highlight one who follows Jesus's teachings versus one who does not. Splitting these verses detracts from these comparisons. The last interesting split by Patte is the removal of v. 20 from Mt. 5:17-19. For Patte, v. 20 serves as an introduction to the antitheses. While the verse does function in this way, it does not function as a standalone phrase. Verse 20 has two verbal clues that tie it to vv. 17-19. There is the similar repetition of beginnings with v. 18 ("For I say to you") and the repetition of the Matthean phrase "kingdom of heaven" of v. 19.[48] It is best to read vv. 17-20 as a unit, especially considering its presence in only Matthew's Gospel.

The next problematic area of Patte's construction is his pairing of Mt. 5:17-19 (C1) and 6:22–7:12 (C2). Patte's rationale for this pairing is that it keeps the *inclusio* of "law and prophets" in place. The problem lies in splitting 6:22–7:12 from the other sections of the body of the Sermon. It is much more plausible to see the body of the Sermon as consisting of three sections composed of relatively similar lengths: 5:21-48, 6:1-18, and 6:19–7:12. Also, each of these three sections speaks of the disciple's relationship to God/others. As with the nomenclature of B1, the wording used here in C2 does not grasp the full meaning of these passages. In the flow of the Sermon, Mt. 5:17-20 function more as a heading to 5:21-48 explaining Jesus's relationship to the Mosaic law while vv. 21-48 illustrate this relationship. In a traditional chiasm, the paired units are typically synonymous in meaning and relatively similar in length. This symmetry is clearly not the case with Mt. 5:17-19 and 6:22–7:12.

Conclusion

Patte's recognition of the key emphases and framing material is commendable. His proposal highlights the Sermon's emphasis on the responsibility of disciples to follow Jesus's teachings. Among the framing devices, Patte notes the connection between the *macarisms* and the conclusion of the Sermon, the "law and the prophets" in 5:17 and 7:12, and 6:1 with 6:19-21. Although these connections are important verbal cues for the Sermon, some of Patte's other inferences are less convincing. Patte's proposal only acknowledges two of the Sermon's three major sections. This reduction assigns a major

---

[48] Hagner's, *Matthew 1–13*, 103–13, comments are helpful here in explaining how these verses can function as individual verses but work best when read together thematically.

section (Mt. 6:22–7:12) to a peripheral position in the chiasm. Additionally, some of Patte's labels do not do justice to the passages they are assigned. Lastly, Patte seems to force unnecessary splits among major sections: Mt. 5:11-12 from 5:3-10, Mt. 5:20 from 5:17-19, and Mt. 7:21-27 from 7:13-20.

Expositional/Structurally Centric

The following approach characterizes structural proposals that use a section of the Sermon and explain the rest of the Sermon in light of it.[49] There are generally two portions of the Sermon that are used as foundations: the *macarisms* and the Lord's Prayer.[50] In both cases, the *macarisms* and the Lord's Prayer are used as a basic outline, while the rest of the Sermon on the Mount is shown to be an exposition or further interpretation of its nuanced points.[51] The *macarisms* and the Lord's Prayer also work as the structuring key for the rest of the Sermon on the Mount as portions of the Sermon are ordered by the focal texts. In this section, we will focus our attention on the work of Walter Grundmann, Günther Bornkamm, and Robert Guelich as representative of those who structure the Sermon on the Mount around the Lord's Prayer.[52]

The Lord's Prayer as Structuring Agent

Three major proposals argue that the Lord's Prayer is central, with the rest of the Sermon structured by the Prayer's petitions.[53] The following table compares these proposals. Each interpreter will be explained in detail below (Table 3.1).

Walter Grundmann

In his theological commentary, *Das Evangelium nach Matthäus*, Walter Grundmann presents his analysis of the structure of the Sermon. Grundmann argues that the center of the Sermon, namely the Lord's Prayer, is not only strategically located but also provides the key to understanding the Sermon's structure. After arguing that the Lord's Prayer is theologically significant to the Sermon, Grundmann shows how each of the petitions of the Prayer corresponds to larger sections of the Sermon.[54] As many

---

[49] The term "expositional" describes the practice of taking a smaller phrase and expounding on its meaning. France uses similar language. See France, *Gospel of Matthew*, 155, fn.8, who describes these suggestions as "the Lord's Prayer is in effect expounded clause by clause in the Sermon."

[50] Traces of this have already been discussed in the above outline of Robert Guelich. Guelich's structural proposal is a hybrid of thematic and expositional/structurally centric. In his commentary, he tends to emphasize the theme of "righteousness," hence the reason for being handled in the thematic/theological section.

[51] In some cases, the Lord's Prayer is used only as an outline for half of the Sermon. This will be charted and discussed below.

[52] For a proposal that uses the *macarisms* as a foundation, see M. D. Goulder, *Midrash and Lection in Matthew* (London: SPCK, 1974), 250. For a similar argument, but slightly different expositional proposal, see Green, *Matthew, Poet of the Beatitudes*.

[53] This approach is not to be confused with Ulrich Luz's proposal to see the Lord's Prayer as central. Luz's proposal does not necessarily see the Sermon as an exposition of the Lord's Prayer, but rather the Sermon is symmetrically wrapped around the Lord's Prayer.

[54] Grundmann, *Matthäus*, 204–6.

Table 3.1 Diagram of Grundmann, Bornkamm, and Guelich's Lord's Prayer as Structuring Agent

	The Lord's Prayer as the Centre		
The Lord's Prayer	Grundmann	Bornkamm	Guelich
1. Our Father in Heaven, hallowed be your Name	5:3-16 and 7:7-12 and other references to our Father in heaven	6:33 Seek first God's reign and justice	
2. Your Kingdom come	5:3-16 Beatitudes and Salt, Light Deeds	6:33 Seek first God's reign and justice	
3. Your will be done on earth as it is in heaven	5:17-48 The better righteousness	6:19-24 Treasures not on earth but in heaven	6:19-24 Treasures not on earth but in heaven
4. Give us this day our daily bread	6:19-34 treasures, food, and clothes	6:25-34 Do not be anxious; God cares	6:25-34 Do not be anxious; God cares
5. And forgive us our debts	7:1-6 Judge not, but repent	7:1-5 Judge not, but repent	7:1-5 Judge not, but repent
6. And do not bring us to the time of trial	7:13-23 false prophets	7:6 dogs, pigs, and holy things	7:6 dogs, pigs, and holy things
7. But deliver us from the evil one	7:13-23 false prophets	7:6 dogs, pigs, and holy things	7:6 dogs, pigs, and holy things
To those who ask*		7:7-11 Ask, seek, and knock (*Inclusio* with 6:7-15)	7:7-11 Ask, seek, and knock (*Inclusio* with 6:7-15)
The Golden Rule*			7:12 Summary clause

interpreters have noted, the Lord's Prayer does stand at the approximate center of the Sermon and, more specifically, at the center of Mt. 6:1-18. As the table above indicates, Grundmann only deals with those sections outside of the three marks of Jewish piety in Mt. 6:1-18. Grundmann states that the tradition behind these verses is borrowed from an earlier source (Q) and displays impressive symmetry notwithstanding the insertion of Mt. 6:7-15.

Grundmann splits the Lord's Prayer into seven petitions with the invocation of "Our Father" being connected to "Hallowed be Thy Name." In Grundmann's structure, the Beatitudes (Mt. 5:13-16) and Mt. 7:7-12 correspond to "your kingdom come" and "hallowed be your name." The organizing principle for these sections with their respective petition is in the repetition of "our Father in Heaven." Additionally, Grundmann argues that the Beatitudes and the salt/light metaphor are descriptive of those who make God's name holy and belong to the kingdom. The next petition ("your will be done") relates to Mt. 5:17-48. In this section, Grundmann finds the heart of the Sermon. The disciples are to carry out God's will by embodying the Mosaic law. As mentioned above, Mt. 6:1-18 already displays organization that Matthew has borrowed from a previous tradition. Therefore, this section is excluded from the formal structure of the Sermon. The rest of the material (Mt. 6:19–7:27) fits with the remaining petitions. Grundmann combines Mt. 6:19-23 with 6:24-35. In both sections, the subject concerns possessions and worrying about possessions. Grundmann links these verses with the petition concerning daily bread. If one diverts their attention from worrying about their daily needs, God will provide just enough. The next combination is the petition on forgiveness and Mt. 7:1-6. The larger section speaks to the issue of judging others, while the petition encourages the forgiveness of those who wrong us. The last section is the assignment of Mt. 7:13-27 to the last two petitions ("lead us not into temptation"; "but deliver us from evil"). Grundmann argues that the presence of false prophets in Mt. 7:13-27 is the evil to which the petitioner is praying to avoid.

Walter Grundmann's Structure Critiqued

Grundmann's structural proposal is a serious contribution to the study of the Sermon on the Mount. Commentators have long noted the presence of the Lord's Prayer in a highly stylized section of the Sermon and its apparent centrality. Grundmann simply tries to explain the Prayer in its present position, highlighting the literary artistry and pointing out the shared theology underlying both texts.

Although Grundmann's proposal has several merits, it has not gained universal acceptance. The first issue is the way in which Grundmann connects the Sermon with some of the Prayer's petitions. Grundmann aligns the first half of the Sermon with the first three petitions, while the second half of the Sermon is paired with individual petitions. This ordering stays consistent until he connects Mt. 7:7-12 with the first petition. Grundmann's rationale for making this connection is the verbal link of "our Father in heaven." This connection in Grundmann's proposal throws off the symmetry that is displayed elsewhere.[55] It also does not explain the other instances in which "Father in heaven" appears. Besides this symmetry disruption, Grundmann's choice to align the first half of the Sermon with the first three petitions is questionable. The first three petitions seem to be more abstract in their application than the corresponding sections of the Sermon. The first three petitions also display a very similar message, whereas the corresponding sections of the Sermon are varied. For example, Grundmann links the Beatitudes with the second petition. Is this link significantly stronger than assigning the Beatitudes to "hallowing God's Name" or "doing God's will"? This difficulty in linkage is especially evident when linking Mt. 5:17-48 and "God's will" (v. 10b). In a Jewish context, the law would be the most obvious expression of the will of Yahweh; *Torah* observance is also thematically related to hallowing God's name and the kingdom coming.

As to the second half of the Prayer and Sermon, most of the issues with Grundmann's proposal will be addressed below in the Bornkamm critique. There is one minor discrepancy that differs in Grundmann and Bornkamm. Grundmann links Mt. 7:1-6 with the petition concerning forgiveness, whereas Bornkamm splits Mt. 7:6 from the teaching of 7:1-5.[56] Commentators have noted the difficulty of interpreting Mt. 7:6 because of the lack of parallel texts. An examination of the verse displays its inherent parallelism and lack of obvious dependence on Mt. 7:5 or 7:7. Guelich notes

---

[55] On p. 206, Grundmann, *Matthäus*, explains that this connection of Mt. 7:7-12 with the first petition will be explained in a later section, but the exegesis section for Mt. 7:11 (p. 224) assumes rather than explains this connection.

[56] The problem with linking Mt. 7:1-5 to the forgiveness petition will be addressed below.

the exegetical problem, "At the heart of this contextual dilemma lies the basic question about what the enigmatic saying meant in its original setting as well as here in 7:6."[57] Matthew has put the verse in its present context, but its connection to the Prayer's petition is difficult to validate. There is not necessarily anything in the verse that clues the reader to interpret the metaphors in a manner consistent with forgiveness unless "forgiveness" is considered the holy thing in Mt. 7:6.

Conclusion

The strength of Grundmann's proposal lies in his location of the Prayer at the center of the Sermon. Many of Grundmann's parallels between the Sermon and the Prayer are illuminating, yet he is arguably being overzealous in linking material. While there is thematic chemistry between the Sermon and the Prayer, it is difficult to establish the Prayer as the structuring agent for the entire Sermon.

Günther Bornkamm

In "Der Aufbau der Bergpredigt," Günther Bornkamm takes a familiar thesis and argues for the Sermon's centrality.[58] Like Grundmann, Bornkamm sees the Lord's Prayer as the center of the Sermon. Unlike Grundmann, Bornkamm argues that the Lord's Prayer orders only the second half of the Sermon, namely Mt. 6:19–7:12.[59]

Bornkamm begins his assessment of the Sermon's structure by showing the highly organized nature of ch. 5, Mt. 6:1-18, and Mt. 7:13-27. If such structuring exists in nearly all the components of the Sermon, why would it be absent in the remaining section of Mt. 6:19–7:12? Bornkamm answers this question by giving a redactional assessment of Matthew's presentation of prayer versus Luke's. Unlike Matthew, Luke does not place his teaching on prayer in his Sermon on the Plain. Luke records his version of the Lord's Prayer in a much later chapter (Lk. 11:2-4) followed by a parable of a midnight visitor (vv. 5-8), "asking, seeking, and knocking" (vv. 9-10), and the Father giving the Holy Spirit (vv. 11-13). Matthew does not include the parable of the midnight visitor. Bornkamm notes that it is interesting that Matthew has placed the "asking, seeking, and knocking" much later (Mt. 7:7-11) instead of as a closing to Matthew's extended presentation of prayer in Mt. 6:5-15. Bornkamm sees in this redactional activity a clue for the reader. Because the beginning of the Sermon displays notable symmetry and Matthew has separated two strands of tradition that stand closely together in Luke's writing (6:7-15 [the Lord's Prayer] and 7:7-11 [ask, seek, knock]), there must be something significant happening between these bookends.

Bornkamm agrees with Grundmann that the second half of the Sermon (Mt. 6:19–7:11) is arranged according to the Prayer's petitions. Unlike Grundmann, Bornkamm splits 6:19-35 into two sections. The first section (Mt. 6:19-24) fits with the first three

---

[57] Guelich, *Sermon on the Mount*, 353.
[58] Bornkamm, "Der Aufbau der Bergpredigt," 419–32.
[59] Schnackenburg, *All Things Are Possible to Believers*, 27–8, is sympathetic to this view, though doubts that it can be proven with certainty. Also Meier, *Matthew*, 59.

petitions of the Lord's Prayer (6:9b-10). In Mt. 6:19-24, the emphasis is on honoring God and putting him first. This connection corresponds to the sentiments of the Prayer's petitions to honor God's name, inaugurate his kingdom, and do his will. In Mt. 6:19-21, there is the contrast between "treasures on earth" and "treasures on heaven" that alludes to the phrase connecting the first three petitions, "on earth as it is in heaven." The remaining half of Mt. 6:19-34 connects with the next petition concerning bread (Mt. 6:11). The subject of Mt. 6:25-34 is not worrying about food, drink, and clothing. These represent the most basic of needs and resound the petition for enough bread to supply today's needs. The fifth petition concerning forgiveness (Mt. 6:12) connects with the section on "judging others" (Mt. 7:1-5). The last petitions of the Prayer (Mt. 6:13, temptation/evil one petition) connect with Mt. 7:6 ("do not give what is holy to dogs"). Bornkamm interprets the metaphors of Mt. 7:6 as symbolic of apostasy. The last petitions for avoiding temptation and deliverance from evil make sense as the petitioner's cry to avoid apostasy. As mentioned, the next section on prayer (Mt. 7:7-11) forms an *inclusio* with the Lord's Prayer and is a reminder that God hears his children's request in living out the second half of the Sermon (Mt. 6:19–7:6).

Günther Bornkamm's Structure Critiqued

Bornkamm's proposal is an excellent example of the value of redaction criticism. His analysis of the disparate material and its union in the Matthean Sermon makes several excellent points. Bornkamm is able to propose a reasonable explanation for Matthew's use of source material in Mt. 6:19–7:12 by noting the comparisons with Luke's Gospel.[60] Bornkamm draws attention to the presence of structure in the second half of the Sermon and the prayer material in Mt. 7:7-11, where most have seen randomness.

Despite these strengths, there are several issues with Bornkamm's proposal. The first issue is the lack of consistency in uniting the second half of the Sermon with the Prayer's petitions. Bornkamm arranges Mt. 6:19-24 with the first three petitions but then splits the remaining material to fit each individual petition (Mt. 6:25-34 to 6:11; Mt. 7:1-5 to 6:12; Mt. 7:6 to 6:13). This disproportionate arrangement is difficult to explain.[61] Why is the first block of texts not also split according to each petition? Splitting the first block of texts would create a more consistent and persuasive proposal. It is also highly tenuous that Bornkamm sees a clear split between Mt. 6:19-24 and vv. 25-34. Both sections have a central message centered on the proper response to possessions and an emphasis on "heaven and earth."

The second problem in Bornkamm's proposal is the interpretation of Mt. 6:19-24 in light of the first three petitions. In the Lord's Prayer, the first three petitions seem to have a dual sense, as indicated by the phrase, "on earth as it is in heaven." The focus of the first three petitions is on the eschatological future and present. If this interpretation is accepted, then the tension between these petitions and the corresponding section

---

[60] Bornkamm asserts that Matthew is making use of the Q tradition. This is beyond the scope of this section, but the traditions do not necessarily have to point to Q as they could be from Jesus's oral teachings. Refer back to our earlier discussion.

[61] For an extended discussion of this point, see Allison, "Structure of the Sermon on the Mount," 426.

to the Sermon are clear. The section of the Sermon under question is concerned with possessions and anxiety in the *present*. Apart from "laying up your treasures in heaven," the predominant temporal element is clearly in the present. This lack of thematic/temporal connection between this section and the Prayer makes Bornkamm's parallel tenuous.

The last point of critique is Bornkamm's handling of Mt. 7:1-6. In contrast to Grundmann, Bornkamm splits the section into two parts, assigning Mt. 7:6 to the last two petitions of the Prayer ("Lead us not into temptation"; "Deliver us from the evil one"). The first problem with this connection is Grundmann and Bornkamm's interpretation of 7:1-5. This section's message can be summarized as follows: "judge not, lest you be judged." The section is straightforward in its message, but the manner in which they parallel the forgiveness petition seems stretched.[62] The petition concerning "forgiveness" is set in a conditional phrase highlighting God's forgiveness in relation to humanity, which extends to interpersonal forgiveness. This triangular shape is deemphasized in both proposals and the parallel of debt language is ignored. The second problem is the interpretation of Mt. 7:6. Although rightly separating Mt. 7:6 from 7:1-5 (contra Grundmann), Bornkamm's interpretation of Mt. 7:6 as parallel to both the sixth and seventh petition seems too ambitious. The last petitions, while similar in meaning, have their own distinctive characteristics. We will argue that Mt. 7:6 parallels the sixth petition thematically although lacking lexical parallels.

Conclusion

By showing Matthew's redactional activity, Bornkamm discovers meaning in the arrangement of the Sermon's second half and highlights the importance of prayer in the Sermon's message (connecting the Lord's Prayer with Mt. 7:7-11). The weakness of Bornkamm's proposal is its inability to establish persuasive textual connections between the Sermon and the Prayer. There are times where Bornkamm finds meaning and thematic connections that would not be immediately identifiable if a structural agenda were not present. Bornkamm's structure causes him to read into various texts meanings that do not stand up under scrutiny.[63] As with Grundmann, Bornkamm highlights the centrality of the Lord's Prayer, but also with Grundmann, his assertion that the Prayer is the structuring unit for the Sermon seems overzealous considering the evidence.

Guelich Revisited

As mentioned above, Guelich's approach to the Sermon's structure highlights the theme of "righteousness" as the central emphasis. This thematic approach is combined with the proposal of Günther Bornkamm. For the second half of the Sermon (Mt.

---

[62] Lambrecht, *Sermon on the Mount*, 164.
[63] Concerning Bornkamm's interpretation of Mt. 7:6, Allison, "Structure of the Sermon on the Mount," 427, comments, "Nonetheless, this is only because the first evangelist has not been very helpful in making plain what he took 7:6 to mean. In addition, one suspects that Bornkamm's exegesis is more a reading in than a reading out."

6:19–7:11), Guelich follows Bornkamm's proposal. The only addition to Bornkamm's handling of the structure is the inclusion of Mt. 7:12 as a summary clause to the entire second half of the Sermon. Guelich's combination of thematic and structural concerns is admirable, although not without its problems. Along with the problems mentioned above with Bornkamm's proposal, there is one notable problem with Guelich's proposal. While noting the importance of the Prayer as a guiding factor in half of the Sermon, Guelich still reasons that righteousness is the central theme of the Sermon. There is little doubt that righteousness plays a central role among other important themes in the Sermon, but by giving the Prayer so much prominence in his structural proposal, one would expect Guelich to show how Prayer is central to the Sermon, or at least how righteousness is related to the Prayer. Guelich's structural proposal does not weigh into his interpretation of the Sermon, and the Prayer's centrality is thus, decentralized.

Concentric Structure

In contrast to the previous proposals that noted the centrality of the Lord's Prayer and its petitions as structuring agents, a concentric proposal does not attribute any structural significance to the petitions in ordering the composition of the Sermon on the Mount (contra Grundmann, Bornkamm, and Guelich). Instead, the concentric model highlights the Sermon's structure as "architectonic symmetry" and "ring-shaped," which uses inclusions that are wrapped around the Lord's Prayer. Each *inclusio* adds a layer of meaning to the Sermon.[64] A concentric structure differs from a chiastic structure in the use of its "rings." As we saw in Patte's structural proposal, the paralleled sections in a chiastic structure function synonymously. In a concentric structure, the wording may be parallel, but other factors are considered for the overall parallels. The "rings" are parallel but do not necessarily reinforce each other's meaning.

Ulrich Luz

In his *Hermeneia* commentary on the Gospel of Matthew, Ulrich Luz proposes a concentric structure.[65] In conjunction with the findings of two earlier studies, Luz focuses his attention on the oral composition of the Sermon.[66] Indicative of an oral composition, Luz argues that Matthew has used verbal inclusions. Luz counts six such inclusions (Mt. 5:1-2//7:28–8:1a; 5:3-16//7:13-27; 5:17-20//7:12; 5:21-48//6:19-7:11; 6:1-6//6:16-18; 6:7-8//6:14-15) surrounding the Lord's Prayer, highlighting the Prayer's centrality. Each *inclusio* creates layered meanings for understanding the Sermon. His proposal is as follows:[67]

---

[64] Another proposal who depends heavily on the *inclusio*, but not to the extent of Luz is Quarles, *Sermon on the Mount*, 13–19. See also Jonathan A Draper, "The Genesis and Narrative Thrust of the Paraenesis in the Sermon on the Mount," *JSNT* 75 (1999): 32–45.
[65] Luz, *Matthew 1–7*, 172.
[66] See fn.49 above.
[67] Luz, *Matthew 1–7*, 173.

Frame

5:1-2   7:28–8:1a

situation   reaction of the hearers

Inclusion: "crowds, teaching, going up (down) . . . mountain"

Introduction/Conclusion

5:3-16   7:13-27

introduction   conclusion

Inclusion: "kingdom of heaven"

twice each: 5:3, 10; 7:21

Other formal parallels: third person 5:3-10; 7:21-27

second person 5:11-16; 7:13-20

Introit/Conclusion of the Main Section

5:17-20   7:12

Inclusion: "law and prophets"

Main Section

5:21-48   6:19–7:11

Parallels in length of sections:

56 Nestle-Aland lines in each

6:1-6   6:16-18

righteousness before God

6:7-8   6:14-15

prayer words

The Lord's Prayer

6:9-13

The first *inclusio* Luz brings attention to is the "kingdom of heaven." Like those before him, Luz sees the kingdom of heaven as a major thrust in the Sermon. The teachings of the Sermon look forward to this future kingdom. The next *inclusio* is the double use of "law and prophets." Luz argues that the "law and prophets" are the central theme of the main section. Luz uses the title "introit" to emphasize the aural characteristics of the Sermon on the Mount. It stands as bookends for the body of the Sermon (Mt. 5:21–7:11). At the center of this main section/body of the Sermon stands the Lord's Prayer. This central position is intentional on Matthew's part to emphasize prayer as the Sermon's central message. As stated above, Luz concludes, "Thus the Sermon on the Mount takes its readers along a way that leads them from God's radical demands into the 'interior' of faith where they experience the Father's nearness in prayer. Then it leads them back into the praxis of renouncing possessions and of love."[68]

There are several divisions within the body itself that Luz notes before emphasizing the Prayer. Surrounding the Lord's Prayer are the extended sections of Mt. 5:21-48 and 6:19–7:11. Luz notes that each of these sections occupies fifty-six lines in the Nestle-Aland. Within these individual sections, Luz splits the first (Mt. 5:21-48) into two sets of three (Mt. 5:21-26, 27-30, 31-32//5:33-37, 38-42, 43-47). Each of the two sets has almost the same number of letters and only slightly differentiates in word total (1131/1130 letters; 258/244 words).[69] There is also a similar introduction to each triad (vv. 21, 33: "you have heard that it was said to the ancients").

Although the second longer section (Mt. 6:19–7:11) is not as symmetrical as Mt. 5:21-48, Luz still argues for structuring. Luz argues that there are two major subsections (Mt. 6:19-34; 7:1-11) that use catchwords to signify their division. The first subsection (Mt. 6:19-34) is concerned with possessions, while the second subsection (Mt. 7:1-11) contains no unifying theme.[70] Inside these longer sections, Luz sees Matthew's hand in shaping ch. 6 into three major divisions. Surrounding Matthew's teaching on prayer (Mt. 6:7-15) are the teachings on almsgiving (Mt. 6:1-6) and fasting (Mt. 6:16-18). The stress in vv. 1-6 and 16-18 is on the righteousness of God, a theme central to the Lord's Prayer. The last *inclusio* is Mt. 6:7-8 and 6:14-15. In both instances, Matthew is using prayer words to surround the Prayer par excellence. Verses 7-8 provide the contrast to proper prayer, mentioning that prayer is more than meaningless babble, while vv. 14-15 repeat the forgiveness petition.

Ulrich Luz's Concentric Structure Critiqued

Ulrich Luz's concentric structuring is a relatively new proposal in terms of the history of Sermon interpretation. Because of its novelty, Warren Carter notes, "His [Luz's] proposal is a strong one and it remains to be seen how much support it will receive from scholars."[71] Luz, like others before him, finds the Lord's Prayer at the center of

---

[68] Luz, *Matthew 1–7*, 172.
[69] Luz, *Matthew 1–7*, 226.
[70] Luz, *Matthew 1–7*, 328. It is interesting that earlier (p. 174), Luz argues the presence of triads throughout the Sermon. In this section, he notes the three parts of Mt. 6:19-24 and 7:1-11, making this section somewhat parallel to 5:21-48 with its two groups of triads.
[71] Carter, *What Are They Saying?*, 43. It is interesting that in his commentary, Luz concedes that his structural proposal does not parallel any contemporary literature or literary structuring in the rest of Matthew. Luz, *Matthew 1–7*, 174.

the Sermon. What differentiates his approach is his noting of *inclusios* throughout the Sermon and how each *inclusio* provides layers of meaning for the Sermon. Luz also points out the thematic consistency between the Lord's Prayer and the rest of the Sermon. The Lord's Prayer does not order the surrounding Sermon, but rather its centrality makes it the key text for understanding the Sermon.

Although most of Luz's structural proposal is convincing, there is one aspect that is relatively weak. Luz's justification for paralleling Mt. 5:21-48 and 6:19–7:11 seems to be forced in light of the other *inclusios*.[72] Up to this point in his proposal and after this division of the body, Luz's inclusions show significant thematic unity, substantial verbal agreement, and/or consistent structuring parallels between the respective sections. In this *inclusio*, the only notable parallel between these larger sections of the body for Luz is that they occupy similar amounts of lines in the Nestle-Aland. In terms of thematic agreement between the sections, one could argue that the material in Mt. 5:21-48 is focused on the same subject, namely the proper interpretation of the Mosaic law. This unity of material is apparently absent in Mt. 6:19–7:11. Luz even comments,

> It is not easy to give it [6:19–7:11] a title that covers its contents. It deals more with questions of community life than do the antitheses. There are two obvious parts: 6:19-34 deals with questions about possessions, while no thematic unity is discernible in 7:1-11. It is difficult to say how the section fits in with the Sermon on the Mount as a whole.[73]

Not only does Luz fail to show the thematic unity between the two sections, but he also does not see unity within the second block itself.

In terms of the structuring within the two major blocks, there is also little agreement. Luz contends that Mt. 5:21-48 is highly structured because of its two sets of triads and similar introduction at the beginning of each triad (vv. 21, 33). He argues that there are also two sets of triads in Mt. 6:19–7:11, but they are found only in Mt. 6:19-24 and 7:1-11. This triadic construction completely leaves out the material in Mt. 6:25-34. Interestingly, Luz states that Mt. 6:19–7:11 should be split into Mt. 6:19-34 and 7:1-11. If this split were the case, the addition of Mt. 6:25-34 to the triad of 6:19-34 would add an additional element, throwing off one of the supposed triads.

These small discrepancies do not throw off the overall effect of Luz's proposal. Luz does not seem concerned that every jot and tittle aligns between these sections of the body. Because of the compositional nature of the Sermon, parallel sections do not have to be "perfect." Yet, there may be more parallelism between the sections than Luz concedes. In the following proposal, we will suggest additional structural parallelism.

---

[72] This concern is also shared by Stanton, *Gospel for A New People*, 298. I believe there is parallelism between the sections but not based on the number of lines shared by the sections.

[73] Luz, *Matthew 1-7*, 328.

Conclusion

In terms of his structural proposal, Luz has created a sensible proposal that attempts to do justice to the structural markers, major themes, and redactional clues in the Sermon. Luz also points out how each *inclusio* gives meaning to the Sermon. A major strength of Luz's proposal is his connection between the literary structuring and the theology of the Sermon. While the majority of Luz's inclusions are thoroughly defensible, his rationale for paralleling Mt. 5:21-48 and 6:19–7:11 is not as developed as his other arguments. Luz's appeal to the total number of lines shared between these major sections is not convincing. These critiques along with Luz's lack of clarity in defining the Prayer's centrality (see Chapter 1, Introduction, Survey of Scholarship, pp. xx) demand an extensive study of the relationship between the Sermon and the Prayer.

Structural Proposals Conclusion

The preceding discussion regarding structure has a twofold purpose. First, the proposals surveyed thus far reveal that there are a variety of different ways commentators and biblical scholars have approached the Sermon on the Mount. Some proposals of the Sermon highlight the historical background, while others emphasize its various literary devices. Still others explore the theology of the Sermon. The second purpose of this survey is to show that any proposal that is too stringent is subject to failure. Because of the variety of teachings in the Sermon and "shape" of each section, a one-size-fits-all approach to the Sermon's structure can be difficult to establish. As Ulrich Luz comments, at times, structure can easily become a pattern that a commentator sees in the Sermon that may not be consistent with the authorial intent.[74] A structural analysis that is consistent with Matthew's compositional techniques must be careful not to force the text into unrealistic strictures. We want to offer some general observations gleaned from the previous structural proposals before giving specific comments regarding the five approaches. The following list moves from structural to thematic concerns:

1. Matthew's most common literary devices in the Sermon are dyads, triads, *inclusios*, *kelals*, and the use of repetition.[75]
2. Matthew has structured the Sermon on the Mount. The sections throughout the Sermon also evidence microstructuring within their respective sections.
3. The Sermon's structure creates a cohesive message by compiling individual sets of teachings. Examples of these individual sections of teaching are the *macarisms*, teaching on "salt and light," Jesus's teaching on the *Torah*, the three marks of Jewish piety, the Lord's Prayer, "treasures in heaven" versus "treasures on earth," the teaching on anxiety, "dogs and pigs," "asking, seeking, and knocking" in prayer,

---

[74] Luz, *Matthew 1–7*, 174, states, "It is striking, however, how often the exegete's discretion is pointed in a certain direction."
[75] These literary devices will be illustrated throughout the book.

the Golden Rule, and the series of contrasts in the conclusion. By piecing these together, Matthew creates a panoramic view for the reader.
4. At the most basic level of structure, the Sermon itself has an introduction, body, and conclusion. The Sermon is signaled by Jesus's ascent of a mountain to teach his disciples (Mt. 5:1-2) and ends with Jesus's descent, followed by the reaction of the crowds (Mt. 7:28–8:1).
5. The beginning of the Sermon (Mt. 5:1–6:18) has a more discernible structure and message than the latter half of the Sermon. The most difficult section of the Sermon in which to discern structure is Mt. 6:19–7:12.[76]
6. Matthew's structuring in the Sermon stresses thematic emphases for the Sermon (see Chapter 2, Methodological Implications, Final Form Focus). At the heart of the Sermon lies the kingdom of heaven. Teaching on the kingdom features prominently throughout the Sermon. Closely related to this kingdom emphasis is righteousness and prayer. These emphases are evidenced in the Sermon's reverence for the *Torah* (Mt. 5:17-48) and being socially responsible (Mt. 6:19–7:12). We will explore these themes more thoroughly in the following chapters.
7. Consistent with his character sketches throughout the Gospel, Matthew uses structuring and literary devices to contrast two different ways of life throughout the Sermon. In an implicit and explicit manner, these contrasting ways of life depict citizens of the kingdom of heaven and the kingdoms of earth.

Regarding the proposals themselves, each of these structural suggestions is helpful in exploring the complexity of the Sermon's literary beauty. The work of Kingsbury and Guelich highlights a major emphasis in the Sermon, namely righteousness. Kingsbury and Guelich argue that righteousness guides the structure for the major sections of the Sermon. The proposal being put forward in the following chapters works in reverse order, with the structure informing the themes. By exploring the structure further, righteousness stands in conjunction with other major themes such as the kingdom and prayer.[77]

Allison has pointed out that the common Jewish literary device of triad is prevalent in the Sermon. Unfortunately, Allison overlooks other devices for the sake of the triad. The following proposal will seek to show how the triad works in conjunction with these other literary devices to provide structuring depth and variety in the Sermon.

In contrast to Patte's chiastic structure, the following proposal will not only seek to retain the natural flow of the Sermon, but also to show intentional parallels between various sections. Patte's structure attempts to show parallel sections in the Sermon but breaks up the natural thought units that run throughout the Sermon.

The expositional approaches help in showing the interconnectedness of the Sermon and its parts. Grundmann and Bornkamm show how the Lord's Prayer plays a central

---

[76] Although the question of sources is beyond the present scope of this book, the difficulty of structuring Mt. 6:19–7:12 may be because of Matthew's source material. In other words, he may have structured it as "tightly" as possible without betraying the integrity of the material. He is treating his source material very carefully.

[77] Kingsbury and Guelich would not dismiss these themes as important to the Sermon but would make them subservient to their major theme of righteousness. The following argument will set out to show that righteousness must be understood considering the other emphases and vice versa.

role in the Sermon's structure. The weakness of these proposals is the difficulty in establishing justifiable relationships between some of the parts of the Sermon and their chosen centerpiece. The *macarisms* do not necessarily connect in a uniform fashion with all of the material in the rest of the Sermon, nor does the Lord's Prayer structure the parts of the Sermon.

Much like Patte's chiastic structure, Luz's proposal helps to see the parallel sections and natural flow of the Sermon material, as well as the centrality of the Lord's Prayer. His work on the Sermon connects literary innovation with theology. In this case, Matthew has used the structure, in addition to the words themselves, to convey the message of the Sermon. While Luz's proposal is helpful in seeing the various *inclusios* throughout the Sermon, there are sections that need further clarity in terms of their parallelism. The following proposal will attempt to provide this clarity, particularly the parallelism between Mt. 5:21-48 and 6:19–7:12.

The Sermon's Prayer: A Structural Proposal for the Sermon

As stated, the following proposal seeks to establish the possibility of the Lord's Prayer as the centerpiece of the Sermon based on internal structuring, thematic consistency, and verbal patterning. Building on Luz's proposal, we will be arguing for the Prayer as the exegetical and thematic key to the Sermon's material based on its structural centrality. For ease of understanding, we have created five levels that illustrate the centering motion of the Sermon. Each level will be explained separately in addition to the parallels within each level.

Level 1

In the first level, Matthew creates a narrative *inclusio* around Jesus's teaching in the Sermon (Mt. 5:1–2//7:28–8:1). Set side by side, Allison points out the parallelism between the beginning and ending of Matthew's bookends:[78]

5:1   τοὺς ὄχλους
7:28 οἱ ὄχλοι

5:1   τὸ ὄρος
8:1   τοῦ ὄρους

5:1   ἀωέβη
8:1   καταβάντος

---

[78] Allison, "Configuration of the Sermon," 174. Allison includes among these verses Mt. 4:23-25 to the beginning of the Sermon. While there is one noticeable parallel phrase with 8:1, 4:23 is repeated almost verbatim in 9:35. We have not included 4:23-25 in the formal structure, but these verses do

5:2   ἐδίδασκεν
7:28 διδαχῇ αὐτοῦ

The narrative sections display shared vocabulary and an introduction to the audience of Jesus's Sermon teaching. Given this parallelism, the simplest outline of the Sermon is Mt. 5:1-2 as introduction *to* the Sermon, Mt. 5:3–7:27 as the Sermon proper, and Mt. 7:28–8:1 as the conclusion *to* the Sermon.[79]

Moving within Matthew's introduction and conclusion to the Sermon, Jesus's teaching begins with a series of *macarisms*/Promises (Mt. 5:3-16) and ends with Warnings (Mt. 7:13-27). The first section (Mt. 5:3-16) begins with what is commonly known as the Beatitudes or *macarisms*. There are eight clearly defined couplets each beginning with the word "μακάριοι." The first eight *macarisms* present human flourishing/the good life to those who possess various dispositions (e.g., being poor in spirit, mourn, meek, etc.), while the second part states the eschatological reward for committed discipleship ("theirs is the kingdom of heaven").[80] A "ninth" *macarism* follows in vv. 11-12 but deviates slightly in form, length, and verb usage. These nine *macarisms* are followed by the twin metaphors of salt and light (Mt. 5:13-16). These metaphors are used to shape the picture of Jesus's disciples. The salt metaphor describes the identity of Jesus's followers, while "light" describes the influence these disciples exhibit to those around them.

In terms of continuity between these sections, Mt. 5:3-10 share a similar catchword and emphasis with Mt. 5:11-12 (μακάριοι). Additionally, these two sections speak of earthly dispositions with the promise of heavenly rewards.[81] The difference in these sections is the break in Mt. 5:11-12 from the couplet form that has dominated the first eight *macarisms*. Verses 11-12 also changes in verb form. Interestingly, vv. 13-16 have the same verb form present in vv. 11-12. Verse 12 and the ending of v. 16 also share the phrase ἐν τοῖς οὐρανοῖς. Matthew has retained the individual character of these three sections (Mt. 5:3-10, 11-12, 13-16) but has grouped them in such a way to create fluency.[82] Seeing the beginning in this fashion creates three sections: Mt. 5:3-10, 11-12, and 13-16. There are verbal and thematic connections throughout these sections and several cues that help the reader to see the unity and diversity in these verses.

The parallel section to the *macarisms*/Promises (Mt. 5:3-16) is Jesus's Warnings in Mt. 7:13-27. This section is laid out similarly to Jesus's teaching in Mt. 5:3-16. First, there are three major sections, each of which consists of contrasting ways of life. The sections speak of two ways (Mt. 7:13-14), two fruits/prophets (Mt. 7:15-20), and two foundations (Mt. 7:21-23). Second, there may be an effort on Matthew's

---

play an important role in their parallels with 8:1 and 9:35. They show the close connection between Jesus's words (chs 5–7) and Jesus's deeds (chs 8–9).

[79] We will argue further that Mt. 5:1-2 is an introduction *to* the Sermon, 5:3-16 is the introduction *of* the Sermon, 5:17–7:12 is the body *of* the Sermon, 7:13-27 is the conclusion *of* the Sermon, and 7:28–8:1 is the conclusion *to* the Sermon.

[80] France, *Gospel of Matthew*, 161–2. See esp. fn.13.

[81] Pennington, *Sermon and Human Flourishing*, 153–61, refers to this section as an important building block for "human flourishing."

[82] See Hagner, *Matthew 1–13*, 84. Hagner agrees that the introduction is best seen as stretching across vv. 3-16.

part to show the contrast of doing and not doing in both sections. In Mt. 5:13-16, Matthew uses the metaphor of useless salt to illustrate nonaction or wrong action on the part of the disciple and follows with the metaphor of light to encourage being a witness for Christ. This order is reversed in Mt. 7:13-27 as Jesus begins with the call to enter the narrow gate and then contrasts this gate with the much wider and popular gate (i.e., nonaction or wrong action). Third, in Mt. 5:3-10 and 7:21-27, Matthew uses the third person. These would be considered the more "outside" sections. As Matthew moves more inward, he switches to the second person in Mt. 5:11-16 and 7:13-20.[83]

By paralleling the narrative sections around the Sermon (Mt. 5:1-2, 7:28–8:1), the reader is drawn into the Sermon. This movement inward is continued with the paralleling of Mt. 5:3-16 and 7:13-27. Within these sections of *macarisms* and Warnings is the *inclusio* of the "law and the prophets" (Mt. 5:17//7:12).[84] This small inclusion marks the beginning and ending of the Sermon Body (Mt. 5:17–7:12) and leads to the next level.

Level 2

Three major sections mark Level 2. The three sections are relatively similar in length with only the center section being slightly shorter.[85] Each section will be dealt with separately.

Matthew 5:21-48

The present section consists of Jesus's teaching on the Mosaic law (Mt. 5:17-20). Jesus comments on six different Jewish laws/interpretations. In each of the six cases, the blocks of teaching share similar themes and form. In some cases, some of the blocks have nearly identical word counts.[86] Although the laws are different and arrive from different sources, Jesus remains consistent in his requirements within the six sections. In each exegesis of the law (Mt. 5:21-47), Jesus explains that to achieve exceeding righteousness (see Mt. 5:17-20), one must resist shallow interpretations of the law that only require outward change.[87] In the six teachings, there is a formulaic statement of a commandment ("you have heard that it was said" . . . [commandment]) followed by Jesus's "but I tell you." Also, among these cues is the use of a verbatim introduction in the first and fourth teaching block (Ἠκούσατε ὅτι ἐρρέθη τοῖς ἀρχαίοις). The fourth teaching block bears the word "again" (Πάλιν) to signal another section of laws. This adverb creates two sets of three teachings on the law (Mt. 5:21-26, 27-30, 31-32//5:33-37, 38-42, 43-47 [48]).

---

[83] This is also noted by Luz, *Matthew 1–7*, 173.
[84] Nearly every interpreter recognizes this *inclusio*.
[85] Mt. 5:21-48: 508 words; Mt. 6:1-18: 344 words; Mt. 6:19–7:12: 513 words.
[86] See Luz, *Matthew 1–7*, 226. The first three paragraphs have 258 words (1131 letters), while the second three paragraphs have 244 words (1130 letters).
[87] See Hagner, *Matthew 1–13*, 111–12.

Matthew 6:1-18 (19-21)

In this set of verses, Jesus deals with the three marks of Jewish piety. The content of the passages is very familiar in that the practices mentioned by Jesus were regular parts of Jewish religious observance. The section is usually titled the "cult-didache" following Betz.[88] The practices mentioned are almsgiving, praying, and fasting. These verses will be detailed below in terms of their content and structure (Level 3).

Matthew 6:19–7:12

As commentators have often noted, the structure in this closing section of the Sermon is more difficult to determine.[89] At the most basic level, this section can be split into two blocks: Mt. 6:19-34 and 7:1-12. The first block of texts begins with some general statements about possessions (vv. 19-24) that become more precise in the succeeding verses (vv. 25-34).[90] Matthew 6:19-21 gives the section an eschatological perspective that becomes more grounded in vv. 25-34. Additionally, the beginning of this first major section (vv. 19-24) speaks of the duality of heaven and earth and uses abstract references to the eye, light, and the body. The next section (vv. 25-34) uses natural examples to explain the cure for anxiety.

The next major block in this section is Mt. 7:1-12. This section is essentially three parts beginning with Mt. 7:1-5. The teaching is clear: be careful how you judge others. The next verse, Mt. 7:6, has been somewhat of an enigma. Commentators have struggled to explain its aphoristic meaning and how it fits with what precedes and with what follows. We will discuss its meaning in more depth in Chapter 6.

Matthew brings the body of the Sermon to a suitable close in Mt. 7:7-12. Picking up on the theme of prayer, Matthew explains the importance of persevering in seeking God. As Mt. 6:19-34 has the themes of heaven and earth, so the closing to this section of the body describes earthly prayer to a Heavenly Father.

In terms of paralleling Mt. 5:21-48 and 6:19–7:12, there is no consensus among scholars. In response to Luz, R. T. France summarizes, "It is, however, not clear in what way, e.g., 5:21–48 and 6:19–7:11, correspond to each other, except in the purely formal sense that each occupies 59 lines in Nestle.'"[91] Although France and others remain skeptical, there are some interesting connections that are often overlooked, not least by Luz.

First, there are several interesting thematic connections. Jesus's teaching on the Mosaic law tends to suggest that there is always more than meets the surface. The Mosaic law is sufficient, but Jesus goes to the heart of the law's teaching ("You have

---

[88] Betz, "A Jewish-Christian Cultic Didache in Matt. 6:1–18: Reflections and Questions on the Problem of the Historical Jesus," in *Essays on the Sermon on the Mount* (Minneapolis: Fortress, 1985): 55–70; *Sermon on the Mount*, 62–4.

[89] Stanton, *Gospel for a New People*, 298, comments, "This part of the Sermon seems to be a 'rag-bag' of sayings, only some of which are loosely related to others." Interestingly in his treatment of the Sermon, Stanton highlights the key sections of the Sermon. He completely leaves out 6:19–7:12.

[90] Hagner, *Matthew 1–13*, 156, notes that the first section of Mt. 6:19-24 consists of three logia (vv. 19-21, 22-23, 24).

[91] France, *Gospel of Matthew*, 155, fn.8.

heard it said . . . but I say to you"). In Mt. 6:19–7:12, there is a similar flow of thought. In each of the individual teachings, Jesus digs to the heart of each issue. For example, Jesus insists in vv. 19-21 that earthly treasure is not sufficient but that one must strive for heavenly rewards. Similarly, Mt. 6:25-34 teaches that disciples must subject earthly desires (food, drink, and clothing) to the Father's kingdom and righteousness (Mt. 6:33).

A second connection in terms of subject matter is the consistency in each section in addressing one broad topic. As Mt. 5:21-48 addresses Jesus's teaching on six different laws, so Mt. 6:19–7:12 considers six basic issues of life with a contrast between heavenly and earthly concerns. Betz comments on these six elements, "The third and last section of the body of the Sermon on the Mount (Matt. 6:19–7:12) concerns . . . the human response to God's generosity in the affairs of daily life."[92] For Betz, those areas are Mt. 6:19-21 ("On gathering treasures"), Mt. 6:22-23 ("On vision"), Mt. 6:24 ("On serving two masters"), Mt. 6:25-34 ("On worrying"), Mt. 7:1-5 ("On judging"), Mt. 7:6 ("On profaning the holy: a cryptic *sentential*"), and Mt. 7:7-11 ("On giving and receiving").[93] Although slightly disagreeing as to the arrangement of the six units, Davies and Allison also see six sections in Mt. 6:19–7:12 dealing with "how to behave in the world at large."[94]

The next overlap between these sections is the relatively similar length. In terms of word count, Mt. 5:21-48 has 508 words with the inclusion of one variant word that is disputed in v. 39. On the other hand, Mt. 6:19–7:12 has 513 words with two minor variants.[95] Although word counts are generally not the strongest arguments for parallelism, it is interesting that this section of the Sermon is not the only place that there is an incredibly close word count connected to structural concerns (Mt. 5:21-32//5:33-48).

In addition to the thematic correlations and word counts, the respective structures of each section evidence a parallel. As mentioned earlier, Mt. 5:21-48 splits nicely into two sections of three. Although Mt. 6:19–7:12 does not retain the internal consistency of Mt. 5:21-48, it does exhibit the same basic split into two sections. As mentioned, the first section consists of Mt. 6:19-34, while the second section consists of Mt. 7:1-12.[96]

---

[92] Betz, *Sermon on the Mount*, 65.
[93] Betz, *Sermon on the Mount*, 54–7.
[94] Davies and Allison, *Matthew 1–7*, 625–7.
[95] The first variant is in v. 25: ἢ τί πίητε. Although these small words have significant attestation in the manuscript evidence (K L N Γ Δ Θ 565. 579. 700. 1241. 1424. *l* 844 𝔐 sy$^{p.h}$), they were most likely added as a secondary emendation to balance the immediately preceding phrase, τί φάγητε (see Davies and Allison, *Matthew 1–7*, 646). This would create continuity with v. 31 in which the two phrases are paired. The other variant is in v. 33 where τοῦ θεοῦ (*1 4–6* ℵ [k] 1 sa bo; Eus) is used to describe the accusative τὴν βασιλείαν. The reason for this inclusion is probably to create consistency in the Synoptic traditions' tendency to use the phrase "kingdom of God." Obviously, the kingdom is an important topic in the Gospel tradition and, in most cases, is followed by the genitival phrase. The scribal inclusion is most likely for explanatory reasons and is not entirely necessary to make the point.
[96] See Davies and Allison, *Matthew 1–7*, 626. As mentioned above, Allison proposes an interesting structure for understanding some internal consistency within 6:19–7:12. Matthew 6:19-34 is mirrored by 7:1-11 with 7:12 serving as a conclusion to both sections. Each section begins with an exhortation (6:19-21//7:1-2). This is followed by two parables, with the first parable teaching

In addition to the splitting of each major section into two smaller sections, there is one additional structural marker that each section shares. In the case of Mt. 5:21-48, Jesus concludes his teaching on the *Torah* with a summary clause on perfection (Mt. 5:48). Similarly, Mt. 6:19–7:12 concludes with the Golden Rule (Mt. 7:12).[97]

Level 3

Having examined the three major blocks (particularly the two outside blocks) and their symmetry, one must follow the shaping of Matthew's structure. Level 3 details the central chapter of Matthew's Sermon (ch. 6). Matthew presents three teachings on Jewish piety: almsgiving, prayer, and fasting. Alfred Perry's chart helpfully lays out the consistency of this section (Table 3.2).[98]

In each of these three teachings, Matthew displays impressive symmetry and shared form. Each section displays a contrast between the practice of hypocrites and righteousness that pleases the Father in heaven. The sections also parallel the reward of hypocrites, which is earthly recognition. The only break in this pattern is the inclusion of an extended section on prayer, namely the Lord's Prayer.[99] The obvious length difference in this middle section draws the reader further into the center of the Sermon.

Level 4

Level 4 details Jesus's teaching on prayer (Mt. 6:5-15). After the general teaching concerning proper prayer (Mt. 6:5-6), Matthew surrounds the Lord's Prayer with two phrases (Mt. 6:7-8//6:14-15). The first phrase (Mt. 6:7-8) links with the previous teaching (Mt. 6:5-6) on prayer. In both cases, there is a warning against improper displays of prayer (v. 5: "And whenever you pray, do not be like the hypocrites"; v. 7: "do not use meaningless repetition as the Gentiles do"). Jesus continues in vv. 9-13 with a contrasting example of proper prayer, the Lord's Prayer proper. The phrase following the Lord's Prayer (Mt. 6:14-15) reiterates the concerns of the forgiveness petition (Mt. 6:12).

Verses 14-15 somewhat breaks the patterning that is inherent in the three shorter blocks of teaching. At first, it seems odd that there is an extended teaching on one of the petitions. The key may be to look at its relationship with vv. 7-8. First, the most obvious link is the appeal to the Father's involvement in the life of the petitioner. In the first case, the Father knows our prayers, and in the second case, the Father grants the petitioner forgiveness. Second, in both sets of verses, there is a contrast. In the first

---

on the eye (6:22-23//7:3-5; 6:24//7:6). The third element in the proposal is an encouragement section emphasizing the heavenly Father's care (6:25-34//7:7-11). In both ending sections, the internal rhetoric of the section is an argument from lesser to greater (*a minori ad maius*). Allison's arrangement breaks his triadic arrangement but is helpful for analyzing Mt. 6:19-34 and Mt. 7:1-12.

[97] Interestingly, both summary clauses contain conditional clauses (ὡς, οὕτως). This grammatical parallel may be incidental but still evidences consistency in the rhetoric of the Sermon.

[98] Alfred M. Perry, "The Framework of the Sermon on the Mount," *JBL* 54.2 (1935): 104.

[99] Compare Luke's placement of the Lord's Prayer (11:2-4) and his Sermon on the Plain (6:20-49).

Table 3.2 Word Similarities in the Sermon's Central Section (Mt. 6:2-18)

6:2-4 Almsgiving	6:5-6 Prayer	6:16-18 Fasting
2. ὅταν οὖν...	5. καὶ ὅταν	16. ὅταν δὲ...
μὴ σαλπίσῃς...	οὐκ ἔσεσθε	μὴ γίνεσθε...
ὥσπερ οἱ ὑποκριταὶ...	ὡς οἱ ὑποκριταί	ὥσπερ οἱ ὑποκριταὶ...
ὅπως δοξασθῶσιν	ὅπως φανῶσιν	ὅπως φανῶσιν
ὑπὸ τῶν ἀνθρώπων	τοῖς ἀνθρώποις	τοῖς ἀνθρώποις...
ἀμὴν λέγω ὑμῖν	ἀμὴν λέγω ὑμῖν	ἀμὴν λέγω ὑμῖν
ἀπέχουσιν	ἀπέχουσι	ἀπέχουσι
τὸν μισθὸν αὐτῶν	τὸν μισθὸν αὐτῶν	τὸν μισθὸν αὐτῶν
3. σοῦ δὲ...	6. σὺ δὲ...	17. σὺ δὲ...
4. ὅπως...	...	18. ὅπως...
...	τῷ πατρί σου	τῷ πατρί σου
ἐν τῷ κρυπτῷ	τῷ ἐν τῷ κρυπτῷ	τῷ ἐν τῷ κρυπτῷ
καὶ ὁ Πατήρ σου	καὶ ὁ Πατήρ σου	καὶ ὁ Πατήρ σου
ὁ βλέπων	ὁ βλέπων	ὁ βλέπων
ἐν τῷ κρυπτῷ	ἐν τῷ κρυπτῷ	ἐν τῷ κρυπτῷ
ἀποδώσει σοι.	ἀποδώσει σοι.	ἀποδώσει σοι.

case, the prayers of the Gentile are contrasted with proper prayers. In the second case, there is a contrast between those who give forgiveness and those who do not. Without orienting one's relationships on earth properly, proper prayer is made impossible. There is an interesting thematic link here with the entirety of ch. 6. The ὑποκριταί, who have been mentioned earlier, continuously practice their righteousness before men to be seen. These admonitions against practicing righteousness before men do not abrogate social relationships (see Mt. 6:19–7:12) but rather serves as a reminder that a disciple must be careful to attend to proper outward practice in conjunction with proper prayer.[100] This addendum to the Lord's Prayer of embodying forgiveness gives an example of this type of outward practice.

Level 5

In the fifth level, the Sermon comes to its proper center. If the aforementioned arguments are judged to be reasonable, the Sermon is highlighting the importance of prayer as one of its major themes. One bit of evidence, though, that is often overlooked in terms of the Sermon's structure is the relevance of the Prayer's own concentric structure.

After the invocation, the Prayer begins with two independent clauses both marked with an equal word count, the same word order, and grammatical pattern (ἁγιασθήτω τὸ ὄνομά σου//ἐλθέτω ἡ βασιλεία σου). In both phrases, the verb is the first word, followed by an article + subject + possessive pronoun "you."[101] Interestingly, if one accepts the seven-petition proposal, the last two clauses also display an equal word

---

[100] For similar comments, see Luz, *Matthew 1–7*, 327.
[101] This word count and patterning is also present in the will petition, although the third petition has the addition of the correlative clause.

count, the same word order, and grammatical pattern (καὶ μὴ εἰσενέγκῃς ἡμᾶς εἰς πειρασμόν//ἀλλὰ ῥῦσαι ἡμᾶς ἀπὸ τοῦ πονηροῦ).[102] Both phrases begin with a conjunction, followed by the verb + possessive plural pronoun used as the direct object + preposition + object. The only difference in these last phrases is the negation added to the verb in the first phrase and the use of the article for the object of the preposition in the second phrase.

Upon closer inspection, there are also some interesting thematic links between the first and last doublets. In the first set of phrases, the emphasis is on God's name and his kingdom. The last set of phrases contrast with these "positive" petitions. Specifically, the last two petitions refer to temptation and the evil one.[103] The subject of these final petitions alludes to the chapter preceding the Sermon. In Matthew 4, Jesus is in the wilderness. The Spirit has led him in a forty-day fast. During this time, Jesus is depicted as being tempted by the devil. This reference to evil in the petition would create a direct link in the first and last set of couplets' emphases on the cosmic forces of God and the evil one, namely the devil. The petitioner would in effect be "positively" praying for God to magnify his name and hasten his kingdom while praying negatively and/or against temptation and the evil one.

Moving inside the first and last set of doublets, one can observe again shared elements between petition three and petition five. In both cases, there is the use of correlative conjunctions. These are the only places in the Prayer where these grammatical constructions are present. While the phrases do not mirror one another in word count and word order, they do retain the patterns present in their respective halves of the Sermon. The positive petition is that God's will be done on earth as it is in heaven,[104] while the negative petition is a plea for God's forgiveness. Present in both petitions is an earthly and heavenly dimension. This dimension is obvious in the first petition as it is explicitly mentioned. It finds a perfect parallel in the fifth petition, as the petitioner is praying for the heavenly Father to forgive his sins "as" he forgives his earthly counterparts. As we will argue in Chapter 5, part of God's will in Matthew's Gospel is the act of forgiveness.

Following these implications and structural indicators, the Prayer would structurally lead to the fourth petition as its center or hinge point. As David Wenham has pointed out, there are elements in this fourth petition that unite it with what precedes and what follows.[105] The fourth petition connects with the first three requests in that it asks God to do something positive, "give us daily bread." The fourth petition also connects with the last three petitions not only in its use of the plural pronoun "we" but also in its concern with earthly matters. The following outline illustrates the proposed structures of the Sermon on the Mount and Lord's Prayer (Table 3.3):

---

[102] See also Lohmeyer, *Lord's Prayer*, 26, who notes the significance of the couplets.

[103] The interpretive decision to translate πονηρὸς as "evil one" will be discussed in Chapter 4.

[104] To clarify, the interpretive decision to see the correlative clauses as parallel does not negate the argument that "on earth as it is in heaven" can modify the first three petitions. We agree with Nolland, *Gospel of Matthew*, 289, "There is little difference in meaning if we link it with the third petition or with all three." In contrast, Pennington, *Sermon and Human Flourishing*, 223–4, argues that the clause definitively links to all three petitions.

[105] Wenham, "Sevenfold Form of the Lord's Prayer," 381–2.

Table 3.3 The Sermon's Prayer

	LEVEL 1	
	Sermon on the Mount (5:1–8:1)	
Sermon Introduction	**Narrative *Inclusio***	Sermon Conclusion
(5:1-2)		(7:28–8:1)
Macarisms: Human Flourishing		Call to Action
(5:3-16)	(Level 2: 5:17–7:12)	(7:13-27)
	Inclusio	
	(5:17-20) "*Law and the Prophets*" (7:12)	
	LEVEL 2	
	Sermon Body (5:17–7:12)	
Living Lawfully	Living Piously	Living Socially
(5:17-48)	(Level 3: 6:1-18 [19-21])	(6:19–7:12)
	LEVEL 3	
	Centre of the Centre (6:1-18 [19-21])	
On Giving	On Praying	On Fasting
(6:2-4)	(Level 4: 6:5-15)	(6:16-18)
	LEVEL 4	
	Prayer as the Centre (6:5-15)	
	The Lord's Prayer in Context	
(6:7-8)	(Level 5: 6:9-13)	(6:14-15)
	LEVEL 5	
	The Sermon's Prayer (6:9-13)	
	The Lord's Prayer	
	6:9-13	
	The Lord's Prayer[a]	
	Invocation (6:9b)	
God's name/kingdom		Temptation/evil one
(6:9c-10a)		(6:13)
Prayer for God's Will	**Correlative Clause**	Prayer for Forgiveness
(6:10b)		(6:12)
	Prayer for Daily Bread	
	(6:11)	

[a] For an extensive chart examining the Lord's Prayer and its structure, see Appendix A.

Structure Conclusion

While these are not entirely new proposals in terms of the Sermon on the Mount or the Lord's Prayer's structure, it does suggest a structure within the Prayer that is consistent with its context—the Sermon on the Mount. Both pieces of writing use internal structuring, thematic consistency, and verbal patterning. These structuring devices evidence Matthew's intentions for reading the Sermon on the Mount. The preceding argument has established the Sermon's structure is a set of *inclusios* that work towards a discernible center, the Lord's Prayer. Likewise, the Lord's Prayer works towards a center or hinge point.[106] In both pieces of teaching, righteousness is a prevailing theme, and there is a concern for heavenly matters over and above earthly affairs. These themes are presented in a balanced and measured literary structure. The following structure establishes the Lord's Prayer as a focal point for lexical and thematic parallels with the Sermon on the Mount. To these textual connections, we now turn.

---

[106] Both centers are important to their respective contexts but differ in function. As we will argue in the proceeding chapters, the Lord's Prayer, as the structural centerpiece, is lexically and thematically parallel to the surrounding Sermon. On the other hand, the bread petition is more of a hinge between the two halves of the Prayer.

4

The Matthean Petitions

An Examination of the Father, Will, and Evil Petitions

In Chapter 3, we argued that the Lord's Prayer is placed at the center of the Sermon on the Mount structurally and becomes a focal point for textual connections. This chapter and the next two builds on the previous structural proposal and begins exploring the lexical and thematic parallels between the petitions of the Lord's Prayer and passages in the Sermon on the Mount. The Matthean version of the Lord's Prayer differentiates itself from the Lukan version with its inclusion of three additional phrases.

Matthew 6:9b-13	Luke 11:2-4
⁹Πάτερ **ἡμῶν ὁ ἐν τοῖς οὐρανοῖς**	²Πάτερ,
ἁγιασθήτω τὸ ὄνομά σου,	ἁγιασθήτω τὸ ὄνομά σου
¹⁰ἐλθέτω ἡ βασιλεία σου,	ἐλθέτω ἡ βασιλεία σου
γενηθήτω τὸ θέλημά σου,	
ὡς ἐν οὐρανῷ καὶ ἐπὶ γῆς	
¹¹τὸν ἄρτον ἡμῶν τὸν ἐπιούσιον	³τὸν ἄρτον ἡμῶν τὸν ἐπιούσιον
δὸς ἡμῖν σήμερον	δίδου ἡμῖν τὸ καθ' ἡμέραν
¹²καὶ ἄφες ἡμῖν τὰ ὀφειλήματα ἡμῶν,	⁴καὶ ἄφες ἡμῖν τὰς ἁμαρτίας ἡμῶν,
ὡς καὶ ἡμεῖς ἀφήκαμεν τοῖς	καὶ γὰρ αὐτοὶ ἀφίομεν παντὶ
ὀφειλέταις ἡμῶν	ὀφείλοντι ἡμῖν
¹³καὶ μὴ εἰσενέγκῃς ἡμᾶς εἰς πειρασμόν,	καὶ μὴ εἰσενέγκῃς ἡμᾶς εἰς πειρασμόν.
ἀλλὰ ῥῦσαι ἡμᾶς ἀπὸ τοῦ πονηροῦ.	

We will begin with these petitions, as they have the strongest case for being "Matthean." These petitions also exhibit the strongest textual connections with the Sermon on the Mount, having significant functional, lexical, and thematic parallels.[1]

---

[1] "Functional" parallels refer to the wording of the invocation being *used* in contexts associated with prayer or in cases where prayer is mentioned.

It is likely that Matthew noted similarities between the Prayer and Sermon from the traditions of the Sermon he received, leading him to make connections between the two texts in his Gospel and to bring them together. Matthew then edited parts of both the Sermon and the Prayer with a desire to increase the parallelism between the two texts.[2] By locating the Lord's Prayer in the Sermon on the Mount and through these increased parallels, Matthew shaped these texts to be read together.[3] Matthew's purpose was, on the one hand, to provide an explanation of the requests in the Prayer via the Sermon on the Mount and, on the other hand, a prayer that by its very presence in the Sermon spoke of where the petitioner anticipated getting power to live out the Sermon.

In arguing this specific thesis, we will deal with each petition in the order of their appearance. We will first show that the Matthean petitions are distinctive in comparison with Luke. Yet, a comparison with Luke only shows that Matthew goes one way and Luke another. So, we will attempt to show how each of the petitions within Matthew's version has wording that is Matthean.[4] Then, we will analyze the distribution of the phrase in question within Matthew's Gospel. In this analysis, we will show that the wording of the phrase under examination is "clustered" into chs 5–7. We will call this the argument from "prominence." The wording of the petition is distinctive, then, by its presence and compared with the other Gospels, and the petition is prominent in chs 5–7. These comparisons with the other Gospels and analysis of the distribution of the phrase signal that the phrases are to be read together. This section will not address the instances of the wording within the Sermon on the Mount, as this will be discussed in section three of each analysis.

In the second section, we will attempt to define each petition and discover its meaning. We will examine Matthew's "cultural milieu" for parallels and ideas associated with the wording and phrase in question. Some petitions have more parallels than others, while others are primarily defined by their presence in Matthew's Gospel. The purpose of this section is to establish a basis for exploring thematic parallels between each petition and the Sermon on the Mount.

In the third section, we will work from the first two sections. In Section 1, we have argued that the petition/passages which share lexical parallels should be read together. So, in Section 3, we will list the Sermon references which have the same wording as the petition under investigation. These lexical parallels are unmistakable. We will then attempt to point out the shared themes (Section 2 findings) to strengthen the argument for proposed allusions. In the cases where it is applicable, we will additionally argue for looser parallels (i.e., echoes) to the petition under investigation.

---

[2] For a discussion of Matthew's redaction, see Nolland, *Gospel of Matthew*, 10–11. We agree with Nolland's assessment that Matthew is a "conservative" redactor.

[3] Matthew could very well have intentioned for this pairing to be vocalized as well. The subtle difference of delivery is of no consequence to the overall argument.

[4] For example, we will argue that the phrases which compose the invocation are throughout Matthew and not in the other Gospels. Therefore, the phrasing appears to be preferential to Matthew's Gospel. For a working definition of "Mattheanisms," see Chapter 2, Methodology.

Finally, after arguing for the various parallels between each petition and passage in the Sermon on the Mount, we will suggest what praying the Lord's Prayer might look like if prayed through the lens of the Sermon on the Mount and vice versa.[5]

Invocation: "Our Father in Heaven"

The invocation stands at the head of the Lord's Prayer and (arguably) carries as much exegetical importance as the petitions themselves. Ulrich Luz agrees, "The address . . . stands over the entire prayer and thus carries great weight."[6] N. T. Wright goes even further in his assessment. He proposes that the entire Sermon on the Mount should be titled, "What It Means to Call God 'Father.'"[7] According to Wright, living Jesus's teachings in the Sermon on the Mount is the ultimate expression of calling God "Father." Wright's assessment acknowledges the role of the invocation as part of what it means to call God "Father" but misses its "central" importance.[8] In the following section, we will examine the invocation and its functional, lexical, and thematic parallels with the Sermon on the Mount.

The Distinctives of "Our Father in Heaven"

This section has a twofold purpose. First, we will examine the specific wording of the Matthean version of the invocation, noting its distinctive characteristics. We will argue that the Matthean version is distinguished by its differences with the Lukan version.[9] The nearly exclusive use of the phrase in Matthew indicates its distinctiveness. Second, we will examine the distribution of the invocation's wording within Matthew's Gospel. A survey of Matthew's uses of "our Father in heaven" evidences a concentration of the terms in chs 5–7. Therefore, the distinctiveness of the invocation and its prominence, generally in Matthew's Gospel and specifically in Matthew 5–7, suggests a literary innovation within Matthew. This distinctive wording and prominence creates lexical parallels between the Lord's Prayer and the Sermon on the Mount, and it will be suggested in Section 3 that these parallels are to be read together.

---

[5] We will ultimately argue that the Sermon and the Lord's Prayer have a bearing on each other's meaning, but only after the lexical and thematic parallels are established. Making claims before establishing the parallels runs the risk of fallacious circular reasoning, as one text is used to understand the other text and then back again.
[6] Luz, *Matthew 1–7*, 309. See also *The Theology of the Gospel of Matthew*, trans. J. Bradford Robinson (Cambridge: Cambridge University Press, 1995), 3.
[7] N. T. Wright, *Matthew for Everyone: Chapter 1–15*, New Testament for Everyone (Louisville: WJKP, 2004), 58–9.
[8] To avoid misunderstanding, we will argue that Wright's statement concerning the rhetorical value of "fatherhood" is correct. We are less concerned about the correctness of his larger argument that the Lord's Prayer has an *Exodus* motif.
[9] The version found in the *Didache* agrees with the Matthean version. This repetition is most likely explained by the *Didache's* dependence on Matthew's Gospel. The direction of borrowing between Matthew and the *Didache* is beyond the scope of this project and will not be discussed at length.

Wording

The Matthean version of the invocation is much longer than its Lukan counterpart (Lk. 11:2). While both versions begin with "Father" (Πάτερ), Matthew has added the possessive pronoun "our" (ἡμῶν) and the description of "one who is in heaven" (ὁ ἐν τοῖς οὐρανοῖς).

Mt. 6:9 Πάτερ ἡμῶν ὁ ἐν τοῖς οὐρανοῖς
Lk. 11:2 Πάτερ

Commentators frequently note that these additions function as liturgical additions.[10] A closer look at the wording reveals more than a liturgical elongation. The wording evidences a Matthean preference.

Within Matthew's Gospel, "father" and "heaven" are combined twenty times.[11] The instances are as follows:

Invocation:
6:9 Πάτερ ἡμῶν ὁ ἐν τοῖς οὐρανοῖς

Group 1 (same word order):
5:16 τὸν πατέρα ὑμῶν τὸν ἐν τοῖς οὐρανοῖς
5:45 τοῦ πατρὸς ὑμῶν τοῦ ἐν οὐρανοῖς
6:1 τῷ πατρὶ ὑμῶν τῷ ἐν τοῖς οὐρανοῖς
7:11 ὁ πατὴρ ὑμῶν ὁ ἐν τοῖς οὐρανοῖς
7:21 τοῦ πατρός μου τοῦ ἐν τοῖς οὐρανοῖς
10:32 τοῦ πατρός μου τοῦ ἐν [τοῖς] οὐρανοῖς
10:33 τοῦ πατρός μου τοῦ ἐν [τοῖς] οὐρανοῖς
12:50 τοῦ πατρός μου τοῦ ἐν οὐρανοῖς
16:17 ὁ πατήρ μου ὁ ἐν τοῖς οὐρανοῖς
18:10 τοῦ πατρός μου τοῦ ἐν οὐρανοῖς
18:14 τοῦ πατρὸς ὑμῶν τοῦ ἐν οὐρανοῖς
18:19 τοῦ πατρός μου τοῦ ἐν οὐρανοῖς

Group 2 (article, **Father**, possessive pronoun, modifier):
5:48 ὁ πατὴρ ὑμῶν ὁ οὐράνιος
6:14 ὁ πατὴρ ὑμῶν ὁ οὐράνιος
6:26 ὁ πατὴρ ὑμῶν ὁ οὐράνιος
6:32 ὁ πατὴρ ὑμῶν ὁ οὐράνιος
15:13 ὁ πατὴρ ὑμῶν ὁ οὐράνιος
18:35 ὁ πατήρ μου ὁ οὐράνιος
23:9 ὁ πατὴρ ὁ οὐράνιος

Group 3 (Vocative [2x], modifier)
11:25 πάτερ, κύριε τοῦ οὐρανοῦ καὶ τῆς γῆς

---

[10] E.g., see Davies and Allison, *Matthew 1–7*, 600.
[11] The frequency of the term "heaven" (οὐρανός) and its derivatives in Matthew's Gospel suggests that it is an important term for him. In terms of usage, only Revelation has more references to heaven.

God is referred to as the "Father who is in heaven" in thirteen instances and the "heavenly Father" in seven. The twenty instances display an impressive consistency. A closely related instance is found in Mt. 11:25. Here, the vocative form of πατήρ is present, but the modifying phrase is slightly different with mention of both heaven and earth.

A comparison of the phrase's usage outside of Matthew's Gospel further reveals the distinctive nature of the phrase within Matthew. The phrase is only found in two other places in the New Testament: Mk. 11:25 (ὁ πάτερ ὁ ἐν [τοῖς] οὐρανοῖς) and possibly Lk. 11:13 (ὁ πάτερ ὁ ἐξ οὐρανοῖς).[12] Both instances mention the "Father" and "heaven" but lack the personal pronoun "our."[13]

Prominence

In the previous section, we noted the distinctive nature of the Matthean invocation. We made passing references to the variety of "father" language in chs 5–7. In this section, we intend to note the prominence of these references within chs 5–7 in comparison to the Gospel as a whole. This clustering of references appears to indicate Matthew's intention to prompt the reader to read these phrases together. We will begin with the father references before examining the Matthean modifiers.

God as Father

The title of "father" is used over 170 times in the Gospels.[14] Except for John's Gospel (109 times), Matthew has the largest number of references at sixty-three. Of these sixty-three references to father in Matthew, forty-four are used to refer to God. Matthew's preference for this title is evident not only in his retention of parallel material but also in material unique to his Gospel. As Pennington notes, "Of the twenty-four occurrences of father which do not use heaven or heavenly, twelve have no parallels in Mark or Luke, nearly all of which are in passages unique to Matthew."[15] Of the forty-four instances of God as Father in Matthew, seventeen of these uses are found within the Sermon on the Mount.[16] Within the Sermon itself, ten of the references are found in 6:1-18, a section unparalleled in Mark and Luke.[17]

---

[12] See Jonathan Pennington, *Heaven and Earth in the Gospel of Matthew* (Grand Rapids: Baker, 2007), 232–3, fn.7. See also 67–76.

[13] Luke's phrasing is translated as the "heavenly Father" in modern English versions. The more literal translation would be "the Father the one *from/out* of heaven." This verse will be discussed in more detail below in which we argue that this is not an actual parallel.

[14] Jeremias, *Prayers of Jesus*, 29, counts "father" in Matthew 63 times [44 times: God//19 times: human fathers]; in John 109 times; in Mark 4 times; and in Luke 17 times.

[15] Pennington, *Heaven and Earth*, 233, fn.10. Pennington lists the following passages: Mt. 6:4, 6 (2x), 8, 18 (2x); 13:43; 20:23; 25:34; 26:42, 53; 28:19.

[16] The uses of πατήρ in the Sermon on the Mount are found in 5:16, 45, 48; 6:1, 4, 6 (2x), 8, 9, 14, 15, 18 (2x), 26, 32; 7:11, 21. This clustering of references equals an impressive 39 percent of Matthew's total usages of God as Father.

[17] One could argue that the "father" language in Matthew is not significant because of the equal importance of the term in the Lukan version of the invocation, yet this interpretation neglects the

Heavenly Father/Father in Heaven/Our Father

In addition to the use of "father," Matthew has added the personal pronoun and the "one who is in heaven." In twenty instances, the terms "heaven" (οὐρανός) and "father" (πατήρ) are combined in Matthew's Gospel. This accounts for almost half of his references to God as "Father" (20 of 44). Interestingly, half of the references to the "father" and "heaven" are found in the Sermon on the Mount, without any other places having a significant concentration.

In his references to the "father," Matthew frequently adds the personal pronoun "my." "My Father" is found in Matthew's Gospel in seventeen different places describing both earthly fathers and God. Interestingly, only one of these examples is found in the Sermon on the Mount. Matthew's more common use of a pronoun with "father" is "our" and "your." "Our/your" with "Father" is used in twenty-two different places throughout Matthew's Gospel. Sixteen of these instances are found in chs 5–7, accounting for almost three-fourths of their uses elsewhere in Matthew's Gospel. Table 4.1[18] summarizes Matthew's use of the phrases under scrutiny.

Conclusion

The statistical data shows that Matthew's choice of wording in the invocation is not only preferred by or distinctive to Matthew but also clustered together in the Sermon on the Mount. The evidence appears to indicate Matthew's intentions that the father passages be read together. Matthew has provided lexical parallels between various passages throughout chs 5–7 as evidence of his intentions. The question remains, are these passages only lexically parallel or thematically parallel as well? In the following section, we will argue that not only are the seventeen references to the "father" linked by shared vocabulary, but they are also thematically coherent.

The Meaning of "Our Father in Heaven"

This section will explore the meaning of the invocation's wording. From our study, we conclude that for Matthew, the wording of the invocation is frequently associated with the concepts of relationship, covenant, community, God's sovereignty, and obedience to God's will. Establishing the meaning of the invocation is important for examining thematic parallels with passages in the Sermon on the Mount. This section will first deal with those themes relevant to calling God "our Father" (relationship, covenant, community), then "the one in heaven" (God's sovereignty). Last, we will examine

---

concentration of the term in the Sermon on the Mount and the modifiers found in the Matthean invocation. See Robert L. Mowery, "From Lord to Father in Matthew 1–7," *CBQ* 59.4 (1997), 648. In ch. 6, "father" appears twelve times among the 653 words in the chapter (1.838% ratio). The only place statistically close to this total is in ch. 11 in which father appears five times among the 493 words in the chapter (1.014% ratio).

[18] The table is organized according to the fivefold structure of Matthew's Gospel (i.e., 1–4, 5–7, 8–9, 10, 11–12, 13, 14–17, 18, 19–22, 23–25, 26–28).

Table 4.1 The Distribution of the Invocation's Wording

Chapters/Words (# of uses in Matthew)	1-4	5-7	8-9	10	11-12	13	14-17	18	19-22	23-25	26-28
Πατήρ (63)[a]	4	17	1	7	6	1	7	4	5	6	5
My Father (17)	0	1 (7:21)	1	2	2	0	2	3	1	1	4
Your/our Father (22)	0	16	0	2	0	0	0	1	0	3	0
Heaven/heavens (89)[b]	4	22	2	3	5	9	10	11	9	11	3
Father in heaven (13)	0	6	0	2	1	0	1	3	0	0	0
Heavenly Father (7)	0	4	0	0	0	0	1	1	0	1	0

[a]Of the sixty-three references, every reference to God as "Father" (forty-four) is by Jesus.
[b]Besides the Sermon on the Mount (Matthew 5 has 11 instances/822 words in chapter [1.338% ratio]; Matthew 6 has 8 instances/653 words in chapter [1.225% ratio]), two other chapters have significant concentrations of references to "heaven/heavens." Matthew 16 has 8 instances among the 526 words in the chapter (1.521% ratio), while Matthew 18 has 11 instances among the 668 words (1.647% ratio).

the combined phrasing "our Father who is in heaven" and its use within Matthew (obligation to perform God's will).

Relationship

The most noted theme connected with the Matthean invocation is relationality. In Jesus's prayer, he almost exclusively refers to God as "Father" (e.g., Mt. 11:25-26; Lk. 22:41-44; 23:34; Jn 11:41-42).[19] Craig Keener suggests that this relationship is one of both intimacy and acknowledgment of God as creator.[20] He states, "Effective prayer is not a complex ritual but a simply cry of faith predicated on an assured relationship (7:7-11)."[21] In Jesus's prayers, one can begin to sense this assurance and love. As God's son, Jesus's cries to the "Father" were undergirded with a sense that the Father was listening and cared. As Mt. 6:8 affirms, "Your Father knows what you need before you ask him." Commentators generally agree that by Jesus teaching his followers to call God "Father," he is inviting them to participate in the same relationship that he enjoys.[22] As

---

[19] The only exception is Mk. 15:34 in which Jesus is quoting Ps. 22:1.
[20] Keener, *Gospel of Matthew*, 216-8. To clarify, intimacy refers to "dependence," i.e., as a son would trust a father. Intimacy is not to be confused with the modern concepts of physicality and emotionally laden definitions akin to "baby talk." For a further description, see Mary Rose D'Angelo, "'Abba and 'Father': Imperial Theology and the Jesus Traditions," *JBL* 111.4 (1992): 612-3. Early definitions of this type of intimacy are rooted in Jeremias's identification of the invocation with ἀββά. Ἀββά was a term used by children to refer to older adults in an enduring and intimate way, as a child would speak to their "Papa." The work of James Barr, "Abba Isn't Daddy," *JTS* 39.1 (1988): 28-47, has helpfully clarified that referring to God as "father" does not denote baby talk but rather reverence. It could be argued that Matthew clarifies his intentions by adding the modifiers to his own invocation, particularly the phrase "who is in heaven." This added phrase will be discussed below.
[21] Keener, *Gospel of Matthew*, 216.
[22] See Davies and Allison, *Matthew 1-7*, 601; Keener, *Gospel of Matthew*, 216; Luz, *Matthew 1-7*, 314-6; Nolland, *Gospel of Matthew*, 501.

Leon Morris states, "We are so accustomed to referring to God as 'the Father' that we do not stop to reflect that this is a revolutionary way of thinking of 'the high and lofty One who inhabits eternity, whose name is Holy' (Isa. 57:15)."[23]

Covenantal

In instances where God is called "Father" in the Old Testament, the title was used in the context of God's covenant with Israel (Deut. 32:4-6; Isa. 63:16, 64:8; Jer. 31:9; 1 Chron. 29:10). Because Israel was God's chosen people, they would call him "Father."[24] This relationship with his people was exclusive in that God is never referred to as "Father" by someone outside of Israel. Jeremias concurs, "In the Old Testament, divine fatherhood is related to Israel alone in a quite unparalleled manner. Israel has a particular relationship to God. Israel is God's first-born, chosen out of all peoples."[25] Mary D'Angelo has noted two major functions of fatherhood that are important for this covenantal relationship with Israel: (1) God becomes the refuge of the afflicted and persecuted, especially when the source of danger is from unbelievers or outsiders (see Ps. 68:5-6, 89:20-29; 3 Macc. 6:3-4, 8; 7:6; 4Q372; Sir. 23:1; 51:10; Wis. 2:16-20); and (2) "Father" is usually used with petitions for forgiveness (Wis. 11:2; 1QH 9:30-35; Josephus Ant. 2.6.8).[26] This covenantal understanding of God's fatherhood parallels similar requests in the Lord's Prayer. "Fatherhood" in the invocation is combined with petitions for forgiveness (fifth petition) and rescue from evil (seventh petition). This parallelism suggests that Jesus is inviting his disciples to the covenantal relationship that Israel enjoyed with God as Father.

Communal

Building on the previous point, God established his covenant with a group of people. In those places in which God is referred to as "Father," these cries are not by individuals but rather by a group (Isa. 63:16; 64:8 ["our Father"]; 1 Chron. 29:10). First Chronicles 29:10 is an especially interesting parallel because it refers to God as "Father" in a

---

[23] Leon Morris, *The Gospel According to Matthew*, PNTC (Grand Rapids: Eerdmans, 1992), 106.
[24] See Alon Goshen-Gottstein, "God the Father in Rabbinic Judaism and Christianity: Transformed Background or Common Ground?," *JEC* 38.4 (2001): 475. Goshen-Gottstein shows that this theme is in continuity from the Old Testament to the Rabbinic literature. See also the covenant established by the "Father" of Israel, God, with the "Father" of Israel, Abraham (Genesis 12).
[25] Jeremias, *Prayers of Jesus*, 13.
[26] According to D'Angelo, there is a third function in that "father" evokes the power and providence that govern the world. See "*Abba* and 'Father,'" 621. D'Angelo's analysis agrees with Bruce Chilton's summary of the Pseudepigrapha and the Targumim, "God as 'Father' in the Targumim, in Non-Canonical Literatures of Early Judaism and Primitive Christianity, and in Matthew," in *The Pseudepigrapha and Early Biblical Interpretation*, ed. J .H. Charlesworth and C. A. Evans (Sheffield: JSOT, 1993), 166. He states, "Within early Judaism, God was known as 'Father' particularly (1) For the purposes of prayer, especially prayer in straits, (2) In reference to the vision or revelation that such a prayer might involve, (3) Because he responds to prayer, (4) In view of his power over the entire creation, and (5) In respect of the peculiar relationship between God and his people." The title "father" is also associated with God's role as creator (Deut. 32:6; Isa. 64:8; Mal. 2:10).

prayer.[27] In the LXX, the prayer begins, "O Lord God of Israel, our Father." Matthew appears to draw on this sense of community in his own invocation. Jesus is giving the prayer as means through which his disciples join to pray to the Father. Barth summarizes this communal theme:

> It ["our"] implies the communion of all humanity praying with Jesus Christ, our existence in the fellowship of the children of God . . . This "us" signifies also the communion of the one who prays with all those who are in his or her company and who are likewise invited to pray; with those who have received the same invitation, the same commandment, the same permission to pray beside Jesus Christ. We pray "Our Father" in the communion of this assembly, of this congregation which we call the church.[28]

Affirmation of God's Sovereignty

One of the distinctive elements of the Matthean invocation is the addition of "the one who is in heaven." As many commentators have noted, Matthew's addition of the "one who is in heaven" establishes God's transcendence and thus an affirmation of his sovereignty.[29] The Old Testament presents a wide variety of possibilities concerning the meaning and place of "heaven."[30] The two most common understandings of heaven are (1) an atmospheric place, commonly referring to the sky, and (2) the place where God and his angels dwell.[31] "Heaven" can also be combined with "earth" as a *merism* to refer to the entire creation (Gen. 1:1; 14:22; Lev. 26:19; 1 Chron. 16:31). The Old Testament is clear that worshipping the creation, or in this case the things that occupy the heavens (sun, moon, and stars) was strictly prohibited (Deut. 4:19; 2 Kgs 17:16; Jer. 44:17-23).

---

[27] The doxology frequently associated with the ending of the Matthean version of the Lord's Prayer is found in the broader context of 1 Chronicles 29 and Dan. 7:13-14. While the doxology is not part of the original text, the point still stands concerning the connections between the Matthean invocation and 1 Chronicles 29.

[28] Karl Barth, *Prayer* (Louisville: WJK, 2002), 43-4.

[29] "Sovereignty" is also implicitly found in "father." "Father" is frequently associated with kingship in Jewish literature. One finds this in the Talmudic prayers, particularly in a prayer dating to the second century attributed to Rabbi Akiba. The context for the prayer is a time in which Rabbi Akiba prays during an occasioned fast because of a continuing drought. During this time of distress, he connects the nomenclature of father and king when he prays, "Our Father, our King, we have no King but You. Our Father, our King, for Your sake have mercy upon us" (*b. Ta'an*. 25b). Translation by Jakob J. Petuchowski, "Jewish Prayer Texts of the Rabbinic Period," in *The Lord's Prayer and Jewish Liturgy*, ed. Jakob J. Peuchowski and Michael Brocke (New York: Seabury, 1978), 39. For an explanation of this juxtaposition of father and king, see Geza Vermes, *Jesus and the World of Judaism* (Minneapolis: Fortress, 2003), 30-43. A closely related prayer and perhaps an elaboration of Rabbi Akiba is the *Abhinu Malkenu*. This prayer precedes the morning recitations of the *Shema* and is a series of requests all beginning with "Our Father, our King." See Simon Lauer, "Abhinu Malkenu: Our Father, Our King!" in *Lord's Prayer and Jewish Liturgy*, 73-80.

[30] This will be discussed later regarding the third petition concerning God's will being done "on earth, as it is in heaven."

[31] Pennington, *Heaven and Earth*, 41-65. Pennington provides an excellent overview of heaven in the extant Jewish literature. In the case of definition 1, references to heaven can refer to the place of meteorological phenomenon, such as rain, thunder, wind, clouds, and so on (Gen. 8:2; Deut. 33:13; Josh. 10:11; Ps. 147:8). In the heavenly place (definition 2), God is often depicted as "sitting on His throne" (Ps. 11:4; 103:19) and the one who sees all things (Gen. 21:17; 28:12). These definitions are consistent with the parallels found at Qumran as well.

Heaven has a variety of nuances within its definitions and underwent changes in the ancient world.[32] This changing is especially true in the book of Daniel. In chs 2–7, Daniel uses heaven as a term to emphasize God's universal authority, as evidenced in the following phrases: "God of heaven" (2:18, 19, 37, 44), "God in heaven" (2:28), "Lord of heaven" (5:23), and "king of heaven" (4:34).[33] Whereas the preexilic uses of heaven referred to an actual place, the postexilic examples of "heaven" began to take on the role of describing God himself. Thus, "heaven" began to be used for the divine name and as an expression of sovereignty.[34] This trend continued into the Second Temple literature. First Maccabees is a primary example in that almost all its uses of "heaven" are references to God himself (3:18-19, 50; 4:10, 24, 40, 55; 5:31; 9:46; 12:15; 16:3).[35]

The affirmation of God's sovereignty provides a balance to the relational aspect of the invocation. Hagner summarizes nicely the dynamics of the invocation and petitions that follow, "The address provides the basis of the possibility of such a prayer: as Father, God is concerned for the needs of his children; as the One in heaven, he is all-powerful."[36]

Obligation to Perform God's Will

A final theme associated with the wording of the invocation is an obligation to perform God's will. Whereas the previous themes were connected to the individual words of the invocation, this theme is within the contexts in which the verbatim invocation is used. For evidence of this theme, we will consider the use of "our Father in heaven" within Matthew's Gospel. Since nearly every instance of the phrase is in Matthew, Matthew's theology is the shaping force for understanding how the title "our Father who is in heaven" is to be understood in the New Testament.

In Matthew's rhetoric, followers of the Father in heaven are differentiated by obediently following God's will. Consider Mt. 7:21: "Not everyone who says to me, 'Lord, Lord,' will enter the kingdom of heaven, but only the one who does the will of my Father in heaven." Doing the will of God is mentioned again in Mt. 12:50: "For whoever does the will of my Father in heaven is my brother and sister and mother". In this example, family allegiances are realigned. When someone does the will of God, they are considered part of God's family (see also Mt. 23:9) over and above biological relationships.[37]

---

[32] See Ulrich W. Mauser, "'Heaven' in the World View of the New Testament," *HBT* 9.2 (1987): 31–51.
[33] See Pennington, *Heaven and Earth*, 47. Pennington helpfully points out these occurrences.
[34] Jonathan Lunde, "Heaven and Hell," in *DJG*, ed. Joel B. Green, Scot McKnight, and I. Howard Marshall (Downers Grove: IVP, 1992), 307. See Gustaf Dalman, *The Words of Jesus*, trans. D. M. Kay (Edinburgh: T&T Clark, 1902), 184–94.
[35] Pennington, *Heaven and Earth*, 51, fn.44, notes, "First Maccabees is almost completely lacking in its use of the traditional biblical categories of heaven, such as in meteorological references and the heaven and earth pair indicating the entire world. Instead, nearly every instance of heaven metonymically refers to God in some way, such as the 'crying out to heaven' and 'lifting voices to heaven' phrases." When surveying the Rabbinic material, instances of "heaven" continued to be used as circumlocutions (*b. 'Abod. Zar.* 18a; *b. Sanh.* 15b; 17a). It also bears noting that the title "Father in heaven" became prevalent during this time (*m. Kil.* 9:8; *m. Yoma.* 8:9; *m. Sotah* 9:15; and *m. 'Abot* 5:20).
[36] Hagner, *Matthew 1–13*, 148.
[37] A similar distinction is made in the story concerning Honi the Circle-Drawer and his grandson Hanin. When approached by the people to provide rain, Honi draws a circle in the sand and vows

Evidence of an obligation to God's will also include confessing Jesus before others and sharing forgiveness. Matthew 10:32-33 serves as evidence: "Everyone therefore who acknowledges me before others, I also will acknowledge before my Father in heaven; but whoever denies me before others, I also will deny before my Father in heaven."[38] Confessing Jesus Christ is motivated by the Father's great care for his children (see Mt. 10:31).[39] Additionally, those performing God's will forgive others. Matthew 18:35 states, "So my heavenly Father will also do to every one of you [torture], if you do not forgive your brother or sister from your heart." In this passage, forgiveness is that which differentiates those who follow the Father and those who do not.[40]

Conclusion

From our analysis, we conclude that the wording of the invocation is associated with relationality, covenant, community, and God's sovereignty, and entails an obligation to do His will. Addressing God as "our Father" emphasizes intimacy, covenant, and community. Addressing God as the one "who is in heaven" emphasizes his sovereignty. Read together, "our Father who is in heaven" expresses a desire to do his will. God's will in these instances requires the prioritizing of spiritual kinship over biological ties and the mandate to forgive others.

"Our Father in Heaven" in the Sermon on the Mount

In the previous section, we argued that the invocation is associated with relationality, covenant, community, God's sovereignty, and an obligation to perform His will. We will argue that in those passages in the Sermon on the Mount that feature lexical parallels with the invocation, similar themes can be found. The passages include the following: Mt. 5:16, 45, 48; 6:1, 4, 6 (2x), 8, 14, 15, 18 (2x), 26, 32; 7:11, 21. Also of note are Mt. 5:9 and 5:21-26. In these latter passages, explicit references to the "father"

---

to stay inside the circle and pray until the rain comes (*m. Ta'an.* 3:8). The same story is told of Hanin years later. The story goes,

> Hanin ha-Nehba was the son of the daughter of Onias the Circle-maker. When the world needed rain, our teachers used to send school-children to him, who seized the hem of his coat and said to him, "Daddy, daddy (אבא אבא) give us rain!" He said to Him (God): "Master of the world, grant it (the rain) for the sake of these who are not yet able to distinguish between a father who has the power to give rain and a father who has not."

Hanin distinguishes between himself as "father" and the heavenly "Father" (*b. Ta'an.* 23b). As a guide on earth, the Rabbi realized his own limitations to act as a father and instead points to the true source of rain and deliverance—the Father in the heavens. Cited in Jeremias, *Prayers*, 61. See also Geza Vermes, *Jesus the Jew* (Philadelphia: Fortress, 1981), 211, and *Jesus and the World of Judaism*, 42, and James H. Charlesworth, "A Caveat on Textual Transmission and the Meaning of *Abba*: A Study of the Lord's Prayer," in *The Lord's Prayer and Other Prayer Texts from the Greco-Roman Era*, ed. James H. Charlesworth, Mark Harding, and Mark Kiley (Valley Forge: Trinity International, 1994), 8-9.

[38] Also Mt. 15:13.
[39] See Gundry, *Matthew*, 198.
[40] This correlation is found also in Mt. 18:19 in the passages on binding and loosing. Here, the "Father in heaven" relates to those who pray in groups of two or three. Interestingly, this passage precedes Peter's discussion of forgiveness (i.e., 70 times 7). See Chapter 5 on the forgiveness petition.

are missing, but the passages use familial language and share similar themes with the invocation.

We will examine the passages according to strength of parallels. These textual connections will be determined by their (1) functional, (2) lexical, and (3) thematic parallels. First, this section will examine the invocation's wording in contexts of prayer (Mt. 6:6, 8, 14-15; 7:11) or in cases where prayer is mentioned (Mt. 5:45; 6:26, 32). In these cases, the Sermon references parallel the invocation in terms of function, wording, and themes. Second, this section will examine those passages that connect calling on the Father with good works (Mt. 5:16, 48; 7:21). In Mt. 5:16 and 7:21, the references to the Father are verbatim with the invocation and have similar themes. Matthew 5:48 shares these themes but with an inverted reference ("heavenly Father"). Third, this section will examine those passages that use the invocation's wording in discussions of righteousness (Mt. 6:1, 4, 18 [2x]). These references are found in Matthew's central section, 6:1-18, which we have argued centers around the Lord's Prayer.[41] Matthew has united this section around the theme of righteousness. Fourth, this chapter will examine those passages that use familial language but without explicit mention of the father (Mt. 5:9, 21-26). In these cases, calling on the "father" is more implied but still reasonably demonstrable. Before discussing the specific parallels, we must address the ways that "father" is used throughout the Sermon on the Mount. "Father" is mentioned in four slightly different ways. We will argue that despite their differences in wording, they carry the same meaning and themes.

Is the "Father in Heaven" the "Father in Secret"?

Before examining the textual connections between the invocation and the Sermon on the Mount, it is important to discuss the ways in which "father" appears in the Sermon. References to the "father" can be arranged into four categories: those with (1) the verbatim wording of the invocation, (2) an inverted wording (ὁ πατὴρ ὑμῶν ὁ οὐράνιος) translated as "our heavenly Father," (3) a shortened reference (ὁ πατὴρ ὑμῶν), and (4) the "Father in secret" (ὁ πατήρ σου ὁ βλέπων ἐν τῷ κρυπτῷ/τῷ πατρί σου τῷ ἐν τῷ κρυπτῷ). The inverted wording ("heavenly Father") and shortened references ("our Father") are simpler to explain. Matthew switches between "heavenly Father" and "Father who is in heaven" when varying his part of speech. The "heavenly Father" is always used as a grammatical subject. "Father who is in heaven" is used as the object of a verb or prepositional phrase and in genitive descriptions.[42] Other than variation in parts of speech, the wording appears to have the same meaning. References to "our Father" are mentioned throughout the Sermon but in contexts where fuller references (i.e., "heavenly Father/Father who is in heaven") are nearby. For example, Mt. 6:15 uses the shortened reference ("your Father"), but in v. 14, the fuller reference ("your heavenly Father") has already been used.

---

[41] See Chapter 3 on structure.
[42] The invocation in Mt. 6:9 is a notable exception to this rule in which the longer reference is used in the vocative case. Exceptions also include Mt. 7:11 and 16:17 in which ὁ πατὴρ ὑμῶν ὁ ἐν τοῖς οὐρανοῖς is the grammatical subject.

Questions arise when one surveys the use of "father" in Matthew's central section of the Sermon on the Mount (Mt. 6:1-18). Specifically, Matthew mentions the "Father who is in secret" and the "Father who sees in secret." At first glance, these references appear to invalidate any type of parallel with the invocation. The only shared word is "father" and the Lord's Prayer begins with communal invocation (i.e., "our"), creating tension with the instruction in ch. 6 to pray "in secret" (Mt. 6:5-6).[43] It is in this "secret" place where the Father is and sees.

A closer examination of the texts in question reveals that this inconsistency is more perceived than actual. In Mt. 6:1-18, the references to the three Jewish practices of piety are partly instruction and partly condemnation. In addition to a critique of the hypocritical actions of the Pharisees, Jesus is commanding his disciples to be careful how they give alms (6:2-4), pray (6:5-15), and fast (6:16-18). Because this group is identified as flaunting their works of "righteousness," Jesus changes the medium of good works. To avoid association with "public" righteousness, Jesus encourages his disciples to ensure that their righteousness is different. "Secret" righteousness is performed away from onlookers, but it is guaranteed to be met by the "Father who sees (perhaps, "*comes to you*") in secret" (ὁ πατήρ σου ὁ βλέπων ἐν τῷ κρυπτῷ). The hypocrites who perform their righteousness publically get the attention they want from the crowds, but they are ignored by the Father. A similar explanation is found in 1 Sam. 16:7, referring to how God sees things ("for the Lord does not see as mortals see; they look on the outward appearance, but the Lord looks on the heart").[44] Matthew 6:1-18 is not condemning public acts of almsgiving, prayer, and fasting but rather encouraging disciples to avoid hypocritical displays of righteousness. The "Father who is in heaven" and the "Father who is/sees in secret" therefore have similar meanings, but they are worded to accentuate the sovereignty of God and the places where the Father meets his children.[45]

In conclusion, Matthew uses four differing ways of referring to the "father." Throughout the Sermon on the Mount, the "Father in heaven" is also referred to as the "heavenly Father," "our Father," and "the Father who is in secret." Changes in form indicate contextual and grammatical concerns, not changes in meaning.

Father and Prayer

The strongest textual connections between the invocation and the Sermon on the Mount are signaled by shared references to prayer or contexts discussing prayer, along

---

[43] The inference for public prayer is made from the instruction to pray communally. The tension arises from Jesus's instruction in ch. 6 to do all things in private.

[44] Pennington, *Heaven and Earth*, 237, notes, "The Father God is in secret/hidden (even as his kingdom is) and at the same time, he sees and rewards the righteousness that his children do in secret." Similarly, Betz, *Sermon on the Mount*, 339, argues that these ideas come from the older idea of God as an all-seeing God and that he is hidden/not able to be seen. Steven E. Runge, *Discourse Grammar of the Greek New Testament: A Practical Introduction for Teaching and Exegesis* (Peabody: Hendrickson, 2010), 323-4, notes that "who is in secret" is a discourse feature that "influences how you think about the Father, based on the particular quality mentioned." These elements appear when the writer wishes the reader to envision a particular quality based on the context.

[45] Pennington, *Heaven and Earth*, 237, agrees, "By its nature that which is in heaven is hidden, unless of course it is divinely revealed (see Mt. 3:16-17). The Father in heaven, then, is virtually synonymous with the Father ἐν τῷ κρυφαίῳ."

with lexical and thematic parallels. Matthew has nine references to the "father" in which prayer is discussed or referenced. The references are as follows: Mt. 5:45; 6:6 (2x), 8, 14, 15, 26, 32; 7:11. In this section, we will categorize these parallels in terms of their contexts of prayer as well as showing the lexical and thematic parallels.

Contexts Associated with Prayer

Prayer is often mentioned in the Sermon on the Mount (Mt. 5:45; 6:5-15, 26, 32; 7:7-11). Whether specifically addressing the topic of prayer or simply mentioning it in instruction to pray, Matthew consistently refers to the heavenly Father.[46] References to the "father" are not functioning as invocations in each of these instances but are always near when the subject of prayer is addressed. Besides the invocation, five of Matthew's nine instances are found in his extended section on prayer in Mt. 6:5-15. This grouping of texts on prayer (Mt. 6:7-15) is headed by Matthew's introduction to the subject in 6:5-6. Here, Matthew warns against hypocritical prayers meant to draw attention to the petitioner and not to the "Father." Matthew 6:7-8 warns against using meaningless phrases in our prayers, while 6:14-15 expounds on the forgiveness petition.[47]

Outside of the central section (Mt. 6:1-18), Matthew first mentions the "father" and prayer in Mt. 5:45. In this context, Jesus is addressing how to love your neighbor. Jesus commands that one not only love their neighbor but also love their enemies and pray for them (see Mt. 5:11-12). Love of enemy and prayers on their behalf is evidence of sonship to the Father who is in heaven.

The next reference appears after Matthew's central section (Mt. 6:1-18). Jesus's teaching on anxiety (Mt. 6:25-32) includes a twofold reference. The first appears in Jesus's analogy concerning his care for small things and his disciples. He explains that the "heavenly Father" feeds the birds (Mt. 6:26) and likewise will take care of his followers. The parallel is strengthened when one considers the petition for bread within the Lord's Prayer. It is precisely this answer to prayer that gives the petitioner comfort that God will provide our most basic needs.[48] The second reference is found in the climax of the passage. Jesus contrasts the Gentiles, who constantly wonder what they will eat and drink and wear, with the assurance that the "heavenly Father" will provide all our needs (Mt. 6:32). Jesus finishes this teaching with the command to "strive" first for his kingdom and righteousness (Mt. 6:33). The word "strive" is similar to how one should pray (see Mt. 7:7-11; Lk. 11:1-13).[49] The parallel is strengthened when one considers the second petition. The invocation heads a prayer that "strives" after the very things that Jesus is encouraging in Mt. 6:33 (i.e., the kingdom, righteousness// second and third petitions).

---

[46] By contrast, Luke only mentions prayer and the "father" in four instances compared to Matthew's nine examples.

[47] We agree with Luz when he argues that Mt. 6:14-15 are "prayer words" because of their structural relationship to the Lord's Prayer. See Chapter 3 on structure.

[48] We will argue this more extensively in the next chapter, which addresses the parallels between the bread petition and Mt. 6:25-34.

[49] See France, *Gospel of Matthew*, 270–1, fn.23.

The last reference to "father" and prayer is in Mt. 7:11. In this passage, Jesus is encouraging his disciples to be persistent by asking, seeking, and knocking. He ends the teaching with the assurance that the "Father" will give good things to those who continue to pray fervently.

Wording

Among the references to prayer and "father," Mt. 5:45 and 7:11 are in verbatim agreement with the invocation. Matthew 6:14, 26, and 32 have "your heavenly Father," while Mt. 6:8 and 6:15 refer to "our Father." Matthew 6:6 (2x) is the only reference to the (a) "Father in secret"/(b) "who sees in secret." The intentionality of the wording becomes more obvious when compared to the Lukan parallels (Table 4.2).

References to "father" are found in Mt. 6:6 (2x), 8, 14, and 15, with which Luke does not have a parallel. Matthew 5:45 parallels Lk. 6:35, but Luke does not mention the "Father." Luke refers to being "sons of the Most High" (υἱοὶ ὑψίστου). Whereas Mt. 6:26 refers to "your heavenly Father," Luke simply appeals to God (ὁ θεὸς) as the source of basic needs. The closest parallels between Matthew and Luke are found in Mt. 6:32//Lk. 12:32 and Mt. 7:11//Lk. 11:13. In the first instance, Mt. 6:32 refers to "your heavenly Father," while Luke refers to "your Father" (Lk. 12:32). The addition of heaven is consistent with Matthew's other references.

In the second instance, commentators will often point to Lk. 11:13, describing the "Father" as "out of/from heaven" (ὁ ἐξ οὐρανοῦ), as the closest parallel to the Matthean references.[50] The phrase is translated as the "heavenly Father," giving the impression that Matthew and Luke agree.[51] Upon closer inspection, the context, Luke's instances elsewhere, and textual variants argue against v. 13 as a close parallel to the invocation. In ch. 11, Luke is describing the reward of persistent prayer (Lk. 11:9-13/Mt. 7:7-11). He concludes by promising that the "Father out of/from heaven" will give the Holy Spirit to those who ask. In the Matthean parallel, the gift resulting from persistent prayer is simply something that is good (Mt. 7:11). Matthew's reference appears to generalize the gift to (1) emphasize the action of asking, and (2) the "Father" who gives instead of the gift itself. Luke's reference draws the reader's attention to the gift by naming the Holy Spirit as its object.

References to the Holy Spirit are common throughout Luke's Gospel as the Spirit is a key theme in Luke's narrative. The mention of the Spirit after the one "out of/from heaven" is important though. Elsewhere in his writing, Luke portrays the Spirit as the one "out of/from heaven." These parallels are found in Lk. 1:35, 3:22, and Acts 4:23-31. Although these parallels offer a possibility of the modifier referring to the Spirit, the inclusion of the article in the Greek mandates that the modifier ([ὁ] ἐξ οὐρανοῦ) describe the "Father" as the one of heaven (ὁ πατὴρ [ὁ] ἐξ οὐρανοῦ δώσει πνεῦμα ἅγιον). Yet, the editors of the NA[28] appear to be split on the inclusion of the article, as indicated by the brackets.[52] The textual tradition is split among the oldest manuscripts. In cases

---

[50] Among others, Guelich, *Sermon on the Mount*, 286–7.
[51] See the ESV, NASB, and NRSV to name just a few.
[52] The textual evidence for the inclusion of the article includes A B D W Θ ƒ¹ 𝔐 sy^h. On the other hand, the evidence for the exclusion of the article is *2 3* 𝔓^75 ℵ L Ψ 33. 892. 2542 *pc* sa bo^pt.

Table 4.2 "Father" Parallels in the Sermon on the Mount/Plain

	Matthean wording	Lukan parallel	Lukan wording
Invocation			
6:9	Πάτερ ἡμῶν ὁ ἐν τοῖς οὐρανοῖς	11:2	Πάτερ
Father and Prayer			
5:45	τοῦ πατρὸς ὑμῶν τοῦ ἐν οὐρανοῖς	6:35	υἱοὶ ὑψίστου
6:6a	τῷ πατρί σου τῷ ἐν τῷ κρυπτῷ	No parallel	
6:6b	ὁ πατήρ σου ὁ βλέπων ἐν τῷ κρυπτῷ	No parallel	
6:8	ὁ πατὴρ ὑμῶν	No parallel	
6:14	ὁ πατὴρ ὑμῶν ὁ οὐράνιος	No parallel	
6:15	ὁ πατὴρ ὑμῶν	No parallel	
6:26	ὁ πατὴρ ὑμῶν ὁ οὐράνιος	Lk. 12:24	ὁ θεὸς
6:32	ὁ πατὴρ ὑμῶν ὁ οὐράνιος	Lk. 12:32	ὁ πατὴρ ὑμῶν
7:11	ὁ πατὴρ ὑμῶν ὁ ἐν τοῖς οὐρανοῖς	Lk. 11:13	ὁ πατὴρ ἐξ οὐρανου
Father and "Good Works"			
5:16	τὸν πατέρα ὑμῶν τὸν ἐν τοῖς οὐρανοῖς	No parallel	
5:48	ὁ πατὴρ ὑμῶν ὁ οὐράνιος	Lk. 6:36	ὁ πατὴρ ὑμῶν
7:21	τοῦ πατρός μου τοῦ ἐν τοῖς οὐρανοῖς	No parallel	
Father and "Righteousness"			
6:1	τῷ πατρὶ ὑμῶν τῷ ἐν τοῖς οὐρανοῖς	No parallel	
6:4	ὁ πατήρ σου ὁ βλέπων ἐν τῷ κρυπτῷ	No parallel	
6:18a	τῷ πατρί σου τῷ ἐν τῷ κρυφαίῳ	No parallel	
6:18b	ὁ πατήρ σου ὁ βλέπων ἐν τῷ κρυφαίῳ	No parallel	
Familial Language			
5:9	υἱοὶ θεοῦ	No parallel	
5:21-26	ὁ ἀδελφός σου	No parallel (includes teaching on judgment)	

where the external evidence is split, the internal evidence becomes determinative. In conjunction with our earlier observations regarding Luke's emphases on the Spirit and other references where the Spirit proceeds from heaven, we are inclined to exclude the article. Therefore, Lk. 11:13 is not a parallel to Matthew's distinctive invocation. In Luke, the "Father" gives the Spirit, who descends "out of/from heaven."[53]

Themes

To review, the wording of the invocation is associated with the themes of relationality, covenant, community, God's sovereignty, and an obligation to perform God's will. In

---

[53] John Nolland, *Luke 9:21–18:34*, WBC (Dallas: Word, 1993), 631, agrees, "On the basis of Acts 2:33 it seems best to speak here of the Holy Spirit given from heaven."

those places in the Sermon where the "father" is mentioned, these themes are similarly represented. In this section, we will show that each of the Sermon passages has one or more themes, creating thematic parallels with the invocation. We will discuss the verses in the order of their appearance in the Sermon on the Mount.

In Mt. 5:45, Jesus provides an example from nature to illustrate God's sovereignty over both the spiritual realm and the natural realm. Matthew 5:45b states, "For he makes his sun rise on the evil and on the good, and sends rain on the righteous and on the unrighteous." This display of sovereignty evidences God's love for all creation and establishes the example for his children to follow. As Allison argues, "For if both the natural realm, on the one hand, and the moral spiritual, on the other, have God as their author and sustainer, there must be genuine affinity between the two."[54] Just as the Father who is sovereign over all creation lavishes grace, so must his sons.[55]

In the case of Mt. 6:6 (2x), the theme of covenant appears. This theme is most apparent in the language of secrecy and merit. Part of God's covenant with his people is his promise to commune and provide for them. In Mt. 6:6, Jesus assures those who pray that God will meet with them "in secret." Also, this teaching guarantees that the "Father" will "repay" them. As Guelich notes, "One's reward includes God's blessing at the future judgment in contrast to the recognition received already by the hypocrites (6:5b)."[56] This future judgment to which Guelich refers is part of God's covenant to end what he has started.[57]

Matthew 6:8 uses the "father" language as a means of affirming God's sovereignty. Jesus states, "Your Father knows what you need before you ask him." This truth is grounded in God's power over all creation. Matthew 6:26, 32 similarly represents this theme. Jesus's teaching to avoid anxiety is followed by the promise that the "heavenly Father" will provide not only for the small animals of the earth (Mt. 6:26) but also for his disciples whom he calls children (Mt. 6:32).

Matthew 6:14-15 is an exposition on the forgiveness petition. Its primary theme is one of covenant and obligation to do God's will. In terms of covenant, Jesus discusses the dynamic between interpersonal forgiveness and divine forgiveness.[58] As God continually forgives, so his disciples will forgive others. Thus, interpersonal forgiveness becomes the norm for children of the "Father." This understanding of forgiveness is also an obligation to God's will. As Mt. 18:23-35 explains, forgiveness is an act that is not only initiated by the "Father" but is also demanded by the "Father." Those who are his children must forgive others as an expression of their commitment to God's will. As Mt. 6:15 warns, "If you do not forgive others, neither will *your Father* forgive your trespasses."

---

[54] Allison, *Sermon on the Mount*, 101.
[55] Verse 45 begins with the status of those who love their enemies and pray for them. Those who perform these actions are considered "sons" of the Father in heaven. Within this enjoined relationship, sons of the Father can enjoy the relationship and comfort of knowing that the Father is ultimately in control of our circumstances.
[56] Guelich, *Sermon on the Mount*, 282.
[57] See Pennington, *Sermon and Human Flourishing*, 102–3.
[58] See Chapter 5 for more discussion on the interrelationship between interpersonal and divine forgiveness.

Matthew 7:11 evidences God's love for his children and sovereign promises. His relationship with those who call on his name is characterized by intimacy. In the broader context (Mt. 7:7-11), Jesus is discussing the results of persistent prayer. After a series of rhetorical questions, Jesus guarantees the Father's answer to those who continually seek after him. These rhetorical questions discuss what a father might give his child if he asks for food. The answer to the question is embedded in a promise. The "Father who is in heaven" will "give good things to those who ask him!" This guarantee is an extension of his sovereign fatherhood.

We have argued in this section that many of Matthew's references to the "father" parallel the invocation in terms of contexts of prayer, wording, and themes. References to the "father" are repeatedly paired with the topic of prayer throughout the Sermon. These textual connections are deepened by the shared themes of relationship, covenant, affirmation of God's sovereignty, and obligation to God's will.

Father and Good Works

In this second set of parallels, we will argue that Matthew has enjoined the invocation to Sermon references emphasizing the importance of good works. The topic of good works is addressed in the Lord's Prayer in the third petition. The petitioner requests that God's will be done "on earth as it is in heaven." God's will is accomplished on earth through the work of his disciples.[59] The Sermon references include Mt. 5:16, 48, and 7:21.[60] These verses and the teaching of which they are a part allude to the invocation with lexical and thematic parallels.

Wording

The Sermon references combining "good works" and the father (Mt. 5:16 and 7:21) have the verbatim wording found in the invocation except in Mt. 5:48 ("Be perfect, therefore, as your heavenly Father is perfect"). In Mt. 5:48, Jesus refers to God as "your heavenly Father."[61] The "heavenly Father" is being used as the grammatical subject. These tightly worded instances in the Sermon reveal lexical parallels with the invocation. These references are not paralleled in the Lukan Sermon, except for

---

[59] The "will of God" will be addressed in more detail in the following section. For the present argument, this shortened explanation will suffice to establish the necessary parallel between the topic of good works found in the Sermon and the Lord's Prayer, of which the invocation is a part.

[60] Mowery, "Lord to Father," 652-3, argues that Mt. 5:16 is structurally positioned to introduce the references to the "father" that appear throughout the rest of the Sermon. He states,

> Since this reference to the Father in 5:16 appears to be redactional, its location cannot be blamed on the influence of sources. The structure of the Sermon on the Mount may provide an important clue regarding its location. Many commentators assume that Matt. 5:16 directly precedes the Sermon's central, which they identify as Matt. 5:17–7:12. Building on this assumption, one can argue that Matthew referred to the Father in 5:16, immediately before the central section, in anticipation of the many references to the Father which would appear in that section.

[61] As argued above, the inverted reference of "heavenly Father" is used when Matthew switches parts of speech.

5:48.[62] Verse 48 reads similarly to Lk. 6:36 ("Be merciful, just as your Father is merciful"). The Lukan reference contains (1) the shortened reference to the Father (ὁ πατὴρ ὑμῶν), (2) Jesus's instruction to the disciples to be merciful, and (3) omits the reference to "heaven."[63] On the other hand, Matthew's inclusion of heaven and command to be perfect in Mt. 5:48 strengthens his lexical and thematic parallels with the invocation.

Themes

In addition to the references to good works, the invocation and Sermon references share the themes of covenant, community, and obligation to God's will. In Mt. 5:48, Jesus commands that his disciples strive for perfection. As Hagner notes, "For Matthew, to be τέλειος means to fulfil the law through the manifestation of an unrestricted love (including even enemies) that is the reflection of God's love. This unrestricted love pre-eminently embodies ethical perfection. This perfection, and nothing less, is that to which Jesus calls his disciples."[64] This command to be perfect is grounded in the perfection of the heavenly Father, a perfection that cannot be wholly achieved until the Father has his work fulfilled in his children.[65] Thus, the ongoing work of the Father among his children is part of his covenant as they follow God's laws (see Mt. 5:21-48).

Matthew 5:16 and 5:48 emphasize the role of the community. The teaching in 5:16 is given to a group of people, as they are instructed to be both salt and light, and work together to perform good works to evidence the Father. As Quarles notes, "The heavenly Father is glorified for the good works of Jesus' followers because He gave them spiritual birth and made them heirs of His character and partakers of the divine nature."[66] As they work together, they manifest the love of the Father. Similarly, Mt. 5:48 instructs this group to be "perfect." Their unity to carry out God's laws provide testimony to the Father's ongoing work. We have argued in Chapter 3 that these verses function as an introduction (Mt. 5:13-16/17-20) and conclusion (Mt. 5:48) to Jesus's teaching on the Mosaic law. This structural clue leads to our third thematic parallel.

Perhaps most obvious is the use of the wording of the invocation and the obligation to God's will. "Being a light" and "being perfect" entail good works through keeping God's commandments. In each of these passages, the emphasis is on right living. In those places in Matthew in which the "father" is mentioned, the will of God is often mentioned (see also Mt. 12:50, 18:14, and 26:42).[67] Similarly, these passages have carefully worded references to the "father" that are enjoined to "good works."

Father and Righteousness

In the previous section, we noted the connection of father and good works. In Matthew, righteousness is frequently related to ethical living and thematically related to "good

---

[62] See Table 4.2.
[63] Luke only refers to the "father" in this manner in one other place (12:32).
[64] Hagner, *Matthew 1-13*, 135.
[65] God's perfection in Mt. 5:48 echoes the reference to sovereignty in Mt. 5:45. In other words, not only is God perfect, but also he controls the heavens and everything beneath.
[66] Quarles, *Sermon on the Mount*, 88.
[67] We will discuss this at greater length below.

works." Because these references to "righteousness" are found in Matthew's central section (Mt. 6:1-18), we will discuss their parallels separately. It is within this section that ten of the seventeen references to the "father" in the Sermon can be found. We have already discussed Mt. 6:6 (2x), 8, 14-15 because of their connection of the "father" and prayer. We will briefly examine the remaining references of Mt. 6:1, 4, 18 (2x).

Matthew 6:1, 4, 18 (2x) are found in a highly structured section of the Sermon on the Mount. As we have argued in Chapter 3, the passage begins with the *kelal* statement in Mt. 6:1 ("Beware of practising your piety [δικαιοσύνην] before others to be seen by them; for then you have no reward from your Father in heaven"). Jesus follows with three examples of the "proper practice" of piety/righteousness (δικαιοσύνην). The examples cover the areas of almsgiving (vv. 2-4), prayer (vv. 5-15), and fasting (vv. 16-18). Each of the examples are structured similarly with only a slight variation in the prayer section (i.e., the inclusion of the Lord's Prayer and its surrounding material [vv. 7-8, 14-15]). Each section begins with a condemnation of public righteousness for publicity (Mt. 6:2, 5, 16). These condemnations are followed by Jesus's promise that they have received all that they are seeking—public attention ("Truly, I tell you, they have received their reward"). Those who seek the approval of men by public "righteousness" are called "hypocrites" (οἱ ὑποκριταί) because of their inward wickedness. Jesus continues in each of these examples with his teaching on the proper "display" of righteousness. In contrast to the public displays that Jesus criticizes, proper almsgiving, praying, and fasting are best done "in secret." The three sections end with summative statements making it clear whom disciples should seek as their audience. The "Father who is in secret" (vv. 4, 6, 18 [2x]) will reward those who practice righteousness "in secret." As Guelich notes, the phrasing functions as conclusions for each unit.[68]

These remaining references parallel the invocation in three ways. First, they maintain the consistent and prominent use of "Father" language within Mt. 6:1-18.[69] Second, the *kelal* (Mt. 6:1) indicates the theme of righteousness as shared among the three teachings that follow (Mt. 6:2-18). Third, each of these references and the invocation share the theme of relationship and covenant. These verses not only refer to the "Father" (i.e., relationship), but Mt. 6:4, 6, 18 (2x), like Mt. 18:20, also indicates that God sees and is present everywhere (i.e., "in the secret"). He seeks them out in their private places and communes with them. Additionally, he rewards them for their righteous behavior. This reference to reward is a mark of God's covenant to bless those who are obedient.

Family of God

In addition to the allusions between the invocation and other references to the "father" in the Sermon on the Mount, Matthew has two additional references within chs 5–7 that echo the invocation. In these passages, the "father" is never explicitly mentioned, but rather familial language is used (Mt. 5:9, 21-26). These echoes also share parallel

---

[68] Guelich, *Sermon on the Mount*, 280.
[69] See the earlier discussion of the wording of the invocation and the "Father who is in secret."

themes with the wording of the invocation. First, Mt. 5:9 states, "Blessed are the peacemakers, for they will be called children of God." For the good work of striving for peace, Jesus's disciples are called "children/sons" (υἱοὶ θεοῦ). In this passage, the emphasis is on an obligation to do God's will and enjoying relationship with God. Second, Jesus uses familial language in his teaching on anger (Mt. 5:21-26). After discussing the connection between anger and murder, Jesus offers several examples of how to avoid these offenses (Mt. 5:23-25). Jesus encourages his disciples to seek reconciliation with their "brothers and sisters" amid animosity. These familial terms indicate that they are operating within the same family, a family under the authority of God the "Father." As with Mt. 5:9, the instruction concerning reconciliation is an obligation to God's will of peace.

Invocation Conclusion

In the preceding sections, we have attempted to illustrate N. T. Wright's suggestion that the Sermon is an exercise in calling God "Father." In doing this, we go further than Wright's approach of simply listing instances of fatherhood and, instead, have begun to argue that the Lord's Prayer is the interpretive center of the Sermon on the Mount. We have examined the instances of "Father" throughout the Sermon on the Mount and showed their shared contexts of prayer, similar wording, and thematic coherence to the Lord's Prayer. We have attempted to show that the Lord's Prayer and the Sermon on the Mount should be read in light of one another. When read in this manner, calling on "our Father in heaven" entails a commitment to Sermon living, for example, to prayer (Mt. 5:45; 6:6 [2x], 8, 14, 15, 26, 32; 7:11), good works and righteousness (Mt. 5:16, 48; 6:1, 4, 18 [2x]; 7:21), and being part of the family of God (Mt. 5:9, 21-26).

Third Petition: "Your Will Be Done, on Earth as in Heaven"

Concerning the *macarisms* and the disciples who heard, Graham Stanton once noted, "In Matthew . . . God's blessing is promised to a rather different group: to those who 'hunger and thirst *after righteousness*' (5:6), that is, to disciples who are 'hungry' to do God's will."[70] Stanton's observations are important for two reasons. First, he notes the relationship of various parts of the Sermon to one another. The will of God is mentioned explicitly in Mt. 6:10 and 7:21. Stanton connects the doing of God's will to the *macarism* found in Mt. 5:6 ("blessed are those who hunger and thirst for righteousness, for they will be filled"). Perhaps more importantly is the second element of Stanton's comment. He reasons that "righteousness" is the accomplishing of God's will in the life of a disciple. Stanton's helpful observations stretch beyond their intended purposes, presenting interesting insights into the Matthean Lord's Prayer. Stanton's remarks are particularly interesting for how we understand the third petition and its relationship

---

[70] Stanton, *Gospel for a New People*, 299. Emphasis his.

to its context, the Sermon on the Mount. In this petition, the pray-er requests that God's will be done but in conjunction with the states of heaven and earth. Unlike the invocation and evil petition, the first half of the will petition ("your will be done") lacks the numerous lexical parallels. Yet, the will of God is featured prominently throughout the Sermon on the Mount in Matthew's emphasis on righteousness. Heaven and earth are the spheres in which God completes his will and evidence Matthew's emphasis on the contrast between the nature of God's will and the nature of man's will. In the following section, we will analyze the will petition, as defined by its distinctive wording and themes, before noting its parallels with the Sermon on the Mount.

The Distinctives of "Your Will Be Done, on Earth as in Heaven"

This section has a twofold purpose. First, we will examine the specific wording of the will petition, noting its distinctive characteristics and relationship to the "Father."[71] Throughout Matthew's Gospel, the "will" is often connected to the Father, as is the case of the Lord's Prayer. Second, we will examine the distribution of the will petition's wording within Matthew's Gospel. A survey of Matthew's uses of "your will be done" and "on earth as in heaven" indicates a concentration of the terms in chs 5–7.

Wording

In this section, we will examine the third petition according to its parts. We will start with the main petition clause ("your will be done") and its relationship to the "Father" before examining the correlative clause ("on earth as in heaven").

Γενηθήτω τὸ θέλημά σου/"Your Will Be Done" and the "Father"

An examination of references to the will of God reveals a liking for the phrase in Matthew's Gospel, especially as it relates to the "Father." Mark and Luke both have only one reference to the "will" in relation to the "Father." Both references are found in the Gethsemane narrative.[72] Beside the instances in the Sermon on the Mount, Matthew has four references to the "will" (Mt. 12:50; 18:14; 21:31; 26:42), wherein each refers to the "Father." In Mt. 12:50, Jesus is questioned about the identity of his true family. He answers that those who do the will of the Father are his relatives. The pledge of obedience closely resembles the wording of the invocation as the Father is the one "who is in heaven." In Mt. 18:14, Jesus again connects the will with the "Father who

---

[71] The petition is found in *Did.* 8:2.
[72] Besides Gethsemane, the only instance of θέλημα in Mark is found in the narrative concerning discipleship (Mk. 3:35). Jesus teaches that those who are his brothers and sisters must do the "will of God." In the Gethsemane narrative, the noun form is changed to a verb (Mk. 14:36).
 There are four instances of the noun form θέλημά in Luke's Gospel (12:47 [2x], 22:42, and 23:25). Two of the instances are found in Lk. 12:47. The references are to the actions of a slave in performing the will of his master. As mentioned, the third reference is found in Luke's version of the Garden of Gethsemane (Lk. 22:42). The last instance speaks of the people's "desire/will" to crucify Jesus (Lk. 23:25).

is in heaven." In this instance, the will of the Father is that one takes care of the little ones.⁷³ In Mt. 21:31, Jesus questions the disciples on who is doing the will of the Father. In this instance, mention of heaven is removed, but doing the will of God relates to entrance to the kingdom.⁷⁴ The last instance of the will is in Mt. 26:42. Like Mark and Luke, Matthew retains the saying of Jesus in the Garden of Gethsemane in which he requests to do the will of the Father. Yet, Matthew's wording is in verbatim agreement with the third petition.

> Third petition of the Lord's Prayer (Mt. 6:11): γενηθήτω τὸ θέλημά σου
>   Mt. 26:42: γενηθήτω τὸ θέλημά σου
>   Mk. 14:36: ἀλλ' οὐ τί ἐγὼ θέλω, ἀλλὰ τί σύ
>   Lk. 22:42: μὴ τὸ θέλημά μου, ἀλλὰ τὸ σὸν γενέσθω

As we have attempted and will continue to show, Matthew "heightens" the parallelism between texts. Matthew 26:42 appears to be one of the clearest examples of Matthew's editing. Both texts are prayers by Jesus and share not only references to God's will but also references to the Father (vv. 39, 42) and deliverance from temptation (v. 41). In creating parallels between these texts, Matthew is giving evidence that he edits his prayer texts.

As the evidence shows, Matthew retains more references to the "will" being done than the other Gospel writers.⁷⁵ In his references, he consistently uses the noun form and interestingly connects it to other themes present in the Lord's Prayer, most notably the Father in heaven and the kingdom.⁷⁶ Mark and Luke refer to the will of God in their versions of the Garden of Gethsemane but without the verbatim wording of the third petition found in Matthew's prayer. Each evidence illustrates the distinctive wording of the first clause in the third petition and the consistent use of the "will" throughout Matthew's Gospel.

Ὡς ἐν οὐρανῷ καὶ ἐπὶ γῆς /"Heaven and Earth"

Appended to the end of the third petition is the clause "on earth as it is in heaven" (ὡς ἐν οὐρανῷ καὶ ἐπὶ γῆς). In the above discussion, we have shown that references

---

⁷³ The broader context is speaking on the issues of "temptation" (Mt. 18:6-9, another reference to the Lord's Prayer?) and church discipline (Mt. 18:15-20). This verse (Mt. 18:14) is found in the parable of the lost sheep in which Jesus teaches his disciples that if but one small sheep strays, the shepherd must seek after him. In doing so, the sheep is spared from the threat of "evil." Collectively, then, Matthew 18 speaks on the issues of the Father who is in heaven, the will of God, temptation, and evil—prominent themes also brought together in the Lord's Prayer.

⁷⁴ This connection is interestingly present in the order of Matthew's version of the Lord's Prayer. The kingdom petition is followed immediately with the request for the will of God to be done on earth as it is in heaven. In ch. 21, Jesus is challenging the religious leaders on how their actions on earth relate to heaven. He is also pointing out their ignorance and inability to see his work as being from heaven. There may be some thematic interplay between these passages.

⁷⁵ Benno Przybylski, *Righteousness in Matthew and his World of Thought*, SNTS Monograph Series 41 (Cambridge: Cambridge University Press, 1980), 79, argues that the use of the phrase in Matthew is purely redaction, concluding that the Matthean use is not based on extant Synoptic sources.

⁷⁶ See Mowery, "Lord to Father," 648.

to God's will are more frequent in Matthew compared to Mark and Luke, and the "will" is often connected to the "Father." The evidence is even more compelling when examining "heaven and earth" pairs. Mark only has two instances of the "heaven and earth" pairing, while Luke has five.[77] In Matthew, the heaven and earth pairing occurs twenty times. Jonathan Pennington has helpfully grouped the uses in Matthew into three categories based on wording and function. The three categories are copulative, implied, and thematic pairs. Copulative pairs are "heaven and earth" pairs without any intervening words or phrases (this excludes conjunctions and articles, i.e., ὁ οὐρανὸς καὶ ἡ γῆ). Copulative references to heaven and earth in Matthew are found in 5:18, 11:25, and 24:35. In 5:18 and 24:35, Matthew is referring to the passing away of heaven and earth. In Mt. 11:25, Jesus uses the word pair to describe God's sovereign rule ("Lord of heaven and earth"). Implied pairs are instances where heaven is used but in conjunction with a synonym for earth.[78] Implied pairs in Matthew appear in 5:16; 6:1, 25-33; 10:32-33 (2x); 11:23; 16:17-19; and 21:25-26 (2x).[79] Thematic pairs are the combination of heaven and earth, but with separation by intervening words or phrases.

Thematic pairings of heaven and earth are the most prevalent pairings in Matthew's Gospel.[80] In these cases, Matthew typically follows a pattern (ἐν οὐρανῷ καὶ ἐπὶ γῆς). Instances of the thematic pairs in Matthew occur in 5:13-16, 34-35; 6:1-21 (6:10, 19-20); 10:33-34; 16:19 (2x); 17:25-18:1; 18:18 (2x); 19:19; 23:9; 24:30; and 28:18. This type of pairing is the form found in the third petition. Particularly interesting is the exclusive usage of this phrase in Matthew's Gospel. Pennington summarizes,

> The thematic pairs come from either distinctly M material or are clear redactional additions to his sources. In the latter category, there are five texts where he has apparently added a thematic heaven and earth pair (5:13-16, 6:10, 19-20, 10:33-34, 24:30). In 5:13-16, similar sayings about the salt of the earth are found in Mark and Luke, but neither connects this with Father in heaven. In 6:10, the heaven and earth phrase is completely missing from the Lukan parallel (11:2), and likewise, no heaven and earth pairing is in view in the Lukan parallel (12:33) to Matt. 6:19-20 or to Matt. 10:33-34 (Lk. 12:51). In 24:30, Matthew alone includes the references both to ἐν οὐρανῷ and the tribes τῆς γῆς (cp. Mk. 13:26, Lk. 21:27). Conversely, the copulative pairs in 5:18 and 11:25 are also found in Luke, and 24:35 is in all three gospels.[81]

It becomes evident from a comparative analysis between the Gospels that Matthew has a liking for the heaven and earth pairing, particularly the thematic pairings. He adds heaven and earth in places where Mark and Luke omit the phrase, and this is no less the case in the Lord's Prayer with the inclusion of the third petition.

---

[77] Pennington, *Heaven and Earth*, 193. Mk. 13:27, 31; Lk. 4:25, 10:21, 12:56, 16:17, and 21:33.
[78] See Pennington, *Heaven and Earth*, 164-5.
[79] Because these pairs are not directly stated, we will reserve comment on their specifics for the sake of brevity. We will examine Mt. 5:16 and 6:1 below in the Sermon parallels section.
[80] Pennington, *Heaven and Earth*, 196.
[81] Pennington, *Heaven and Earth*, 198.

Table 4.3 The Distribution of the Third Petition

Chapters/ Words	1-4	5-7	8-9	10	11-12	13	14-17	18	19-22	23-25	26-28
Your will be done	0	2	0	0	1	0	0	1	0	0	1
Heaven/earth	0	8	0	3	2	0	5	2	3	3	1

Prominence

In the previous section, we argued for the distinctive wording and increased presence of "your will be done" and "on earth as in heaven" in Matthew's Gospel compared to Mark and Luke. A closer look at the evidence reveals a concentration of the terms within the Sermon on the Mount (Table 4.3).

Five examples of the will are present in Matthew's Gospel. Two of the five references are within the Sermon on the Mount. The stronger argument relies on the second phrase in the will petition. Heaven and earth pairings are found in eight different places throughout the Sermon on the Mount (5:3-12, 13-16, 18, 20, 34-35, 45; 6:1-21 [10, 19-21], 25-34). The only place with a comparable amount is chs 14-17 and chs 23-25. In chs 14-17, five of the six "heaven and earth" pairings are contained in three verses (Mt. 16:17-19). These verses are a climactic moment in Matthew's narrative in which Peter is given the keys to the kingdom of heaven. These keys give Peter the authority to bind and loose on earth and subsequently bind and loose in heaven.[82] In some senses, this depiction of Peter is the fulfilment of the Sermon's teachings, as he is an archetype of Sermon-based discipleship. In this regard, these instances in chs 14-17 do not detract from the concentration of heaven and earth in the Sermon but rather provide an example of an individual disciple embodying the heaven and earth theme.[83] In chs 23-25, Jesus is condemning the hypocrisy of the Pharisees. The section has eight "woes" (Mt. 23:13, 14, 15, 16, 23, 25, 27) addressing various sins.[84] The instances of heaven and earth in Matthew 24 are suitable to the subject matter of Jesus's return to earth (24:30, 35). The mentions of heaven provide a fitting contrast to the "earthly" living of the Pharisees condemned in ch. 23.

Conclusion

The statistical data indicates that Matthew's choice of wording is not only preferential to Matthew but also featured prominently in the Sermon on the Mount. Particularly,

---

[82] The pairing of heaven and earth are used as contrasts in the narrative. The Sermon on the Mount similarly contrasts heaven and earth and gives instructions to disciples on how to live in a "heavenly" manner despite being on "earth."

[83] This connection is also noted by Kari Syreeni, "Between Heaven and Earth: On the Structure of Matthew's Symbolic Universe," *JSNT* 40 (1990): 5-6. Note also what he describes as the "institutional fulfilment" of God's will on heaven and earth in Mt. 18:18-19.

[84] Most likely, Matthew's section of woes parallels Luke's introduction to the Sermon on the Plain (Lk. 6:20b-26). Matthew has displaced his woes for a later chapter in which he condemns the Pharisees for their hypocrisy.

Matthew uses thematic pairings of "heaven and earth" throughout the Sermon. The repetition of the terms provides lexical parallels between the third petition and various passages throughout chs 5–7. As with the invocation, the third petition has not only lexical parallels but also thematic parallels. In the following section, we will establish a basis for thematic parallels before turning to the parallels themselves in Section 3.

The Meaning of "Your Will Be Done, on Earth as in Heaven"

This section will explore the meaning of the will petition. As with the invocation, establishing the meaning of the third petition is important for examining thematic parallels with passages in the Sermon on the Mount and the centrality affirmed. From our studies, we conclude that for Matthew, "your will be done, on earth as in heaven" is primarily an ethically oriented prayer asking for God's help to empower the petitioner to live righteously as outlined in the Sermon on the Mount. In the following section, we will discuss the eschatology of the will petition, the relationship of God's will and righteousness in Matthew, and the ethical import of performing God's will "on earth as in heaven."

Eschatology of the Will Petition

The modern consensus is that the will petition has an entirely eschatological future focus.[85] The verb γενηθήτω is an aorist passive imperative, typically understood as a divine passive. The divine passive suggests that God is the only one who can bring about his "will." In the same way that God's name is sanctified, and his kingdom comes, so the will is accomplished. The "will" is, as Brown translates, "God's design of salvation effected through Jesus and extended to men through the apostles."[86] The correlative clause ("on earth, as in heaven") is understood as accomplished in heaven, and now the petitioner longs for the future consummation on earth. As Calvin argues, in one sense, the will petition then contains "nothing new" because it repeats the requests of the first two petitions (i.e., Name, kingdom).[87]

As we have argued in Chapter 3, the structure gives clues to the temporal element of the will petition. We have argued that the will petition is influenced by not only petitions 1–2 (i.e., Name, kingdom) but also petition 5 (i.e., forgiveness).[88] This context would indicate an interpretation of the will petition as not only a request for the

---

[85] Among others, Brown, "Pater Noster," 191–4.
[86] Brown, "Lord's Prayer," 192.
[87] Calvin, *Institutes* 3.20.42.
[88] Nolland, *Gospel of Matthew*, 289, fn.326, notes,

> There may be something of "in heaven" and "on earth" in Matt. 6:12b, with God's act of forgiving taking place in heaven and forgiveness of one another taking place on earth. If so, then we may note an artistry in that in v. 10 the "as" phrase relates to the existing heavenly state of affairs and comes before the linked phrase, whereas in v. 12 the "as: clause relates to the existing earthy state of affairs and comes after the linked clause (a double inversion).

> We will argue similarly in Chapter 5.

consummation of God's will in the future but also empowerment for daily living and discipleship.[89] Davies and Allison insightfully note, "Perhaps it is wrong to see here any antithesis [between the eschatological future and the present]. In the biblical tradition, God's will is usually accomplished through his people. So, do not the eschatological and ethical interpretations go hand in hand?"[90] The Matthean parallels help answer this question.

The most convincing piece of evidence for a dualistic temporal understanding of the will petition is Mt. 26:42. In Mt. 26:42, both the eschatological future and present are emphasized.[91] In praying, Jesus recognizes the gravity of the forthcoming crucifixion.[92] It is through his death that Jesus guarantees the completion of God's will for the future. Also, Jesus negates his own will in order to perform the will of the Father. As Young notes, "Jesus did not succumb but performed the will of God. A person overrules his own volition in order to do God's will."[93] He understands that it is God's will for him to act in a disciplined way in the present.[94]

The Will of God and Righteousness in Matthew's Gospel

In the previous section, we argued from the Matthean parallels that the third petition refers not only to the eschatological future but also to the right conduct of the disciples empowered to live faithfully until the final consummation. In this section, we will argue that in Matthew's Gospel, Jesus uses the terms for will (θέλημα) and righteousness (δικαιοσύνη) to refer to right conduct and obedience to God's commandments. While each word has its own nuances, their meanings have significant overlap in Matthew's Gospel.[95] As Young notes, doing God's will is rooted in *Torah* observance.[96] Young illustrates with examples from Ps. 40:8 ("I delight to do your will, O my God; your law

---

[89] Young, *Jewish Background to the Lord's Prayer*, 20, notes, "The teaching of the Jewish sages can enhance our understanding of Jesus' teaching here by increasing our knowledge of the ancient Jewish world. This supplication does not deal with *discerning* the will of God in a person's life, but in God's will being *accomplished*." Emphasis mine.

[90] Davies and Allison, *Matthew 1–7*, 606.

[91] The other references in Matthew refer to the Father's *will* (7:21; 12:50; 18:14; 21:31) as ongoing obedience in the present and the future. Guelich, *Sermon on the Mount*, 290, notes that these references express the "conduct characteristic of sonship, namely, obedience to the Father's *will*." Emphasis his.

[92] Nolland, *Gospel of Matthew*, 1094, notes, "In prayer he [Jesus] regains renewed confidence about the Father's will, and by v. 46 is ready to face his future."

[93] Brad Young, *The Jewish Background to the Lord's Prayer* (Austin: Center for Judaic-Christian Studies, 1984), 21.

[94] Quarles, *Sermon on the Mount*, 201–2, notes that it is Jesus's predetermined plan to follow God's will (see also Mt. 18:14). He differentiates Mt. 18:14 and 26:39 from 7:21, 12:50, and 21:31. Quarles argues that the first two references refer to God's predetermined will, therefore being eschatological, and the last three have moral connotations. This distinction does not seem warranted given the similarity in the requests. Each of the references are linked to the Father. Additionally, 18:14 and 26:36 do not automatically signal an eschatological understanding even if they are references to predetermined events (i.e., predestined does not equal eschatological).

[95] The notable difference is an emphasis on law-keeping that is associated with righteousness. The will of God would include this but does not specify "law" specifically in the instances throughout Matthew.

[96] Young, *Jewish Background to the Lord's Prayer*, 20.

is within my heart") and Rabban Gamaliel (*Avot.* 2:4—"Do His will as if it were your will").[97] A close reading of "righteousness" in Matthew reveals a similar meaning.[98]

Scholars have debated the meaning of righteousness, especially in the Sermon on the Mount: (1) Some have argued that the term is used univocally throughout the New Testament and Matthew's references are akin to Paul's soteriological usage.[99] (2) Others have argued that righteousness refers to God's vindication as anticipated in Isaiah's eschatological promises.[100] This understanding of the term accords with the *macarisms* (Mt. 5:3-12) and background of Isaiah 61 in which the "poor in spirit" and "mourning" are finally comforted.[101] (3) Many scholars have argued that Matthew is using the term ethically.[102] In what follows, we will address each of these aspects with the intention of showing the overlap with the "will of God."

In view of these three options, it is best to see aspects of each within Matthew's use of "righteousness."[103] In Matthew's Gospel, righteousness is defined by obedience to God. We will reserve comment on the instances of righteousness in the Sermon on the Mount for below, but Matthew offers two instances of righteousness in action (Mt. 3:15, 21:32) outside of the Sermon.[104] In Mt. 3:15, Jesus insists on his own baptism by John the Baptist as a means of "fulfilling" all righteousness (see Mt. 5:17-20). Jesus's obedience to the will of God through baptism is the means of fulfilling righteousness. Matthew 21:32 similarly connects the term "righteousness" with John the Baptist. The verse states, "For John came to you in the way of righteousness." Two pieces of evidence suggest that "righteousness" in Mt. 21:32 is to be understood in the same manner as in 3:15. First, the Lukan parallel to Mt. 21:32 suggests that righteousness is synonymous to the purposes of God.[105] Luke 7:30 states, "But the Pharisees and the lawyers rejected God's purpose for themselves, not having been baptized by John." In other words, the rejection of baptism by the Pharisees is their noncompliance to the "way of righteousness" (Mt. 21:32). Second, the context of Mt. 21:32 connects

---

[97] Young, *Jewish Background to the Lord's Prayer*, 20.
[98] Matthew uses the term δικαιοσύνη on seven occasions: 3:15; 5:6, 10, 20; 6:1, 33; and 21:32.
[99] Among others, Guelich, *Sermon on the Mount*, 157, argues that Matthew includes the soteriological aspect in his definition of righteousness. Also, Hagner, *Matthew 1-13*, 56. Hagner acknowledges an ethical side to "righteousness" in Matthew's Gospel but thinks that interpreters ignore the aspect of "grace" as a vital aspect of the term. Hagner's argument for grace alludes to the soteriological understanding of righteousness. Roland Deines, "Not the Law but the Messiah: Law and Righteousness in the Gospel of Matthew—An Ongoing Debate," in *Built Upon the Rock: Studies in the Gospel of Matthew*, ed. Daniel Gurtner and John Nolland (Grand Rapids: Eerdmans, 2008), 81, describes righteousness in Matthew as "Jesus-righteousness." In his essay, he specifically deals with Mt. 5:17-20 and explains that the *Torah* "will function as a guide to know what sin is (cf. Rom. 3:19) and what it means that God wants the obedience of all humans in all aspects of their personal and social life," 82.
[100] E.g., Gundry, *Matthew*, 70.
[101] Most recently, Wenham, "Beatitudes: Observations on Structure," 208-11.
[102] Davies and Allison, *Matthew 1-7*, 499; France, *Gospel of Matthew*, 119, 271; Keener, *Gospel of Matthew*, 206-7.
[103] Similarly, Guelich, *Sermon on the Mount*, 84-7.
[104] Kari Syreeni, *The Making of the Sermon on the Mount: A Procedural Analysis of Matthew's Redactoral Activity, Part I, Methodology and Compositional Analysis*, AASF (Helsinki: Suomalainen Tiedeakatemia, 1987), 207, argues that the frequency and its use throughout the Sermon show its importance for understanding chs 5-7.
[105] See Przybylski, *Righteousness in Matthew*, 95.

righteousness with the will of the Father (Mt. 21:31).[106] The will of the Father is describing obedience and response to Jesus's call. In this context, Jesus praises the tax collectors and prostitutes for responding and exhibiting the righteousness described by John.

The second view is praiseworthy for its acknowledgment of the Old Testament background to the *macarisms*. As we will argue in Chapter 5, Isaiah 61 is beneficial for understanding the poor in spirit, mourning, and so on, and their relationship to the kingdom. A brief examination of Isaiah 61 shows the progression of righteousness coming to the earth. The chapter begins with several lexical parallels to the *macarisms*. Isaiah 61 promises that the "poor" will be given good news and those who mourn will be "oaks of righteousness" (vv. 1-4). Similarly, Mt. 5:3-10 promises blessings to the "poor in spirit," comfort for the "mourning," and the kingdom of heaven to those who pursue righteousness. The metaphors of "hunger and thirsting" emphasize a spiritual longing for doing God's will (i.e., pursuing righteousness).[107] This is similarly anticipated in the final verses of Isaiah 61, in which the prophet proclaims,

> I will greatly rejoice in the Lord, my whole being shall exult in my God; for he has clothed me with the garments of salvation, he has covered me with the robe of righteousness, as a bridegroom decks himself with a garland, and as a bride adorns herself with her jewels. For as the earth brings forth its shoots, and as a garden causes what is sown in it to spring up, so the Lord God will cause righteousness and praise to spring up before all the nations. (vv. 10-11)

Wenham helpfully summarizes, "This focus on restored righteousness and justice especially in the second half of Isaiah 61 makes perfect sense, as an integral part of the joyous salvation which Yahweh's anointed one has been announcing."[108]

The third view argues that righteousness refers to moral conduct. This view is the most commonly held view among scholars regarding the definition of righteousness in Matthew's Gospel. As we have argued above, Jesus's obedience to John's baptism is a means of fulfilling Scripture.[109] In so doing, Jesus fulfills the Messianic expectation that he will obediently follow God's will. God's will, then, is the accomplishing of salvation (i.e., Pauline soteriology), the vindication of God's kingdom (i.e., Isaiah 61), and the mandate to moral living. We will address this in more detail below as we show the connections between righteousness and the third petition.

Before proceeding to the next section, one additional issue requires attention. As we have argued, in Matthew's Gospel, the "will of God" and "righteousness" are closely related in meaning. Yet, does Matthew *use* these concepts in the same way, in a functional sense? Przybylski argues in the negative:

---

[106] This connection provides additional support for understanding the "will of God" and righteousness as having similar referents.

[107] See Pss. 42:2, 63:1, 143:6; Amos 8:11. Davies and Allison, *Matthew 1-7*, 451, also point out the Rabbinic reference, *b. Sanh.* 100a: "Him who starves himself for the sake of the study of *Torah* in this world, the Holy One, blessed be He, will fully satisfy in the next."

[108] Wenham, "Beatitudes: Observations on Structure," 211.

[109] Davies and Allison, *Matthew 1-7*, 327.

Righteousness and doing the will of the Father, though not identical in meaning, are related in meaning. They are not, however, related in *use*. Matthew's religious understanding as a member of the church is that of a disciple doing the will of the Father and not that of a righteous person doing righteousness. The term is reserved strictly for contexts in which Jesus is involved in polemical situations and/or is dealing with non-disciples or audiences compromising both disciples and non-disciples.[110]

Przybylski states that "righteousness" is used when Jesus is in contexts of conflict with religious leaders, and "will of God" is exclusively used to encourage discipleship.[111] Although Przybylski's treatment of righteousness in Matthew's Gospel has become the standard on the topic, his discussion of functionality does not hold up to scrutiny. Specifically, Przybylski's comments regarding Mt. 6:10 and 7:21 are not correct, as he states that neither example is used in contexts of conflict. First, Mt. 6:10 references the "will of God" within a section focused on righteousness (see Mt. 6:1). Matthew uses three examples of proper righteousness in comparison with the practices of hypocrites. The middle example is prayer (Mt. 6:5-15), of which the Lord's Prayer is used as an exemplar. Even if Mt. 6:5-6 is not acknowledged as evidence of conflict (i.e., righteous prayer versus hypocritical prayer), the verses directly before the Lord's Prayer (6:7-8) present the prayers of the Gentiles and their meaningless phrases. The example of the Gentiles of Mt. 6:7-8 provides a fitting context of "conflict."

Additionally, Przybylski argues that Mt. 7:21 refers to the entrance requirements to the kingdom for disciples without any signs of conflict.[112] The wording of Mt. 7:21 closely parallels the wording of Mt. 5:16. Verse 16 states, "Let your light shine before men in such a way that they may see your good works, and glorify your Father who is in heaven." Matthew 5:16 and 7:21 share references to the Father in heaven and the importance of good works. Interestingly, the larger context of Mt. 5:16 connects being "salt" and "light" with those who are persecuted for righteousness' sake (Mt. 5:10). Like those in Mt. 7:21 who do the will of God, those who are persecuted for righteousness' sake (Mt. 5:10) are promised the kingdom of heaven. Matthew 5:10-16 and 7:21 present several parallel ideas.[113] First, being "salt and light" is the righteousness that leads to persecution. Second, persecution for righteousness' sake is rewarded with the kingdom of heaven. Third, the kingdom of heaven is promised to those who do the will of God. If these three are true then, lastly, the will of God is used similarly to the righteousness that leads to persecution.[114] This conclusion brings the "will of

---

[110] Przybylski, *Righteousness in Matthew*, 113. Emphasis mine.
[111] Przybylski, *Righteousness in Matthew*, 114.
[112] Przybylski, *Righteousness in Matthew*, 114.
[113] W. J. Dumbrell, "The Logic of the Role of the Law in Matthew 5:1–20," *NovT* 23.1 (1981): 10–6.
[114] See also Paul Foster, *Community, Law and Mission in Matthew's Gospel*, WUNT 177 (Tübingen: Mohr Siebeck, 2004), 201, who states,

> Although Matthew does not explain what "doing the will of the Father" means in the context of 7:21, when it is seen as an entrance requirement to the kingdom in the same way as δικαιοσύνη is in 5:10, it is reasonable to conclude that there is some overlap for Matthew

God" in Mt. 7:21 into the context of conflict (i.e., "persecution for righteousness' sake") presented in Mt. 5:10-16, which Przybylski argues is absent.

This section has addressed two major issues regarding the third petition. First, we have argued that the will of God and righteousness are closely related terms in Matthew's Gospel. Second, we have refuted the argument that Matthew is using the "will of God" and righteousness differently. Both terms are used in "contexts of conflict" (contra Przybylski). Establishing this close connection between these two terms and refuting the argument that they are used differently is important for textual connections between the third petition and the Sermon's emphasis on righteousness.

The Heavenly Will and the Earthly Will

As we have illustrated above, the heaven and earth pairing is a prominent feature of the Sermon on the Mount. Matthew's grouping of these instances into the Sermon on the Mount signal a literary innovation. Our initial explanation of heaven and earth stopped short of explaining the purpose of these pairings. In this section, we will examine the role of this phrase in relationship to "your will be done." We will argue that heaven and earth are signaling a contrast. The petition for God's will to be done "on earth as in heaven" is the petitioner's acknowledgment that the world is not as it should be. It is only until the will of God, as already accomplished in heaven, comes to earth that all things will be made right.[115] In the meantime, petitioners will pray for God's will and the empowerment to be "heavenly" representatives on earth.

As stated above, a helpful starting point for understanding heaven and earth pairings in Matthew's Gospel is the work of Jonathan Pennington. Pennington has provided a comprehensive study of the instances of "heaven and earth" pairings throughout Matthew's Gospel.[116] In his proposal, the instances of heaven and earth function in two ways in Matthew. The first function of heaven and earth is merismatic. Merismatic pairs refer to the totality of the creation and are the most common usage in the Old and New Testament.[117] Despite the widespread merismatic usage in the testaments, Matthew only uses heaven and earth in this manner on three occasions (Mt. 5:18, 11:25, and 24:35).[118] Matthew's more common usage of "heaven and earth" is antithetical. The fourteen thematic combinations (Mt. 5:13-16, 34-35; 6:1-21 [6:10*, 19-20]; 10:33-34; 16:19 [2x]; 17:25–18:1; 18:18 [2x]; 19:19; 23:9; 24:30; and 28:18) and ten implied pairs (Mt. 5:16; 6:1, 25-33; 10:32-33 [2x]; 11:23; 16:17-18, 19; and 21:25-26

between "doing the will of the Father" and the practice of "righteousness" by members of his community.

[115] A similar statement could be made regarding the hallowing of God's name and the coming kingdom.
[116] As we showed earlier, heaven and earth pairings are common to Matthew but not the other Synoptics.
[117] "Heaven and earth" pairings are common throughout the Old Testament and Pseudepigrapha/Apocrypha. Heaven and earth is used 185 times in the Old Testament. Among the Pseudepigraphal/Apocryphal works, 1 Enoch is most concerned with heaven and earth dualism. Examples include 1 En. 2:1-2; 8:4; 39:3; 84:2; 102:3b, d.
[118] Pennington, *Heaven and Earth*, 199–200, notes that these three uses are Matthew's only three copulative uses of heaven and earth (article-heaven-καὶ-article-earth).

[2x]) of heaven and earth all function in this manner.[119] The degree of contrast may vary depending on the context, but each of these passages is meant to show the divide between heaven and earth. The specific wording of the will petition places it squarely in the antithetical pattern. Read in this manner, God's will is accomplished in heaven but has not been accomplished on earth. Syreeni aptly notes, "The Lord's Prayer expresses an ideal correspondence or equivalence which would bring the two realms of reality together into a harmonious whole."[120] With the degree of separation between the heavenly will and the earthly will, disciples pray to live as sons and daughters of the Father on earth.[121] It is only when the heavenly will has been accomplished on earth that the petition has found its answer.

Conclusion

In the previous sections, we have discussed the temporality of the will petition, the relationship of God's will and righteousness in Matthew, and the ethical import of performing God's will "on earth as in heaven." From our analysis, we conclude that for Matthew, "your will be done, on earth as in heaven" is primarily an ethically oriented prayer asking for God's help to empower the petitioner to live righteously as outlined in the Sermon on the Mount. Additionally, in the interim between God's kingdom finally coming, disciples are to live the "heavenly" will on earth.

"Your Will Be Done on Earth as in Heaven" in the Sermon on the Mount

This section will examine those passages in the Sermon on the Mount that have shared references to the "will of God/righteousness" and/or "heaven and earth." As we argued above, references to righteousness must also be included in these parallels because of its relationship with the "will of God" in Matthew's Gospel. Mention of these phrases include Mt. 5:3-12, 13-16, 20; 5:34-35, 45, 48; 6:1, 19-21, 25-34; and 7:12, 21. In addition to lexical parallels, the third petition and Sermon parallels share similar

---

[119] Pennington, *Heaven and Earth*, 195, fn.8, is hesitant about labeling Mt. 6:25-33 as an implied pairing. He labels the grouping as Mt. 6:26-30. Consideration of the broader teaching in Mt. 6:25-33 shows that the implied pair is between the kingdom of the Father in heaven and things that people worry about on earth. Extending the parameters to vv. 25 and 33 develops this theme further.

[120] Syreeni, "Between Heaven and Earth," 4.

[121] Pennington, *Heaven and Earth*, 155, insightfully notes,

> Specifically, 6:9–10 shows that for Matthew, the current tension or contrast between heaven and earth is *not* part of God's creative and redemptive plans. The great Christian prayer is that the disjuncture between the two realms will *cease* to be: God's Name will be hallowed, his will done, and his kingdom manifested *not only in the heavenly realm but also in the earthly*. This is important because when emphasizing the contrast between heaven and earth it would be a mistake to understand this as a permanent and divinely designed state. The contrast between heaven and earth is a result of the sinfulness of the world and is thus unnatural. The eschatological goal, according to 6:9–10, is that this unnatural tension will be resolved into the unity of God's reign over heaven and earth. As the entire Gospel seeks to show, it is in Jesus Christ that the eschatological reuniting of heaven and earth has begun (see especially 28:18), and it will be consummated at his Parousia. (Emphasis his)

themes, most notably an emphasis on infusing the heavenly way of life into the earthly realm. As the third petition is closely wed to the second petition ("kingdom come"), many of the passages in the following analysis pair the two ideas ("will/righteousness/ heaven/earth" and "kingdom"), highlighting the overarching theme of "kingdom righteousness" within the Sermon.[122]

Matthew 5:3-12

As we have noted and will note in other sections, the *macarisms* have several parallels with the Lord's Prayer. In addition to parallels with the Father and kingdom, the *macarisms* have strong connections to the will petition. Before discussing the specific parallels, it is important to note some of the previous discussion. First, the *macarisms* are distinguished by their similar wording and form. Second, Mt. 5:3 and v. 10 share the phrase "for theirs is the kingdom of heaven," creating an *inclusio* around the first eight *macarisms*. Third, the point of view changes from third person to second person in Mt. 5:11-12 to ease the transition into Mt. 5:13-16, where the second person becomes prominent. Fourth, the *macarisms* collectively describe a portrait of "kingdom" disciples.[123]

The connections between the *macarisms* and the third petition are twofold. First, the passages share similar vocabulary and an emphasis on obedience. The *macarisms* have two references to "righteousness" (Mt. 5:6, 10)[124] as well as references to "heaven and earth." "Heaven" is mentioned in the *inclusio* of "kingdom of heaven" (Mt. 5:3, 10)[125] and is promised to those who are persecuted (Mt. 5:12). The "earth" is given to the meek as an inheritance (Mt. 5:5). The mention of "earth" alludes to Ps. 37:11 ("But the meek shall inherit the land, and delight themselves in abundant prosperity"). While Ps. 37:11 describes the future possession of the Promised Land, Matthew's reference to "earth" is a probable expansion of the inheritance beyond the land of Canaan to the ends of the earth.[126] The petition's content provides a starting point for this in-breaking of the heavenly "will" into these new expanses.

Second, the third petition and the *macarisms* have thematic parallels. As we argued above, the will petition looks to the eschatological future of God's name and kingdom coming to earth, as well as the present. The present is emphasized in the pray-er's participation in the ongoing process of the will being completed. This temporal understanding of the third petition parallels the temporal elements of the *macarisms*. The first line of each *macarism* addresses the current disposition of a

---

[122] Guelich, *Sermon on the Mount*, 32–3, has argued that the overarching theme of the entire Sermon is "kingdom righteousness." Also, Nolland, *Gospel of Matthew*, 288–9.
[123] It is beyond the scope of the present argument to discuss each *macarism* in depth. For a helpful overview, see Pennington, *Sermon and Human Flourishing*, 41–67, 137–68.
[124] Stanton, *Gospel for a New People*, 299, has pointed out that in Mt. 5:6, the addition of "righteousness" evidences the hand of Matthew. The phrasing is not paralleled in the similar *macarism* of Lk. 6:21 ("Blessed are the hungry, for they will be filled"). It is possible that this addition is precisely for the parallel mentioned above.
[125] Stanton, *Gospel for a New People*, 299, has argued that these *macarisms* are Matthean. If this is the case, the intentionality of the connections with the Lord's Prayer is strengthened.
[126] For an extended discussion, see Quarles, *Sermon on the Mount*, 55–8.

disciple, while the second line addresses the future. For example, "Blessed are those who mourn, for they will be comforted." "Those who mourn" (οἱ πενθοῦντες) is a present active participle referring to the ongoing activity of mourning. "They will be comforted" (παρακληθήσονται) is a future passive verb referring to God's comfort in the future.[127]

Matthew 5:13-16

Matthew 5:13-16 records Jesus's teaching to be "salt and light." The passage flows from the *macarisms* (Mt. 5:3-12) and leads to Jesus's teaching on the Mosaic law (Mt. 5:17-48). Concerning the metaphors of salt and light, interpretations have typically focused on the practical uses of each element. Yet, Allison has argued, "Matthew's words do not tell us how to become salt or light or lamp, nor exactly what those things mean."[128] The variety of interpretations validate Allison's concerns. Interpretations of salt have ranged from its job as a preservative,[129] a seasoning,[130] a fertilizer,[131] and a purifying agent.[132] Still others have preferred to see the metaphor of salt as broad and inclusive, referring to any number of these different aspects.[133] The light metaphor is equally allusive. Having a wide semantic range, light has often symbolized the law, joy, righteousness, the divine presence, and revelation.[134] Although these disagreements may encourage one to side with Allison, Matthew has provided context to limit the possibilities.

First, the main ideas in vv. 13 and 14 are set in a parallel structure. The dual metaphors appearing together (salt/light) are unique to Matthew's sermon.[135]

Matthew 5:13a: Ὑμεῖς ἐστε τὸ ἅλας τῆς γῆς
Matthew 5:13b: useless salt
Matthew 5:14a: Ὑμεῖς ἐστε τὸ φῶς τοῦ κόσμου
Matthew 5:14b: dark light

Both phrases begin with the second-person pronouns, followed by the second-person plural form of "be." This parallelism continues with genitive modifiers referencing

---

[127] A third parallel may exist in the ordering of the *macarisms* and the Lord's Prayer. The *macarisms* begin with references to heaven (Mt. 5:3), mentions of earth (Mt. 5:5) and righteousness (Mt. 5:6), and then concludes with an *inclusio* (5:10, "kingdom of heaven"). Verses 11-12 also mention heaven and form a concluding note to the *macarisms*. Similarly, the Lord's Prayer (6:9-13) begins with a reference to heaven (6:9, "our Father in heaven"), mentions earth and righteousness (6:10, "your will be done, on earth as in heaven"), and ends in an *inclusio* fashion but without an additional reference to heaven. We have argued above for a concentric structure to the Lord's Prayer. Verses 14-15 mention the "Father in heaven" and form a concluding note to the Lord's Prayer. Pennington, *Heaven and Earth*, 74, notes this similarity but neglects to see this as a parallel.
[128] Allison, *Sermon on the Mount*, 31.
[129] D. A. Carson, *Matthew 1–12*, EBC (Grand Rapids: Zondervan, 1995), 138–9.
[130] Luz, *Matthew 1–7*, 205–6.
[131] Gundry, *Matthew*, 75–6.
[132] Quarles, *Sermon on the Mount*, 77–83.
[133] Hagner, *Matthew 1–13*, 99.
[134] H. Conzelmann, "φῶς," in *TDNT*, vol. 9, 310–58.
[135] A "salt" saying is found in Mk. 9:50 and Lk. 14:34-35. Hagner, *Matthew 1–13*, 98, notes,

the ground/world (τῆς γῆς/τοῦ κόσμου).¹³⁶ Both lines of text ("you are salt/you are light") are followed by contrasts. Salt that is useless becomes tasteless and is thrown on the ground (Mt. 5:13).¹³⁷ A light is not visible if it is put in a hiding place (Mt. 5:15). This tightly structured section indicates that these phrases are best read as having a similar meaning. The references are probably referring to the identity ("salty salt") and influence ("being a light") of Jesus's disciples on earth.¹³⁸ As Quarles notes, "The disciples of Jesus will be characterized by righteousness and purity and that their righteousness will move others to glorify God and seek to be transformed by Him in a similar way."¹³⁹

These verses parallel the third petition in two ways. First, Mt. 5:13-16 references "heaven and earth." The references to heaven and earth are thematic and implied.¹⁴⁰ The modifiers ("of the earth"/"of the world") added to salt and light function as a thematic contrast with the Father in heaven. One must be salt and light in the earth/world because of the absence of those very elements. This explicit comparison is repeated in an implicit manner in v. 16. The verse states, "Let your light shine before others, that they may see your good deeds and glorify your Father in heaven." Jesus's teaching implies that your light will shine before those on earth to glorify the heavenly Father. Second, the metaphors themselves describe how a disciple lives according to God's will. Being salt and light in the earth/world brings the heavenly will to the earthly realm. It is through the embodiment of the *macarisms*, specifically righteous living, that one is "salt and light." This "salt and light" living parallels the contrasting heaven and earth theme and the present orientation of the third petition to follow God's commands.

Matthew 5:17-20

In Mt. 5:17-20, Jesus's teaching addresses the accusation that he wants to abolish the "law and the prophets" (Mt. 5:17). Jesus declares that he has come to fulfil the

"Luke 14:34 seems dependent on the Markan parallel, although, in one word (μωρανθῇ, 'loses its taste'), Luke agrees with Matthew against Mark. Luke's second verse (14:35) is not found in Mark but is similar in content to Matt. 5:13c, especially in the reference to 'casting out' tasteless salt. Mark alone has the corresponding comment: 'Have salt in yourselves and be at peace with one another' (9:50)."

Matthew has a similar comment regard peace only a few verses earlier (Mt. 5:9). The "light/lamp" saying has parallels in Mk. 4:21 and Lk. 8:16 (also 11:33).

¹³⁶ Among the Synoptics, Matthew is unique in his inclusion of "τῆς γῆς" in the salt metaphor. For the significance of this phrase, see Don Garlington, "'The Salt of the Earth' in Covenantal Perspective,' *JETS* 54.4 (2011): 715–48; Paul S. Minear, "The Salt of the Earth," *Int* 51 (1997): 31–41.

¹³⁷ Glen Stassen and David P. Gushee, *Kingdom Ethics: Following Jesus in Contemporary Context*, 1st ed. (Downers Grove: IVP, 2003), 468–73, have suggested that this metaphor may be referencing the sand that is used metaphorically in ch. 7. In this (chiastic?) arrangement, the fool builds his foundation on sand and the overall effect is uselessness. This useless sand mimics the "bad" salt. Sand resembles the shape of granular salt but is unsalted and trampled under the feet of man. On the other hand, the wise man builds his house on a rock. This metaphor connects with the light that is set on the hill. In this high place, it is most capable of shining brightest. The suggestion is at least plausible considering the similar wording and themes.

¹³⁸ Scot McKnight, *Sermon on the Mount*, The Story of God Bible Commentary (Grand Rapids: Zondervan, 2013), 57.

¹³⁹ See Quarles, *Sermon on the Mount*, 79.

¹⁴⁰ See the earlier discussion for definitions of "thematic" and "implied" heaven and earth pairs.

Mosaic law and instructs his disciples to rebuke anyone who sets aside even the least commandment (Mt. 5:18-19). Verse 20 states, "For I tell you, unless your righteousness exceeds that of the scribes and Pharisees, you will never enter the kingdom of heaven." In what follows (Mt. 5:21-48), Jesus is interpreting the teachings of the Old Testament through his own person and life.

Jesus's introduction to the Mosaic law (Mt. 5:17-20) has four parallels to the third petition. First, the will of God and righteousness are paralleled. The righteousness of Mt. 5:20 is characterized by the keeping of God's commandments. This insistence on obedience parallels the emphasis of the third petition. Second, Mt. 5:18 picks up on the "heaven and earth" theme, using the phrase in a merismatic fashion. Although the wording is similar, the function is different. A closer parallel is found in v. 20. Although it is not explicitly mentioned, "heaven and earth" is implied. The disciples are being commended to display "surpassing righteousness," and they will enter the kingdom of heaven. The "kingdom of heaven" is contrasted with the works of the Pharisees on earth. This depiction of the Pharisees leads to the third parallel, namely both passages blend the eschatological future with the present. Actions in the present are spoken of in consideration of the future kingdom of heaven. Jesus warns that teachers cannot relax the Mosaic law but must teach and act according to their precepts. The Pharisees are used as the foil and representative of those who do not perform the "will of God." They are therefore not guaranteed the kingdom of heaven. Fourth, the will petition and Mt. 5:17-20 evidence the contrasting nature of heaven and earth. As we argued above, Jesus's followers must define their righteousness on earth by the pattern of "heavenly" righteousness (Mt. 5:20). This heavenly righteousness contrasts with the "righteousness" of the Pharisees, who receive their rewards on earth (see Mt. 6:1-21).

Matthew 5:33-37

In Jesus's teaching on oaths, he presents a "heaven and earth" pair (Mt. 5:33-37). The teaching on oaths requires that a disciple of Jesus tell the truth in all things and avoid swearing according to objects. Certain Rabbinic teachings permitted dishonesty in cases where oaths were not sworn to God.[141] One could swear by Jerusalem or "by the earth" and the severity of breaking the oath was nullified.[142] Jesus's teaching subverts this teaching with the commendation to be honest always.

The parallels with the third petition are twofold. First, Mt. 5:33-37 and the third petition share references to "heaven and earth." "Heaven and earth" are mentioned in vv. 34-35. It is difficult to discern the function of this heaven and earth pairing. Charles Quarles has argued that the pairing is merismatic.[143] According to this interpretation, Jesus's teaching is commanding one not to swear an oath according to heaven or earth because God sits on his heavenly throne and uses the earth as his footstool. The implication is that one should not swear on anything within the created sphere, that

---

[141] References include *m. Šebu.* 4:13, *m. Ned.* 1:3, *t. Net.* 1.2.3, *m. Sanh.* 3:2, *b. Ned.* 14b.
[142] For an extended discussion of this teaching, see the Name section in Chapter 6, and Quarles, *Sermon on the Mount*, 135–44.
[143] Quarles, *Sermon on the Mount*, 140.

is, on heaven or earth. In this interpretation, heaven and earth are read together as complementary spheres, expressing the totality of creation. While Quarles's reading is possible, this would present the only case in Matthew in which a heaven and earth pairing functions as a *merism* but lacks the copulative form (i.e., article-heaven-καὶ-article-earth). If the wording is an indication of its function, the more probable reading is an antithetical pairing, similar to the function of the phrase in the third petition. Jesus's teaching would therefore say, "Do not swear on heaven or the opposite, which is earth." The point is the same as Quarles's but with the proper stress on the antithesis of heaven and earth. Second, Jesus's teaching is commending the observance of the "will of God" regarding truth-telling. Jesus explains that obedience to the Mosaic law is a form of righteousness (see Mt. 5:20). For this reason, truth-telling becomes a means through which disciples live righteously.

Matthew 5:45, 48

In Jesus's final teaching on the Mosaic law (Mt. 5:43-47 [48]), he provides double references to the third petition. The first is found in Mt. 5:45, in which Jesus commends his disciples to love their enemies. After commanding the love of enemies and prayers on their behalf (Mt. 5:44), Jesus appeals to the Father in heaven as the example for disciples. The Father in heaven causes the sun to rise on the evil and the good, and rain on the righteous and unrighteous (Mt. 5:45). After a series of rhetorical questions (Mt. 5:46-47), Jesus instructs his disciples to emulate the perfection of the heavenly Father (Mt. 5:48). The instruction to be perfect as the Father is the second reference.

Matthew 5:45 and v. 48 parallel the third petition, each sharing an emphasis on the accomplishing of God's will. In Mt. 5:43-47, the Father in heaven is used as the example for disciples. The Father in heaven loves both neighbor and enemy and sends rain on the righteous and unrighteous. The implication is that as rain falls on all humans, so the Father showers his love equitably. Matthew 5:48 presents a parallel teaching in which the Father is used again as an example for the disciples. Considering the verse's summative function, the perfection of the Father is linked with the fulfilment of Jesus's teaching on the Mosaic law.[144] At the very least, the commended perfection

---

[144] Within the Sermon itself, specifically in its three major sections (Mt. 5:21–7:12), Matthew has inserted/retained phrases to help the reader pause or transition between sections. The first occurrence is Mt. 5:48:"Ἔσεσθε οὖν ὑμεῖς τέλειοι ὡς ὁ πατὴρ ὑμῶν ὁ οὐράνιος τέλειός ἐστιν. This phrase has a twofold function in its respective discourse, signaled by the conjunctive adverb οὖν. The first function is summative. Normally translated as "therefore," Matthew is both summarizing (1) the immediate teaching (5:43-47) and (2) Jesus's teaching concerning the Mosaic laws (5:21-47). The emphasis in both sets of passages is that disciples are to seek perfection, because in doing this, they are emulating their heavenly Father. The second function is that it marries the earthly and heavenly dimensions that have been prevalent thus far in the Sermon. The use of οὖν is typically used to denote consequence. If the hearer of Jesus's teachings follows him in fulfilling the law in the present, they will in effect be perfect in the eschatological future.

One could argue that Jesus's initial teaching on the Mosaic law (Mt. 5:17-20) is the first use of an introductory phrase. We are not diminishing the use of this phrase as an introduction to the formal teaching on the Mosaic law found in vv. 21-48. Matthew tends to use phrases and paragraphs for multiple functions and purposes. We will argue later that Mt. 7:12 has a summative function as well

parallels the love of neighbor and enemy. "Perfection" in Mt. 5:48 carries the same ethical emphasis as the third petition and the Sermon's emphasis on righteousness.[145]

Matthew 6:1, 19-21

Matthew 6:1 states, "Be careful not to practice your righteousness in front of others to be seen by them. If you do, you will have no reward from your Father in heaven."[146] Commentators have noted the *kelal* function of Mt. 6:1 as its message summarizes the teaching which follows (Mt. 6:2-18). In the following verses, Jesus explains three areas of Jewish piety/righteousness (i.e., almsgiving, prayer, and fasting).

Although Mt. 6:1 begins a new section, it is not without thematic parallels to the previous section.[147] This *kelal* on Jewish piety picks up on the theme of righteousness implied in Mt. 5:48's mention of "perfection" and *inclusio* with Mt. 5:17-20. In Matthew's vocabulary and the context of the Sermon, "perfection" and "righteousness" share similar connotations.[148] In addition to the similar concepts of "righteousness," Matthew retains the heaven/earth duality. In Mt. 6:1, Jesus commands his disciples that their practices on earth are not for an audience but rather for their heavenly Father.

The emphasis in Mt. 6:1 on the duality of heaven and earth is repeated in 6:19-21. Matthew 6:19-21 states:

> Do not store up for yourselves treasures on earth, where moths and vermin destroy, and where thieves break in and steal. But store up for yourselves treasures in heaven, where moths and vermin do not destroy, and where thieves do not break in and steal. For where your treasure is, there your heart will be also.

The popular understanding of Mt. 6:19-21 is to read these verses as a "beginning" to the disparate teaching in the latter half of the Sermon (Mt. 6:19–7:12).[149] If read exclusively with 6:22–7:12, vv. 19-21 begin the discussion of physical possessions and the accumulation of wealth through the end of ch. 6.[150] A closer look at the wording and thematic elements in these verses reveals its dual function as not only a "beginning"

---

as an *inclusio* function with Mt. 5:17-20 (i.e., repetition of "law and prophets"). It is easy to see that in this case, both functions are acceptable. The same can be said about the dual function of Mt. 5:17-20.

[145] McKnight, *Sermon on the Mount*, 147, says that "perfect" means to "love all humans, Jews and Romans, as neighbours." McKnight argues that this interpretation lines up with Jesus's instruction that the *Torah* hang on the commandments to love God and to love one's neighbor as oneself. While McKnight's interpretation captures the ethical element of the word, "perfect" appears to mean more, particularly as it relates to the Mosaic law (Mt. 5:21-47).

[146] The Greek reads: Προσέχετε δὲ τὴν δικαιοσύνην ὑμῶν μὴ ποιεῖν ἔμπροσθεν τῶν ἀνθρώπων πρὸς τὸ θεαθῆναι αὐτοῖς· εἰ δὲ μή γε, μισθὸν οὐκ ἔχετε παρὰ τῷ πατρὶ ὑμῶν τῷ ἐν τοῖς οὐρανοῖς.

[147] See Luz, *Matthew 1-7*, 296.

[148] See Davies and Allison, *Matthew 1-7*, 563–6, 575–8. Also of note is the similarity of function. While the imperative sense of "to be" is implied in Mt. 5:48, Mt. 6:1 makes it clear that righteousness is not to be paraded before men.

[149] This view is found almost exclusively in the commentaries available, with the exception of Pennington, *Heaven and Earth*, and J. C. Fenton, *Saint Matthew*, Pelican Gospel Commentaries (London: Penguin Books, 1963). For the majority view, see Davies and Allison, *Matthew 1-7*, 625; Gundry, *Matthew*, 111; Keener, *Gospel of Matthew*, 162–3, 228.

[150] See Guelich, *Sermon on the Mount*, 322–9, as representative of this view.

to Matthew's third major section in the Sermon's body (Mt. 6:19–7:12) but also as a closing to the teaching on Jewish piety (Mt. 6:1-18).

Two commentators have noted the dualistic function of Mt. 6:19-21. First, J. C. Fenton has observed, "To practice piety (alms, prayer, and fasting) in order to be seen by men is to lay up treasures on earth, in the praise and approval of men; but to practice piety in secret is to lay up treasures in heaven, with God, and to wait for his praise and approval at the last judgment."[151] Similar to this interpretation has been the work of Jonathan Pennington. In *Heaven and Earth in the Gospel of Matthew*, Pennington has argued that the themes of heaven and earth are crucial ordering themes in Matthew's Gospel.[152] According to Pennington, Mt. 6:1 is a negative statement that finds its positive counterpart in vv. 19-21, thus forming an *inclusio*. Matthew 6:1 argues against practicing your righteousness before men in which one's reward is nullified. The ultimate reward is given to those who practice righteousness before their Father in heaven. Verses 19-21 continue this teaching with an imperative to store up treasures in heaven. "Treasures" is a metaphor for the gift to those who practice proper righteousness.[153] The reading of vv. 19-21 as a conclusion to ch. 6 completes an already highly stylized section.[154]

The parallels with the third petition are twofold. First, the *inclusio* found in Mt. 6:1, 19-21 shares several lexical parallels with the third petition. Both teachings speak of the will of God/righteousness and have the repetition of "heaven and earth." Second, both passages share a concern for the ethical aspect of the will of God. Przybylski summarizes the thrust of Mt. 6:1: "The rationale behind 6:1 thus appears to be that even if one knows the nature of true righteousness, one will not receive a reward unless one adheres to the proper practice of righteousness. Theory and practice must go in hand in hand."[155] Matthew 6:19-21 reiterates this emphasis on practice in its twin imperatives concerning proper and improper storage of treasures ("Do not store up"/"Store up"). The concluding note brings the discussion back to the genesis of good

---

[151] Fenton, *Matthew*, 103.
[152] Pennington, *Heaven and Earth*, 242–7. See also Chapter 3 on structure.
[153] Pennington, *Sermon and Human Flourishing*, 102–3, elaborates on "treasures" in his most recent book. For a detailed analysis of Matthew's use of "treasures" and its relationship to Second Temple literature, see Nathan Eubank, "Storing Up Treasure with God in the Heavens: Celestial Investments in Matthew 6:1–21," *CBQ* 76 (2014): 77–92. Eubank additionally shows the how Matthew's understanding of "treasure" is parallel to sins as "debts," a concept also found in the Lord's Prayer, *Wages of Cross-Bearing and Debt of Sin: The Economy of Heaven in Matthew's Gospel*, Beihefte zur Zeitschrift für die neutestamentliche Wissenschaft 196 (Berlin: De Gruyter, 2013), 25–85; Jack R. Lundbom, *Jesus' Sermon on the Mount: Mandating a Better Righteousness* (Minneapolis: Fortress, 2015), 217–22.
[154] In addition to the thematic connections mentioned above, this understanding of vv. 19-21 as a conclusion would also make ch. 6 parallel to Jesus's teaching on the Mosaic law (with Mt. 5:48 being a conclusion) and the Sermon conclusion in ch. 7 (with the Golden Rule functioning as an ending). The Sermon would then have three major sections, each with summary verses and close in length. Pennington goes on to argue that while vv. 19-21 functions as a conclusion, it does not necessarily entail an ending point. This small section is a "bridge" that connects 6:1-18 with 6:22–7:12. Just as 5:13-16 (salt and light) in Allison's scheme bridges the *macarisms* with Jesus's teaching on the Mosaic law, similarly, 6:19-21 works as a transitional unit between the second and third major sections in the Sermon. We have also argued above that 5:48 has transitional value that 6:1 picks up on.
[155] Przybylski, *Righteousness in Matthew*, 88.

works, the heart in which righteousness begins. Additionally, both passages emphasize the contrasting nature of heaven and earth. Proper righteousness in Mt. 6:1, 19-21 is presented as those things with earthly significance versus those things rewarded by the Father in heaven. Specifically, vv. 19-21 explain that earthly treasure will rust and decay, but heavenly treasure will not be consumed by earthly wear.

Matthew 6:22-24

As we argued above, Mt. 6:19-21 has a dual function. It not only provides a suitable closing to the highly structured teachings in the beginning of ch. 6 but also begins the third and last section of the body of the Sermon (Mt. 6:19–7:12). In the teachings that follows, Jesus addresses several topics, including a variety of financial and social concerns. Following Mt. 6:19-21 are the dual metaphors in Mt. 6:22-24. Matthew 6:22-24 is often broken into two separate sections. The reasons for this split center on the difficulty of finding a connection between the respective metaphors (healthy/unhealthy eye [6:22-23] and God/money [6:24]) and the presence of a command that makes a separate point in v. 24 (Οὐδεὶς δύναται δυσὶ κυρίοις δουλεύειν). This split is unwarranted when the underlying premise is considered.

As we will argue in more depth below, the reference in both passages is to the contrasts between good and evil. In this case, a "healthy eye" refers to a wholesome, generous eye, while an "evil eye" refers to duplicity of sight (see Mt. 20:15).[156] With the introduction of Mt. 6:19-21, the desire of the "eye" is directed toward heavenly and earthy treasures. This understanding of vv. 22-23 leads straight to the point in v. 24. The strong antithesis is retained in v. 24, and the metaphors of healthy and evil eyes find particularity in Jesus's warning against attempting to worship both God and mammon. Jesus warns that a disciple can only love one master, for he or she will hate the other.

The parallels with the third petition primarily center around the antitheses of vv. 22-24 and the heaven and earth duality. The message of Mt. 6:22-24 is a prescription for wholeness and singularity of desire. The healthy eye will love God and seek heavenly treasure (Mt. 6:19-21). As we have argued above, Mt. 6:19-21 has several parallels to the third petition. As vv. 22-24 continue the theme of Mt. 6:19-21, one can discern the insistence that God's will is an unequivocal devotion to kingdom priorities. Additionally, vv. 22-24 maintain the antithesis of heaven and earth, as represented in the third petition. The "evil eye" and mammon represent things of the earth, while disciples are called to have "healthy sight" and devotion to God.

Matthew 6:25-33

We have summarized the subject matter of Mt. 6:25-34 and its connections with the invocation in the Father section.[157] For the sake of brevity, we will simply point

---

[156] In other words, the contrast is between single-mindedness and duplicity. See Lundbom, *Jesus' Sermon on the Mount*, 224.

[157] We will further discuss this section of the Sermon in accordance with the fourth petition.

out the parallels with the third petition without reiterating the content summary. The parallels between the third petition and Mt. 6:25-33 are threefold. First, the two passages share an emphasis on pursuing the will of God. In Mt. 6:25-34, the pursuit of righteousness includes striving for the kingdom and avoiding worry (Mt. 6:33). Second, the two passages share references to heaven and earth (Mt. 6:26-33). The birds of the air and the lilies of the ground are representative of earthly creatures. Additionally, bread, drink, and clothing are "earthly" concerns. The Father in heaven provides for these earthly concerns (Mt. 6:32), but Jesus teaches that the kingdom and righteousness must be pursued first (Mt. 6:33). Thus, heaven is emphasized through the work of the Father and the prioritizing of the kingdom and righteousness over the earthly concerns of bread, drink, and clothes. Third, the two passages share *contrasting* pairs of heaven and earth. We have mentioned the implied pairing above (bread/drink/clothing/birds/lilies versus Father in heaven/kingdom/righteousness) but without reference to the function of the pairing. In Mt. 6:25-34, the things of earth are the things that the "Gentiles" pursue. "Gentiles" function as a foil in this context and they only focus on earthly concerns. Jesus's disciples must pursue the Father in heaven and his kingdom/righteousness (Mt. 6:33). In the broader context of the Lord's Prayer, the "Gentiles" are similarly used as a foil (Mt. 6:7). With the inclusion of the third petition, the Prayer is given as a means through which one pursues heavenly concerns.

Matthew 7:12

Although Mt. 7:12 lacks direct lexical parallels to the third petition, its message echoes the emphasis of the third petition. The verse states, "In everything do to others as you would have them do to you; for this is the law and the prophets." As numerous commentators have pointed out, the "therefore" in Mt. 7:12 signals a summative function of the Sermon's preceding teachings.[158] In this, the righteousness prescribed by the Sermon is encapsulated in the command to treat others as one would want to be treated. As Quarles notes,

> 7:12 summarizes and concludes Jesus' interpretation and application of the Law (5:17-48), his instruction related to deeds of righteousness (6:1-18), and his instruction for life in this world including both one's relationship to possessions (6:19-34) and to people (7:1-6), as well as 7:7-11.[159]

In this regard, the teaching in Mt. 7:12 thematically parallels the emphasis in the Prayer on righteousness and the will of God.

---

[158] Davies and Allison, *Matthew 1-7*, 685; Guelich, *Sermon on the Mount*, 379-81; Nolland, *Gospel of Matthew*, 330.
[159] Quarles, *Sermon on the Mount*, 306.

Matthew 7:21

The final parallel to the third petition is Mt. 7:21. The verse states, "Not everyone who says to me, 'Lord, Lord,' will enter the kingdom of heaven, but only the one who does the will of my Father in heaven." The context for this verse is 7:21-23 in which Jesus describes a scene of judgment. In these verses, many come to God and proclaim the great things they have done. Works of supposed "righteousness" include prophecy, driving out demons, and performing miracles (Mt. 7:22). Jesus proclaims, "I never knew you. Away from me workers of lawlessness!" (7:23).[160] The Matthean version differs in its inclusion of the phrase "will of God" and connects it with the "Father in heaven."

This verse is the strongest parallel to the third petition. The addition of "will of God" and "Father in heaven" signal lexical parallels between Mt. 7:21 and the third petition. Along with references to the "will of God" and the "Father in heaven," the kingdom of heaven is mentioned (Mt. 7:21) with heaven and earth being implied. The implied heaven and earth pairing is found in the contrasts between the Father in heaven/kingdom and the works of false disciples. They conduct their work on earth but do not have access to the kingdom. This contrast presents thematic parallels as well. The phrase translated "evildoers" is οἱ ἐργαζόμενοι τὴν ἀνομίαν. The term is more accurately translated as "workers of lawlessness."[161] The translation presents a contrast with those who are true disciples and perform the proper will of God. As we have argued above, the will of God and righteousness in Matthew are integrally related to the keeping of God's commandments.

Will Petition Conclusion

In the preceding sections, we have examined the third petition. The third petition is notable for its distinctive phrasing and prominence within the Sermon on the Mount. Particularly of note is the third petition's verbatim agreement with Jesus's cry in Gethsemane (Mt. 26:42). The repetition in the third petition and Gethsemane prayer evidence the hand of Matthew in shaping the wording of each phrase to reflect his purposes. The third petition is closely related to righteousness, a term that is central to the Sermon on the Mount. The will of God and righteousness refer to the keeping of God's commands. With the addition of "heaven and earth," a central theme in its own regard within the Sermon on the Mount, the third petition is enhanced in its parallels with the Sermon. When the third petition is read together with the Sermon on the Mount, its aim is seen to express a desire to embody the *macarisms* (Mt. 5:3-12), be salt and light (Mt. 5:13-16), live according to God's laws (Mt. 5:17-20), speak truthfully (Mt. 5:33-37), love enemies and emulate the perfection of the Father (Mt. 5:45, 48), practice righteousness by storing up heavenly treasure (Mt. 6:1, 19-21, 22-24), seek the

---

[160] Luke parallels the teaching here, but only briefly and in combination with the parable of the wise and foolish builders (Lk. 6:46.49). The Matthean and Lukan versions put emphasis on not only calling on the Lord but also doing what he says. We have translated "workers of lawlessness" instead of the NRSV "evildoers" to highlight a Matthean emphasis.

[161] We will discuss this translation in more depth in conjunction with the seventh petition.

kingdom among earthly desires (Mt. 6:25-33 [esp. v. 33]), do good to others (Mt. 7:12), and rightfully confess "Lord, Lord" (Mt. 7:21).

Seventh Petition: "Rescue Us from the Evil One"

The Lord's Prayer comes to a suitable closing with the seventh petition.[162] Betz insightfully notes that this line of the Lord's Prayer forms the "climax of all [the] petitions."[163] In this petition, the pray-er requests deliverance from evil/the evil one. Debate concerning the seventh petition centers on the translation of τοῦ πονηροῦ. The -ου ending can be read as a masculine singular about the "devil" or a neuter singular referring to generic evil. In addition to this interpretive question, an overlooked aspect of the seventh petition is how the petition parallels its Matthean context, the Sermon on the Mount. One notable exception to this overlooked aspect is the work of Mark Kiley.[164] He has recently argued that the seventh petition (as well as the rest of the Lord's Prayer) connects to material that follows in the Sermon on the Mount (Mt. 6:19–7:23). To correct an early version of this argument by Günther Bornkamm, Kiley argues that the connections of the Lord's Prayer to the Sermon stretch from 6:19 to 7:23. We will argue that Kiley's basic argument is correct, yet, like Bornkamm, he ignores the connections of the seventh petition to the first half of the Sermon on the Mount. Several references to "evil" are found within the first half of the Sermon on the Mount (Mt. 5:11, 37, 39, 45).

The Distinctives of "Rescue Us from the Evil One"

This section will establish the distinctives of the seventh petition in the Matthean version of the Lord's Prayer in terms of wording and prominence. First, we will argue that the seventh petition is carefully worded to create lexical parallels with passages in the Sermon on the Mount, thus reaffirming the centrality of the Lord's Prayer. Second, we will examine the distribution of the petition's wording within Matthew's Gospel. A survey of Matthew's references to "evil" indicates a concentration of the terms in chs 5–7. The distinctiveness of the seventh petition and its prominence in Matthew 5–7

---

[162] This statement may seem unusual to those accustomed to the liturgical doxology. The earliest manuscript evidence of the Lord's Prayer (ℵ B D Z 0170 f¹ l 2211 lat mae bo^pt; Or) does not contain the doxology and therefore appears to indicate that petition seven is the ending of the prayer. For an extended discussion of the doxology, see Matthew Black, "The Doxology to the Pater Noster with a Note on Matthew 6:13B," in *A Tribute to Geza Vermes: Essays on Jewish and Christian Literature and History*, JSOTSupp Series 100, ed. Philip R. Davies and R. T. White (Sheffield: JSOT, 1990); Andrew J. Bandstra, "The Original Form of the Lord's Prayer," *CTJ* 16 (1982): 88–97; Jacob Van Bruggen, "The Lord's Prayer and Textual Criticism" *CTJ* 17 (1981): 78–87.

[163] Betz, *Sermon on the Mount*, 405. Whether as a reference to the devil or to anonymous evil, evil is foundational to all the petitions. Concerning the first half of the Lord's Prayer, that which takes the Lord's name in vain, thwarts the kingdom and turns man against the God's will is evil. The results are the same concerning the second half of the Lord's Prayer. Evil causes man to doubt God's provision, not forgive others, and not trust God in temptation.

[164] Kiley, "Lord's Prayer and Matthean Theology," 15–27.

indicate a literary innovation within Matthew in which the references should be read together.

Wording

Matthew's version of the Lord's Prayer ends with an "added" petition, which is only found in Matthew's Gospel. In this petition, the pray-er requests rescue from evil/evil one. In this section, we will examine the wording found in the seventh petition to establish a basis for lexical connections. Matthew has a lexical preference for ὁ πονηρὸς compared to the other Gospels.

Ῥύομαι/"Rescue"

Before considering the references to evil, it is important to note that Matthew is the only Gospel writer to employ the imperatival form of "rescue." While this is not necessarily indicative of distinctiveness or Matthean redaction, the way that Matthew connects it with ὁ πονηρὸς is interesting. The verb ῥύομαι is only used in two other places in the Synoptic Gospels. Matthew has a reference in 27:43 in which Jesus's assailants are taunting him during his crucifixion: "He trusted in God; let him deliver (ῥυσάσθω) him now, if he will have him: for he said, I am the Son of God." The assailants quote Ps. 22:8, which states that the one who trusts in God will be "rescued" if he believes. The other reference is found in Lk. 1:74, which describes God's covenant with his people to rescue them from evil (see Gen. 22:16-18).[165] The imperative form of "rescue" is common in the Old Testament, particularly in the Psalmist's prayers of Israel (6:5; 7:2; 16:13, etc.). While Matthew may not be directly borrowing the term, his usage echoes the Psalmic pattern.[166]

Ὁ πονηρὸς /"Evil/Evil One"

The word for evil (ὁ πονηρὸς) appears forty-one times in the Synoptic Gospels. On word statistics alone, one can see the prevalence of references to evil in Matthew with twenty-seven of the forty-one instances, including the Lord's Prayer.[167] In the Sermon

---

[165] Luke 1:74 states, "that we, being rescued (ῥυσθέντας) from the hands of our enemies, might serve him without fear."

[166] The Psalmic background and argument for Matthean distinctiveness are difficult to substantiate because of the common usage of ῥύομαι. The imperative form is also necessitated by the context.

[167] Mark has three references to evil, all in the same passage. The three references are to generic evil, an evil eye (envy), and to evil things that come from within. Luke has fourteen references to evil. Of the fourteen instances, four are paralleled in the Sermon on the Mount in Matthew (Lk. 6:22/Mt. 5:11-12; Lk. 6:35/Mt. 5:39-42 [39]; Lk. 11:13/Mt. 7:7-11 [11]; Lk. 11:34/Mt. 6:22-23). The remaining instances are to evil people (Herod, 3:19; Pharisees, 11:39; a slave, 19:22; generic man, 6:45), evil spirits (7:21, 8:2, 11:26), evil treasure (6:45), generic evil (6:45), and an evil generation (11:29). Of these remaining ten references, five are directly paralleled in Matthew (Lk. 6:45/Mt.12:35; Lk. 11:26/Mt.12:45; Lk. 11:29/Mt.16:4). Of the remaining five references to "evil" in Luke (Lk. 3:19; 7:21; 8:2; 11:39; 19:22), Matthew has parallel passages but removes the references to "evil." Therefore, Luke only speaks of "evil" in an unparalleled way in five instances. There is an emphasis as well on evil spirits (Lk. 7:21 and 8:2).

on the Mount references, Matthew has five additional references to evil compared to Luke, which includes the seventh petition.[168] Among his eighteen other references, only six are paralleled in Luke.[169] The other twelve references to "evil" are original to Matthew. Matthew uses his references to "evil" to describe a variety of things. He refers to evil thoughts/intentions (9:4; 15:19; 22:18), evil people (Pharisees, 12:34; generic men, 13:49; a slave, 18:32; wedding guests, 22:10), evil generations (12:39, 45), the evil one (13:19), children of the evil one (13:38), and an evil eye (20:15).

Interestingly, Matthew is the only Synoptic Gospel that refers to the devil as ὁ πονηρὸς. These instances are in Mt. 13:19 and 13:38. In the parallel passage to Mt. 13:19, Mark has "evil" with ὁ σατανᾶς (Mk. 4:15).[170] Mark refers elsewhere to the devil as ὁ σατανᾶς in 1:13; 3:23 (2x), 26; 4:15; and 8:33. Luke uses ὁ σατανᾶς in 10:18; 11:18; 13:16; and 22:3, 31. Matthew only uses the term ὁ σατανᾶς to refer to the devil in 4:10, 12:26 (2x), and 16:23. The reference in Mt. 4:10 may well be borrowed from Mark (see 1:13) as well as the direct quote in 16:23 (see Mk. 8:33). This leaves only two instances in Matthew where he uses ὁ σατανᾶς (12:26 [2x]) instead of ὁ πονηρὸς.

In Mt. 13:38, the evil one is identified as "the devil" (ὁ διάβολος) in v. 39. Matthew uses the phrase (ὁ διάβολος) on six occasions (4:1, 5, 8, 11; 13:39; 25:41) elsewhere.[171] Only two of these instances are without parallel (Mt. 13:39 and 25:41). In Luke, references to the devil as ὁ διάβολος are found in 4:2, 3, 6, 13 and 8:12. The references in Luke 4 are paralleled in Mt. 4:1-11.

In conclusion, Matthew has both generic references to evil and references to the evil one, that is, the devil. In the cases that Mark and Luke prefer the devil (ὁ διάβολος) or Satan (ὁ σατανᾶς), Matthew prefers ὁ πονηρὸς. Matthew does have references to ὁ διάβολος and ὁ σατανᾶς, but they are less frequent than the other Gospel writers. The use of ὁ πονηρὸς is therefore distinctive in Matthew's Gospel. As we will show in Section 3, the repetition of ὁ πονηρὸς indicates lexical parallels between the seventh petition and the Sermon on the Mount.

Prominence

In the previous section, we noted the distinctive wording of the seventh petition. The evidence for this includes the multiple references to ὁ πονηρὸς throughout Matthew's Gospel in comparison to Mark's and Luke's. Matthew has twenty-seven total references to evil including the petition in the Lord's Prayer. In this section, we intend to note the prominence of these references within chs 5–7 in comparison to the Gospel as a whole. This clustering of references indicates Matthew's intention that these phrases be read together.

---

[168] Matthew 5:37, 45; 6:13; 7:17; and 7:18.
[169] Matthew 12:35/Lk. 6:45 (3), Mt.12:45/ Lk. 11:26 (Matthew includes an additional reference to an "evil generation" not included in this Lukan parallel), Mt. 16:4/Lk. 11:29, Mt.25:26/19:22.
[170] The reference in Lk. 8:12 is paralleled in Mt. 13:19. Both Matthew and Luke contain a similar explanation of the role of the devil in handling the seed that is thrown near the road. Yet, Matthew has ὁ πονηρὸς, snatching what has been sown in the heart, while Luke has ὁ διάβολος, doing the snatching.
[171] Mark only uses ὁ σατανᾶς to refer to the devil.

Table 4.4 The Distribution of the Seventh Petition

Chapters/Words	1–4	5–7	8–9	10	11–12	13	14–17	18	19–22	23–25	26–28
ὁ πονηρὸς	0	9	1	0	7	3	2	1	3	1	0

In Matthew's twenty-seven references to ὁ πονηρὸς, nine are found in the Sermon on the Mount. In these Sermon references, Matthew has five additional references to evil compared to Luke (5:37, 45; 6:13; and 7:17, 18). In addition to the instances in the Sermon on the Mount, chs 11–12 have seven references to ὁ πονηρὸς. The instances of ὁ πονηρὸς are all found in ch. 12 and in four verses. Matthew 12:34-35 has four of the seven instances and parallels Mt. 7:6-10. The other three references are found in Mt. 12:39 and 12:45 (2x). The reference in Mt. 12:39 refers to Jonah as a sign to a wicked generation (also Mt. 16:4). Matthew 12:45 continues the discussion of the "wicked" generation with an additional reference to evil spirits. Obviously, the clustering of words often reflects the subject matter, but it can also be important to note in statistical arguments (Table 4.4).[172]

Conclusion

In this section, we set out to examine the wording of the seventh petition and the prominence of its wording within the Sermon on the Mount. The wording found in the seventh petition is preferred by Matthew in comparison to the other Synoptic writers. Additionally, Matthew has clustered his references to ὁ πονηρὸς in chs 5–7. Here, nine of his twenty-seven total references can be found.

The Meaning of "Rescue Us from the Evil One"

This section will explore the meaning of the seventh petition. As with the invocation and will petition, establishing the meaning of the seventh petition is important for establishing a basis for thematic parallels with passages in the Sermon on the Mount and reinforcing the parallels with the Lord's Prayer. Before examining these themes, we will consider the traditional starting point for understanding the seventh petition: Is ὁ πονηρός neuter or masculine? Next, we will look at other prayers that are worded similarly to the seventh petition. From our study, we conclude that for Matthew, evil is used to refer to the evil one, that is, the devil. Closely related are a variety of topics, ranging from literal embodiments of evil (evil agents and evil spirit) to symbolic things (evil eye, fear, hand of wickedness). Petitions against evil are an affirmation of God's power over evil. Also, these requests are offered so that evil will not separate the petitioner from God.

---

[172] The table is organized according to the fivefold structure of Matthew's Gospel.

Evil or Evil One?

An important question about the seventh petition is the identity of "evil." Considerable debate surrounds the question regarding the gender of ὁ πονηροῦ in Mt. 6:13. If the gender is neuter, then the reference would be to general evil, thus a petition for "rescue from evil." If the gender is masculine, the translation would be "evil one," that is, the devil. In his now classic treatment of the Lord's Prayer, Ernst Lohmeyer has argued for the "evil one."[173] His argument is as follows: (1) References to the devil as the evil one are consistent with the rest of the New Testament (2 Thess. 3:3, Eph. 6:16, 1 Jn 2:13, etc.);[174] (2) Matthew is the only Synoptic writer who refers to the devil as the "evil one" (5:37; 13:19, 38);[175] (3) The sixth petition refers to eschatological temptation; therefore, the seventh petition must refer to the devil as the one who ushers in the last days;[176] and (4) The allusion in Jn 17:15 (ἀλλ᾽ ἵνα τηρήσῃς αὐτοὺς ἐκ τοῦ πονηροῦ) is the closest parallel to the Lord's Prayer in which a prayer refers to the devil.[177]

Lohmeyer's argument is helpful for several reasons. First, Lohmeyer is sensitive to the strength of parallels when presenting his case. Arguably, Jn 17:15 is a close parallel to the seventh petition in the Gospels and represents a strongest defense for the evil one. Second, Lohmeyer helpfully draws attention to the interplay between the sixth and seventh petitions.[178] Third, Lohmeyer acknowledges the uniqueness of Matthew's mention of the evil one, among the Synoptic writers.

Notwithstanding these strengths, Lohmeyer's argument is not decisive in its current form. In what follows, we will provide a more balanced presentation of the evidence as well as suggest further evidence for "evil one." We will address Lohmeyer's arguments in the order in which they were listed. First, the consistency of the New Testament witness is not univocal on the identity of ὁ πονηρὸς. Other passages such as Lk. 6:45; Rom. 12:9; Gal. 1:4; and 2 Tim. 4:18, suggest a neuter reading. Particularly interesting is the parallel in 2 Tim. 4:18.[179] In this passage, the petitioner requests rescue from evil, uses the adjectival form of ὁ πονηρὸς, and refers to entrance into the heavenly kingdom (καὶ σώσει εἰς τὴν βασιλείαν αὐτοῦ τὴν ἐπουράνιον). This creates a closely worded parallel to the Lord's Prayer, with allusions to both the seventh and second petitions (i.e., kingdom). Second, Matthew is the only Synoptic writer to refer to the evil one, but he also predominantly refers to evil in the more generic sense. In Matthew's twenty-seven references to ὁ πονηρὸς, only two are unequivocal references to the evil one (Mt. 13:19, 38). Matthew 5:37 is a reference to the evil one but is translated as "of evil" in various translations. The specific wording of the Lord's Prayer is found in Mt. 12:35, and this is most certainly a reference to an "evil person" but not the devil. Third,

---

[173] Lohmeyer, *Lord's Prayer*, is followed by a host of scholars who agree: see Guelich, *Sermon on the Mount*, 297; Gundry, *Matthew*, 104; Keener, *Gospel of Matthew*, 224. For a thorough discussion, see Davies and Allison, *Matthew 1–7*, 614–15.
[174] Lohmeyer, *Lord's Prayer*, 214–15.
[175] Lohmeyer, *Lord's Prayer*, 215.
[176] Lohmeyer, *Lord's Prayer*, 216.
[177] Lohmeyer, *Lord's Prayer*, 209. This is also noted by W. O. Walker, "The Lord's Prayer in Matthew and in John," *NTS* 28 (1982): 246–7; and Wenham, "Sevenfold Form of the Lord's Prayer," 381, fn.20.
[178] Lohmeyer, *Lord's Prayer*, 26–7.
[179] See Luz, *Matthew 1–7*, 323, considers this the tipping point for the argument.

Lohmeyer's eschatological future reading is more assumed than proven. By positing a future interpretation of the sixth petition, Lohmeyer assumes that the seventh must refer to the end times. Yet, evidence for an eschatological future reading of the sixth petition is based on a misappropriated parallel with Rev. 3:10 ("Because you have kept my word of patient endurance, I will keep you from the hour of trial that is coming on the whole world to test the inhabitants of the earth"). It is highly improbable that the temptation referred to in the sixth petition, with its lack of the definite article, is referring to the final judgment, as in Rev. 3:10. There is also nothing within the context of the sixth petition that necessitates a completely future interpretation, as in the context of Revelation.[180]

Charles Quarles has pointed out the close affinities between the sixth petition and the temptation of Christ in Mt. 4:1-10.[181] Quarles's argument is important to consider because he argues for the evil one without appealing to the argument for the eschatological future. Quarles has shown the extensive lexical parallels between the temptation narrative and the sixth petition. Quarles rightly concludes that not only is the sixth petition focusing on present temptation, as in Christ's, but also, the seventh petition's mention of ὁ πονηρός is paralleling ch. 4's mention of the devil. Therefore, the seventh petition is requesting rescue from the evil one.

An often-neglected piece of evidence for understanding the seventh petition is found in the structure of the Lord's Prayer. As we have argued above in conjunction with David Wenham, the last two petitions are juxtaposed to the first two petitions of the Lord's Prayer in a concentric structure. In this case, the Name and kingdom are "positive" petitions, which are parallel to the "negative" petitions of temptation and the evil/evil one. Translating the seventh petition as a masculine singular noun creates a more suitable parallel to the first petition. As the Name refers to the Father in Heaven specifically, so the reference to evil finds specificity in the evil one.

In consideration of the above arguments, we conclude that Lohmeyer was right. Yet, some of his arguments do not consider the full scale of evidence, and in some cases, he has neglected other key evidence. Matthew is distinctive among the Synoptic writers in his references to the evil one. Other key evidence to the identity of "evil" includes the immediately preceding temptation narrative (Mt. 4:1–10) and the structure of the Lord's Prayer. This reference would parallel other references to evil, as the devil is linked with varying forms of evil as their cause.[182]

Jewish Lexical Parallels to "Rescue Us from Evil/Evil One"

In this section, we will analyze those passages in Jewish literature that have similarities in wording with the seventh petition, particularly found in prayers. The following table takes the various words in the seventh petition and examines the LXX and Second Temple literature for possible parallels (Table 4.5). We will also consider the Hebrew

---

[180] For a fuller discussion, see Chapter 6 on the temptation petition.
[181] For a fuller discussion, see Chapter 6 on the temptation petition.
[182] This question is dismissed by Gerhardsson. He, "Matthean Version," 217 states, "The familiar question whether τοῦ πονηροῦ is to be understood as masculine or neuter is difficult to answer

Table 4.5 Jewish Parallels to the Seventh Petition According to Similar Wording

Phrase Combinations/ Verses	ῥῦσαι/πονηροῦ	ῥῦσαι/ἀπὸ (object)	ῥῦσαι/ἡμᾶς	ἀπὸ τοῦ πονηροῦ
	Esth. 4:17	Ps. 16:13 (ἀσεβής/"ungodly"; ἐχθρός/"enemy")	Esth. 4:8 (ἐκ θανάτου/"death")	Deut. 23:10 (φυλάσσω/"beware/guard")
		Ps. 139:2	Ps. 21:21 (ῥομφαία/"sword"; κύων/"dog")	Esth. 4:17 (emphasis is God as deliverer without reference to specific evil)	2 Sam. 13:22 (antithesis of good)
	PsSol. 12:1 (synonyms for evil: "lawless man," "lawless tongue," "slander," "liar," and "deceit")	Ps. 38:9 (ἀνομία/"lawlessness")	Isa. 63:16 ("Our Redeemer/Rescuer")	Ps. 139:2 (ἐξαιρέω/"deliver" in addition to "rescue")
		Ps. 42:1 (ἀνθρώπου ἀδίκου καὶ δολίου/"unrighteous and deceitful men")	Ps. 78:9 (emphasis is God as deliverer without reference to specific evil)	Job 1:1 (ἀπέχω/"be distant from")
		Ps. 119:2 (χειλέων ἀδίκων καὶ γλώσσης δολίας/"lying lips and deceitful tongue")		Job 1:8 (ἀπέχω/"be distant from")
				Sir. 4:20 (φυλάσσω/"beware/guard")
				PsSol. 12:1 (ῥῦσαι/rescue)
				1 Thess. 5:22 (ἀπέχω/"be distant from")
				2 Thess. 3:3 (φυλάσσω/"beware/guard")
				2 Tim. 4:18 (ῥύσεται/"rescue"; σῴζω/"save")

and Aramaic equivalents in the sections that follow.[183] An extensive word search for parallels reveals that πονηρὸς and its cognates can refer to a variety of things. Jewish prayers for deliverance include rescue from "temptation, shame, evil impulse, evil events, and sickness, evil thoughts and dreams."[184] This deliverance can also include rescue from evildoers and death.

Three passages in the Septuagint have the aorist ῥῦσαι and a form of πονηρός paired (Est. 4:17, Ps. 139:2, and PsSol. 12:1). In each of these passages, prayers are offered to avoid "evil or evil men." Psalms of Solomon 12:1 has an interesting list of "evils" included in its reference to generic evil. The list includes a "lawless man," a "lawless tongue," "slander," a "liar", and "deceit." Psalms 139:2 requests rescue from evil men who do violence.

In the next set of parallels, we examine those passages that enjoin ῥῦσαι and ἀπὸ. In this set of examples, there are a variety of objects to be *rescued from*. Psalms 16:13 asks to avoid both the "ungodly" (ἀσεβής) and the "enemy" (ἐχθρός). Psalms 21:21 presents two objects as foils to rescue, the "sword" (ῥομφαία) and the "dog" (κύων). Psalms 38:9 refers to lawlessness (ἀνομία). Psalms 42:1 and 119:2 both refer to differing forms of unrighteousness. Psalms 42:1 refers to unrighteous and deceitful men, while Ps. 119:2 makes mention of unrighteous lips and deceitful tongues. Tobit 12:8-10 states, "For almsgiving delivers from death (ἐκ θανάτου ῥύεται)." Interestingly, the phrase is couched in instructions on prayer. The instruction begins, "Prayer is good when accompanied by fasting, almsgiving, and righteousness." This listing of works is reminiscent of the wider context of the Lord's Prayer.

In the third category, we examine passages that ask for rescue (ῥῦσαι/ἡμᾶς), but without reference to "evil," and do not mention "from" (Isa. 63:16; Est. 4:8, 17; Ps. 78:9). In Isa. 63:16, God is called "our Redeemer." Isaiah 63:16 is also one of the few places in the Old Testament in which "our Father" is used in a prayer. This assimilation of God as the "one who rescues" and the "Father" provides a closely worded parallel to the Lord's Prayer. A similar reference to God's delivering is found in Est. 4:8 and Ps. 78:9. Esther 4:8 expresses the desire to be rescued "out of death." Like Isa. 63:16 above, Ps. 78:9 presents possible parallels with the Lord's Prayer. In addition to the request for deliverance (ῥῦσαι ἡμᾶς), Ps. 78:9 refers to the glorifying of God's name, a probable parallel to the first petition (ἕνεκα τῆς δόξης τοῦ ὀνόματός σου) and requests for forgiveness (καὶ ἱλάσθητι ταῖς ἁμαρτίαις ἡμῶν).[185]

In the fourth category, we examine "from the evil one" (ἀπὸ τοῦ πονηρου). An examination of the instances shows a variety of synonyms for "rescue" in order to be rid of "evil." Deuteronomy 23:10, Sir. 4:20, and 2 Thess. 3:3 use the wording for "beware/guard (φυλάσσω)." Psalms 139:2 (LXX) prays for "deliverance" (ἐξαιρέω) in addition to "rescue." Job 1:1, 8 (LXX) and 1 Thess. 5:22 refer to "being distant from"

---

with any degree of probability, the choice is however, of little significance." We are arguing that the chief significance is not in the identity of the evil but in the lexical parallels it creates.

[183] In the Old Testament, the Greek word πονηρός is typically parallel to the Hebrew word רע.

[184] G. Harder, "πονηρός, πονηρία," in *TDNT*, vol. 6, ed. G. Kittle and G. Friedrich, trans. G. W. Bromiley (Grand Rapids: Eerdmans, 1964–76), 561.

[185] The verb ἱλάσκομαι refers to the desire of the petitioner to receive mercy or propitiation. As we will argue, forgiveness and mercy are closely related in Matthew's Gospel. See also Lk. 18:13.

(ἀπέχω) evil. Second Timothy 4:18 uses "rescue" and "save" (σῴζω) in synonymous parallelism.[186] In 2 Sam. 13:22, "evil" is used as the antithesis of good.

When examining these parallel verses, two themes emerge. First, "evil" refers to the conceptual opposite of the Father and his goodness. The Jewish parallels describe multiple facets of opposition, whether from within a person (i.e., deceit and lawlessness) or outside a person (i.e., temptation or evil people). Prayers are a means through which the petitioner avoids the separation that evil causes with the Father. Second, prayers against evil are an affirmation of God's power over evil. In the following section, we will explore these two themes further.

Evil Stands at Odds with the Father

Among the various references to evil, the definition and purpose of evil is clear. Evil is the conceptual opposite of God, and its purpose is to separate God and his children. The first set of evidence includes texts that equate evil with godlessness, such as Ps. 16:13 (see also *Tg. Isa.* 11:4).[187] Also, the synonyms of evil are opposites of God's attributes. Texts such as PsSol. 12:1, Ps. 38:9, 42:1, 119:2, and Est. 4:8 closely associate evil with lawlessness, slander/deceit, unrighteousness, and lying lips.

This set of opposites is represented well in the literature of Qumran in which references to evil are used to refer to the eschatological dark lord. In these texts, the Hebrew cognate of evil is used to refer to the one who is seeking to rule men.[188] This eschatological figure is given a curse as punishment for his opposition to the Father.[189] These texts refer to the Angel of Light fighting Melki-resha, who is the Angel of Darkness. Related texts include 4QLevib ar frag.1 and 11QPs^a. In the latter text, a similar request is made where the petitioner prays, "Let not Satan rule over me, nor an evil spirit."

Evil is also intent on drawing the petitioner away from God. Two examples in the Rabbinic literature closely parallel the seventh petition and evidence this separation. The petitioner prays so that he may not be led away. *B. Ber.* 60b reads: "Bring me not in the grasp of sin, iniquity nor of temptation or disgrace. Let the good inclination rule over me and let the evil inclination not rule over me."[190] Similar sentiments can be found in *b. Ber.* 16b: "May it be Your will to deliver me from arrogant men and from

---

[186] To reiterate, the following parallels are for comparison only. It is quite likely that 1 Thess. 5:22 and 2 Tim. 4:18 may have been influenced by the Lord's Prayer and therefore do not necessarily present something unique or distinctive.

[187] *Tg. Isa.* 11:4 uses the Hebrew word translated as ἀσεβής in the LXX. Ἀσεβής is translated as "godless" and is a synonym for evil. Cited by Black, "Doxology to the *Pater Noster*," 333.

[188] See 4Q544 frg. 2.3, the text reads: "[…] and Melki-resha' (רשע מלכי). [Blank] And I said: My Lord: What is the ru[ling…]." All translations of the Qumran text by F. Garcia Martínez, "4Q 'Amram B 1, 14: Melki-resha or Melki-sedeq?" *RevQ* 12.45 (1985): 114. See also F. G. Martinez and E. J. C. Tigchelaar, eds., *The Dead Sea Scrolls: Study Edition*, vol. 2 (Brill: Leiden, 1998), 1089, for a fuller context and description of the Angel of Darkness versus the Angel of Light (Michael).

[189] See 4Q280 frg. 2.2, the text reads: "[And they will say: Accur]sed are you, Melki-resha' (רשע מלכי), in all the pla[ns of your blameworthy inclination. May]."

[190] David Flusser, "Qumran and Jewish Apotropaic Prayers," *IEJ* 16 (1966): 198–200. It is important to note that this passage is a substantive parallel to the Lord's Prayer. In both passages, prayers concerning temptation are followed by requests to flee from evil.

arrogance from bad man and bad company from mishap from the evil inclination . . . and from Satan who is bent on destruction."[191] In both instances, the petitioner realizes the impending consequences of evil and its divisive agenda.

Prayers against Evil Are an Affirmation of God's Power over Evil

Parallels to the seventh petition also reveal a second theme. Requests for rescue from evil are grounded in an affirmation of God's power over evil. Often, God is given distinct roles as Redeemer and Deliverer in response to evil. Three closely related parallels to the seventh petition are Est. 4:17, Isa. 63:16, and Ps. 78:9. In each of these passages, God is referred to as the "Redeemer." In these cases, the emphasis is less on the object to be rescued from but more on the God who saves. Closely related to God's role in redemption is God as "Deliverer." God is described in this manner in Ps. 79:9,[192] Est. 4:17,[193] and *Did.* 11:5.[194] In these instances, God acts in accordance with his own reputation. It is for his own glory that he delivers those who cry out (see esp. Ps. 79:9). Other instances of God's power over evil are found in prayers for God's strength to overcome evil men. In a closely worded parallel to the seventh petition, Ps. 139:2 requests God's strength to overcome violent men (see Ps. 16:13; PsSol. 12:1). The closest parallel in the New Testament to the seventh petition is 2 Tim. 4:18. As argued above, the passages share references to deliverance from evil and the kingdom. In 2 Tim. 4:18, Paul asks God to save him "from every work of evil" (ἀπὸ παντὸς ἔργου π ονηροῦ).[195]

Conclusion

In the previous section, we have examined the meaning of the seventh petition. From our analysis, we conclude that for Matthew, evil is probably used to refer to the evil one, that is, the devil. Closely related are a variety of topics, ranging from literal embodiments of evil (evil agents or evil spirit) to symbolic things (evil eye, fear, hand

---

[191] Samuel T. Lachs, *A Rabbinic Commentary on the New Testament: The Gospels of Matthew, Mark, and Luke* (Hoboken: KTAV, 1987), 122–4. The reference to the evil inclination (*yezer hara*) is the Rabbinic expression concerning the internal "desire for evil" (see also, *b. Hag.* 16a; *b. Bat.* 16a). See also A. Edward Milton, "'Deliver Us from the Evil Imagination': Matt. 6:13B in Light of the Jewish Doctrine Yêser Hârâ," *RelStTh* 13 (1995): 60–3.

[192] Psalm 79:9 LXX reads, "Help us, O God of our salvation, for the glory of your name; deliver us, and forgive our sins, for your name's sake." (βοήθησον ἡμῖν ὁ θεὸς ὁ σωτὴρ ἡμῶν ἕνεκα τῆς δόξης τοῦ ὀνόματός σου κύριε ῥῦσαι ἡμᾶς καὶ ἱλάσθητι ταῖς ἁμαρτίαις ἡμῶν ἕνεκα τοῦ ὀνόματός σου).

[193] Esther 4:17 LXX has similar wording as Ps. 79:9. The Septuagint includes an extended ending to ch. 4. The text reads as follows: ὁ θεὸς ὁ ἰσχύων ἐπὶ πάντας εἰσάκουσον φωνὴν ἀπηλπισμένων καὶ ῥῦσαι ἡμᾶς ἐκ χειρὸς τῶν πονηρευομένων καὶ ῥῦσαί με ἐκ τοῦ φόβου μου (Est. 4:17). In this case, the petitioner is requesting deliverance out of the "hand of wickedness" and "my fear."

[194] *Didache* 11:5 requests deliverance from evil and to perfect it in the love of God. It states, "Remember your church, Lord, to deliver it from all evil and to make it perfect in your love." For Greek text and translation of the *Didache*, see Michael Holmes, ed., *The Apostolic Fathers: Greek Texts and English Translations* (Grand Rapids: Baker, 2007), 361.

[195] See Luz, *Matthew 1–7*, 323. As stated, the close parallelism between this verse and the Lord's Prayer may be due to reliance on the same tradition.

of wickedness). Petitions against evil are an affirmation of God's power over evil and for the purpose of avoiding the separation from God which evil causes.

"Rescue Us from Evil" in the Sermon on the Mount

This section will examine those passages in the Sermon on the Mount that share lexical and thematic parallels with the seventh petition, thus reaffirming the centrality of the Lord's Prayer within the Sermon on the Mount. The verses are as follows: Mt. 5:11, 37, 39, 45; 6:23; 7:11, 17-18, and 23. The uniting feature of these references and the seventh petition is the shared references to "evil." Additionally, each of these Sermon passages share similar themes with the seventh petition. We will examine each in the order in which they appear.

Matthew 5:11

Matthew 5:11 functions as the ninth *macarism* and transition to Jesus's teaching on salt and light (Mt. 5:13-16). In this verse, Jesus is extending blessings to include those who face evil. The verse describes insults, persecution, and falsehoods as the norm for those who pursue the kingdom of heaven (see Mt. 5:10). This list culminates in a reference to spoken evil here (πᾶν πονηρὸν). In the previous verse (Mt. 5:10), Jesus explains that a disciple should expect such evil because of their righteousness (ἕνεκεν δικαιοσύνης).[196] In addition to this lexical parallel, Mt. 5:11 shares both themes associated with the seventh petition. An examination of the list shows the contrary nature of evil. Each of the vices listed in Mt. 5:11 contradicts the righteousness of the disciples and ultimately the righteousness of the Father/kingdom of heaven. As we argued above, prayers for deliverance are an affirmation of God's power over evil. The affirmation of God's power comes in the form of a promise in Mt. 5:11. Those who "rejoice and stay glad" in the face of evil will have their reward in heaven (Mt. 5:12).[197] This promise is confirmation that the Father ultimately has power over evil and persecution will cease in the eschatological future (see Isa. 61:10-11).

Matthew 5:37

In Mt. 5:33-37, Jesus commands, "Let your word be 'Yes, Yes' or 'No, No'; anything more than this comes from the evil one."[198] Making vows beyond these simple answers are ensuring falsehoods and disciples must guard against dishonesty. Jesus notes that the source of these falsehood is the evil one (ἐκ τοῦ πονηροῦ).[199] Evil is frequently associated with falsehood in the Jewish parallels and represents that which is at odds

---

[196] See also Mt. 10:22 where Jesus makes it clear that persecution will often be on his account.
[197] Matthew 5:10-12 is reminiscent of the third petition as well. God's will on earth is accomplished when his disciples rejoice in the face of evil.
[198] We will explore this passage in more depth in the Name section. Matthew 5:37 is without a Lukan parallel.
[199] This phrasing is found in Mt. 12:34-35, in which ὁ πονηρὸς is frequently cited. In each of these cases, the reference is to "evil persons."

with the Father (see PsSol. 12:1; Ps. 119:2). The wording in Mt. 5:37 is the same as 6:13 but employs the preposition ἐκ (see Jn 17:15). The reference may very well point to the source of falsehood, or father of lies, the devil, and provide the closest lexical parallel to the seventh petition in the Sermon. This explicit contrast shows the divide between the Father and the evil one, evidencing thematic coherence.

Matthew 5:39

In the next section of teaching on the Mosaic law (Mt. 5:38-42), Jesus again refers to evil. Following the reiteration of the *lex talionis* (Mt. 5:38), Jesus urges his disciples to avoid retaliation. He commands, "But I say to you, 'Do not resist an evildoer. But if anyone strikes you on the right cheek, turn the other also.'" The source of insults and physical harm is an "evildoer" (τῷ πονηρῷ). Even if the assault is from an "evil" person or generic evil, Jesus teaches that a disciple must not resist. The translation of "evil" is difficult in v. 39. The articular reference (τῷ πονηρῷ) suggests a specific person, but clearly it does not refer to the evil one, that is, Satan.[200] The reference may refer to a generic "evildoer" but could be a play on words with the *lex talionis*. As Jesus has instructed to avoid an eye for an eye and a tooth for a tooth, so evil cannot be returned to an evil person. The context (Mt. 5:38-42) models the theme of God's power over evil. The children of the Father (see Mt. 5:45) can resist retaliation because the battle has already been won. Justice is in the hands of the Father.[201] The prayers of deliverance from evil would parallel the affirmation of God's power over the insults and physical harm of an evildoer in these situations.

Matthew 5:45

Matthew 5:45 is found in the context of Jesus's teaching on how to love enemies.[202] The reference to evil is found in Jesus's metaphor concerning farming. Jesus teaches that the sun rises on both the evil and good. Here, he is instructing his followers to love both neighbors and enemies in the same way that God is sovereign over both good and evil, that is, "like Father, like son." As Hagner notes, "To love one's enemies is, then, to treat them as God treats those who have rebelled against him. Thus, the children, the disciples, should imitate their heavenly Father."[203] The reference to evil refers to enemies (Mt. 5:44 [τοὺς ἐχθροὺς]),[204] those who persecute (Mt. 5:44 [τῶν διωκόντων ὑμᾶς]), and the unrighteous (Mt. 5:45 [ἀδίκους]). Connecting these concepts is reminiscent of Pss. 16:13, 42:1, and 119:2. In addition to the lexical parallels, Mt. 5:45

---

[200] Hagner, *Matthew 1–13*, 130.
[201] See also Rom. 12:9, 21; 2 Cor. 11:20; and 1 Thess. 5:15.
[202] The text states, "so that you may be children of your Father in heaven; for he makes his sun rise on the evil and on the good, and sends rain on the righteous and on the unrighteous."
[203] Hagner, *Matthew 1–13*, 134.
[204] Luke refers to "enemies," but he does not mention evil. Instead, Luke equates the "enemies" with "sinners." "Sinners" are referred to four times in the passage (Lk. 6:27-28, 32-35) and appears to be a central theme in Luke 6. Matthew only refers to "sinners" on five occasions (Mt. 9:10, 11, 13; 11:19; 26:45). Except for Mt. 26:45, "sinners" have a positive connotation in Matthew, as the Matthean

shares thematic parallels with the seventh petition. As mentioned above, Mt. 5:45 affirms God's sovereignty over evil. In v. 45, the Father causes the sun to rise over all of creation and he is above all peoples of the earth, whether righteous or evil.

Additional parallels in this verse and the Lord's Prayer include allusions to prayer (v. 44) and the repetition of the invocation's wording (v. 45). Those who oppose evil are considered children of the Father. They are also expected to pray for those who are evil. The Lord's Prayer offers the perfect petition, "rescue us" from this evil and, in this case, the evil of retaliation and resistance to offer love.

Matthew 6:23

Matthew 6:22-23 refers to the belief that the eye was the window to the soul ("The eye is the lamp of the body. So, if your eye is healthy, your whole body will be full of light; but if your eye is unhealthy (πονηρὸς), your whole body will be full of darkness. If then the light in you is darkness, how great is the darkness!"). If the eye is evil, then the body, of which it is a part, is also evil. *BDAG* understands the reference to "evil" as "sick, in poor condition (in a physical sense)."[205] The context suggests an alternate meaning to that which *BDAG* suggests. The contrasting metaphor in v. 22 describes the body as one of "light." While the body can be sick, "light" is never used to describe health. The metaphor in v. 22 describes the healthy eye as ἁπλοῦς. As Gundry points out, the reference is to a singular view of sight.[206] The contrasting metaphor of the "evil eye" would therefore refer to duplicity of "sight" and not to being "sick." This interpretation is confirmed when read in light of Mt. 20:15. Matthew 20:15 describes an "evil eye" as one that is greedy. Considering Mt. 6:19-21 and v. 24 as context, Matthew appears to suggest that the "evil eye" is seeking treasures on earth instead of heavenly treasure, thus implying its duplicitous desires. Thematically, the reference to the "evil eye" parallels the seventh petition in its emphasis on those things that separate a disciple from the Father. Greed takes root in the accumulation of earthly treasure, treasures that are described as "darkness" (Mt. 6:23) and ultimately rust and decay. A similar message is found in 1 Jn 1:5, which seems to reference the teaching of Jesus: "This is the message we have heard from him and proclaim to you, that God is light and in him there is no darkness at all." The answer to duplicitous "sight" is found in the following passage (Mt. 6:25-34). Jesus commends his disciples to "strive first for the kingdom of God and his righteousness" (Mt. 6:33).

Matthew 7:11

As we have argued above and will argue in other sections, Mt. 7:7-11 closely parallels the Lord's Prayer in multiple ways. These textual connections include the lexical

---

Jesus chooses to fellowship with sinners. Luke, on the other hand, refers to "sinners" on eighteen occasions (Lk. 5:8, 30, 32; 6:32, 33, 34 [2x]; 7:34, 37, 39; 13:2; 15:1, 2, 7, 10; 18:13; 19:7; and 24:7) and in varying senses.

[205] *BDAG*, 852. The NRSV quoted above also agrees with this translation.
[206] Gundry, *Matthew*, 113.

parallel to evil in Mt. 7:11. As Mt. 7:11 states, if evil people know how to give good gifts to their children, how much more will the Father give to those that love him? In this verse, "evil" is being used as a contrast to the goodness of God. In previous examples, references to "evil" have been to things that are blatantly against the Father, but here the disciples are being called "evil." Gundry helpfully explains, "Here πονηροί modifies the disciples *considered as human beings*."[207] This aspect of the disciples refers to internal evil, that is, their sinful nature. As Allison helpfully points out, all human beings are sinners and struggle accordingly. He writes,

> Sinners persecute saints (5:10–12, 38–48). People kill (5:21), get angry (5:22–26), commit adultery (5:27), divorce their spouses to marry others (5:31), and take oaths because the lie is so prevalent (5:33). They use religion for their selfish glorification (6:1–18), occupy themselves with storing up earthly treasures (6:19–21), fail in generosity (6:22–23), serve mammon (6:25), foolishly worry about secondary matter (6:25–34), and pass judgment on others (7:1–5).[208]

Matthew 7:11 shares the seventh petition's reference to "evil." These evils ultimately separate children from the Father's good gifts.

Matthew 7:17-18

Matthew 7:17-18 falls in the middle section of Jesus's tripartite ending to the Sermon on the Mount (Mt. 7:13-14, 15-23, 24-27). In this section, Jesus refers to fruit that is "evil," in contrast to good fruit (see also Mt. 12:33-35). Jesus is using the metaphor to address the contrast between true and false prophets (Mt. 7:15-16). The text states, "Beware of false prophets, who come to you in sheep's clothing but inwardly are ravenous wolves. You will know them by their fruits. Are grapes gathered from thorns, or figs from thistles?" Although their outward appearance may be the same, the work of false prophets reveals their identity.[209] The false prophets are described as "ferocious wolves," whose work seeks to destroy true disciples (see also Zeph. 3:3, Isa. 65:25, Acts 20:29) and spread lies.[210] Thematically, Mt. 7:17-18 is reminiscent of the Jewish parallels to evil men who seek to separate people from God's truth (PsSol. 12:1; Pss. 16:3, 42:1, 119:2). Yet, Mt. 7:19 makes clear that judgment is guaranteed to those who lead people away from the Father. They are "cut down and thrown into the fire." The seventh petition parallels the desire to avoid the separation caused by this "bad/evil fruit."[211]

---

[207] Gundry, *Matthew*, 125. Emphasis his.
[208] Allison, *Sermon on the Mount*, 157.
[209] See Grundmann, *Matthäus*, 233, "Es gibt ein wurzelhaftes Gutsein des Menschen und ein wurzelhaftes Bösesein, das sich in seinen Äußerungen enthüllt."
[210] In each of these parallel passages, "wolves" are used symbolically to refer to the work of evil men causing death and destruction.
[211] Luke 6:43-45 parallels Mt. 7:15-20, although the parallels are loose. Luke does not develop the tree and fruit metaphor as extensively as Matthew. Matthew also puts more emphasis on actions (Mt. 7:20), while Luke focuses on the heart and speech (Lk. 6:45).

Matthew 7:23

Matthew 7:23 continues the teaching of 7:17-18 but without an explicit lexical parallel to the seventh petition. The previous metaphor of vv. 17-18, concerning "evil" fruit, continues into v. 23, "Then I will declare to them, 'I never knew you; go away from me, you workers of lawlessness.'" Despite their efforts to do things in the name of God, Jesus describes these people as "workers of lawlessness" (οἱ ἐργαζόμενοι τὴν ἀνομί αν).[212] The phrase is also used in Mt. 13:41, 23:28, and 24:12.[213] In each of these cases, the "workers of lawlessness" are synonymous with the deeds of false prophets and both are evil. In addition to this emphasis on evil, this verse and its context have several catchwords with the Lord's Prayer. These "workers of lawlessness" are not children of the Father in heaven and therefore will not enter the kingdom of heaven (Mt. 7:21).[214]

Evil Petition Conclusion

In the previous sections, we have analyzed the seventh petition. The seventh petition is defined by its distinctive phrasing and prominence within the Sermon on the Mount. Specifically, Matthew prefers ὁ πονηρὸς when addressing the antithesis of the Father in heaven, particularly in his distinctive references to the devil (Mt. 13:19, 38). In Matthew's Gospel, the devil is closely tied to varying forms of evil, creating lexical parallels between the seventh petition and passages throughout the Sermon on the Mount (contra Bornkamm and Kiley). These lexical parallels are strengthened with shared themes between the respective passages under investigation. Particularly, requests against evil show the contrast between the Father in heaven and the evil one, as well as affirm the power of God over evil. The lexical and thematic parallels signal Matthew's increased parallelism and "prayerful" reading strategy for the Sermon on the Mount. When read in this manner, the seventh (evil) petition prays to avoid slander (Mt. 5:11), falsehood (Mt. 5:37), retaliation (Mt. 5:39), hating your enemy (Mt. 5:45), duplicitous desires (Mt. 6:23, "evil eyes"), doubting God's good gifts (Mt. 7:11), bearing bad fruit (Mt. 7:17-18), and being a worker of lawlessness (Mt. 7:23).

Chapter Conclusion

This chapter has argued that Matthew's understanding of the added petitions is made clear by their parallels with the Sermon on the Mount. These parallels reaffirm the

---

[212] Noted by Kiley, "Lord's Prayer and Matthean Theology," 22.
[213] See also Ps. 38:9; PsSol. 12:1.
[214] Luke has an interesting parallel to this passage. The teaching in Mt. 7:15-23 is found in two separate places in Luke (6:43-45 and 13:25-27). In the Lukan parallel to Mt. 7:23 (Lk. 13:25-27), Luke combines the exclamation, "Go away from me, all you evildoers," with the teaching on the wide/narrow gate (see Mt. 7:13-14). The expression in Luke is a pronouncement of judgment on "evildoers," but more correctly "workers of unrighteousness" (ἐργάται ἀδικίας). Translations conflate these references without noting the nuances of both Mt. 7:23 and Lk. 13:27 (i.e., the NRSV translates both instances as "evildoers"). The Matthean reference to "workers of lawlessness" (οἱ ἐ ργαζόμενοι τὴν ἀνομίαν) retains the importance of law-keeping, a theme central to the Matthean Sermon, and may echo the will petition, both lexically and thematically.

structural centrality of the Lord's Prayer, as shown in Chapter 3. As we have argued throughout this chapter, Matthew shows preference for certain words and phrases, which in turn build continuity between the Lord's Prayer and the Sermon on the Mount. Specifically, the Father, will, and evil petitions feature Matthew's preferred vocabulary, as indicated by word statistics and Synoptic comparisons, and those words are prominent in the Sermon on the Mount compared to the rest of Matthew's Gospel. In conjunction with the preferential wording and prominence of each petition, we have analyzed each petition's meaning. By examining these petitions within Matthew's cultural milieu, a basis for thematic parallels with the Sermon on the Mount is established. By analyzing the functional, lexical, and thematic parallels between the Lord's Prayer and the Sermon on the Mount, it becomes evident that Matthew is shaping these texts so that they are read together. Matthew's purpose was, on the one hand, to provide an explanation of the requests in the Prayer via the Sermon on the Mount and, on the other hand, a prayer that by its very presence in the Sermon spoke of where the petitioner anticipated getting power to live out the Sermon.

To review, calling on "our Father in heaven" entails a commitment to Sermon living, for example, to prayer (Mt. 5:45; 6:6 [2x], 8, 14, 15, 26, 32; 7:11), good works and righteousness (Mt. 5:16, 48; 6:1, 4, 18 [2x]; 7:21), and being part of the family of God (Mt. 5:9, 21-26). The third (will) petition, among other things, is asking the Father to help us to embody the *macarisms* (Mt. 5:3-12), be salt and light (Mt. 5:13-16), live according to God's laws (Mt. 5:17-20), speak truthfully (Mt. 5:33-37), love enemies and emulate the perfection of the Father (Mt. 5:45, 48), practice righteousness by storing up heavenly treasure (Mt. 6:1, 19-21, 22-24), seek the kingdom among earthly desires (Mt. 6:25-33 [esp. v. 33]), do good to others (Mt. 7:12), and rightfully confess "Lord, Lord" (Mt. 7:21). The seventh (evil) petition prays to avoid slander (Mt. 5:11), falsehood (Mt. 5:37), retaliation (Mt. 5:39), hating your enemy (Mt. 5:45), duplicitous desires (Mt. 6:23, "evil eyes"), doubting God's good gifts (Mt. 7:11), bearing bad fruit (Mt. 7:17-18), and being a worker of lawlessness (Mt. 7:23).

5

Matthew's "Slightly" Different Petitions

An Examination of the Kingdom, Bread, and Forgiveness Petitions

In Chapter 4, we began with an examination of the invocation, will, and evil petitions and their respective parallels to the Sermon on the Mount. These petitions have the highest probability of being Matthean and evidence some of the strongest parallels between the Lord's Prayer and the Sermon on the Mount. These parallels consist of functional, lexical, and thematic textual connections. In addition to these parallels, the wording of each petition is featured prominently in Matthew 5–7. In this chapter, we will examine the next set of petitions within Matthew's version of the Lord's Prayer. These petitions are closely related to the Lukan version but have slight differences.

Matthew 6:9b–13	Luke 11:2–4
⁹Πάτερ ἡμῶν ὁ ἐν τοῖς οὐρανοῖς ἁγιασθήτω τὸ ὄνομά σου,	²Πάτερ, ἁγιασθήτω τὸ ὄνομά σου
¹⁰**ἐλθέτω ἡ βασιλεία σου,** γενηθήτω τὸ θέλημά σου, ὡς ἐν οὐρανῷ καὶ ἐπὶ γῆς	**ἐλθέτω ἡ βασιλεία σου**
¹¹τὸν ἄρτον ἡμῶν τὸν ἐπιούσιον δὸς ἡμῖν σήμερον	³τὸν ἄρτον ἡμῶν τὸν ἐπιούσιον δίδου ἡμῖν τὸ καθ' ἡμέραν
¹²καὶ ἄφες ἡμῖν τὰ ὀφειλήματα ἡμῶν, ὡς καὶ ἡμεῖς ἀφήκαμεν τοῖς ὀφειλέταις ἡμῶν	⁴καὶ ἄφες ἡμῖν τὰς ἁμαρτίας ἡμῶν, καὶ γὰρ αὐτοὶ ἀφίομεν παντὶ ὀφείλοντι ἡμῖν
¹³καὶ μὴ εἰσενέγκῃς ἡμᾶς εἰς πειρασμόν, ἀλλὰ ῥῦσαι ἡμᾶς ἀπὸ τοῦ πονηροῦ.	καὶ μὴ εἰσενέγκῃς ἡμᾶς εἰς πειρασμόν.

The differences in the bread and forgiveness petitions are more obvious as they have different wording. The kingdom petition, on the other hand, has the same wording as the Lukan parallel but differentiates itself because of its close relationship to the will petition. This juxtaposition with the will petition influences the meaning of the kingdom petition. The kingdom petition also displays the extensive lexical parallels present in the invocation, will, and evil petitions. To reiterate, it is likely that Matthew noted similarities, as with the invocation/will/evil petitions, between the kingdom/bread/forgiveness petitions and Sermon from the traditions of the Sermon he received, leading him to make connections between the two texts in his Gospel and to bring them together. Matthew then edited parts of both the Sermon and the Prayer with a desire to increase the parallelism between the two texts.

Matthew's purpose was, on the one hand, to provide an answer to the requests in the Prayer via the Sermon on the Mount and, on the other hand, a prayer which by its very presence in the Sermon spoke of where the petitioner anticipated getting power to live out the Sermon's prescribed lifestyle.

In arguing this thesis, we will deal with each petition in the order of its appearance. As in the previous chapter, we will similarly order the analysis of each petition.[1] We will first attempt to examine the distinctives of each petition in comparison to Luke's version of the Lord's Prayer.[2] A comparison with Luke is not necessarily indicative of distinctiveness, yet it provides a helpful starting point for noting differences in the Matthean version. If the wording is prominent in Matthew's Gospel or has unique characteristics found only in Matthew's Gospel, then the wording is arguably Matthean. These word distinctives create a basis for establishing lexical parallels with the Sermon on the Mount, which will be explored in more depth in the third section.

In the second section, we will attempt to define each petition and discover its meaning. We will examine Matthew's cultural milieu for parallels and ideas associated with the wording and phrases in question. Some petitions have a long history in Jewish thought, while others are primarily defined by their presence in Matthew's Gospel. The purpose of this section is to establish a basis for identifying thematic parallels between each petition and the Sermon on the Mount.

In the third section, the work of sections one and two are brought together. We will examine the Sermon references that have lexical and thematic parallels with the petition under examination. We will begin with lexical parallels and then reinforce these initial textual connections by illustrating thematic parallels. In the cases where it is applicable, we will additionally argue for looser parallels (i.e., echoes) to the petition under investigation.

Finally, after examining the textual connections between the kingdom, bread, and forgiveness petition with the Sermon on the Mount, we will suggest what occurs when the Lord's Prayer is acknowledged as the centerpiece of the Sermon on the Mount.

---

[1] One will immediately notice that the kingdom petition is missing a "distinctives" section. The reason for this omission is explained below.
[2] To review, we will define distinctives by the following criteria: dissonance, repetition, prominence, consistency, and internal structuring. For a fuller explanation of "distinctiveness," see Chapter 2 on methodology.

Second Petition: "Your Kingdom Come"

Although the nature of the "kingdom" is one of the most hotly debated topics in Jesus studies, one point of which scholars agree is its centrality to Jesus's teaching.[3] It should be no surprise then that the prayer that Jesus taught would have a request concerning the kingdom. In the prayer, Jesus instructs his disciples to pray that the kingdom would come. The kingdom is "of you" (σου), that is, of "the Father in heaven." The kingdom petition is followed by the request that God's will be done, "on earth, as in heaven." In the following sections, we will examine the kingdom petition by exploring these key points. We will first consider the wording of the petition before examining its meaning within Matthew's cultural milieu. These sections will establish a basis for demonstrating lexical and thematic parallels with the Sermon on the Mount, which we will examine in the last section.

Wording of "Your Kingdom Come"

In previous chapters, and in those sections and chapters that follow, we have begun our study of each petition by noting its distinctive features. Unlike the previous petitions, the request for the coming of God's kingdom is not distinctive by the aforementioned criteria. The petition is in verbatim agreement with both Lk. 11:2 and *Did.* 8:2 and refers to a topic (i.e., the kingdom) addressed throughout the Synoptic Gospels. Perhaps the only thing that might differentiate the kingdom petition from its extant parallels is its relationship with the will petition in Matthew's version of the Lord's Prayer. As we will argue in a subsequent section, the will petition suggests something about Matthew's understanding of the kingdom petition. Before considering the meaning of the second petition, it is worth noting the statistically "commanding" number of references to the kingdom and their distribution throughout Matthew's Gospel and the unusual description of the "kingdom" as "coming."[4]

Kingdom

The most popular reference in Matthew's Gospel to the kingdom is the "kingdom of heaven" (3:2; 4:17; 5:3, 10, 19 [2x], 20; 6:10; 7:21; 8:11; 10:7; 11:11, 12; 13:11, 24, 31, 33, 44, 45, 47, 52; 16:19; 18:1, 3, 4, 23; 19:12, 14, 23; 20:1; 22:2; 23:13; 25:1).[5] Other kingdom references include the singular reference to the kingdom (Mt. 13:19, 38), the good news of the "kingdom" (Mt. 4:23, 9:35, 24:14), the kingdom of darkness (Mt.

---

[3] Of course, this centrality is where the agreements end. For a helpful overview of the direction of kingdom studies, see Scot McKnight, *A New Vision for Israel: The Teachings of Jesus in National Context* (Grand Rapids: Eerdmans, 1999), 70–155.
[4] Dennis C. Duling, "Kingdom of God/Kingdom of Heaven," in *Anchor Bible Dictionary*, vol. 4, ed. D. N. Freedman (New York: Doubleday, 1992), 57, notes the "commanding" emphasis in Matthew's Gospel in comparison with the other Synoptics.
[5] For an overview of the kingdom of heaven, see Jacob Neusner, "The Kingdom of Heaven in Kindred Systems, Judaic and Christian," *BBR* 15.2 (2005): 279–305; and Margaret Pamment, "The Kingdom of Heaven According to the First Gospel," *NTS* 27 (1981): 211–32.

8:12), the kingdom "of God" (Mt. 12:28; 19:24; 21:31, 43),[6] the kingdom "of the Son of Man" (Mt. 13:41, 16:28),[7] Jesus's kingdom (Mt. 20:21), Satan's kingdom (Mt. 12:26), and kingdoms of the earthly world (Mt. 4:8, 12:25, 24:7 [2x]). Matthew even has references to the Father's kingdom (Mt. 6:10, 33; 13:43; 25:34; 26:29) (Table 5.1).[8]

As the table illustrates, Matthew prefers to call the kingdom one "of heaven" and heavily discusses the "kingdom" in his discourses (31 of 55). Interestingly, Mark and Luke do not use the phrase "kingdom of heaven."[9] This accumulation of references, particularly in the discourses, signals Matthew's redaction and desire for these texts to be read together. In this regard, the second petition and Sermon passages illustrate Matthew's retention of parallel material.

The Kingdom "Coming"

Although the kingdom is quite common throughout Jesus's teaching, the juxtaposition of the "kingdom" with "coming" (ἐλθέτω) is not as common. Although we will explore the meaning of this phrase below, it is notable how unusual this phrase is in parallel literature. Besides the second petition in Lk. 11:2, the only closely worded parallels to the kingdom "coming" are found in Mk 11:10 (εὐλογημένη ἡ ἐρχομένη [participle, present, middle, nominative] βασιλεία τοῦ πατρὸς ἡμῶν Δαυίδ· ὡσαννὰ ἐν τοῖς ὑψίστοις) and Lk. 22:18 (…ἡ βασιλεία τοῦ θεοῦ ἔλθῃ) and 23:42 (Ἰησοῦ, μνήσθητί μου ὅταν ἔλθῃς εἰς τὴν βασιλείαν σου).[10]

The only reference to the kingdom "coming" in the Old Testament is found in Mic. 4:8 LXX.[11] The verse states, "And you, O tower of the flock, hill of daughter Zion, to you it shall come, the former dominion (ἡ πρώτη βασιλεία) shall come (εἰσέρχομαι), the sovereignty of daughter Jerusalem." We will argue below that this lexical parallel

---

[6] Robert Foster, "Why on Earth Use 'Kingdom of Heaven'?: Matthew's Terminology Revisited," *NTS* 48.4: 494–5, draws attention to the fact that "kingdom of God" in Matthew is always used in the context of disputes, garnishing a negative connotation. It is typically being rejected by an individual.

[7] These references are particularly important to the current argument because of the uses of the Danielic phrase "Son of Man." We will argue that Daniel's understanding of the kingdom is influential in Matthew's understanding of the term.

[8] Note that Mt. 6:10 is placed in both the "kingdom of heaven" and the "Father's kingdom" categories.

[9] The only closely related passage in which kingdom and heaven are brought together outside of Matthew is Lk. 19:38. Otherwise, Mark refers to the kingdom in two ways, "of God" (1:15; 4:11, 26, 30; 9:1, 47; 10:14, 15, 23, 24, 25; 12:34; 14:25; 15:43) and singular instances (3:24 [2x], 6:23 [of Herod], 11:10 ["coming"], 13:8 [2x]). Luke has a larger variety of kingdom references. They include the kingdom of God (4:43; 6:20; 7:28; 8:1, 10; 9:2, 11, 27, 60, 62; 10:9, 11; 11:20; 13:18, 20, 28, 29; 14:15; 16:16; 17:20 [2x], 21; 18:16, 17, 24, 25, 29; 19:11; 21:31; 22:16, 18; 23:51), singular references to the kingdom (1:33; 11:17; 12:31, 32; 21:10 [2x]; 22:29, 30; 23:42), the kingdom of the Father (11:2), the kingdom of the world (4:5), and the kingdom of Satan (11:18). Of Luke's references, five of the references parallel Matthew's Sermon on the Mount including the line of the Lord's Prayer (6:20; 11:2; 12:31, 32; 21:31).

[10] Luke 23:42 is a less likely parallel as it describes Jesus entering the kingdom after his crucifixion. In this case, Jesus is "going," instead of "coming" as the second petition states. Kiley, "The Lord's Prayer and Matthean Theology," 18, has pointed to three potential echoes in Matthew itself. These instances include 9:28, 13:38, and 17:25. In these passages, Jesus *comes* into a house. Immediately afterward, discussions of the kingdom occur. As Kiley notes concerning the kingdom, "In chapter 10, the focus is on its [the kingdom's] healing; in chapter 13, on its [the kingdom's] mystery; in chapter 18, on its [the kingdom's] exaltation of the child/little ones."

[11] This lexical parallel was helpfully pointed out by Pitre "Lord's Prayer and the New Exodus," 81.

Table 5.1 "Kingdom" in Matthew's Gospel

Chapters/Words (# of uses in Matthew)	1–4	5–7	8–9	10	11–12	13	14–17	18	19–22	23–25	26–28
Kingdom of heaven (33)	2	7	1	1	2	8	1	4	5	2	0
Kingdom (3)	0	1	0	0	0	2	0	0	0	0	0
Kingdom of God (4)	0	0	0	0	1	0	0	0	3	0	0
Kingdom of the Father (5)	0	2	0	0	0	1	0	0	0	1	1
Good news of the kingdom (3)	1	0	1	0	0	0	0	0	0	1	0
Kingdom of Son of Man (2)	0	0	0	0	0	1	1	0	0	0	0
Jesus's kingdom (1)	0	0	0	0	0	0	0	0	1	0	0
Satan's kingdom (1)	0	0	0	0	1	0	0	0	0	0	0
"Kingdom" of the earthly world (4)	1	0	0	0	1	0	0	0	0	2	0
Kingdom of darkness (1)	0	0	1	0	0	0	0	0	0	0	0
Totals (57)	4	8[a]	3	1	5	12	2	4	9	6	1

[a] In the Lord's Prayer, the "kingdom" is a singular reference (Mt. 6:10), yet implicitly (1) of the Father [see Mt. 6:9b] and (2) of heaven ["on earth, as in heaven"].

warrants an examination of the message of Micah 4.[12] In the broader context, Micah describes a "coming" kingdom given to the lame and afflicted, and dispersed (v. 6), in which the group is rescued from its enemies.[13] We will expand on this parallel in the following section as well as examining other references concerning the "coming" of Yahweh and the Day of the Lord.

The Meaning of "Your Kingdom Come"

This section will explore the meaning of the kingdom petition. The kingdom is a prominent topic not only in Matthew's writings but also throughout Old Testament and Second Temple literature.[14] We will not attempt to cover every aspect of the kingdom but rather those aspects that prove to be thematically significant within the Sermon on the Mount.[15] As Norman Perrin notes, the kingdom can "have a set of meanings that

---

[12] A similar argument is made in Pitre, "Lord's Prayer and the New Exodus," 81–7.
[13] The wording of Micah 4 has several thematic connections to the Lord's Prayer. Both passages describe a "coming kingdom" (Mic. 4:8), rescue from evil/enemies (Mic. 4:10), and profaning God's name (Mic. 4:11).
[14] Contra Marcus J. Borg, *Jesus in Contemporary Scholarship* (Valley Forge: Trinity International, 1994), 48–68.
[15] This statement is not intended to imply that we will avoid evidence if it disagrees with the main thesis. A full exploration of the kingdom is beyond the scope of the present work. For a fuller account, see G. R. Beasley-Murray, *Jesus and the Kingdom of God* (Grand Rapids: Eerdmans, 1986); Dunn, *Jesus*

can neither be exhausted nor adequately expressed by any one referent."[16] Establishing the meaning of the second petition is important for examining thematic parallels with passages in the Sermon on the Mount. From our study, we conclude that for Matthew, "your kingdom come" is primarily a future-oriented prayer asking for God to bring his rule and kingdom into the world, but it is also a prayer related to the present and to Christian living expressing a longing and crying out for kingdom-shaped living, such as the Sermon on the Mount portrays. To explain this conclusion, we will examine the good news of the kingdom, the kingdom which will come and is here, the contrasting nature of the kingdom, and the ethics of the kingdom.

The Good News of the Coming Kingdom

It is indisputable that the kingdom is a commanding theme in Matthew's Gospel and particularly in the Sermon on the Mount. Leading up to the Sermon on the Mount, Jesus announces the kingdom as inaugurated in his own presence: "Repent, for the kingdom of heaven has come near" (Mt. 4:17).[17] Also, the framing device around the Sermon on the Mount (i.e., Mt. 4:23, 9:35; see also 24:14) explains that the kingdom is one of "good news," that is, the gospel. To understand these references to the kingdom, one should look no further than the Old Testament. Matthew echoes this Jewish story of God's rule and promise of eschatological fulfilment throughout his Gospel. While numerous texts illustrate this connection, we will focus on Isa. 52:7, Zech. 14:9, and the already mentioned Mic. 4:8.

The first text that proves useful for understanding the kingdom in Matthew's Gospel is Isa. 52:7 ("How beautiful upon the mountains are the feet of the messenger who announces peace, who brings good news, who announces salvation, who says to Zion, 'Your God reigns'"). This passage, like Mt. 4:23 and 9:35 (i.e., the ellipsis around the Sermon and chs 8–9), lexically parallels the kingdom as "good news" (εὐαγγέλιον in Matthew and its verbal form in Isaiah [LXX]).[18] As this verse makes clear, the coming of the kingdom is the coming of God's reign.[19] God's reign was an important part of Jewish conviction as they believed that the coming kingdom would not necessarily be a

---

Remembered, 383–487; N. T. Wright, *Jesus and the Victory of God*, COQG 2 (Minneapolis: Fortress, 1996), 198–474.

[16] Norman Perrin, *Rediscovering the Teachings of Jesus* (New York: Harper & Row, 1967), 47–8. Perrin uses the Lord's Prayer as one of his examples. See also Perrin, "Eschatology and Hermeneutics: Reflections on Method in the Interpretation of the New Testament," *JBL* 93 (1974): 10–11. Perrin's point is that the kingdom is not a true sign. A sign has a one-to-one correspondence to reality, but the kingdom has many different aspects and things to which it points. We do not intend to go as far as Perrin in affirming that the kingdom has no referent at all.

[17] This statement is, of course, preceded by John's prophetic message in 3:2. Scholars have debated the meaning of ἤγγικεν, but the perfect tense of the verb suggests that the presence of the kingdom is at least in some sense accomplished in Jesus's earthly arrival. The verb is also found in Mt. 26:46 in which "drawing near" clearly denotes something accomplished. In ch. 26, Jesus is referring to the work of Judas as his betrayer, an event that precedes the prayer in Gethsemane.

[18] See Mk 1:15.

[19] Michael F. Bird, *The Gospel of the Lord: How the Early Church Wrote the Story of Jesus* (Grand Rapids: Eerdmans, 2014), 15, states, "Jesus took up the Isaianic script about the good news of God's

spatial thing but rather God coming as king over his creation.[20] Additionally, God was to be king over his covenantal people.[21]

The second useful text for understanding the kingdom in the Gospels' account of Jesus's teaching, including Matthew's Gospel, is Zech. 14:9, which states, "And the Lord will become king over all the earth; on that day the Lord will be one and his name one." The Jewish hope was that their acknowledged reign of God from Zion would extend beyond the people of Israel. This fulfillment of prophecy would be the conquering of Israel's enemies and expansion of God's reign over all the world.[22] The second petition may be alluding to this expansion with the appending of the phrase, "on earth, as it is in heaven" (ὡς ἐν οὐρανῷ καὶ ἐπὶ γῆς). As God's reign is already present in all of heaven, so his reign will extend also to all the earth.

As stated above, the closest Old Testament lexical parallel to the second petition is Mic. 4:8 ("to you it shall come . . . the kingdom").[23] An examination of its broader context (Mic. 4:1-8) reveals several aspects of the coming kingdom:[24]

> In days to come the mountain of the Lord's house
> shall be established as the highest of the mountains,
> and shall be raised up above the hills.
> Peoples shall stream to it,
> and many nations shall come and say:
> "Come, let us go up to the mountain of the Lord,
> to the house of the God of Jacob;
> that he may teach us his ways
> and that we may walk in his paths."
> For out of Zion shall go forth instruction,
> and the word of the Lord from Jerusalem . . .
>
> In that day, says the Lord,
> I will assemble the lame
> and gather those who have been driven away,
> and those whom I have afflicted.
> The lame I will make the remnant,
> and those who were cast off, a strong nation;
> and the Lord will reign over them in Mount Zion

---

coming reign and declared that this reign was now becoming a reality in and through his work as the messianic herald of salvation."

[20] See also Pss. 44:4, 68:24, 146:10, 149:2; Isa. 41:21, 44:6; Zeph. 3:15. Jesus's unparalleled reference to the "Great King" in Mt. 5:35 may be a direct reference to this Jewish conviction. Dunn, *Jesus Remembered*, 544, fn.3. So also Duling, *Anchor Bible Dictionary*, 57.
[21] See Chapter 4 in which we argue that the invocation is similarly covenantal.
[22] See Isa. 24:21-23; Ezek. 20:33; and Zech. 14:16-17.
[23] Contra Meier, *Mentor, Message, and Miracles*, 362, fn.39.
[24] Dunn, *Jesus Remembered*, 393. Dunn, on pp. 393–6, lists fourteen sorts of expectations that may have been evoked by Jesus's proclamation of the "coming kingdom." Pitre, "Lord's Prayer and the New Exodus," 81–4. As we will argue below, Daniel 2–7 is a key text for understanding the nature of the kingdom in Matthew's Gospel. Quarles, *Sermon on the Mount*, 45–7.

now and forevermore.
And you, O tower of the flock, hill of daughter Zion,
to you it shall come, the former dominion shall come,
the sovereignty of daughter Jerusalem.

Micah links the coming of the kingdom to the "latter days," God's universal rule, the ingathering of the nations to Zion, the implementation of the temple, and the healing of those who are afflicted (see Lk. 4:18-19).[25] Those who return to Zion are said to worship the God of Jacob, walk in his "paths," and receive God's word. In this regard, Pitre rightly notes, the kingdom "coming" is not simply an eschatological event but also a *liturgical* and *ecclesial* event.[26] Those who assemble will worship the Lord and walk in his ways. In the latter days, the king will gather the nations and separate those who have walked according to his instruction and those who have not (see Mt. 7:21-23). The *Exodus* imagery within this chapter parallels the image of Jesus as the new Moses in Matthew 1-4. In the Sermon on the Mount, Jesus assumes the role of "the prophet greater than Moses" in giving the law (see esp. Mt. 5:21-48).

The Kingdom That Will Come and Is Here

The Lord's Prayer looks both to the eschatological future and present. Jeffrey B. Gibson's most recent book on the Lord's Prayer has challenged the eschatological future reading of the kingdom petition.[27] He has argued that the kingdom petition does not refer to the future coming of God's reign, but, rather, the petition implores God "for divine aid for the obedience that renders one worthy of [the kingdom], and against apostasy."[28] Gibson presents three arguments against the future aspect of the second petition followed by four arguments for an entirely "present" interpretation of the petition.[29] First, Gibson denies any relationship between the Lord's Prayer and the *Kaddish*.[30] Further, he argues that if one could positively establish a connection, the *Kaddish* is not a future-oriented prayer.[31] Second, the association of the "kingdom" with Old Testament parallels commits the "token-word fallacy." This fallacy asserts that the interpreter assumes words are uniform and invariable. Gibson appeals here to

---

[25] See also Isa. 29:18; 35:5-6.
[26] Pitre, "Lord's Prayer and the New Exodus," 83.
[27] Gibson, *Disciples' Prayer*; "Matthew 6:9-13//Luke 11:2-4: An Eschatological Prayer?" *BTB* 31 (2001): 96-105. See also John Dominic Crossan, *The Greatest Prayer: Rediscovering the Revolutionary Message of the Lord's Prayer* (New York: HarperCollins, 2010), 73-95; Douglas E. Oakman, "The Lord's Prayer in Social Perspective," in *Jesus, Debt, and the Lord's Prayer: First-Century Debt and Jesus' Intentions* (Eugene: Cascade, 2014), 42-91.
[28] Gibson, *Disciples' Prayer*, 113.
[29] Gibson, *Disciples' Prayer*, 109, presents a minor argument concerning the aorist tense in the second petition. He argues that the aorist imperative in the request does not refer to a "once-only" event but, rather, that something should happen in a specific situation. In other words, the request does not look forward to a climactic event in the future. Gibson's argument does not take into account that the aorist tense is the normal usage in Hebrew prayers translated into Greek. Therefore, the tense cannot be pressed too far in terms of meaning as it is consistently used throughout the Lord's Prayer as the standard verb form. Gerhardsson, "Matthean Version," 213.
[30] So also, David Baumgardt, "*Kaddish* and the Lord's Prayer," *JBQ* 19.3 (1991): 164-9.
[31] Gibson, *Disciples' Prayer*, 48-62, 106-9.

the wisdom of George Caird.[32] Caird states, "If the Synoptic Gospels are right to insist that Jesus spent much of his time explaining what *he* meant by the kingdom, would it not follow that he did not mean what everybody else meant by it?"[33] This rhetorical question leads to Gibson's next claim. Third, Gibson denies any Old Testament parallels to the second petition. To be a proper parallel, the quoted text would require a reference to God's reign, spoken to God (i.e., "You yourself reign over us"), or an indirect construction (i.e., "may your kingdom be manifested").[34]

Further, Gibson provides four arguments for an ethical reading of the second petition. First, Gibson argues that the wording of the petition closely resembles those Rabbinic texts (*B. Bat.* 10a and *Yoma* 86b) that seek God's aid to be "rendered worthy of the deliverance that was faithful Israel's inheritance."[35] These Rabbinic texts are focused solely on the present. Second, the "come" in the second petition refers to "the petitioner [to] be "turned from" disobedience and conformed to the person who is called upon to "come." Gibson appeals to the parallel text of Rev. 22:20c concerning this direction of "coming" ("The one who testifies to these things says, 'Surely I am coming soon.' Amen. *Come* (ἔρχου), *Lord Jesus!*").[36] Third, Gibson appeals to Brant Pitre's argument that the parallel of Mic. 4:8 is actually about a "kingdom" that is to come, which is a people, and not a "reign" or a territory.[37] The petition, then, is about how people live in the here and now and not a coming reign. Fourth, the kingdom petition is heavily influenced by the will petition. Gibson argues that read together, the petitions could be paraphrased, "may we be made worthy of your reign by being conformed not to our own will but to yours."[38]

Gibson's claims are important for understanding at least one aspect of the kingdom's meaning. We agree that the kingdom petition does have an ethical component that is strengthened by appeals to the Rabbinic parallels and addition of the will petition, yet this does not have to negate the future. Although the phrase "kingdom come" is unusual in the Old Testament,[39] the concept of the kingdom is very common. As Davies and Allison state, "There are no parallels to the idea of the "coming kingdom," though the coming day of Yahweh was a common OT idea."[40] The coming day of Yahweh is described in 1 Chron. 16:33; Pss. 96:13, 98:9; Isa. 13:6, 26:21; Joel 2:1; Mic. 1:3; Zech. 14:1; and Mal. 4:5. First Chronicles 28:5-7 talks about the kingdom that will have Solomon on the throne of the kingdom. In v. 7, this kingdom is described as a forever kingdom. Other allusions to God's future kingdom include Isa. 24:23, 33:22, 52:7; Zeph. 3:15; and Zech. 14:9. In these texts, God is described as king over all creation. Daniel 7:13-14 describes a future kingdom with all peoples, nations, and languages gathered together under an eternal King.

---

[32] Gibson, *Disciples' Prayer*, 110.
[33] G. B. Caird, *New Testament Theology*, ed. L. D. Hurst (Oxford: Clarendon, 1995), 367. Emphasis his.
[34] Gibson, *Disciples' Prayer*, 111.
[35] Gibson, *Disciples' Prayer*, 111.
[36] Gibson, *Disciples' Prayer*, 112.
[37] Gibson, *Disciples' Prayer*, 112–3. Pitre, "Lord's Prayer and the New Exodus," 83.
[38] Gibson, *Disciples' Prayer*, 113.
[39] As noted above, Mic. 4:8 is the exception.
[40] Davies and Allison, *Matthew 1–7*, 604.

In the literature of the Second Temple, the understanding of the future kingdom is consistent with the Old Testament.[41] Consider the following: *Apoc. Bar.* 44:12: "there cometh . . . the new age" and *Tg. Mic.* 4:8: "to thee shall the kingly sovereignty come." Despite Gibson's hesitations, there are several reasons to see textual connections between the *Kaddish* and the Lord's Prayer.[42] As is often noted, the beginning lines read very similarly to the first three petitions of the Lord's Prayer.

> Exalted and *hallowed* be his great *name*
> > in the world which he created according to his *will*.
>
> May he let his *kingdom* rule
> > in your lifetime and in your days and in the lifetime
> > of the whole house of Israel, speedily and soon.
>
> And to this, say: Amen.

Additionally, the date of the *Kaddish* is not necessarily an argument against the parallels to the Lord's Prayer. The content of the *Kaddish* is symptomatic of common first-century Jewish thought. While the argument for direct dependence may be difficult to establish, the argument for a close connection between the prayers as representative of Jesus's time is not.

Before considering those parts of Gibson's argument with which we agree, it is important to note a major flaw in Gibson's methodology. On three occasions, Gibson picks a line from an author's work that makes his point but does not fairly represent the author's view. The first example is his appeal to John Nolland that the *Kaddish* does not look to the future.[43] While Nolland does dismiss the *Kaddish* as an example of prayers for the future, Nolland still concludes that the second petition is "clearly . . . eschatologically oriented." Gibson's appeal to Nolland's authority appears to suggest that Nolland agrees with an ethical interpretation of the second petition. Next, Gibson appeals to Brant Pitre that the second petition is more about the people of God living ethical lives than the future coming reign of God. Unfortunately, Gibson picks an example in Pitre's work that speaks of the people of God but ignores the context. Pitre's overarching argument is that the second petition evokes a typological eschatology that envisions the hope of a new *Exodus*. This interpretation squarely places Pitre's work among those who see the petition addressing the eschatological future. Lastly, Gibson compares the use of the verb in the second petition to Rev. 22:20c ("Come, Lord Jesus"). Revelation 22:20c is within a context that is highly eschatological, making the ethical interpretation highly unlikely. Verses 7, 10, and 12 refer to the coming of Jesus as an eschatological event connected to final judgment.[44]

When one turns to the New Testament, specifically the Gospels, the ethical aspect for which Gibson argues is present. The kingdom is present in the person of Jesus Christ.

---

[41] Rabbinic references include *b. Ber.* 40b. See also *As. Mos.* 10:1–3; *m. Cant. R.* 2:13; *Tg. Isa.* 31:4, 40:9; *Tg. Zech.* 14:9; *y. Ber.* 9, 12d. (30).
[42] See also the *Tefillah*, the sixth *berakh*.
[43] Gibson, *Disciples' Prayer*, 54–62. For quotation, see Nolland, *Gospel of Matthew*, 286–7.
[44] See Quarles, *Sermon on the Mount*, 198–9.

1. As we will argue below, the *macarisms* (Mt. 5:3-12) refer to the present and future reign of God over those who follow him.
2. Matthew 12:28 suggests that the work of Jesus was a sign of the present kingdom.[45] The text reads, "But if it is by the Spirit of God that I cast out demons, then the kingdom of God has come to you."[46]
3. Some references speak of the kingdom as a present reality to those who submit to Jesus in the here and now (Mt. 19:14, 21:31).[47]

In light of these Jewish and Matthean texts, we disagree with Gibson's view that the second petition only focuses on the present. The kingdom in Matthew's Gospel is to be identified with the coming day of Yahweh in the Old Testament. God will establish his reign upon earth, as it is already in heaven. While Matthew does describe the kingdom as inaugurated in the coming of Jesus Christ, particularly his words and deeds/miracles/exorcisms, his references still look to the eschatological consummation of time.[48] Therefore, a proper understanding of the second petition must account for both the eschatological future and the present.

The Kingdom of Contrast

As Wenham,[49] Viviano,[50] Pennington,[51] and Quarles[52] have noted, the kingdom in Matthew's Gospel is highly influenced by Daniel 2–7. Evidence for reading Matthew's kingdom references in light of Daniel include his numerous lexical parallels. Matthew refers specifically to the Danielic concepts of the Son of Man (Mt. 8:20; 12:8, 38-42; 13:37, 41-42; 16:27-28; 18:11; 20:17-19; 24:30; 25:31-32; 26:64) and Abomination of Desolation (Mt. 24:15-16). He also has at least thirty allusions to various passages throughout Daniel.[53] Reading Matthew's kingdom in light of Daniel's descriptions illustrates that the kingdom of God contrasts with the kingdoms of earth.[54] Because of

---

[45] See McKnight, *New Vision*, 7. George E. Ladd, *The Gospel of the Kingdom: Scriptural Studies in the Kingdom of God* (Grand Rapids: Eerdmans, 1959), 14, 18.
[46] Paul, who wrote under the influence of Jesus's teachings, also refers to the present kingdom. See Col. 1:13-14; Rom. 14:17; 1 Cor. 4:20; and Col. 4:11. See Wenham, *Paul*, 34–103.
[47] Beasley-Murray, *Jesus and the Kingdom*, 162–3.
[48] Additional clues for this mixed temporality of the second petition are found in the third petition. In this petition, the petitioner requests God's will to be "on earth, as in heaven" (Mt. 6:9-10). The assumption is that God's will is already accomplished in heaven, and therefore the request is that it will be similarly accomplished on earth. While the petitioner requests that they may participate in carrying out the "will" of God now, they also pray that God will finally accomplish his "will" in the future.
[49] David Wenham, "The Kingdom of God and Daniel," *ExpTim* 98.5 (1987): 132, observes, "The full significance of the Danielic background has not usually been recognized, and that in fact the book of Daniel may be the primary background to the Gospels' teaching about the Kingdom."
[50] B. T. Viviano, "The Kingdom of God in the Qumran Literature," in *The Kingdom of God in 20th Century Interpretation*, ed. Wendell L. Willis (Peabody: Hendrickson, 1987), 97–107.
[51] Pennington, *Heaven and Earth*, 268–278. Pennington, 271, notes, "This important section of Daniel provides the most extensive and elaborate development of the heaven, earth, and kingdom themes found anywhere in the Jewish literature."
[52] Quarles, *Sermon on the Mount*, 46, fn.34.
[53] Statistics taken from index of NA 28 Greek text.
[54] A thorough defense of reading the "kingdom of heaven" through the lens of Daniel is provided by Pennington, *Heaven and Earth*, 285–93.

its importance for understanding the "kingdom" in Matthew's Gospel, we will consider Daniel 2–7 in detail.

Daniel 2–7[55]

The prominent theme in Daniel 2–7 is the contrast between God's kingdom and its saints and the rulers and kingdoms of earth (Table 5.2). This theme is not unique to Daniel 2–7, but Daniel presents the most comprehensive treatment of the subject.[56] Following the lead of John J. Collins,[57] John Goldingay,[58] and Jonathan Pennington,[59] we will examine these chapters according to their chiastic structure, noting the contrasts between these kingdoms of heaven and earth.

Daniel 2 begins with Nebuchadnezzar's dream. The contrasts between heaven and earth emerge immediately in the narrative. Nebuchadnezzar demands that his wise men interpret a dream, yet they reply, "There is not a man on earth who can tell the king's matter" (Dan. 2:10). In contrast, Daniel is presented next in the narrative as a representative of the "God of heaven" (Dan. 2:18, 19, 28). Daniel interprets the dream and explains the significance of four kingdoms (Dan. 2:31-43). Each of these four kingdoms represent earthly superpowers. Amid these kingdoms is one more kingdom, a kingdom that "shall never be destroyed" (Dan. 2:44). Chapter 7 parallels the vision in ch. 2 but with slightly different apocalyptic images. Chapter 7 depicts four beasts, each with different heads of animals (Dan. 7:1-8). The fourth beast is depicted as one who will tower above the others because of his strength and great evil (Dan. 7:7-8). Later, he is described as "on earth" and devouring "the whole earth" (Dan. 7:23). This beast speaks pompously to the Most High and persecutes the saints (Dan. 7:25). In Daniel's visions, the beast is destroyed by the Ancient of Days (Dan. 7:9, 13, 22) and the Son of Man (Dan. 7:13), and an everlasting kingdom is established. In chs 2 and 7, the contrast between things of heaven and earth is clear. In both instances, the kingdom of heaven overtakes the kingdom of earth.

In chs 3 and 6, the themes of heaven and earth are not as developed. These chapters recount Nebuchadnezzar erecting a golden statue and the three Jewish children refusing to bow in worship (Dan. 3:1-18). Their punishment is the fiery furnace. The victor of the fiery furnace is the "God of Shadrach, Meshach, and Abednego" (Dan. 3:28). The flow of ch. 3 has Nebuchadnezzar as the "king of the earth" and the Most High God (Dan. 3:26) in a battle for allegiances. In ch. 6, Daniel is faced with a similar incident as Shadrach, Meshach, and Abednego. King Darius is coerced into establishing a decree that no one should pray to anyone except the king (Dan. 6:7-8). Daniel rejects the decree and is thrown in a lion's den (Dan. 6:10-18). Like Shadrach, Meshach, and

---

[55] For a discussion of Daniel 2–7 as a thematic and structural unit, see Pennington, *Heaven and Earth*, 270–1.

[56] Other texts that contrast the kingdom of God and the kingdom of heaven include: Isa. 14:19, 23:17, 37:16, Jer. 15:4, 29:18, 50:41. See especially Ps. 2 and the book of Judith.

[57] John J. Collins, *Daniel: A Commentary on the Book of Daniel*, Hermeneia (Minneapolis: Fortress, 1994), 35.

[58] John Goldingay, *Daniel*, WBC (Waco: Thomas Nelson, 1989), 270–1.

[59] Pennington, *Heaven and Earth*, 279–82.

Table 5.2 Daniel's Contrasts of "Kingdoms"

"Kingdoms of Earth"	"Kingdom of God"
Daniel 2 and 7	
Nebuchadnezzar's wise men (2:10)	"God of heaven" (2:18-19, 28)
Dream of the Four kingdoms (2:31-43)	Kingdom "shall never be destroyed"
Dream of the Four beasts (7:1-8)	(2:44)
"from the earth" (7:18)	Ancient of Days (7:9, 13, 22)
"devouring whole earth" (7:23)	Son of Man (7:13)
Speaks against the Most High and persecutes saints (7:25)	Everlasting Kingdom (7:14)
Dan. 3–4:3 and 6	
Nebuchadnezzar's statue (3:1-18)	Nebuchadnezzar's confession: "Blessed is
Nebuchadnezzar, "king to all the peoples, nations, and men of every language that live in all the earth" (4:1)	the God of Shadrach, Meshach, and Abednego" (3:28)
	Most High God, kingdom is everlasting (4:2-3)
Darius' decree (6:7-8)	Daniel's deliverance (6:19-24)
Lion's den (6:10-18)	Darius' confession: "For he is the living
"Conspirators, "all the presidents of the kingdom, the prefects and satraps, the counsellors, and the governors (6:7)	God, enduring forever. His kingdom shall never be destroyed and his dominion has no end" (6:26, see 4:1-3)
Daniel 4 and 5	
Dream of the Tree, which is visible to the ends of the earth (4:10-11)	Angel cuts down the tree (4:13-17)
Nebuchadnezzar becomes an animal (4:15-17, 25-27, 28-33)	Nebuchadnezzar's confession: "I, . . ., praise, exalt, and honour the King of heaven" (4:37)

Abednego, Daniel is saved by God (Dan. 6:22). The conspirators are described as "all the presidents of the kingdom, the prefects and satraps, the counsellors and the governors" (Dan. 6:7). After his decree is foiled, Darius extols the God of Daniel, "For he is the living God, enduring forever. His kingdom shall never be destroyed and his dominion has no end" (Dan. 6:26, see 4:1-3).[60] The narratives of chs 3 and 6 continue the contrasting visions of heaven and earth first depicted in Daniel 2 and 7.

Daniel's contrasts of the kingdoms of earth and kingdoms of heaven come to a climax in chs 4 and 5. In ch. 4, Daniel recounts Nebuchadnezzar's second dream and his interpretation. Nebuchadnezzar sees a tree growing in the center of the earth that is visible to the ends of the earth (Dan. 4:10-11). The tree is representative of the expanse of Nebuchadnezzar's earthly kingdom. Yet, the tree in the dream is cut down by an angelic figure (Dan. 4:13-17), and the "tree" becomes as an animal. This point of humiliation and defeat of his earthly kingdom is reemphasized throughout the dream narrative (Dan. 4:15-17), Daniel's interpretation (Dan. 4:25-27), and, finally, the actual event of Nebuchadnezzar becoming an animal of the field (Dan. 4:28-33). After Nebuchadnezzar's humiliation, he returns to his senses and praises the "king of heaven" (Dan. 4:37).

---

[60] Daniel 4:1-3 LXX is part of ch. 3 in the Masoretic text. Read in this manner, the closing notes for both chs 3 and 6 speak of the eternal kingdom.

The description of the kingdom in Daniel 2–7 not only reinforces our earlier observations concerning the future coming of God's reign, but also the teachings in Daniel 2–7 illustrate the contrasting nature of the kingdom of God with the kingdoms of earth. Throughout these chapters, kingdom, heaven, and earth are often mentioned. Matthew shares this vocabulary with Daniel, creating a probable background for Matthew's "kingdom" references.[61] Richard Bauckham helpfully summarizes, "Jesus was at pains to avoid the implication that God rules in the way that earthly kings rule. In fact, much of Jesus' teaching seems designed precisely to show how God's rule differs from earthly rule."[62] Daniel 2–7 clearly evidences Bauckham's point.

The Ethics of the Kingdom

As we have noted above, Matthew's understanding of the kingdom petition is influenced by the addition of the will petition ("Your will be done, on earth as it is in heaven"). Additionally, we have addressed the aspect of the eschatological future and the present in the kingdom petition. Particularly in Matthew's Gospel, following Jesus's words and deeds (i.e., the will being done) are required for membership in the kingdom of heaven. As Guelich notes, "The personal-ethical dimension of the Kingdom is seen in the confrontation between Jesus, his ministry, and the individual."[63] Outside of the Sermon on the Mount, those who identify with the kingdom of heaven are those who hear God's words and do them (see Mt. 12:50; 13:19, 22-23). In several passages, the metaphor of fruit is used to express obedience to Jesus's teaching (Mt. 12:33-37; 13:23; 21:43). The kingdom is also integrally related to righteousness (see Mt. 5:6, 6:33), and Matthew defines righteousness as the proper observance of God's laws.[64] Other passages in Matthew reveal an emphasis on care for the underprivileged, who are often depicted as children (Mt. 25:31-46; see also 18:6-14). In these instances, kingdom membership is closely wed to the completion of God's will on earth.

Conclusion

From our analysis, we conclude that for Matthew, your "kingdom come" is primarily a future-oriented prayer asking for God to bring his rule and kingdom into the world, but it is also a prayer related to the present and to Christian living expressing a longing and crying out for kingdom-shaped living, such as the Sermon on the Mount portrays. After clarifying the "kingdom" as the coming of God's reign on earth, we

---

[61] Pennington, *Heaven and Earth*, 285–93, argues that Daniel 2–7 is the probable origin of Matthew's heaven and earth language. Daniel's phrases "God of heaven + kingdom," "God of heaven," and "God of heaven in contrast with earthly kings" becomes Matthew's "kingdom of heaven," "Father in heaven," and "kingdom of heaven in contrast with earthly kingdoms," respectively.

[62] Richard Bauckham, "Kingdom and Church According to Jesus and Paul," *HBT* 18.1 (1996): 5.

[63] Guelich, *Sermon on the Mount*, 79.

[64] We have examined the relationship of righteousness and "God's will" in Chapter 4. Pennington, *Heaven and Earth*, 267, shows the continued emphasis on law-keeping and the kingdom in Rabbinic literature. The one who "takes upon himself the yoke of the kingdom of heaven" (*m. Ber.* 2:2) is obliging himself to love God and keep his commandments. Additionally, the one who ceases to cite the *Shema* daily would cast off "the yoke of the kingdom of heaven" (*m. Ber.* 2:5).

have considered the temporality, contrasting nature, and ethics of the kingdom. This analysis is important for identifying thematic parallels with the Sermon on the Mount. In conjunction with the findings of Section 1, we now turn to the textual connections between the Lord's Prayer and the Sermon on the Mount.

"Your Kingdom Come" in the Sermon on the Mount

As Betz notes, the "principal theological concept in the Sermon on the Mount is that of the 'kingdom of heaven.'"[65] We will argue that Betz is correct in his assertion. In this section, we will examine those instances in the Sermon that discuss the kingdom and argue that where the kingdom is referenced (i.e., lexical parallels), similar themes are paralleled. We will begin with those places that specifically refer to the "kingdom" (Mt. 5:3-10, 17-20; 6:33; 7:21-23), before considering a looser parallel (Mt. 7:13-14).

Matthew 5:3-10

The first instances of the kingdom of heaven are mentioned in Mt. 5:3 ("Blessed are the poor in spirit, for theirs is the kingdom of heaven") and 5:10 ("Blessed are those who are persecuted for righteousness' sake, for theirs is the kingdom of heaven").[66] These verses form an *inclusio* around the beginning section of the Sermon on the Mount (Mt. 5:3-10).[67] Matthew 5:3-10 pronounces the blessing of God on those whose identity reflects kingdom priorities.[68] Each phrase starts with μακάριοι followed by a participle or adjective. The second half of the isocolon is signaled by the ὅτι, followed by a promise. Matthew 5:3 and 5:10 pronounce flourishing to the "poor in spirit" and those who are "persecuted for "righteousness' sake" with the promise of the "kingdom of heaven." These references function as a lexical parallel with the second petition.[69]

> Blessed are the poor in spirit, for theirs is the *kingdom* of heaven
> (μακάριοι οἱ πτωχοὶ τῷ πνεύματι, ὅτι αὐτῶν ἐστιν ἡ βασιλεία τῶν οὐρανῶν)
> [Six *Macarisms*]
> Blessed are those who are persecuted for righteousness' sake, for theirs is the *kingdom* of heaven
> (μακάριοι οἱ δεδιωγμένοι ἕνεκεν δικαιοσύνης, ὅτι αὐτῶν ἐστιν ἡ βασιλεία τῶν οὐρανῶν)

In addition to the lexical parallel between the second petition and Mt. 5:3 and v. 10, both passages evidence thematic parallels. As we argued above, the second petition

---

[65] Hans Dieter Betz, "Cosmogony and Ethics in the Sermon on the Mount," in *Essays on the Sermon on the Mount* (Philadelphia: Fortress, 1985), 120.
[66] See Grundmann, *Matthäus*, 120, 132–5.
[67] As we have argued in Chapter 3 on structure, vv. 11-12 continue the introduction but have a slightly different form that creates continuity with vv. 13-16.
[68] It is unnecessary to discuss each of the *macarisms* in depth. For the present argument, it is enough to show how they function together and the characteristics common among them.
[69] The mention of righteousness also closely parallels the emphasis of kingdom and its close relationship with the will petition, as we have argued immediately above and in the previous chapter.

primarily relates to the future, but is also concerned with the present. The concern for the present is manifested in the keeping of God's laws and living a life that is in contrast with "earthly" living. The teaching in Mt. 5:3 and v. 10 evidences these themes in two ways. First, the structure of the *macarisms* parallels the temporality of the second petition. Each *macarism* implies *flourishing* for the present, with a *promise* for the future.[70] For example, those who are *presently* "poor in spirit" are promised the future kingdom of heaven.[71] Second, both passages describe the requirements of the kingdom. "Poor in spirit" refers to Isa. 61:1 ("oppressed, broken-hearted, captives") and 66:2 ("This is the one to whom I will look, to the humble and contrite in spirit"), in which flourishing is guaranteed to those who are oppressed and persecuted.[72] This emphasis on persecution likely explains the close parallelism with Mt. 5:10 and shared promise of the kingdom of heaven to those who are persecuted. In Mt. 5:10, the reason for persecution is for "righteousness' sake." In Matthew's Gospel, righteousness is closely associated with keeping God's laws and performing God's will.[73]

Matthew 5:17-20

The second instance of the kingdom is found in a cluster of references in Mt. 5:17-20.[74] The term is mentioned in three separate but parallel instances (Mt. 5:19 [2x], 20).

> Do not think that I have come to abolish the law or the prophets; I have come not to abolish but to fulfil. For truly I tell you, until heaven and earth pass away, not one letter, not one stroke of a letter, will pass from the law until all is accomplished. Therefore, whoever breaks one of the least of these commandments, and teaches others to do the same, will be called least in the *kingdom* of heaven; but whoever does them and teaches them will be called great in the *kingdom* of heaven. For I tell you, unless your *righteousness* exceeds that of the scribes and Pharisees, you will never enter the *kingdom* of heaven.

In this passage, Jesus is explaining his relationship to the teaching of the "law and prophets." He instructs his disciples that he has not come to destroy or abolish the teaching of the Mosaic law but rather to fulfil its teachings (Mt. 5:17-18). Matthew 5:19

---

[70] See France, *Gospel of Matthew*, 164.
[71] As Pennington, *Sermon and Human Flourishing*, 101, notes, "To frame the Beatitudes and to open the Sermon with references to God's heavenly reign is to use a megaphone to communicate that Jesus' ministry is looking forward to the eschaton."
[72] See Gundry, *Matthew*, 67–8. Most recently, Charles Quarles, "The Blessings of the New Moses: An Examination of the Theological Purpose of the Matthean Beatitudes," *JSHJ* 13.2/3 (2015): 302–27, has argued that the proper background for the *macarisms* is found in Deuteronomy 27–30. Even if Quarles is correct, his main point agrees with the thrust of the present argument.
[73] The parallels between righteousness and the will of God have been examined in Chapter 4. If one considers the source of persecution, then another possible thematic parallel emerges. While the text does not specify the source or identity of persecution, it is reasonable to assume that it is by those who are opposed to the kingdom of heaven. This implied contrast parallels the consistent division between the kingdom of God and kingdoms of earth.
[74] Matthew 5:17-20 functions as an introduction to the Mosaic law in Mt. 5:21-48. Therefore, this cluster of references to the "kingdom" are placed in a structurally pivotal location.

details the differing approaches to the law of Moses. Those who break the laws and teach others to do the same will not enter the kingdom of heaven, while those who obey the laws and teach others likewise will be great in the kingdom of heaven (Mt. 5:19). Verse 20 serves as a transitional verse uniting the law of Moses (Mt. 5:17-19) and the teachings of Jesus (Mt. 5:21-48). Jesus's commendation is to obey not only the law of Moses but also the righteousness that "exceeds that of the scribes and Pharisees" (Mt. 5:20, 21-48).[75]

The parallels between the second petition and Mt. 5:17-20 are threefold. First, as we have mentioned, both passages refer to the kingdom. This lexical parallel is the most obvious connection, but further lexical echoes are present among the contexts. The people mentioned in each context are frequently associated with one another in Matthew's Gospel. The Lord's Prayer is given as an alternative to the prayers of the "hypocrites" (see also Mt. 6:5-8). The righteousness commanded by Jesus in Mt. 5:17-20 is an affront to the scribes and Pharisees. It is quite likely that Jesus's reference to "hypocrites" and "scribes/Pharisees" are referencing the same group (see Mt. 23:1-12).[76] Second, the temporal aspects of Mt. 5:17-20 parallel the temporal aspect of the second petition. Both passages emphasize the present, while reminding the reader of the eschatological future. Third, the kingdom and righteousness are paralleled in Mt. 5:17-20 in much the same way that the Lord's Prayer enjoins the coming kingdom and the will of God. In Mt. 5:17-20, whoever keeps the commandments will enter the kingdom of heaven, and whoever does not keep the commandments (i.e., righteousness that does *not* "exceed that of the scribes and Pharisees") is barred from the kingdom of heaven (Mt. 5:20).

Matthew 6:33

Matthew 6:33 states, "Strive first for the *kingdom* of God and his *righteousness*, and all these things will be given to you as well." Jesus's teaching here concludes a section on worry and anxiety. Instead of fixating on earthly things, Jesus encourages his disciples to rightly align their priorities on things above (Mt. 6:25-34). Although the verse is short, it has significant textual connections with the second petition.

First, vv. 10 and 33 share lexical parallels. The "kingdom" (Mt. 6:10//6:33) and the heavenly Father (Mt. 6:9//6:32) are mentioned in both verses and their contexts. Second, both verses emphasize prayer. The second petition is found in a prayer, while v. 33 begins with the instruction to "strive" (ζητεῖτε), a word often used synonymously for prayer (see Mt. 7:7). Although the reference here is to our aims in life, the reference would certainly include prayers. Third, the kingdom and righteousness are

---

[75] Before examining the parallels between the second petition and this passage, it is important to note the Mattheanism throughout Mt. 5:17-20. The distinctive nature of this passage suggests Matthew's shaping and heightens the probability of intentional parallelism. Gundry, *Matthew*, 78–82, provides an extensive sampling of the distinctive words within this passage.

[76] Another, but less probable, parallel between the second petition and Mt. 5:17-20 is the "action" in both passages. As the kingdom is described as "coming" (ἐλθέτω) in Mt. 6:10, so Jesus is described as "coming" (ἦλθον) in Mt. 5:17. Both verbs are aorist active indicatives from ἔρχομαι. Examples of the coming of Jesus paralleling the kingdom's coming are found elsewhere in Mk. 1:15; and Lk. 4:43, 10:9, 11:20, and 17:21.

conceptually linked in both verses. Verse 33 commands the seeking of the "kingdom and righteousness." As we have argued above, Matthew's understanding of the second petition is made clear in part by the will petition. The will petition is synonymous with righteousness in Matthew's Gospel, creating a substantive thematic parallel. Fourth, both verses have implicit contexts of contrast. In Mt. 6:32, Jesus contrasts the "Gentiles" (ἔθνη) with those who follow the Father in heaven. The Gentiles worry about earthly things like food, drink, and clothing, while followers of the "Father in heaven" seek the "kingdom and righteousness" (Mt. 6:33). The second petition is part of a prayer that is given as an alternative to the meaningless prayers of the Gentiles (οἱ ἐθνικοί). The second petition prays for God's kingdom to come, while the Gentiles are content with their earthly kingdoms, receiving their earthly rewards (Mt. 6:5).

Matthew 7:21-23

Matthew 7:21-23 discusses the end of time. The teaching is part of Matthew's concluding section to the Sermon in which the eschatological judgment is in view (7:13-27). The explicit reference to the "kingdom of heaven" is found in v. 21: "Not everyone who says to me, 'Lord, Lord,' will enter the *kingdom* of heaven." Jesus is contrasting those who enter the kingdom of heaven and those who do not. The entry requirement for the kingdom is doing the will of the Father. On the other hand, some will prophesy, exorcise demons, and perform duties in God's name but will ultimately be declared "workers of lawlessness (οἱ ἐργαζόμενοι τὴν ἀνομίαν)."

Matthew 7:21-23 and the second petition share several textual connections. First, the passages and their contexts share lexical parallels. Both teachings refer to the kingdom (Mt. 6:10//7:21), the name (Mt. 6:9//7:22), the will of the Father (Mt. 6:10//7:21), the Father in heaven (Mt. 6:9//7:21), and evil (Mt. 6:13//7:23).[77]

> Matthew 7:21-23
> Not everyone who says to me, 'Lord, Lord,' will enter the *kingdom* of heaven, but only the one who does the *will* of my *Father in heaven*. On that day many will say to me, '*Lord, Lord*, did we not prophesy in your *name*, and cast out demons in your *name*, and do many deeds of power in your *name*?' Then I will declare to them, 'I never knew you; go away from me, you *evildoers*.

> Matthew 6:9b-13
> Our *Father in heaven*,
> Hallowed be Your *name*
> Your kingdom come.
> Your *will* be done, on earth as it is in heaven.

---

[77] The parallels are even more distinctive when the Lukan parallels are considered. Luke's parallel to Mt. 7:21-23 is found in Lk. 6:46 (Mt. 7:21) and Lk. 13:25-27 (Mt. 7:22-23). Luke 6:46 states, "Lord, Lord," but excludes the reference to the kingdom, will of the Father, and the Father in heaven. Luke 13:25-27 enjoins the teaching found in Mt. 7:22-23 with the teachings on the wide and narrow door (see Mt. 7:13-14). In this differing arrangement, Luke mentions the "kingdom of God" twice (13:28-29). Matthew parallels these kingdom references a chapter later and changes them to his preferred "kingdom of heaven" (8:11).

Give us this day our daily bread.
And forgive us our debts, as we also have forgiven our debtors.
And do not bring us to the time of trial,
But rescue us from the *evil one*.

Second, the temporal aspect is paralleled in both passages. As we argued above, the second petition is primarily focused on both the eschatological future and present. In Mt. 7:21-23, the future is firmly in mind as the scene is one of eschatological judgment. Yet, the verses allude to the disciples doing the will of God in the present (Mt. 7:21). The iterative stress in the participial phrase (ὁ ποιῶν τὸ θέλημα τοῦ πατρός μου) is the ongoing activity of kingdom ethics. Third, both passages present a context of contrast. The implied contrast in the second petition is explicit in Mt. 7:21-23. Jesus outlines those who will enter the kingdom of heaven and those who will not. The guarantee of heaven is for those who do the will of the Father in heaven (Mt. 7:21). Those who will not enter the kingdom of heaven attempt to do the will of the Father in heaven but are declared "workers of lawlessness."[78]

Matthew 7:13-14

The previous section discussed those passages in the Sermon on the Mount that displayed lexical and thematic parallels with the second petition. These parallels were evidenced by shared references to the "kingdom" and the shared themes of temporality, contrast, and ethical conduct. Mark Kiley has argued that another possible connection with the second petition is found in Mt. 7:13-14.[79] In this passage, Jesus employs the metaphors of wide and narrow gates to depict contrasting ways of life. Matthew 7:13-14 states, "Enter through the narrow gate; for the gate is wide and the road is easy that leads to destruction, and there are many who take it. For the gate is narrow and the road is hard that leads to life, and there are few who find it." Kiley argues that the broad and narrow gates of Mt. 7:13-14 is explained by the parable of the camel squeezing through the needle's eye (Mt. 19:24) and the rich man entering the kingdom of heaven (Mt. 19:16-30). The difficulty of the rich man and camel (Mt. 19:23, "πλούσιος δυσκόλως εἰσελεύσεται εἰς τὴν βασιλείαν τῶν οὐρανῶν") are thematically paralleled to the difficulty of entering the narrow gate (τεθλιμμένη ἡ ὁδὸς ἡ ἀπάγουσα εἰς τὴν ζωήν).[80] If these intratextual parallels explain Mt. 7:13-14, these verses function as a sayings commentary on the second petition.

Kiley's sensitivity to other passages in Matthew's Gospel to inform how we understand the kingdom petition and Sermon on the Mount is commendable. Unfortunately, Kiley misses some of the more direct thematic links already present in Mt. 7:13-14. While Mt. 7:13-14 does not mention the kingdom, it does present two thematic parallels with the second petition. First, the kingdom petition and Mt. 7:13-14 describe the future consummation of God's kingdom and the present. The metaphor

---

[78] For a discussion of "workers of lawlessness," see Chapter 4 on the seventh petition.
[79] Kiley, "Lord's Prayer and Matthean Theology," 17.
[80] Kiley, "Lord's Prayer and Matthean Theology," 17.

of the gate describes the eschatological judgment, but Matthew refers also to the "road" that leads to the gate. As Gundry notes, "We are to think not only of travelling a roadway *to* one or the other gate at the final judgment, but also of travelling a road and entering through a gate as independent figures, both of which stand for the present life of discipleship."[81] Gundry's insights evidence another textual connection. The kingdom petition and Mt. 7:13-14 contain contrasts, and those contrasts include ways of living (i.e., kingdom ethics versus earthly living). Ethics as defined by the kingdom of heaven is characterized by a way toward the narrow gate, while the way of destruction (i.e., earthly living) is through the wide gate.

Kingdom Petition Conclusion

In the previous sections, we have analyzed the kingdom petition. To accomplish this task, we have examined its wording and meaning. We have argued that the second petition is primarily a future-oriented request for God's rule, but it also a prayer related to the present, expressing a longing for kingdom-shaped living displayed in the Sermon on the Mount. We have examined the instances of the kingdom in the Sermon on the Mount and showed their textual parallels with the second petition. In so doing, we have argued that these texts should be read in light of one another. When read in this manner, praying "your kingdom come" entails embodying the *macarisms* (Mt. 5:3-10), fulfilling the law and prophets (Mt. 5:17-20), seeking the kingdom and righteousness (Mt. 6:33), and performing the will of God (Mt. 7:21-23). The petition may also imply a desire to avoid the easy way of life that leads to destruction (Mt. 7:13-14).

Fourth Petition: "Give Us This Day Our Daily Bread"

Perhaps Colin Hemer said it best when describing the fourth petition: "It is a sobering reflection that the origin and meaning of a word in a passage so familiar as the Lord's Prayer remain uncertain and debated."[82] Hemer is referring to the word ἐπιούσιος within the bread petition of the Lord's Prayer. The petition is a request for the simplest of foods yet contains a notoriously difficult word to translate.[83] The difficulty of this word has often overshadowed the significance of the entire petition, especially as it relates to the rest of the Lord's Prayer and its context, the Sermon on the Mount. In Chapter 3, we argued for a concentric structure for the Lord's Prayer, centering around the fourth petition as a hinge between petitions 1-3 and petitions 5-7. Building on this

---

[81] Gundry, *Matthew*, 127, also argues for the connection of Mt. 7:13-14 with 6:10-11, 13.
[82] Colin Hemer, "ἐπιούσιος," JSNT 22 (1984): 81.
[83] The lack of uses of ἐπιούσιος has been noted by prominent scholars such as Bruce Metzger, "How Many Times does 'epiousios' Occur Outside the Lord's Prayer?," *ET* 69 (1957): 52-4. Metzger alludes to one possible reference to the word in a now-lost manuscript. Metzger's mention of the possibility was evidence enough for *BDAG*, which states, "wenigstens in einem Fall nachgewiesen ('proven in at least one case')." M. Nijman and K. A. Worp, "'ΕΠΙΟΥΣΙΟΣ' In a Documentary Papyrus?," *NovT* 41 (1999): 231-4, have since debunked this possible reference. This will be discussed in more detail below.

argument, we will examine the fourth petition by examining its lexical, thematic, and structural parallels with the Sermon on the Mount.[84]

The Distinctives of "Give Us This Day Our Daily Bread"

This section will establish the distinctives of the fourth petition in terms of wording. We will argue that the fourth petition is carefully worded to create lexical parallels with the Sermon on the Mount. The most obvious lexical parallel is the shared references to bread. We will analyze the meaning of ἐπιούσιος and its consequences for understanding the fourth petition. This section will begin with the minor word differences before interpreting the *crux interpretum* (ἐπιούσιος) of the fourth petition.

The primary differences in the Matthean and Lukan versions of the fourth petition are lexical. There are two differences in the second half of the petition (δός/δίδου; σή μερον/καθ' ἡμέραν).

Matthew 6:11a/Luke 11:3a: τὸν ἄρτον ἡμῶν τὸν ἐπιούσιον
    Matthew 6:11b: δὸς ἡμῖν σήμερον
    Luke 11:3b: δίδου ἡμῖν τὸ καθ' ἡμέραν

In the fourth petition, Matthew and Luke diverge on the verb tense for "give" and have different wording for daily provisions ("today/day after day").

By Luke's use of the present imperative verb and accompanying adverbial phrase τὸ καθ' ἡμέραν, the meaning of Luke's bread petition is easier to envision. The request in Luke is for day-to-day bread. As Keener notes, "This one is most naturally uttered by the poor of this world, a condition that characterized many Galilean peasants and artisans who followed Jesus."[85] Luke has arguably generalized the temporal element (ἡμέραν) within the petition to emphasize sustenance for daily survival. It is interesting to note the phrase's prevalence elsewhere in Luke's Gospel. Luke has seven total uses of the word ἡμέραν (2:37, 9:23, 11:3, 16:19, 19:47, 22:53, and 24:21).[86] Of these seven instances, six occur with the corresponding preposition καθ'.[87] Among the six uses in Luke, two are changes from his Markan source. As Robert Guelich notes, "This change most likely stems from Luke's redaction, since he has introduced the same use of 'day after day' in Mark 8:34, see Luke 9:23, and Mark 11:18, see Luke 19:47."[88]

In Matthew's wording, the verb tense is more appropriate to the temporal adverb σήμερον.[89] The Matthean wording may be intended to provide some artistic beauty to

---

[84] A structural parallel refers to the connection between the context of the Lord's Prayer and Mt. 6:31-34. Both passages share lexical parallels that are similarly ordered. Therefore, the "form" of these texts, or overall shape, is paralleled. This ordering will be discussed below.
[85] Keener, *Gospel of Matthew*, 222.
[86] In Matthew's Gospel, there are only four examples of ἡμέραν, and only one of these has the corresponding preposition.
[87] There are also six additional examples in Acts (2:46, 47; 3:2; 16:5; 17:11; and 19:9).
[88] Guelich, *Sermon on the Mount*, 291. Another example of Lukan redaction or uniqueness is his recording of the teaching on prayer in ch. 11. In v. 13, Luke records that the Father gives the Holy Spirit. In the Matthean recording, the Father simply gives "good gifts" (Mt. 7:11).
[89] The wording is certainly not suggestive of a Mattheanism, because σήμερον only appears nine times in his Gospel compared to the eleven times in Luke.

the fourth petition. If the fourth petition is read as two phrases paralleling one another, the endings of each line provide aural resonance. Both lines end with the -ον sound, presenting some poetic beauty in the fourth petition.[90] Another possibility is that the wording provides a lexical parallel with Matthew's chosen context, the Sermon on the Mount. Σήμερον appears in Mt. 6:30 in Jesus's teaching on avoiding worry. This same passage addresses concerns for daily sustenance and will be discussed in more detail below. It is likely that Matthew noted the wording in his source and the possibility of parallels.

Interpreters are divided on the meaning of the enigmatic word ἐπιούσιος, translated as "daily" in most English versions. Because the term remains without parallel, the interpretations have split along three lines. John Nolland provides a helpful summary of these interpretations:[91]

1. The meaning derives from the Greek noun οὐσία, which is typically translated as "that which exists and therefore has substance, property, wealth."[92] With the combination of ἐπί, the new meaning could be (1) "supersubstantial" (i.e., surpassing all that belongs to the substantial world), (2) "for substance," (3) "above and beyond wealth/property," or (4) "essential."[93] Origen argued that the combination of ἐπιούσιος with "bread" refers to heavenly bread (*On Prayer* 27.13). Others have preferred this same etymology, but they interpret the wording as referring to the *Eucharist*.[94] Both definitions are symbolic readings that look to the future.
2. The term is a derivation of the feminine participle εἶναι. In this case, the feminine gender of the participle (ἐπιοῦσα) indicates an understood ἡμέρα, and the sense is "for the present day." Frequently commentators will dismiss this reading because of its supposed tautology, as well as accusing Matthew of using an unusual word when more basic terms for "daily" were available.[95]
3. The term is a derivation of the participle form of ἰέναι. Like option 2, ἡμέρα is understood, and the meaning would be something akin to "for the coming day."[96] This understanding of the word can take on two separate connotations: (1) The first meaning has become very popular among those who read the prayer as related to the eschatological future. The argument follows that this future reading is in keeping with the first three petitions.[97] Jerome remarks that in his reading of the *Gospel of the Nazarenes*, the Greek word ἐπιούσιος is represented by the Hebrew/Aramaic word מחר (*Commentary on Matthew*). This term's semantic

---

[90] This consonance has also been suggested by Michael Wade Martin, "Poetry of the Lord's Prayer," *JBL* 134.2 (2015): 365.
[91] John Nolland, *Luke 9:21–18:34*, WBC, vol. 35b (Dallas: Word, 1993), 615–7; *Gospel of Matthew*, 289–90.
[92] *BDAG*, 740.
[93] List taken from Nolland, *Luke 9:21–18:34*, 615.
[94] Connecting the Lord's Prayer and the *Eucharist* has a historical precedent in *Didache* 8–9.
[95] See Luz, *Matthew 1–7*, 320.
[96] See Werner Foerster, "ἐπιούσιος," in *TDNT*, vol. 2, ed. G. Kittel and G. Friedrich, trans. G. W. Bromiley (Grand Rapids: Eerdmans, 1964–76), 593–5.
[97] Brown, "Pater Noster as an Eschatological Prayer," 194.

range includes references to the future. The requested bread would then be for the heavenly future bread, a desire for feasting at the eschatological table in the kingdom of heaven. (2) The second option is to see the word, as a reference to the next day, preferring a literal rendering of the phrase.

Colin Hemer has argued persuasively for option 2. Hemer's argument is anticipated in the work of J. B. Lightfoot.[98] Lightfoot argued that the feminine participle ἐπιοῦσα had become a substantive by the time of the New Testament writings, referring to the "coming" or "following" day.[99] Hemer points to several convincing parallels that use ἐπιοῦσα as a substantive in parallel literature to the New Testament. Particularly interesting is the use of synonyms and derivatives of ἐπιοῦσα in the book of Acts (7:26, 16:11, 20:15, 21:26), in which participles are used substantively. The presence of these instances in Acts is corroborated by ἐπιούσιος in Lk. 11:3, reflecting the consistency of a common author.[100] It appears reasonable to assume that Matthew and Luke drew from the same tradition in choosing this derivate. Although the word is not common, its use before the writings of the Gospels reflects a reverence for the liturgical material of an earlier period. If Hemer's conclusion is correct, this understanding of ἐπιούσιος within the Matthean prayer provides an additional basis for parallels within the Sermon on the Mount. Matthew's retention of the difficult wording from his tradition most likely stems from his noting of similarities between the fourth petition and his chosen context, the Sermon. "Bread," which is "for tomorrow," is a prominent subject in two passages in the Sermon on the Mount (Mt. 6:25-34; 7:7-11).[101] We will explore these textual connections in the third section.

The Meaning of "Give Us This Day Our Daily Bread"

This section will explore the meaning of the fourth petition's wording in Matthew's cultural milieu. By locating the fourth petition in Matthew's cultural milieu, a basis for thematic parallels is established. Lengthy treatments have been devoted to the requests for bread in antiquity.[102] This section does not intend to replicate those treatments but rather to argue that the request for bread is common among Jewish prayers in which food was a necessity for everyday life. These requests evidence belief in the sovereignty of God at work. He is the provider of bread, steadfast in his provision, and sufficient in what he provides. Among those texts addressing the giving of bread, Exodus 16 and Mt. 4:1-4 present the strongest parallels to the fourth petition and statements concerning God's sovereignty.[103] Each text and its themes will be examined before considering its parallels to the Lord's Prayer and fourth petition in Section 3.

---

[98] J. B. Lightfoot, *On a Fresh Revision of the English New Testament*, 2nd ed. (London: Macmillan, 1872), Appendix "On the Words ἐπιούσιος, περιούσιος," 195–242, esp. 199.
[99] Lightfoot, *Fresh Revision*, 199.
[100] Hemer, "ἐπιούσιος," 87–8.
[101] A. H. M'Neile, *The Gospel According to St. Matthew* (London: Macmillan, 1957), 79, helpfully notes, "In liturgical use 'bread for the coming day' could denote either 'bread for the day then in progress,' or 'bread for the morrow,' according as the Prayer was used in the morning or in the evening."
[102] See esp. Edwin M. Yamauchi, "The 'Daily Bread' Motif in Antiquity," *WTJ* 28 (1966): 145–56.
[103] See Garland, "Lord's Prayer in the Gospel of Matthew," 222.

Exodus 16

Exodus 16:1-36 LXX describes the wilderness wanderings of Israel and the giving of the heavenly manna. In v. 4, the Lord instructs Moses, "I am going to rain bread from heaven for you, and each day (ἡμέρας εἰς ἡμέρα LXX) the people shall go out and gather enough for that day. In that way I will test them, whether they will follow my instruction or not." The phrase ἡμέρας εἰς ἡμέραν refers to this daily provision. Israel was instructed to go out and collect the day's offering. Despite their failings and complaining, God continued to supply this daily portion of bread. Exodus 16:11-12 states, "The Lord spoke to Moses and said, 'I have heard the complaining of the Israelites'; say to them, 'At twilight you shall eat meat, and in the morning, you shall have your fill of bread (ἄρτος); then you shall know that I am the Lord your God.'" At the giving of this word to Israel, the bread began to fall from heaven. The Israelites collected the bread, each according to his need. Even though Israel would continue to complain and eventually be barred from entry into the Promised Land, God provided for the needs of his people through the giving of daily bread.

An examination of Exod. 16:1-36 reveals several themes. First, God is sovereign over his people. This sovereignty is displayed in his giving of sustenance to Israel in the wilderness. Second, God's provision was steadfast. Not only did God provide daily bread, but he did so despite Israel's complaining. Third, God's provision was sufficient. God knew how much Israel needed for each day and provided a double portion on the sixth day for the observance of Sabbath (see vv. 17-18).[104]

The fourth petition is reminiscent of Exodus 16 for two notable reasons. First, the two passages share several lexical parallels. Both passages refer to "giving," "daily/today," "testing," and "bread."[105] Second, God is the giver of daily bread from *heaven* in Exodus 16. Similarly, the fourth petition requests daily bread from the Father who is in *heaven*. With these parallels in mind, the Lord's Prayer echoes Exodus's emphasis of God's provision. The request for daily provision would evoke God's steadfastness and sufficiency.

Matthew 4:1-10

In addition to Exod. 16:1-36, the closest parallel to the fourth petition is the temptation of Jesus found in Mt. 4:1-4. Verses 1-4 state,

> Then Jesus was led by the Spirit into the wilderness to be tempted by the devil. After fasting forty days and forty nights, he was hungry. The tempter came to him and said, "If you are the Son of God, tell these stones to become bread." Jesus

---

[104] Exodus 16 is not alone in emphasizing God's sovereignty regarding his provision. Other texts include Pss. 107:4-9; 146:5-7; and Prov. 30:7-9. Proverbs 30:8-9 is an especially important text. In v. 8, the last half reads σύνταξον δέ μοι τὰ δέοντα καὶ τὰ αὐτάρκη. As Yamauchi, "'Daily Bread' Motif in Antiquity," 154, points out, the prayer is not only a request for a sufficient amount but also an affirmation that the sufficient amount is exactly what God will provide. See also Garland, "Lord's Prayer in the Gospel of Matthew," 222-3.

[105] See M'Neile, *Gospel According to St. Matthew*, 80.

answered, "It is written: 'Man shall not live on bread alone, but on every word that comes from the mouth of God.'"

Jesus refuses the temptation and explains that bread is secondary to the word of God. It is important to note that Jesus is not forsaking bread; rather, he is remaining faithful to God's will through fasting.

Matthew 4:1-4 is thematically linked with Exodus 16 and for that reason evidences similar themes.

1. Before beginning his ministry in Galilee, Jesus was led by the Spirit into the wilderness. In Exodus 16, Israel is led by God into the wilderness.
2. Jesus begins a fast for forty days. Israel was in the wilderness for forty years and complained because of their lack of food.
3. A key difference in these texts is the responses of Jesus and Israel. Whereas Israel demanded bread from heaven, Jesus continued to fast. Israel complained of their needy state, while Jesus affirmed the will of God. Israel ultimately caved to the temptation of complaining, while Jesus resisted the temptations of the devil. When tempted with the devil's provision of bread, Jesus exclaims, "Man cannot live on bread alone, but by every word that proceeds from the mouth of God." He trusts that God is sovereign within this temptation and ultimately is in control. By continuing the fast, Jesus additionally affirms that God's provision is steadfast and sufficient. Jesus's statement makes clear that earthly needs must be rightly ordered behind the word of God.

The connections between Mt. 4:1-4 and the Lord's Prayer are threefold. First, the broader context of Mt. 4:1-4 brings together bread, kingdom, temptation, and the source of evil. Similarly, the Lord's Prayer references bread, kingdom, temptation, and the source of evil. Second, the structure of the Lord's Prayer shows that bread is secondary to God's name, kingdom, and will. Jesus's response to the devil also subordinates bread to God's will.[106] Third, both texts appear to draw on the themes present within Exodus 16. If these connections are tenable, then the same themes present in Exodus 16 and in Mt. 4:1-14 inform our understanding of the fourth petition.

Conclusion

From our analysis, we have argued that the fourth petition is primarily rooted in a trust of God's sovereignty and provision of daily bread. God's provision is both steadfast and sufficient. These themes prove to be thematically significant to other passages throughout the Sermon on the Mount. In conjunction with our earlier observations concerning the distinctive wording, we will now turn to the textual connections between the fourth petition and the Sermon on the Mount.

---

[106] See Chapter 3 on structure of the Lord's Prayer.

"Give Us This Day Our Daily Bread" in the Sermon on the Mount

In his article, "'Daily Bread' Motif in Antiquity," Edwin Yamauchi insightfully notes,

> Even . . . in its most mundane sense, that petition [fourth petition] as seen in the light of the associations of "daily bread" in antiquity is not lacking in spiritual significance. It teaches the lessons of dependence upon a Father who provides for his children their basic needs, of confidence that day by day without fail he will provide, and of contentment with all that he does provide.[107]

Yamauchi persuasively argued for similar themes to those examined in the previous section. The aim of this section is to combine Yamauchi's insights and the fourth petition's relationship to the Sermon on the Mount. We will examine those passages in the Sermon on the Mount that have textual connections with the fourth petition. The strongest parallels to the fourth petition are Mt. 6:25-34 and 7:7-11, signified by lexical and thematic parallels. Other passages that are more loosely paralleled to the fourth petition include Mt. 5:6; 6:19-21; and 6:24. These passages do not explicitly mention bread or daily provision, but they share similar themes to the fourth petition ("hunger and thirst," "treasures in heaven," and "mammon"). We will begin with the strongest parallels (Mt. 6:25-34; 7:7-11) and then go on to the weaker parallels (Mt. 5:6; 6:19-21, 24).

Matthew 6:25-34

In Mt. 6:25-34, Jesus addresses the temptation of anxiety. He begins, "Do not worry about your life, what you will eat or what you will drink, or about your body, what you will wear. Is not life more than food, and the body more than clothing?" (v. 25). Encouragement comes through a set of rhetorical questions (vv. 26-30). In this section, Jesus uses examples from nature. If the Father cares for the birds, the lilies, and the grass of the field, then how much more will he care for his children?[108] Jesus concludes, "Do not worry" (v. 31). After establishing the love of the Father for his children, Jesus teaches that his disciples should not distress over what they will eat, drink, or wear (vv. 31-34). The heavenly Father knows what they need, and his kingdom is more important (v. 33) than food, drink, and clothing.[109] The following sections highlight the shared wording, structure, and themes in the fourth petition and Mt. 6:25-34.

Wording

Matthew 6:25-34 has four direct lexical parallels with the fourth petition. The first parallel is in each passages' reference to daily sustenance. Although Mt. 6:25-34 does

---

[107] Yamauchi, "'Daily Bread' Motif in Antiquity," 156. Yamauchi is addressing a common criticism from those who favor the eschatological reading of the fourth petition that the fourth petition is too simple and mundane to only mean a request for bread.
[108] See Davies and Allison, *Matthew 1-7*, 650.
[109] See Prov. 30:8-9.

not explicitly refer to "bread," two verses allude to bread. Verse 25 asks a rhetorical question concerning the value of food (τροφή). It is obvious that the food that one would worry about includes "bread." Several verses later, Jesus assures the disciple that God will provide all "these things" (v. 32). The phrase guarantees the disciples that he or she need not worry about what he will eat, drink, or wear. Second, both passages mention "daily/today." In the fourth petition, Matthew uses ἐπιούσιος and σήμερον to refer to each day and "for the following day." References to the day in Mt. 6:25-34 occur in v. 34 (αὔριον/ἡμέρᾳ), in which Jesus refers to "tomorrow." Third, both passages link the "giving" nature of God to prayer. In the fourth petition, the reference is an aorist imperative (δὸς), whereas Mt. 6:33 refers to the future giving (προστεθήσεται) of bread, drink, and clothing if the disciples' priorities are rightly ordered. In order to achieve rightly ordered priorities, disciples must "strive" after the kingdom and righteousness. The command to "strive" (ζητεῖτε) is used to describe prayer elsewhere in the Sermon (see Mt. 7:7-11). Fourth, lexical parallels are present between Mt. 6:25-34 and the Lord's Prayer in general, of which the fourth petition is a part. As mentioned, both passages share references to the heavenly Father (Mt. 6:9//6:26, 32) and the kingdom (Mt. 6:10//6:33).

Structure

In addition to the lexical parallels noted above, the framing of the Lord's Prayer and its immediate context parallel the ordering of Mt. 6:25-34. M. F. Olsthoorn has illustrated this argument from structure. As the following table demonstrates, when Mt. 6:7-11 is read alongside the latter half of Mt. 6:25-34, the passages evidence impressive lexical parallels:[110]

Matthew 6:7-11	Matthew 6:31-34
[7]But when you pray use not vain repetitions	[31]Therefore, have no anxiety, saying, "what are we to eat?" or "what are we to drink?" or "what are we to wear?" [32]All
as *the Gentiles* (οἱ ἐθνικοί) do,	these are things *the heathens* (ἔθνη) seek.
for they think they shall be heard for their much speaking. [8]Do not be like them,	
for your Father knows	*For your* heavenly *Father*

---

[110] M. F. Olsthoorn, *The Jewish Background and the Synoptic Setting of Mt. 6:25-33 and Lk. 12:22-31*, SBFA 10 (Jerusalem: Franciscan, 1975), 71. The following table is adapted from Olsthoorn.

what you need	*knows*, that *you need* all these things.
(οἶδεν γὰρ ὁ πατὴρ ὑμῶν ὧν χρείαν ἔχετε	(οἶδεν γὰρ ὁ πατὴρ ὑμῶν ὁ οὐράνιος
πρὸ τοῦ ὑμᾶς αἰτῆσαι αὐτόν)	ὅτι χρῄζετε τούτων ἁπάντων)
Before you ask Him.	
[9]This is the way you should *pray*	[33]But *seek* (ζητεῖτε)[111]
(προσεύχεσθε):	
Our Father ...	
[10]*Your kingdom* (ἡ βασιλεία σου) come,	first *his reign* (τὴν βασιλείαν)
Your will (τὸ θέλημά σου) be done	and *his righteousness*;
on earth as it is in heaven.	(τὴν δικαιοσύνην αὐτοῦ)
[11]*Give us* (δὸς ἡμῖν) our daily bread	then all these things will *be given* (προστεθήσεται ὑμῖν) you as well.
today (σήμερον).	[34]Have no anxiety about *tomorrow* (τὴν αὔριον).

Verse 7 begins with warnings against vain repetitions to the Father. Similarly, Mt. 6:31 gives a series of questions concerning food, drink, and clothing that Jesus dismisses as unnecessary. The similar wording continues with references to the "Gentiles/heathens." The references are from the ἔθνος word group. Next, there is an affirmation of not only "your Father" but also with his knowledge of present needs. The passages continue with references to prayer and to shared concepts of the content of prayer. Kingdom parallels kingdom (βασιλεία//βασιλείαν), will parallels righteousness (θέλημά//δικαιοσύνην),[112] and each passage refers to God's giving nature. The parallels are finalized in references to the "day."

A comparison with Luke reveals that this framing device is not as extensive as the Matthean version. Luke parallels the teaching on anxiety in 12:22-34 in this manner:

Luke 11:2-4	Luke 12:30-32
	[29]And do not keep striving for what you are to eat and what you are to drink, and do not keep worrying.

---

[111] This parallelism also strengthens the suggestion above that "strive" in Mt. 6:33 is part of Matthew's prayer motif. See p. 219.

[112] The connection between God's will and righteousness is explored in Chapter 4. The structural outline above strengthens the already proposed textual connection.

	³⁰For it is the nations of the world that strive after all these things,
²*Father* (Πάτερ), hallowed be your name	and your *Father* (πατὴρ) knows that you need them.
Your *kingdom* (ἡ βασιλεία) come,	³¹Instead, strive for his *kingdom* (τὴν βασιλείαν),
³*Give us* (δίδου ἡμῖν) each day our daily bread as well.	and these things will be *given to you* (προστεθήσεται ὑμῖν) ³²" Do not be afraid, little flock, for its your Father's good pleasure to give you the kingdom

Luke does not preface his version of the Lord's Prayer with the warning against meaningless phrases (Mt. 6:7-8). Interestingly, the teaching on prayer also does not affirm the Father's knowledge of our needs, although his teaching on anxiety does include this affirmation (Lk. 12:30). The parallels begin with the references to the kingdom (Lk. 11:2//Lk. 12:31). Luke omits the petition for God's will and interestingly does not include "righteousness" alongside the kingdom in his instruction to "strive" (Lk. 12:31). The parallels resume and end with references to "giving" in Lk. 11:3// Lk. 12:31. Luke 12 does not include a parallel to Mt. 6:34 ("So do not worry about tomorrow, for tomorrow will bring worries of its own. Today's trouble is enough for today").[113]

The structure of Mt. 6:7-11//6:31-34 appears to be from Matthew's hand or in the tradition in which he received. As we have suggested above, Matthew edits parts of the Sermon and the Prayer to increase the parallelism between the two texts. This ordering of concepts strengthens the parallels between the Lord's Prayer and Mt. 6:25-34 in a manner not found in Luke. This distinctive parallelism in turn increases the textual connections of the Lord's Prayer and Mt. 6:25-34.

Themes

A glossary reading of the Sermon appears to offer contradictory themes in the fourth petition and Mt. 6:25-34.[114] Namely, the fourth petition's appeal to bread "for tomorrow" (ἐπιούσιος) appears to be at odds with Jesus's later teaching to avoid "worrying about tomorrow." This apparent contradiction does not explore the range of parallel themes

---

[113] Interestingly, Mt. 6:34 includes the references to "day/today/tomorrow." The inclusion of v. 34, with its supposed redundancy, strengthens the lexical parallels with the fourth petition.

[114] This objection is anticipated in Hemer, "ἐπιούσιος," 90-1. Hemer argues from an etymological perspective that the passages are not incongruous. He states, "The accent is upon immediate sequence rather than on chronological date. As a morning prayer, it is naturally a petition for 'today's' need. There is no conflict with the caution against fretting over the unknown future." This explanation provides additional evidence to the suggestions in this section.

between the fourth petition and teaching on anxiety. First, this argument misrepresents the teaching in the fourth petition and Mt. 6:25-34. While Mt. 6:34 does instruct the disciple not to worry about tomorrow, this instruction is not at odds with the emphasis of the fourth petition. The fourth petition is a petition expressing not only a need but also a dependence on the Father in heaven. Similarly, Mt. 6:25-34 instructs disciples to seek first the kingdom and righteousness (v. 33). The emphasis of ἐπιούσιος is on the immediacy of the bread, not necessarily the temporal sequence of its being given. Therefore, the petition is not a sign of worry but of trust that God will provide (see Mt. 6:32).[115] In other words, the fourth petition and Mt. 6:25-34 share the theme of dependence on God as an expression of his sovereignty.

In addition to this dependence on God, the fourth petition and Mt. 6:25-34 emphasize God's role as provider. This understanding of God's provision is perhaps the most obvious parallel between the fourth petition and Sermon material. The petitionary nature of the request for bread acknowledges that the Father in heaven will give bread to those who ask (see also Mt. 7:7-11). In Mt. 6:25-34, Jesus continually refers to the Father as the one who provides (vv. 26, 30, 32, 33). This shared theme of God as provider leads to the third theme.

The fourth petition and Mt. 6:25-34 share the theme of properly ordered desires. We have argued above that the structure of the Lord's Prayer indicates that God's name, kingdom, and will are sought before bread.[116] In Mt. 6:25-34, Jesus begins with discussions of food, drink, and clothing but ends with the command to seek "first" the kingdom and righteousness (Mt. 6:33).[117] As Yamauchi states, "Food is the most pressing human need—a need which occurs day after day. Yet in God's sight when compared with spiritual needs (Matt. 4:4) it is a need which is the least important of all (Matt. 6:30–32)."[118] In both passages, the consistent theme is God's kingdom above earthly needs but not necessarily at the expense of literal bread.

The last shared theme is the affirmation of God as steadfast and sufficient in his provision. The fourth petition implicitly shows its trust in God's steadfast provision by only requesting enough bread for the "coming" day. The Father in heaven will provide daily and the daily amount is enough. This provision is similarly affirmed in Mt. 6:34 ("So do not worry about tomorrow, for tomorrow will bring worries of its own. Today's trouble is enough for today") but with one additional key. In Mt. 6:30, Jesus uses the phrase "you of little faith," which serves as a contrast to the type of behavior Jesus is commanding. The phrase occurs only five times in the Biblical corpus.[119] Four of these examples are in Matthew, and one is found in the Lukan parallel to Mt. 6:30. In the three examples outside of ch. 6, each is a critique

---

[115] As Luz, *Matthew 1–7*, 321, states, "Prayer and 'worries' are two completely different things."
[116] The petition itself suggests this ordering of priorities. The petitioner comes to God "daily" for bread, so that he does not accumulate too much and circumvent his Godward desires (see Mt. 6:24).
[117] It is interesting to note that Matthew includes the reference to "first," which is lacking in the Lukan parallel. The addition of this word serves as an emphasis on properly ordered needs. See Guelich, *Sermon on the Mount*, 341–2, for further commentary.
[118] Yamauchi, "Daily Bread Motif," 154.
[119] Matthew 6:30, 8:26, 14:31, 16:8; Lk. 12:28. Especially interesting is the instance in Mt. 16:8. Jesus is referring to the feeding of the multitudes in ch. 14 where "bread" is central to the discussion. In each of these instances, Jesus is condemning the disciples for their lack of faith in God's provision.

of disciples who lack faith in God's provision. The use of the phrase here in Mt. 6:30 appears to have the same meaning. Jesus is contrasting the type of trust in God's steadfastness and sufficiency with those "who have little faith." Both petition and Sermon material are instructing the disciple to have "great faith" that God is steadfast and sufficient in his provision.

Matthew 7:7-11

Matthew 7:7-11 instructs Jesus's followers to be persistent in their prayer lives. To make this point, Jesus uses two rhetorical questions that describe an evil father feeding his children. If the child asks for a loaf of bread or fish, will the evil father give him a stone or snake? The answer is a resounding, "No!" In contrast, Jesus explains the results of continual prayer.[120] The Father in heaven will give good gifts to those who ask persistently. The parallels between this teaching and the fourth petition are threefold. The initial parallel is signaled by the function of each respective passage. Both teachings are instructions on prayer. This section will argue that this initial parallel is coupled with both lexical and thematic parallels. As we have argued throughout this book, prayer is central to the Sermon on the Mount. It would only be fitting that these extended teachings on prayer share detailed textual connections and the Sermon's body would conclude with a reminder of prayer's centrality, as articulated in the Lord's Prayer.

Wording

The lexical parallels between the fourth petition and Mt. 7:7-11 are signaled by shared references to bread (Mt. 6:11//7:9) and bread as a gift (Mt. 6:11//7:9-11). In Mt. 7:9, bread is used in a rhetorical question to make a greater point, but it is assumed that God will be the provider. References to the giving nature of God in the fourth petition are paralleled in the threefold references to giving in Mt. 7:9-11. In addition to these specific parallels to the fourth parallel, Mt. 7:7-11 has several lexical parallels to the Lord's Prayer in general. Matthew 7:11 mentions "your Father in heaven" and "evil."[121]

Themes

In addition to the lexical parallels, the fourth petition and Mt. 7:7-11 share thematic parallels. The themes present are the affirmation of God as sovereign provider and God's provision as steadfast and sufficient. First, the fourth petition and Mt. 7:7-11 affirm God as the sovereign provider. One must remember the introductory preface to the Lord's Prayer, "Do not be like them, for your Father knows what you need before you ask him" (Mt. 6:8). The wording of the fourth petition echoes this confidence that

---

[120] Jesus uses the iterative sense of "asking, seeking, and knocking." This verbal aspect refers to "continuing" action.

[121] These lexical parallels were explored in depth in Chapter 4.

God is in control of all circumstances and has set aside provision before our petitions are uttered. Matthew 7:8 and v. 11 similarly repeat this affirmation of God as sovereign provider. Verse 8 explains that God gives to those who ask. While the verse is used as a command to be persistent, it is assumed, from God's perspective, that he has already prepared the answer. Verse 11 repeats, the giver of good things is the Father who is in *heaven*.[122]

Second, the fourth petition and Mt. 7:7-11 evidence God's provision as steadfast and sufficient. This point has been argued above concerning the fourth petition's insistence on daily sustenance. In Mt. 7:8, Jesus guarantees that those who continually ask, seek and knock will receive, find, and have their door opened. Jesus is not conceding flippancy in prayer though (i.e., whatever you ask, you will receive). Rather, Jesus gives examples that draw on daily provisions of food that a father provides for his family (vv. 9–10). As an earthly father provides daily, so the heavenly Father will provide to those who seek.

This section has argued to this point that Mt. 6:25-34 and 7:7-11 present the clearest Sermon parallels to the fourth petition. Beyond these passages, there are three looser parallels. These passages include Mt. 5:6; 6:19-21; and 6:24. The textual connections are signaled by implicit lexical parallels and shared themes.

Matthew 5:6

The first possible link to the fourth petition is found in the *macarisms*. Jesus instructs the disciples to hunger and thirst for righteousness' sake, for they will be filled (Mt. 5:6).[123] Elsewhere, Matthew has joined references to food and righteousness, namely in the structure of the Lord's Prayer ("your will be done"//"give us daily bread")[124] and in Mt 6:25-34 ("food, drink, clothing"//"strive first for his righteousness"). One must be careful, though, because of the literal reference to bread in Mt. 6:10 and the metaphorical/spiritualized reference to food in Mt. 5:6. The object of desire (hunger/thirsting) in Mt. 5:6 is righteousness. It could be the case that the fourth petition implies a hunger and thirst for God's name, kingdom, and will implicitly in addition to "hunger and thirst" for daily sustenance.[125] Thematically, one could argue for shared concepts between the fourth petition and Mt. 5:6. In both cases, God is the provider. In Mt. 5:6, Jesus uses the passive verb to imply that God is the one who "fills" those who hunger and thirst. In Mt. 6:11, the mouths of the disciples are filled by the Father in heaven. Additionally, the fourth petition is part of Jesus's explanation of what true righteousness looks like (Mt. 6:1-18). Undoubtedly, a hunger and thirst for righteousness would encompass proper prayer (Mt. 6:11).

---

[122] Emphasis mine.
[123] Matthew 5:6 states, "Blessed are those who hunger and thirst for righteousness, for they will be filled."
[124] As we have argued in Chapter 4, God's will is frequently associated with righteousness. See esp. Mt. 7:21.
[125] Arguably, each of these texts share the background text of Mt. 4:1-4. This shared background would provide an additional parallel. See Keener, *Gospel of Matthew*, 170.

Matthew 6:19-21

In Mt. 6:19-21, Jesus instructs his disciples to seek "treasures in heaven."[126] This "treasure in heaven" is contrasted with "treasures on earth." "Treasure in heaven" does not rust or decay, but "earthly treasure" does. As we have argued above, Mt. 6:19-21 serves a dual function of concluding 6:1-18 and introducing 6:22-34. This dual function assists in discerning the meaning of the verses. First, the verses provide a conclusion to Mt. 6:1. Matthew 6:1 teaches the disciples to beware of practicing righteousness before men. Outward righteousness receives a just reward from the Father in heaven, a reward characterized by judgment. Verses 19-21 reiterate this instruction to avoid earthly "treasures" (i.e., earthly practice of righteousness and earthly rewards) and rather seek heavenly treasure (i.e., rewards from the Father in heaven). Second, vv. 19-21 function as an introduction to 6:22-34. In the verses that follow, Matthew gives a literal referent to "treasure on earth." Matthew 6:22-34 addresses earthly wealth and its pursuit. The passages do not discourage wealth but the "storing up" (θησαυρίζω) of wealth. As Allison notes, "the verb, 'to treasure', refers to accumulation, not simple possessions."[127]

With the close connections of the fourth petition to Mt. 6:25-34, it is reasonable to suspect some thematic coherence between the fourth petition and Mt. 6:19-21. While the fourth petition seeks literal bread, it does not assume that its request subverts the desire for God's name, kingdom, and will. The fourth petition only asks for sustenance for the coming day. Within this affirmation of God's sufficient provision, the disciple excludes the chances of lavish living. David Garland makes a similar point, "The prayer for physical sustenance frees disciples from becoming mired in futile worry over their subsistence (Matt. 13:22) and frees them for the task of seeking first the kingdom of heaven."[128] It can be inferred that those who have sufficient bread in answer to the fourth petition will not be distracted in their pursuit of "heavenly treasure."

Matthew 6:24

Like Mt. 6:19-21, Mt. 6:24 contrasts heavenly and earthly things.[129] Specifically, Jesus states that one cannot be a slave to both God and money. In both cases, God and money demand holistic devotion. Jesus states, you will "either hate the one and love the other, or be devoted to the one and despise the other." Within this short teaching, there are two possible parallels with the fourth petition. First, Jesus references μαμωνᾶς in v. 24, a term of Aramaic origins that likely refers to "wealth, property."[130] This definition closely parallels the connotation of "bread" (ἄρτος) in the fourth petition. "Bread"

---

[126] Matthew 6:19-21 reads in full, "Do not store up for yourselves treasures on earth, where moth and rust consume and where thieves break in and steal; but store up for yourselves treasures in heaven, where neither moth nor rust consumes and where thieves do not break in and steal. For where your treasure is, there your heart will be also."
[127] Davies and Allison, *Matthew 1–7*, 630.
[128] Garland, "Lord's Prayer in the Gospel of Matthew," 222.
[129] Matthew 6:24 reads, "No one can serve two masters; for a slave will either hate the one and love the other, or be devoted to the one and despise the other. You cannot serve God and wealth."
[130] BDAG, 614. As Lundbom, *Jesus' Sermon on the Mount*, 226–7, notes, the term does not always have a negative connotation. Jesus's condemnation is becoming a slave to provision.

echoes the concept of sufficient provision. In this regard, those who seek God trust him for daily bread, but those who do not seek God desire wealth and property. Second, the emphasis in Mt. 6:24 is on rightly ordered priorities. The teaching makes clear that devotion to God supersedes and subverts all other allegiances. The meagre requests in Mt. 6:11 similarly subject all earthly provision to God's name, kingdom, and will (also Mt. 6:33).

This section, then, has argued for three additional parallels (Mt. 5:6; 6:19-21, 24) to the fourth petition. These parallels only loosely connect to the fourth petition, not bearing the combination of lexical, structural, and thematic affinities found in the fourth petition and Mt. 6:25-34//7:7-11. Yet, each of these passages has thematic parallels as well as implicit lexical parallels. In each instance, the emphasis is on rightly ordered priorities, which is prominent in the fourth petition.

Bread Petition Conclusion

In the previous sections, we have analyzed the fourth petition. We have attempted to make sense of this difficult yet familiar petition as it relates to the Sermon on the Mount. In addition to studying the enigmatic ἐπιούσιος, we have examined the lexical, structural, and thematic parallels with the Sermon on the Mount. In so doing, we have attempted to show that these texts should be read together. When read in this manner, the bread petition is a request and affirmation of fully trusting that God will provide daily sustenance (Mt. 6:25-34; 7:7-11) but not at the expense of God's kingdom and righteousness (Mt. 6:33). The request may also loosely parallel the instruction to the disciples to "hunger and thirst" after righteousness (Mt. 5:6), seek heavenly treasures above earthly treasures (Mt. 6:19-21), and worship God over wealth (Mt. 6:24).

Fifth Petition: "Forgive Our Debts, As We Forgive Our Debtors"

Commentators typically reason that the forgiveness petition in Matthew has the same rhetorical effect as Luke's petition, but with older diction. Donald Hagner states, "Matthew's fifth petition is basically the same as in Luke except for his use of τὰ ὀφειλήματα ἡμῶν, 'our debts,' where Luke has τὰς ἁμαρτίας ἡμῶν, 'our sins.'" He continues, "Matthew's language at a number of points is the more original (e.g., ὀφειλήματα, 'debts,' for Luke's ἁμαρτίας, 'sins')."[131] These historical observations often overshadow an important aspect of understanding the forgiveness petition and one of its functions. The wording and shape of the forgiveness petition parallels several passages in the Sermon on the Mount. The juxtaposition of ὀφείλημα and ἀφίημι highlights the themes of forgiveness and debts/obligation.[132] Obligation is part of

---

[131] Hagner, *Matthew 1-13*, 145, is likely right concerning the wording (i.e., the wording is more archaic), but the point is that these historical questions dominate the discussion of the Lord's Prayer at the expense of the context of the Sermon on the Mount.

[132] On the economic language in Matthew, see Eubank, *Wages of Cross-Bearing and Debt of Sin*, 25–85.

Matthew's retention of "debt" language in both clauses of the fifth petition, whereby the petitioner requests forgiveness for their debts and exclaims their own forgiveness of debtors. God will forgive us our debts (to him) when we ask, but only when we forgive those people indebted to us.[133] By joining interpersonal forgiveness and divine forgiveness, a triangular shape is formed between God, the debtor, and the indebted.[134] These aspects of the forgiveness petition—forgiveness, obligation, and its triangular shape (divine and interpersonal)—have thematic parallels with six passages in the Sermon on the Mount: Mt. 5:7, 21-26, 38-42, 43-47; 6:14-15; and 7:1-5. In the following sections, we will analyze the fifth petition within the Sermon on the Mount, as defined by its distinctive words and thematic parallels.

The Distinctives of "Forgive Our Debts, As We Forgive Our Debtors"

This section will examine the specific wording of the Matthean version of the forgiveness petition, noting its distinctive characteristics. The primary differences between the Matthean and Lukan versions are lexical.[135] Both requests contain parallel lines and similar emphases but with slightly different wording.

Matthew 6:12
καὶ ἄφες ἡμῖν τὰ ὀφειλήματα ἡμῶν,
ὡς καὶ ἡμεῖς ἀφήκαμεν τοῖς ὀφειλέταις ἡμῶν·

Luke 11:4b
καὶ ἄφες ἡμῖν τὰς ἁμαρτίας ἡμῶν,
καὶ γὰρ αὐτοὶ ἀφίομεν παντὶ ὀφείλοντι ἡμῖν·

In the first clause, the Matthean version employs the term τὰ ὀφειλήματα, or "debts," whereas the Lukan version refers to ἁμαρτίας, or "sins." Both Matthew and Luke have references to "debts" in their second clauses. Second, the Matthean version has the unusual conjunction ὡς καὶ whereas the Lukan version contains καὶ γάρ. Third, the

---

[133] It could be argued that we are in a constant state of "debt" to both God and others. It is not necessary for the present argument to clarify to what extent we are in "debt" but rather to illustrate that we are indebted to both God and man.

[134] David Aune, "The Forgiveness Petition in the Lord's Prayer: First Century Literary, Liturgical and Cultural Contexts," in *Jesus, Gospel Tradition and Paul in the Context of Jewish and Greco-Roman Antiquity*, Wissenschaftliche Untersuchungen zum Neuen Testament 303 (Tübingen: Mohr Siebeck, 2013), 62, proposes a helpful model for understanding the petition called "triangular reciprocity." In his model, "triangular reciprocity" refers to three principles being intimately linked: "'God' (to whom the petition for forgiveness is addressed), the Christian who prays (addressing a petition for forgiveness to God), and others, perhaps Christians themselves (who are somehow indebted to, or have sinned against, the Christian who prays)."

[135] The forgiveness petition is also found in the *Didache* version of the Lord's Prayer. Its fifth petition reads as follows: καὶ ἄφες ἡμῖν ὀφειλὴν ἡμῶν, ὡς καὶ ἡμεῖς ἀφήκαμεν τοῖς ὀφειλέταις ἡμῶν. *Didache* 8:2 contains elements found in both Matthew and Luke. Particularly striking in the *Didache* version is the retention of the reference to "debts" in the comparative clause as well as the unusual conjunction ὡς καὶ. Both elements are found in the Matthean version and argue for a common source or the *Didache*'s dependence on Matthew.

Matthean version uses the aorist tense of ἀφίημι, whereas the Lukan version has the present tense.[136] The fifth petition refers to "debts" in relation to forgiveness, an unusual juxtaposition in parallel literature. As we will argue below, the joining of the two terms is explained by Mt. 18:23-35. Additionally, the petition contains a comparative/conditional particle (ὡς καί), which links interpersonal and divine forgiveness. We will examine the changes in conjunction and verb tense, before examining Matthew's use of "debt" language in both clauses of the fifth petition.

Ὡς καί and ἀφίημι

Matthew has the unusual conjunction ὡς καί and the aorist tense of ἀφίημι in the second clause. Matthew is the only Synoptic writer to use the phrase ὡς καί (Mt. 6:12, 18:33, and 20:14). Luke's phrasing employs καὶ γάρ with the present tense of ἀφίημι. Luke's use of the conjunctions καί and γάρ is found elsewhere throughout his Gospel.[137] Each writer appears to be familiar with the phraseology used by the other. Acts has several instances of ὡς καί. Instances include Acts 10:47, 11:17, 13:33, 17:28, 22:5, and 25:10. Matthew uses the phrase καὶ γάρ in 8:9, 15:27, and 26:73. This evidence suggests that each of the writers have chosen their words carefully or followed the tradition available to them. We will explore the meaning of Matthew's conjunction below. In terms of verb usage, Matthew's aorist verb is appropriate for the temporal adverb, while Luke's present tense verb is appropriate for his serial/distributive phrase. Matthew's use of the aorist is also consistent with his other petitions.[138] We will note the implications of the aorist verb tense below.

"Debts/Sins"

Matthew and Luke's versions of the Lord's Prayer refer to forgiveness of "debtors" (ὁ φειλέταις/ ὀφείλοντι) in their second clause, but the Matthean version also refers to "debts" in its first clause. In the Lukan version, the first clause refers to "sins" as an apparent explanation of the "debt" language in its second clause. Brad Young helpfully summarizes: "When Luke uses the word 'sin,' he seems to be explaining and clarifying the word 'debts' to his readers."[139] With Luke's Gentile audience, the Semitic nuances of "debt" may have created difficulties in understanding the nature of forgiveness. Without completely ridding the petition of "debt" language, the Lukan version gives an interpretation of petitions for forgiveness.

In Matthew's Gospel, there are several references to "debt."[140] Besides the reference in the Lord's Prayer, "debt" language is referenced in seven places. Matthew 18 has five

---

[136] An extended discussion of the aorist tense of ἀφίημι is found below.
[137] Lk. 1:66; 6:32, 33; 7:8; 11:4; 22:37; and 22:59.
[138] Charles Quarles, *Matthew*, EGGNT (Nashville: B&H, 2017), 64.
[139] Young, *Jewish Background to the Lord's Prayer*, 30.
[140] Luke has the term ὀφείλημα five times throughout his Gospel including the verbal form (ὀφείλοντι) found in the forgiveness petition (11:4; 13:4; 16:5, 7; 17:10). Luke 13:4 references the falling of the tower of Siloam on eighteen people. Jesus asks if these people were worse debtors, or, rather, culprits than any man who does not repent in Jerusalem. The "culprits" are called sinners in 13:2.

references to debt (18:24, 28, 30, 32, 34), while ch. 23 has two references to that which is "owed" (23:16, 18). Matthew 23:16-23 contains a critique of Pharisees who break their oaths by swearing on different objects. The references in ch. 23 use the verbal from of "debt" (ὀφείλω). In this context, the verb reflects an aspect of "debt," as there is obligation to uphold sworn oaths. Matthew 18:23-35, like the fifth petition, connects the concept of debt with forgiveness (ἀφίημι). Interestingly, this parable in ch. 18 is only found in Matthew. Besides Matthew's two references (Mt. 6:12; 18:23-35),[141] 1 Maccabees is the only instance in parallel literature in which ἀφίημι and ὀφείλημα appear together.[142] These comparisons between Matthew and parallel literature evidence the distinctive nature of the wording in Matthew's version. As we will argue below, this distinctive wording in the fifth petition parallels several passages in the Sermon on the Mount.

The Meaning of "Forgive Our Debts, As We Forgive Our Debtors"

This section will explore the meaning of the forgiveness petition. From our study, we conclude that for Matthew, the fifth petition is first and foremost about relationships, particularly those in need of healing. We will start with an examination of Mt. 18:23-35, since it is the closest parallel to the forgiveness petition outside the Sermon on the Mount. Matthew 18:23-35 functions as a "commentary" on the debt/forgiveness relationship.[143] The use of "debt" language narrows the scope of forgiveness to financial obligations and "sins" in general. Second, the fifth petition connects the need for interpersonal forgiveness with divine forgiveness. If the Father has forgiven us, then we, as sons of the Father, will constantly seek to forgive others. As the petition suggests, our forgiveness functions as a prerequisite to requesting God's forgiveness. Third, this petition explicitly connects prayer and human action, an aspect we have argued is implicit throughout the other petitions. Evidence for this connection includes not only the petition itself but also the Prayer's concentric structure, which pairs the forgiveness petition with the will of the Father.

Matthew 18:23-35

Matthew 18:23-35 recounts the story of a servant who owes a large sum of money. The debt is forgiven by a gracious king. Upon receiving his debt forgiveness, the

---

In this case, the reference is to the men being crooks that have robbed and perhaps owe society. Luke 16:5, 7 are in a parable concerning how to act wisely. The scene is of a manager and a rich man. They are discussing monetary debts owed, or, rather, what "debts" might typically refer to. The last reference in 17:10 is Jesus teaching his disciples. By way of metaphor, Jesus asks a rhetorical question concerning the actions of a slave and how the slave's obedience relates to true discipleship. The "debt" is paid when the disciples exhibit true obedience. In this sense, "debts" is akin to "ought-ness" or obligation. In each of Luke's instances, the "debt" language is never used in relationship to "forgiveness" or as a metaphor for "sin" except in the instance of 13:4. In this instance, "debts" is used as a metaphor for "sin" but without reference to forgiveness.

[141] As Betz, *Sermon on the Mount*, 402, fn.488, notes, "In the NT this expression is rare."
[142] Noted in Davies and Allison, *Matthew 1–7*, 611.
[143] According to Betz, *Sermon on the Mount*, 402, fn.488, Matthew 18 "illustrates the doctrines underlying the fifth petition of the Lord's Prayer."

servant goes and finds a man who owes him an insignificant amount compared to his previously forgiven debt. When the man does not pay back the debt, the forgiven servant throws his debtor into prison, demanding that the last cent be paid. Onlookers witness the injustice and immediately report the events back to the king. The king brings the forgiven servant before him and punishes him by means of torture for his unrepentance and inability to show mercy. Matthew 18:23-35 is parallel to the forgiveness petition in three ways.

First, as we have illustrated above, Mt. 18:23-35 is the only example in the New Testament of "debt" language being discussed in relation to "forgiveness" besides the fifth petition. Second, the Lord's Prayer and Mt. 18:23-35 share several lexical parallels. Besides the repetition of forgiveness and debts, the king (Mt. 18:23) is compared to the heavenly Father (v. 35: ὁ πατήρ μου ὁ οὐράνιος). Although the wording is slightly different, the comparison of the king to the "heavenly Father" reminds us of the invocation (Πάτερ ἡμῶν ὁ ἐν τοῖς οὐρανοῖς) and the kingdom he will bring about (i.e., Mt. 6:10: the kingdom "of you/Father").[144] Verse 33 also contains the unusual conjunction ὡς καὶ. Third, Mt. 18:33 connects interpersonal and divine forgiveness. This interplay is shown in the comparison of the forgiveness of the Father/king and the unforgiving servant. The unforgiving slave is held accountable for his lack of mercy. The parable makes clear that it is the responsibility of being fellow slaves under the same king that one must show forgiveness to his or her debtors.[145] In the fifth petition, the conditional phrasing suggests that one must not expect forgiveness which he is not able to give to others.

An examination of Mt. 18:23-35 and its parallels with the fifth petition present a fuller picture of the petition's meaning. Matthew 18:23-35 refers to monetary "debts" to signify something that is "owed." In both ch. 18 and the fifth petition, the image of literal debt represents "sin."[146] Chapter 18 makes it clear that failure to show mercy closes the door to God's forgiveness. As Nolland notes, "Prophetic religion insisted on a consistency between the godward dimension of religious life and behaviour in the human community, and Matthew insists on the same here."[147] It is therefore incumbent upon those who profess the Father as king to make forgiveness and mercy a hallmark of their witness.

Debts Include Money and Moral Failure

As we have argued above, Matthew's connection of forgiveness with "debts" is what is distinctive about the wording of the fifth petition. The combination of the two terms

---

[144] As we argued in a previous chapter, the invocation has sovereign undertones and is frequently used in conjunction with references to God as king.

[145] See Hauck, "ὀφείλω," in *TDNT*, vol. 5, ed. G. Kittel and G. Friedrich, trans. G. W. Bromiley (Grand Rapids: Eerdmans), 563, states,

> The word σύνδουλος in Matt. 18:28f. is a reminder of the binding interrelation of men and of their common and very serious subjection to the same Lord and Judge. If there is a refusal to remit the debt of one's brother, then God for His part will replace grace by the pitiless justice which casts one back quite hopelessly into the state of inability to pay.

[146] See Nolland, *Gospel of Matthew*, 290.

[147] Nolland, *Gospel of Matthew*, 291.

is borrowed from the world of law and commerce.[148] As we will demonstrate, the wording in the fifth petition refers to both monetary debts and moral sin. As Young notes, "The word 'debts' is... flexible... Personal debts or moral obligations connected to interpersonal relationships, as well as sins, are encompassed by Jesus' words."[149] An examination of the history of the word "debts" confirms this suggestion. In the Old Testament, references to debts referred almost exclusively to monetary loans. Deuteronomy 15:2 and Isa. 24:2 refer to "debts," with subtle allusions to the remission of sins. Deuteronomy 15:2 states, "And this is the manner of the remission: every creditor shall remit the claim that is held against a neighbour, not exacting it of a neighbour who is a member of the community, because the Lord's remission has been proclaimed." The teaching of Deuteronomy is taken up in the proclamation of Isaiah 61. In this chapter, the "anointed" one inaugurates the "year of the Lord's favour" (v. 2). During this time, the remission of all debts occurs. The Lord's remission includes "debts," both financial and moral, as a means of restoring justice (vv. 10-11).[150] As we noted above, Wenham shows that the focused attention on righteousness and justice in the second half of Isaiah 61 is an "integral part of the joyous salvation which Yahweh's anointed one has been announcing."[151] It is likely that Matthew understood this background of "debts," as Isaiah 61 is a pivotal text for understanding earlier parts of the Sermon on the Mount (also Mt. 5:3-10).[152]

Like the Old Testament, the writings at Qumran almost exclusively use "debt" language to refer to monetary concerns.[153] The Aramaic word for "debt" is חיב /הבו. Although the examples that refer to "sins" as debts are rare, it is not completely absent. Anderson notes two passages. The first is *CD* 3:9-12. In the third column of the writing, the writer speaks of those who have turned to their own whims (v. 11). Those who were a part of the covenant were given to the sword because of their debts (הבו).[154] In this context, the "debt" is clearly not of monetary value but instead a reference to sin.[155]

---

[148] Betz, *Sermon on the Mount*, 402. See also Oakman, "Lord's Prayer in Social Perspective," 71-7. Oakman points out the context but presses the literal meaning of the terms too far. He ignores the addition of Mt. 6:14-15 to the end of the Lord's Prayer in Matthew's Gospel. As we will argue, the reference to "debts" refer to both money and sin.

[149] Young, *Jewish Background to the Lord's Prayer*, 30.

[150] Contra Lyndon Drake, "Did Jesus Oppose the *Prosbul* in the Forgiveness Petition of the Lord's Prayer?," *NovT* 56 (2014): 233-44, who argues that the focus of Jesus's teaching is on literal debts. Drake argues that Jesus's hearers would have heard the fifth petition as Jesus's opposition to the *prosbul* in relation to the *Jubilee*. Marius J. Nel, "The Forgiveness of Debt in Matthew 6:12, 14–15," *Neot* 47.1 (2013): 92, rightfully notes that if Jesus wanted to make this understanding of debt part of the fifth petition, he has left it unclear. See also Nolland, *Gospel of Matthew*, 290, who argues similarly to Nel.

[151] Wenham, "Beatitudes: Observations on Structure," 211.

[152] For additional arguments examining Isaiah's importance for understanding the Sermon, see Wenham, "Beatitudes: Observations on Structure," 208–11.

[153] Gary A. Anderson, *Sin: A History* (New Haven: Yale University, 2009), 34. As Anderson notes, the "pronounced and nearly ubiquitous usage of debt language like that found in Rabbinic literature or the New Testament is not found at Qumran."

[154] For the full context, see F. G. Martinez and E. J. C. Tigchelaar, eds., *The Dead Sea Scrolls: Study Edition*, vol. 1 (Leiden: Brill, 1997), 555.

[155] See Anderson, *Sin*, 34.

A second text in which debts refers to moral guilt is 11QMelchizedek.[156] In this passage, Melchizedek is depicted as a royal figure and leader of the "children of light" (v. 8). In the flow of the passage, Melchizedek appeals to the texts of Lev. 25:8-17 and Deut. 15:1-11 (see above) in exacting a release for the debts of his men. Deuteronomy 15 describes a monetary debt release at the end of every seven years. Leviticus 25, on the other hand, prescribes a monetary debt release at the end of forty-nine years. In both cases, the instructions are given to landowners in relationship to their tenants. In the present passage, interestingly, this debt is owed to Belial, the leader of the sons of darkness.[157] When reflecting on the release of debts, Melchizedek "proclaims liberty for them to set them free and make atonement for their sins (vs. 6)." The writer here uses the monetary debt language of Leviticus and Deuteronomy in the first half of the phrase but applies its principles of monetary release to the moral failures of Melchizedek's men.[158]

In the Rabbinic literature, "debt" became a standard reference to sins. Although the English translation can be difficult, according to McNamara, the fundamental meaning is something akin to "sin" or "guilt."[159] In *Tg. Neof. Ex.* 32:31, Moses says: "This people have sinned great sins (חוֹבָא)" In the *Tg. OnkE.* 10:17, the Hebrew phrase is rendered as "pardon now my guilt" in the Aramaic שְׁבוֹק כְּעַן לְחוֹבַי)). Other examples of "debts" as sins include: *Gen. Rab.* 85:2; 92:9; *Ex. Rab.* 25:6; 31:1; *Pesiq. R.* 11:23; 51:8.[160]

In conclusion, "debts" can refer to both monetary and moral guilt. The term transformed over time and throughout various literature, but both meanings stayed intact. Until the Rabbinic literature, examples of "debts" referring to moral guilt were relatively few. Within the Rabbinic literature, "debt" became the standard term for sin. The symbolism of "debts" is apt given its broad meaning of "obligation," whether financial concerns or moral failure before God.

Interpersonal and Divine Forgiveness

As we have noted above, interpersonal and divine forgiveness are linked in the fifth petition. The petitioner offers forgiveness to his debtors, while requesting forgiveness from God concerning his own debts. These bilateral relationships are interconnected in their execution. This concept was widespread in Judaism. *Sirach* 28:2-4 states, "Forgive your neighbour the wrong he has done, and then your sins will be pardoned when you pray. Does a man harbour anger against another, and yet seek for healing from the Lord? Does he have no mercy toward a man like himself, and yet pray for his own

---

[156] For a full reading and translation of this text, see M. DeJonge and A. S. Van Der Woude, "11Q Melchizedek and the New Testament," *NTS* 12 (1965–6): 301–26.

[157] See 11Q Melchizedek 13. It is interesting that this idea of debt is juxtaposed with the concept of an agent of darkness. This combination of concepts is certainly present in the Lord's Prayer in its appeal to forgiveness of "debts" and deliverance from the "evil one."

[158] See also Joseph A. Fitzmyer, "Further Light on Melchizedek from Qumran Cave 11," *JBL* 86 (1967): 25–41. Pitre, "Lord's Prayer and the New Exodus," 89–90.

[159] Martin McNamara, *Targum and Testament-Aramaic Paraphrases of the Hebrew Bible: A Light on the New Testament* (Grand Rapids: Eerdmans, 1972), 120.

[160] See Keener, *Gospel of Matthew*, 223. McNamara, *Targum and Testament*, 120. The major difference is the presence of a conditional clause in the forgiveness petition.

sins?"¹⁶¹ A similar teaching is found in *m. Yoma* 8.9: "God will not affect atonement for the sins of a person against his fellow human beings until he has received the forgiveness of the fellow human beings."¹⁶²

Before moving to the next section, it is important to sort out the relationship of interpersonal and divine forgiveness. The matter is complicated by the interrelatedness of the conditional phrasing of the fifth petition with the use of the particle ὡς καὶ and the translation of the verb in the second clause. If the verb in the second clause is translated as a perfect verb, as Hans Dieter Betz has asserted, the second clause is typically translated, "as we also have forgiven."¹⁶³ The completed action as denoted by the perfect tense, suggests that the petitioner is offering his completed forgiveness as cause for God to act. The causal relationship between interpersonal and divine forgiveness is relieved in the Lukan version. The conjunction is purely coordinating (καὶ γὰρ), and Luke uses the present tense verb in the second clause to describe the ongoing process of forgiveness (i.e., an iterative emphasis). God is forgiving a disciple's sins, while the disciple continues to forgive. Both actions are happening concurrently.

A close examination of the fifth petition reveals more similarity in meaning with the Lukan version than initially perceived. First, Betz mistakenly identifies the tense of the verb as perfect.¹⁶⁴ The consequence of the perfect parsing is the assumption that the completed acts of forgiveness merit God's forgiveness. The verb tense is more accurately parsed as an aorist active indicative. As Mounce notes, three μι verbs form their aorist active indicatives with -κα instead of -σα.¹⁶⁵ Among those three instances, ἀφίημι takes on the -κα stem in the athematic conjugation.¹⁶⁶ In this regard, Matthew and Luke's understanding of divine and interpersonal forgiveness would be similar. The aorist is consistent with Matthew's other petitions and does not necessarily signify completed action in a punctiliar sense. Matthew's usage should be translated along the lines, "forgive us like we forgave" or "as we are also forgiving" to deemphasize the "completed act of forgiveness as cause/merit for God's forgiveness."¹⁶⁷ Second, an examination of ὡς καὶ reveals that the phrase is conditional but not in a causal sense. As we have noted above, the particle is used in two other places in Matthew's Gospel. In Mt. 20:14, Jesus discusses the pay for workers in the field. Jesus is asked a question about the fairness of his agreement to pay one denarius. He answers that he intends to pay the workers in a comparable fashion ("I choose to give to this last the same *as*

---

[161] Richard B. Hays, *Echoes of Scripture in the Gospels* (Waco: Baylor, 2016), 123–4, argues that *Sirach* is the closest parallel to the fifth petition.
[162] Quoted in Luz, *Matthew 1–7*, 322.
[163] The ESV.
[164] It appears that Betz, *Sermon on the Mount*, 404, mistakenly assumes a perfect tense from the κα– morpheme.
[165] William D. Mounce, *The Morphology of Biblical Greek* (Grand Rapids: Zondervan, 1994), 101. He explains, "Ἀφίημι is a compound of ἀπό and ἵημι. In the formation of the present tense, the ο elides and the π aspirates to a φ. The η therefore represents the stem vowel." 101, fn.1.
[166] As Quarles, *Sermon on the Mount*, 210, fn.361, has noted, "The verb is clearly an aorist, which often uses the κα– morpheme in the athematic conjugation." See also, Gundry, *Matthew*, 108; Luz, *Matthew 1–7*, 322; BDAG, 156; and Davies and Allison, *Matthew 1–7*, 611–12. "Athematic" refers to having a suffix at the end of a verb without a connecting vowel.
[167] See Quarles, *Matthew*, 64.

I give to you"). In the second instance (Mt. 18:33), the wording and connotation are almost identical to Mt. 6:12. As we have argued above, Mt. 18:23-35 is important for understanding the fifth petition. Verse 33 states, "Should you not have had mercy on your fellow slave, as (ὡς κἀγώ) I had mercy on you?" The king asks the unforgiving servant if he is exempt from showing forgiveness. The king shows mercy to this servant earlier in the narrative and then finds out later that the forgiven servant is not showing mercy to others. The children of God must be marked by forgiveness, both in being given forgiveness and in giving subsequent forgiveness.

In this regard, the fifth petition prays to a God who forgives. God's forgiveness becomes the standard by which the petitioner forgives (i.e., as the Father, so his children). The petitioner then offers their forgiveness as evidence of being God's children and God may continue to show forgiveness to those who ask. As Davies and Allison state, "God's forgiveness, although it cannot be merited, must be received, and it cannot be received by those without the will to forgive others."[168]

Forgiveness Is the Will of God

As we have argued in Chapter 3 and illustrated in Chapter 4, the forgiveness and will petitions are structurally and thematically connected. In addition to this structural link, Matthew 18 links the will of God and forgiveness. In Mt. 18:14, Jesus discusses the "will of your Father in heaven" (τοῦ πατρὸς ὑμῶν τοῦ ἐν οὐρανοῖς). This teaching (Mt. 18:10-14) is found between Jesus's teaching on stumbling blocks (Mt. 18:6-9) and reproving a brother or sister who has sinned (Mt. 18:15-22). The interplay between these passages indicates that they should be read together. The teaching on stumbling blocks (Mt. 18:6-9) warns that one should avoid causing a "little one" to stumble. Matthew 18:10-14 instructs that the "will of the Father" is caring for the "little ones." The "little one" is a sheep who is lost, and the shepherd seeks him out, even if he is one out of a hundred sheep. Verse 15 picks up on this idea of seeking out a "lost one." The lost one has gone astray in sin. Church members are encouraged to go after him in the same way that the shepherd seeks after their lost sheep. This teaching (Mt. 18:15-20) is followed by Peter's question concerning forgiveness (18:21-22: "Lord, if another member of the church sins against me, how often should I forgive?") and the parable of the unforgiving servant (Mt. 18:23-35). Matthew 18:21-22 makes clear that the one who has gone astray must be forgiven for his sins (i.e., forgiven "seventy-seven" times) in the same manner that the Father in heaven forgives (18:23-35). These conceptual links within ch. 18 suggests that the chapter is one continuous narrative about forgiveness as the will of the Father.[169] Therefore, the will of

---

[168] Davies and Allison, *Matthew 1–7*, 611. Gundry, *Matthew*, 108–9, similarly argues that Matthew has changed the "for" in Luke's conditional phrasing. He states,

> Theologically, the change produces an interpretation of the original "for" as indicating a paradigm of forgiveness rather than a reason for forgiveness; i.e. forgiveness of others presents God with an example of the forgiveness sought from him, not with a meritorious act by which God's forgiveness might be earned. Forgiveness of others demonstrates sincerity in asking forgiveness from God.

[169] Additional links include the heaven and earth language throughout Matthew 18 (heaven: vv. 3, 4, 10, 18, 19, 35/earth: vv. 2 [implied], 12 [implied], 18) and the will petition. See Kiley, "The Lord's

the Father in heaven (Mt. 6:10//18:14) is to forgive as the Father in heaven forgives (Mt. 6:12//18:27, 35).

Additional evidence for this linkage between forgiveness and doing the will of God is found in a comparison between the fifth petition with similar Jewish prayers mentioned above (see esp. *Sir.* 28:1-7). These Jewish prayers do not contain the emphasis on human action contained in the fifth petition. Luz agrees, "In my opinion, there is no case where human action is taken into a central prayer text in this way . . . [P]rayer and human action are not mutually exclusive."[170] Jesus gives the fifth petition with the prescription, even expectation, that prayers for God's forgiveness will be accompanied with ever-giving forgiveness from the petitioner. Throughout the book, we have suggested that the praying of the Lord's Prayer engages one in the teachings and moral conduct prescribed by the Sermon on the Mount. In this regard, the fifth petition is the most explicit connection of prayer in "action."

Conclusion

From our analysis, we conclude that the forgiveness petition is primarily concerned with broken relationships, particularly broken by indebtedness. In this section, we have analyzed the concepts of "forgiveness," "debts," and the relationship between interpersonal and divine forgiveness. Our analysis has showed the significance of Matthew 18 for understanding these important concepts and their relationship to the forgiveness petition. In this section, we have argued that "debts" refers to both financial obligations and moral guilt. Also, the fifth petition intricately links interpersonal and divine forgiveness. The petition makes clear that failure to forgive others will result in a lack of forgiveness from the Father (see Mt. 6:14-15; 18:35). Lastly, we have argued that forgiveness is part of the will of God. The forgiveness petition brings human action explicitly into the praying of the Lord's Prayer.

"Forgive Our Debts, As We Forgive Our Debtors" in the Sermon on the Mount

In the previous section, we argued that the fifth petition is primarily explained by Matthew 18 and comparable texts within Matthew's cultural milieu. These texts suggest that the fifth petition concerns forgiveness for all sorts of "debts," both financial and moral. The fifth petition also joins prayer and human action by way of comparing interpersonal and divine forgiveness. Lastly, forgiveness is closely linked with the will of God. In this section, we will analyze those passages in the Sermon on the Mount that share textual connections with the fifth petition (Mt. 5:7, 21-26, 38-42, 43-48;

Prayer and Matthean Theology," 18. Kiley connects the will petition with Mt. 18:10-14 but does not extend the connections to the rest of ch. 18.

[170] Luz, *Matthew 1-7*, 322. Also, I. Abrahams, *Studies in Pharisaism and the Gospels*, 2nd ed. (Cambridge: Cambridge University Press, 1924), 98, states, "This would involve a *nuance* unfamiliar if not unknown to Jewish theology. [...] This particular petition in the Lord's Prayer emanates, not from Jewish models, but from the peculiar thought of Jesus himself." Emphasis his.

6:14-15; 7:1-5). These connections are defined by lexical and thematic parallels. Although none of the Sermon passages explicitly mention ὀφείλημα, debt imagery is still arguably present. The parallels within the Sermon on the Mount also closely relate to Mt. 18:23-35 in the same manner as the forgiveness petition. The debt imagery and shared allusions to Mt. 18:23-35 then strengthen the parallelism with the fifth petition and the respective Sermon passages. We will begin with Mt. 6:14-15 as it functions as a sayings commentary on the fifth petition and then examine the references in their order of appearance (Mt. 5:7, 21–26, 38–42, 43–47; 7:1–5) throughout the Sermon on the Mount.[171]

Matthew 6:14-15

The closest parallel to the fifth petition, by definition and proximity, is found in Mt. 6:14-15. The text reads, "For if you forgive (ἀφῆτε) others their trespasses (παραπτώματα), your heavenly Father will also forgive (ἀφήσει) you; but if you do not forgive (ἀφῆτε) others, neither will your Father forgive (ἀφήσει) your trespasses (παραπτώματα)." The structure of the Sermon on the Mount, specifically Mt. 6:5-15, has vv. 7-8 and 14-15 as an *inclusio* around the Lord's Prayer. As we have argued in Chapter 3, these verses are considered "prayer words" because of their connection with the Lord's Prayer.[172] Mark 11:25 ("Whenever you stand praying, forgive, if you have anything against anyone; so that your Father in heaven may also forgive you your trespasses") places similar teaching on forgiveness in a context of prayer (Mk 11:22-26). It is probable that Matthew is connecting the sayings in Mt. 6:14-15 with prayer in the same manner as his Markan source. The message of vv. 14-15 sets forth positive and negative teachings concerning forgiveness. God will forgive those who forgive (v. 14) and will withhold forgiveness from those who do not forgive (v. 15). The conditional phrasing makes man's forgiveness a prerequisite for God's forgiveness, but not the cause. Matthew 6:14-15 reiterates the teaching of the fifth petition and brings forgiveness to the forefront of the Lord's Prayer. As we have argued throughout this book, other parts of the Lord's Prayer are explained by sections of the Sermon on the Mount and Matthew's Gospel, but none of the petitions are featured in the immediate context in the manner of the teaching on forgiveness. As Davies and Allison state, the question of Matthew's placement of vv. 14-15 is often ignored.[173] Davies and Allison argue that the placement puts communal reconciliation at the center of the Lord's Prayer. As the disciples pray to "our Father," so they must be defined by interpersonal forgiveness.[174] This suggestion is certainly correct, but vv. 14-15 also reiterate the heaven and earth theme prevalent throughout the rest of the Sermon. Matthew's placement of teaching for the community (vv. 14-15) forms the "earthly" counterpart to the "heavenly" teaching in vv. 7-8. Verses 7-8 depicts the assurance that the Father in heaven knows the answer to our prayers (i.e., the Lord's Prayer) before we even ask him.

---

[171] A closely worded parallel to Mt. 5:7 is found in Lk. 6:36 ("Be merciful, just as your Father is merciful"), but the form suggests a more substantive parallel with Mt. 5:48.
[172] Also, Luz, *Matthew 1–7*, 173.
[173] Davies and Allison, *Matthew 1–7*, 616.
[174] Davies and Allison, *Matthew 1–7*, 617.

The connections between the fifth petition and Mt. 6:14-15 are twofold. First, both passages discuss the forgiveness of "debts." The key link between the passages is the lexical parallel of ἀφίημι. Verse 14 describes the object of forgiveness as trespasses (τὰ παραπτώματα αὐτῶν).[175] *BDAG* defines "παραπτώματα" as a "misstep, particularly in violation of a moral standard."[176] As Nolland notes, the switch from "debts" to "transgressions," which is only used here in Matthew, confirms the definition of debts as any type of wrongdoing.[177] Second, both passages intertwine interpersonal and divine forgiveness. As Garland notes, "Forgiveness is not dependent on our having forgiven others first. But persons should not expect to receive from God what they are not prepared to bestow on others."[178] It is within this understanding of God's shared mercies that one seeks reconciliation with their brother or sister.[179] The conditionality of vv. 14-15 reiterates the emphasis in the fifth petition that one must show forgiveness to others before seeking God's forgiveness.

Matthew 5:7

The next instance of Sermon material that parallels the fifth petition is found in the *macarisms*. Matthew 5:7 states, "Blessed are the merciful, for they will receive mercy" (μακάριοι οἱ ἐλεήμονες, ὅτι αὐτοὶ ἐλεηθήσονται). The key term in v. 7 is "merciful" (ἐλεήμων) and its cognate (ἐλεέω). Ἐλεήμων is only found here in Matthew's Gospel and Heb. 2:17. The imagery in Heb. 2:17 is of Christ as a merciful priest who gives pardon for sin. The mercy of the priest is showed by his offering on behalf of a guilty party (i.e., offering remission/propitiation of the guilty party's sin). Other instances of mercy and its cognates in Matthew's narrative include 9:13, 27; 12:7; 15:22; 17:15; 18:33; 20:30-31; 23:23. These instances fall into two groups. The first group refers to God's display and prescription for justice (Mt. 9:13; 12:7; 23:23). Jesus's desire is that his followers would show mercy (and "not sacrifice") to others. The second group are in instances of healing (Mt. 9:27; 15:22; 17:15; 20:30-31). Those who desire Jesus's healing come to him requesting mercy.[180] As Davies and Allison helpfully summarize, mercy "is a fundamental demand (see 9:13; 12:7; 23:23) which is fleshed out both by Jesus' words (5:43-48; 18:21-35; 25:31-46) and by his example (9:27-31; 15:21-28; 17:14-18; 20:29-34)."[181] In the second clause of Mt. 5:7, the verb is the future passive ἐλεηθήσονται. The future passive verb is commonly seen as a "divine" passive in this

---

[175] See also Eph. 1:7 ("In him we have redemption through his blood, the forgiveness of our trespasses, according to the riches of his grace.").
[176] *BDAG*, 770.
[177] Nolland, *Gospel of Matthew*, 293. Compare Lk. 11:4.
[178] Garland, "Lord's Prayer in the Gospel of Matthew," 223.
[179] As France, *Gospel of Matthew*, 252, notes, "In these verses the conditional element which was apparently implicit in v. 12 becomes quite explicit and is emphasized by being stated both positively and negatively. Only the forgiving will be forgiven." France also connects the teachings here with ch. 18 and Mt. 5:23-24, as we are arguing. Krister Stendahl, "Prayer and Forgiveness," *SEÅ* 22 (1957): 75, calls the parallel between the fifth petition and vv. 14-15 the "law of mutuality."
[180] See also Mt. 25:31-46 where the word "mercy" is not used, but care for the hungry, thirsty, naked, and sick is described. These actions constitute acts of mercy.
[181] Davies and Allison, *Matthew 1-7*, 454.

context. God is inferred to be the one giving mercy. This mercy is shown to those who are merciful.[182]

This verse shares several textual connections with the fifth petition. The wording of this *macarism* parallels both debts and forgiveness, along with the connection of interpersonal and divine forgiveness. In Matthew's Gospel, mercy and forgiveness are closely related terms.[183] This relationship is made explicit in the petition and *macarism's* shared pretext, Matthew 18. In this story of forgiveness (Mt. 18:23-35), the terms are used interchangeably. Verse 33 states, "Should you not have had *mercy* on your fellow slave, as I had *mercy* on you?" The question regarding mercy is referencing the previous example of forgiveness shown by the king to an indebted servant.

In addition to this parallel of meaning, the combination of the merciful and the one who shows mercy (i.e., God) in Mt. 5:7 evidences the interconnectedness of interpersonal and divine forgiveness found in the fifth petition. The teaching in Mt. 5:7 instructs Jesus's disciples to be merciful, while suggesting that they will be shown mercy by God in the future. Divine mercy in this case is conditioned on the disciple showing mercy to others. Quarles explains, "Showing mercy does not earn mercy from God, but it does express the humble repentance that is essential to receiving divine mercy."[184] As we argued above, the same insistence on disciples being a merciful/forgiving group is explained in Mt. 6:14-15 and 18:35.

Matthew 5:21-26

In Mt. 5:21-26, Jesus addresses the subject of anger toward a brother or sister. As with the other so-called "antitheses," Jesus begins with a reference to the Old Testament (v. 21) followed by a clarification of its intended purpose. Jesus teaches (v. 22) that avoiding murder is not enough and even anger toward another is liable to judgment (see Deuteronomy 16-18; 2 Chron. 19:5-10). The examples of wrongdoing (showing anger, insulting, cursing) toward one's brother or sister are followed by three parallel judgments (liable to judgment, liable to council, liable to hell fire).

Angry with a brother or sister	liable to judgment
Insult a brother or sister	liable to the council
Say "You fool"	liable to hell

Jesus summarizes these paralleled wrongdoings in v. 23 as offenses (τι κατὰ σου) and subsequently instructs his disciples to leave their offerings at the altar until the offense has been reconciled. Verse 23 states,

---

[182] Davies and Allison, *Matthew 1-7*, 454, similarly point out the concept of pardon.
[183] "Mercy" can also refer to giving to the poor/almsgiving, see Mt. 6:2-4 ("ἐλεημοσύνην/acts of mercy").
[184] Quarles, *Sermon on the Mount*, 63. Contra Luz, *Matthew 1-7*, 196.

So, when you are offering your gift at the altar, if you remember that your brother or sister has something against you, leave your gift there before the altar and go; first be reconciled to your brother or sister, and then come and offer your gift.

Once this forgiveness has been sought, one is able to properly offer gifts to God. Jesus's teaching implies a sense of debt to one's brother or sister. The language of reconciliation hints at this implication. As Hagner notes, "Perhaps we are to understand a reciprocal resentment. When reconciliation has been made, 'then' (τότε) the gift may be offered and, the implication is, then God will accept it; see Mark 11:25)."[185] In vv. 25-26, this debt language is made more explicit. The judgment associated with not reconciling with a brother or sister is imprisonment. Keener notes that Matthew "may use the custom of debt imprisonment as another image in the parable. No mercy would be shown: the amount of money to be repaid extended to the last (literally) *quadrans*, almost the least valuable Roman coin, the equivalent of only a few minutes' wages."[186] The debt metaphor ("last penny" [τὸν ἔσχατον κοδράντην]) is used hyperbolically here to stress the importance of reconciliation (also Mt. 18:34). Jesus's point is that right relationship with someone is of utmost importance regardless of the wrongdoing. It is interesting that no mention is made of the actual wrongdoing; it is just assumed that disciples would seek reconciliation regardless of the offense.[187]

The connections with the fifth petition and Jesus's teaching on anger begin with the need for repairing broken relationships. Forgiveness serves as a foil to anger and the inability to reconcile with one's brother or sister. In Mt. 5:21-26, debt language is used throughout to express the need for reconciliation and forgiveness.[188] Second, Mt. 5:21-26 joins interpersonal and divine activity. In this case, one must seek reconciliation with his or her brother or sister before offering his gift at the altar. If a disciple does not reconcile with the offender, judgment will ensue. This conditional statement leads to the next parallel. Third, the fifth petition and Mt. 5:21-26 share parallels with Mt. 18:23-35. Matthew 5:21-26 connects with this chapter by way of the repetition of ἀδελφός and the satiation of judgment.[189] Matthew 5:26 refers to a repayment of the "last cent" (τὸν ἔσχατον κοδράντην)," while Mt. 18:34 calls this payment a "debt" (πᾶν τὸ ὀφειλόμενον). This association of "debt" to the "last cent" closely parallels the "owing/debt" language in the forgiveness petition. Fourth, the *movement* of the fifth petition is mimicked by Mt. 5:21-26. It is assumed that one has forgiven his fellow brother in the fifth petition *before* he or she prays to God for his or her own "debts."[190] Similarly, in Mt. 5:21-26, one must leave his or her gift before God and reconcile with a brother or sister *before* giving a proper offering.

---

[185] Hagner, *Matthew 1-13*, 117.
[186] Craig S. Keener, *The IVP Bible Background Commentary: New Testament*, 2nd ed. (Downers Grove: IVP, 2014), 58.
[187] This is noted by Nolland, *Gospel of Matthew*, 232. He states, "It is no accident that Matt. 5:21-22 does not show the slightest interest in whether the person who is the object of the anger deserves it."
[188] Hagner, *Matthew 1-13*, 117.
[189] The reoccurrence of ἀδελφός is noted by France as a connection between Mt. 5:21-26 and 18:23-35. See Mt. 18:15, 21, 35 for references to ἀδελφός.
[190] Interestingly, the movement of ch. 18 is the forgiveness of God before the forgiveness of the indebted.

Matthew 5:38-42

Strained relationships are taken up again in Mt. 5:38-42. Here, Jesus addresses retaliation. The teaching begins with a reiteration of the *lex talionis* followed by Jesus's exhortation to love evildoers (τῷ πονηρῷ). This exhortation is followed by five instructions on how to love well. In each of these examples, Jesus does not demand what one might expect but rather to go above and beyond the normal reaction. Instead of giving someone what is due, a disciple is to give much more. The five examples include turning the other cheek, giving your last bit of clothing, walking the extra mile, giving to beggars, and lending to borrowers.

This teaching parallels the fifth petition in three ways. First, the examples of proper love for evildoers is laden with debt and obligation language.[191] Each of these examples works from the principle of one-to-one reciprocity. Jesus's teaching subverts the normal obligation of reciprocity within God's shared grace. Jesus's disciples do not simply repay the debt that is owed but are indebted to share God's abundant love to evildoers. In other words, one says no to retaliation but yes to mending strained relationships by being merciful (Mt. 5:7) and forgiving (Mt. 6:14-15) as the Father. Second, Mt. 5:38-42 shares lexical parallels with the Lord's Prayer, of which the fifth petition is a part. Besides the implicit references to "debt," both passages refer to evil (Mt. 5:39//6:13). Third, the fifth petition and Mt. 5:38-42 find a common parallel in Matthew 18. This connection is not immediately evident until one considers the parallels between Mt. 5:38-42 and 5:43-47, a set of teachings closely related to Matthew 18.[192]

1) Matthew 5:38-42 and 5:43-47 share similar references and responses to evil. Mercy is to be shown through non-retaliation and love of enemy.
2) In both Mt. 5:38-42 and 5:43-47, Jesus is encouraging supererogatory actions, that is, going up and above the normal obligation. It is not enough to return an eye for an eye or love your neighbor; instead, a disciple of the Father in heaven must love their enemy and give to them as they ask—tasks that evidence the Father's love.[193]

---

[191] Parallels include v. 40, "sue you" (καὶ τῷ θέλοντί σοι κριθῆναι); v. 41, "forces into service" (καὶ ὅστις σε ἀγγαρεύσει); v. 42, "and do not refuse anyone who wants to borrow from you (καὶ τὸν θέλοντα ἀπὸ σοῦ δανίσασθαι μὴ ἀποστραφῇς). Davies and Allison, *Matthew 1-7*, 545-6, point out that Matthew and Luke have switched the ordering of the tunic and garment in their respective versions. The context of Luke is of a disciple being robbed, with the outer garment being the first piece to go. After this is gone, the disciples should give his inner garment as a statement of going above the normal obligation. Matthew is thinking of a court scene in which one is required to give the inner garment because the outer garment cannot be legally requisitioned. Yet, in Matthew, the outer garment is to be given as well. Matthew's version is stressing the legal/debt imagery with its ordering.

[192] Allison, *Sermon on the Mount*, 93, even notes the continuity between Mt. 5:21-26 and 5:38-42. He states, "In 5:21-26 Jesus forbids anger, an emotion that would make the actions of 5:38-42 impossible."

[193] The point of the teaching is not indiscriminate giving but mimicking the Father's love for humanity (v. 45).

Matthew 5:43-47

Matthew 5:43-47 continue the teaching of Mt. 5:38-42 with lessons on how to love others. Whereas Mt. 5:38-42 functions as a negation prohibiting retaliation, vv. 43-47 encourages the love of neighbors and enemies.[194] This love of enemy is to be coupled with prayers on their behalf. Jesus provides the example of the Father's ("in heaven") love over the righteous and unrighteous as a precedent for the disciples' love. Just as the Father in heaven loves, so his disciples will love. The teaching ends with a series of rhetorical questions concerning the obligation of love. The implied answer to these questions is that a disciple will always mimic the Father.

This teaching continues the themes mentioned in Mt. 5:38-42 and for this reason shares many of the same parallels with the fifth petition. The instruction to love others, even enemies, must embody the ethic of forgiveness encouraged in Mt. 5:7; 6:12; and 6:14-15. The mention of prayer for enemies alludes to the rhetorical function of the Lord's Prayer. Prayers for those who persecute disciples might include not only delivery from enemies (Mt. 6:13) but also strength to forgive their "transgressions" (Mt. 6:12).[195] The connection of interpersonal and divine forgiveness in the fifth petition is also found in Mt. 5:43-47. As the Father in heaven (Mt. 5:45//6:9) loves the righteous and unrighteous, so his disciples must love their neighbors and enemies (Mt. 5:44). Quarles captures these ideas well:

> Jesus' concern in this text was not with the status of sonship but with the characteristics of sonship. Jesus recognized that just as the son of an earthly father will resemble his father in many ways—his appearance, his mannerisms, his gait, and so forth—so the children of God will resemble their heavenly Father in their character and behaviour.[196]

Matthew 7:1-5

The last parallel to the fifth petition is found in Mt. 7:1-5. Matthew 7:1-5 deals with the topic of judging others.[197] Jesus begins his discussion with a metaphor concerning measurements ("For with the judgment you make you will be judged, and the measure you give will be the measure you get"). The analogy is illustrative of the comparative

---

[194] The text reads in full,
> You have heard that it was said, "You shall love your neighbour and hate your enemy." But I say to you, "Love your enemies and pray for those who persecute you, so that you may be children of your Father in heaven; for he makes his sun rise on the evil and on the good, and sends rain on the righteous and on the unrighteous. For if you love those who love you, what reward do you have? Do not even the tax collectors do the same? And if you greet only your brothers and sisters, what more are you doing than others? Do not even the Gentiles do the same?"

[195] The parallel with the seventh petition is examined in Chapter 4.
[196] Quarles, *Sermon on the Mount*, 163.
[197] To clarify, Jesus is not condemning all judging. Instead, he is condemning unfair and unbalanced assessments of other's actions. McKnight, *Sermon on the Mount*, 227, insightfully notes, "We must learn to distinguish moral discernment from personal condemnation."

aspect of judgment. To the extent one measures, one will be measured. In vv. 3-4, Jesus issues two rhetorical questions based on his analogy of measurements. The questions center around the speck in a neighbor's "eye" and the "log" in one's own eye. Verse 5 finishes the teaching with an exhortation to restrain from unfair judgments because of the disproportionate guilt one should acknowledge in their own life. It states, "You hypocrite, first take the log out of your own eye, and then you will see clearly to take the speck out of your neighbour's eye."

These verses connect with the fifth petition in three ways.[198] First, the bilateral relationship is explicit in both passages. As Keener notes, the idea of a measuring scale was used in Jewish tradition for the Day of Judgment.[199] In other words, with the same measure one uses with a brother or sister, so one will be measured by God. Second, the concept of reciprocity is evoked in both passages. Matthew 7:1-5 is explaining the relationship between equals and arguing that judgment is unnecessary because everyone has his or her own faults. Jesus evokes the hyperbolic examples of a "log" and a "speck" to make his point. One's "log" is his faults before God, and therefore, one cannot evaluate another's failures (i.e., "speck"). Therefore, do not judge, for you will be judged (Mt. 7:1). Third, the teaching in Mt. 7:1-5 and the fifth petition share the background of Matthew 18. Matthew 18:23-35 explores the topic of differing amounts of indebtedness. Similarly, Mt. 7:1-5 takes up the topic of unproportioned faults. In these verses, one is advised to avoid harsh judgments for fear that one's own indebtedness far outweighs the debts of others.

Forgiveness Petition Conclusion

In what has preceded, we have analyzed the forgiveness petition, as it is an integral petition of the Lord's Prayer. The forgiveness petition is defined by its distinctive phrasing, specifically the juxtaposition of "debts" and "forgiveness." The forgiveness petition is also distinctive in its close connection between prayer and human action, along with the petitioner's responsibility to forgive others as he or she has been forgiven by God. This connection between interpersonal and divine forgiveness gives the fifth petition a triangular shape in which petitioners are to show forgiveness to their debtors before approaching God for forgiveness. At the heart of the forgiveness petition is a request to repair broken relationships (Mt. 6:14-15). Therefore, when the fifth petition is prayed within the context of the Sermon on the Mount, it entails a request to be merciful (Mt. 5:7, 6:14-15), seek reconciliation with others (Mt. 5:21-26), resist retaliation (Mt. 5:38-42), love and pray for enemies (Mt. 5:43-47), and avoid unfair judgments (Mt. 7:1-5).

---

[198] Contra Lambrecht, *Sermon on the Mount*, 164. Guelich, *Sermon on the Mount*, 324, states, "Matt. 7:1–5 on Judging, begins to make sense in its present location, since it now provides the counterpart to the fifth petition concerning forgiveness (6:12)."

[199] Keener, *Gospel of Matthew*, 241.

Chapter Conclusion

This chapter has argued that Matthew's understanding of the kingdom, bread, and forgiveness petition is made clear by their location with the Sermon on the Mount. Matthew establishes textual connections between these petitions with his chosen context by using lexical and thematic parallels. These parallels reaffirm the structural centrality, as we argued in Chapter 3, of the Lord's Prayer. As we have continued to argue in this chapter, Matthew has distinctive wording and verbal preferences, which establish continuity between the Lord's Prayer and the Sermon on the Mount. The distinctives of these petitions are not as pronounced as the invocation, will, and evil petitions but, nevertheless, evidence parallels. These lexical parallels are reinforced by an analysis of each petition's meaning within Matthew's cultural milieu. While some of the petitions evidence wording found throughout Jewish literature, some of the wording is heavily shaped by Matthew himself. By analyzing the proposed textual connections between the petitions and passages in the Sermon on the Mount, it becomes evident that Matthew is shaping these texts to be read together.

To review, when read in this manner, praying "your kingdom come" implies embodying the kingdom ethics of the *macarisms* (Mt. 5:3-10), fulfilling the law and prophets (Mt. 5:17-20), seeking the kingdom and righteousness (Mt. 6:33), and performing the will of God (Mt. 7:21-23). The request may also imply a desire to avoid the easy way of life that leads to destruction (Mt. 7:13-14). The bread petition is a request and affirmation of fully trusting that God will provide daily sustenance (Mt. 6:25-34; 7:7-11) but not at the expense of God's kingdom and righteousness (Mt. 6:33). The request may also loosely parallel the instruction to the disciples to "hunger and thirst" after righteousness (Mt. 5:6), seek heavenly treasures above earthly treasures (Mt. 6:19-21), and worship God over wealth (Mt. 6:24). The forgiveness petition is a request to repair broken relationships in the same manner that God has restored relationship with his disciples (Mt. 6:14-15). This triangular shape demands that petitioners will be merciful (Mt. 5:7, 6:14-15), seek reconciliation with others (Mt. 5:21-26), resist retaliation (Mt. 5:38-42), love and pray for enemies (Mt. 5:43-47), and avoid unnecessary judgment (Mt. 7:1-5).

6

The Remaining Petitions

An Examination of the Name and Temptation Petitions

In Chapters 4 and 5, we have argued for various parallels between the Lord's Prayer and the Sermon on the Mount. The invocation, will, and evil petitions displayed extensive lexical and thematic parallels with the Sermon on the Mount. In addition to these parallels, the wording of these petitions is clustered into Matthew 5–7, signaling that the petitions and Sermon references should be read together. The kingdom, bread, and forgiveness petitions similarly display lexical and thematic parallels, but lack the prominence of the invocation, will, and evil petitions within Matthew 5–7. Whether as an added phrase prominently featured in chs 5–7, distinctive wording, or shared theme, the petitions signal the hand of Matthew in shaping his version of the Lord's Prayer as the centerpiece of the Sermon on the Mount. The two remaining petitions differ from those mentioned in the previous chapters.

Matthew 6:9b-13	Luke 11:2-4
⁹Πάτερ ἡμῶν ὁ ἐν τοῖς οὐρανοῖς	²Πάτερ,
ἁγιασθήτω τὸ ὄνομά σου,	**ἁγιασθήτω τὸ ὄνομά σου**
¹⁰ἐλθέτω ἡ βασιλεία σου,	ἐλθέτω ἡ βασιλεία σου
γενηθήτω τὸ θέλημά σου,	
ὡς ἐν οὐρανῷ καὶ ἐπὶ γῆς	
¹¹τὸν ἄρτον ἡμῶν τὸν ἐπιούσιον	³τὸν ἄρτον ἡμῶν τὸν ἐπιούσιον
δὸς ἡμῖν σήμερον	δίδου ἡμῖν τὸ καθ' ἡμέραν
¹²καὶ ἄφες ἡμῖν τὰ ὀφειλήματα ἡμῶν,	⁴καὶ ἄφες ἡμῖν τὰς ἁμαρτίας ἡμῶν,
ὡς καὶ ἡμεῖς ἀφήκαμεν τοῖς	καὶ γὰρ αὐτοὶ ἀφίομεν παντὶ
ὀφειλέταις ἡμῶν	ὀφείλοντι ἡμῖν
¹³**καὶ μὴ εἰσενέγκῃς ἡμᾶς εἰς**	**καὶ μὴ εἰσενέγκῃς ἡμᾶς εἰς**
πειρασμόν,	**πειρασμόν.**
ἀλλὰ ῥῦσαι ἡμᾶς ἀπὸ τοῦ πονηροῦ.	

In the Matthean and Lukan versions, the phrases are verbatim.[1] Interestingly, this absence of distinctive elements in these two petitions results in a lack of extensive parallels with the Sermon.[2] However, the Name and temptation petitions do share themes with various passages throughout the Sermon. In the following analysis, we will focus on these thematic parallels to establish textual connections between the remaining petitions and the Sermon on the Mount. We will first examine the meaning of each petition by looking to Matthew's cultural milieu for ideas associated with the wording of each petition. This analysis will establish a basis for identifying thematic parallels between the Lord's Prayer and the Sermon on the Mount. In the next section, we will examine the parallels between the petition under consideration and the passages in the Sermon. In considering the parallels, we will focus on those parallels with the Sermon on the Mount that have been previously unexamined.[3] Finally, after arguing for the various parallels between each petition and passage in the Sermon, we will suggest what praying the Lord's Prayer might look like if prayed through the lens of the Sermon on the Mount and vice versa.

First Petition: "Hallowed Be Your Name"

The Lord's Prayer begins with the request to hallow the name of God. Although simple in form, the petition establishes the emphasis for the first half of the prayer, an emphasis that focuses the petitioner godward.[4] Unfortunately, the importance of the first petition is often subordinated by commentators to the invocation and second petition. Interpreters will see the Name petition as an application of the invocation,[5] calling for the "hallowing" of the Father in heaven, while others read the petition as referring to the eschatological future and anticipating the emphasis of the second petition.[6] In effect, the first petition becomes almost identical in meaning and function to whichever line of the Prayer it is being paralleled. An often-neglected aspect of the first petition is its relationship to the Sermon on the Mount. In the following sections, we will examine the Name petition by examining its meaning within Matthew's cultural milieu. We will begin with an analysis of the petition's keywords, followed

---

[1] See also *Did.* 8:2. This statement is also true of the kingdom petition, but the kingdom petition has numerous lexical parallels with passages in the Sermon on the Mount, making the petition more fitting for the previous chapter.
[2] The only distinctive element of each petition is its proximity to other distinctive elements in the Matthean version of the Lord's Prayer. By extensive, we are referring to structural, lexical, and thematic parallels working in tandem.
[3] As we have stated elsewhere, it is likely that Matthew noted parallels between the Lord's Prayer and the Sermon on the Mount and even increased the parallelism in some instances. Therefore, it should be expected that various parallels can be established between one petition and several Sermon passages and one Sermon passage can parallel several petitions.
[4] James Swetnam, "Hallowed be thy Name," *Bib* 52.4 (1971): 558, calls it a "deceptively simple phrase."
[5] Norman Metzler, "The Lord's Prayer: Second Thoughts on the First Petition," in *Authentication the Words of Jesus. NT Tools and Studies*, ed. Bruce Chilton and Craig Evans (Leiden: Brill, 1999), 187–202; Swetnam, "Hallowed Be Thy Name," 556–63; E.-J. Vledder, "'Laat uw Naam geheilig worden': Een uiting van eerbied aan God," *HTR* 67.1 (2011): 1–6.
[6] Davies and Allison, *Matthew 1–7*; Nolland, *Gospel of Matthew*, 287.

by a discussion of its temporality, and then its connection to ethics/discipleship. This analysis will establish a basis for identifying thematic parallels with passages in the Sermon on the Mount (Mt. 5:16, 33-37; and 7:21-23).[7]

The Meaning of "Hallowed Be Your Name"

To understand the first petition, we will explore the meaning of its two keywords. A study of the "Name" and "hallow" shows that the first petition is concerned with the proper reverence of God.

Hallowing and Profaning the Name

Scot McKnight aptly begins his study of the first petition noting, "Those who love God long for him to be honoured."[8] The first petition then establishes the proper emphasis for the petitions that follow by requesting the hallowing/revering of God's name. The first key term in the first petition is the instruction to "hallow." The word translated "hallow" is from the Greek word ἁγιάζω. The word is associated with being "set apart" or "sacred."[9] It is part of a larger vocabulary associated with the Jewish sacrificial system.[10] Hallowing God's name was fundamental to Jewish ethics, along with its opposite, profaning the name (see Lev. 18:21; 19:12; 20:3; 21:6; 22:2, 32; Ps. 74:7; Jer. 34:16; Ezek. 36:20; 39:7; 43:7-8; Amos 2:7). The key text for understanding the Old Testament background of honoring the name of God and avoiding the profaning of the Name is Exod. 20:7. Exodus 20:7 states, "You shall not make wrongful use of the name of the Lord your God, for the Lord will not acquit anyone who misuses his name." The Hebrew word used for "in vain" is לַשָּׁוְא. The phrase refers to bringing emptiness to the name of God or "causing it to be worthless." In the broader context of ch. 20, God is giving Israel directions on how to live among the surrounding nations and how to remain holy. The conclusion is that the Israelites can profane God's name through their actions and, conversely, "hallow" that name through keeping God's commandments. It would have been unthinkable to honor God's name and then immediately profane the same name. Consider the wisdom of Prov. 30:7-9:

> Two things I ask of you;
>> do not deny them to me before I die:
> Remove far from me falsehood and lying;

---

[7] While the following passages exhibit demonstrable parallels with the first petition, arguably, the entire Sermon is concerned with the "setting apart" of God's name. The discipleship prescribed by the Sermon defines Christian identity. As Luz, *Matthew 1-7*, 318, notes, "The petition is not a disguised challenge to oneself; it is still a request: human knowledge, human action, and human experience are made possible, encouraged, and supported by God." By extension, the name of God is made known in the world through Christian presence, as it is empowered by God.
[8] McKnight, *Sermon on the Mount*, 176.
[9] *BDAG*, 10, defines the word, "to treat as holy, reverence." The first petition already retains this concept of reverence by using the circumlocution of "Name" for God.
[10] O. Procksch, "Holiness," in *TDNT*, vol. 1, ed. G. Kittel and G. Friedrich, trans. G. W. Bromiley (Grand Rapids: Eerdmans, 1964-76), 89.

> give me neither poverty nor riches;
> feed me with the food that I need,
> or I shall be full, and deny you,
> and say, "Who is the Lord?"
> or I shall be poor, and steal,
> and profane the name of my God.

The words of Agur record an individual who prays for daily food and to avoid falsehood. He then records a hypothetical event in which the person who has been given food questions the source or steals instead of waiting for provision. In so doing, the person profanes the name of God and poses an affront to the God we confess.[11]

When one turns to the New Testament, the idea of hallowing God's name is not common. Possible parallels among the Gospels include Lk. 1:49 and Jn 12:28.[12] In Lk. 1:49, Mary sings about the holiness of God's name (καὶ ἅγιον τὸ ὄνομα αὐτοῦ). In this clause, holy is an adjective for God's name and not in the imperatival form found in the first petition. John is the closest parallel to Matthew's reference to the name. In Jn 12:28, Jesus gives instruction to his disciples to pray that the Father may glorify his name (δόξασόν σου τὸ ὄνομα). John's connotation refers more to the concept of "showing forth" or "magnifying" God's name (see Mt. 5:16) but retains the sense of "hallowing."[13]

Among the epistles, there are two references in which the name is set apart, although the language of "holiness" (ἁγιάζω) is not used. Romans 15:9 quotes from Ps. 18:49. The verses states, "and in order that the Gentiles might glorify (τῷ ὀνόματί σου ψαλῶ) God for his mercy. As it is written: 'Therefore, I will confess to you among the Gentiles, and sing praises to your name.'" The Psalmist proclaims that they will sing praises to God's name to exalt and set his name apart. The second instance is Heb. 13:15: "Through him, then, let us continually offer a sacrifice of praise to God, that is, the fruit of lips that confess his name" (Δι' αὐτοῦ [οὖν] ἀναφέρωμεν θυσίαν αἰνέσεως διὰ παντὸς τῷ θεῷ, τοῦτ' ἔστιν καρπὸν χειλέων ὁμολογούντων τῷ ὀνόματι αὐτοῦ). The author of Hebrews encourages his audience to use their lips to offer "sacrifices of praise" (ἀναφέρωμεν θυσίαν), and in so doing, confess God's name. The author evokes sacrificial language reminiscent of the Old Testament and its connection to hallowing and the temple. Although the verse does not explicitly refer to hallowing, the language of Hebrews is reminiscent of the third commandment's implicit instruction to use the name of God properly.

---

[11] Rick W. Byargeon, "Echoes of Wisdom in the Lord's Prayer (Matt. 6:9–13)," *JETS* 41.3 (1998): 362–4, has argued similarly. The reference תָּפַשְׂתִּי שֵׁם אֱלֹהָי in Prov. 30:9 is a probable parallel to the first petition of the Lord's Prayer. The phrase is translated as "profane the name of God." Byargeon argues that the literal translation of תפשׂ ("to grab hold of") implies "stealing." In the context of Proverbs 30, "profaning the name of God" is the "theological consequence" of stealing. The implied means through which one sanctifies the Name is by living a life of contentment.

[12] M'Neile, *Gospel According to St. Matthew*, 78.

[13] See also Jn 17:6 in which he uses the term Ἐφανέρωσά in reference to the name. Again, the emphasis is on the separate and unique nature of God's name. Wenham, "Sevenfold Form of the Lord's Prayer," 381, fn.20.

The closest extracanonical parallel to the first petition, and arguably the Lord's Prayer, is the *Kaddish* prayer.[14] It reads:

> Exalted and hallowed be his great name
>> In the world which he created according to his will.
>
> May he let his kingdom rule
>> In your lifetime and in your days and in the lifetime
>> Of the whole house of Israel, speedily and soon.
>
> Praised be his great name from eternity to eternity.
>> And to this say: Amen.

Like the Lord's Prayer, the *Kaddish* refers to the hallowing of God's name, the coming kingdom, and mentions God's will. The *Kaddish* refer to the holiness of God's name in reference to both the eschatological future kingdom (i.e., the kingdom comes "speedily and soon") and present ("in your lifetime and in your days"). We will discuss this parallel in more depth below, specifically noting its temporal elements and parallels to the Lord's Prayer.

The second keyword in the first petition is the "Name." The name is a substitute term for the *Tetragrammaton* (Exod. 3:13-14; see also Jn 12:28; Rom. 9:17).[15] "Names" in the Old Testament were virtually inseparable from the being to which they referred.[16] Therefore, misuse of someone's name was equivalent to defaming the individual. It is likely that Matthew has retained a circumlocution from his tradition to reflect both reverence for God and also to avoid breaking the third commandment.

Besides the first petition, Matthew uses "name" to refer to God in Mt. 7:22, 10:22, 12:21, 18:5, 18:20, 19:29, 21:9, 23:39, 24:5, 24:9, and 28:19. These verses refer to both God the father and Jesus himself. Allison additionally notes, "Matthew may have thought more specifically in terms of the revealed name of power which the Father shared with Jesus and the Spirit—'the name of the Father and of the Son and of the Holy Spirit' (Mt. 28:16-20; see Jn 17:11; Phil. 2:9)."[17] Jesus's equality with God is also confirmed by the prayers in Matthew's Gospel that are directed toward Jesus to save or heal (see 8:8, 25; 14:30; 15:22, 25; 17:15; 20:30-33).[18]

In the Lord's Prayer, the petition prays that the Name of "you" be hallowed. The "you" refers to the immediately preceding invocation, in which the "Name" parallels the "Father in heaven."[19] As Robert Mowery has observed, chs 1-7 in Matthew's

---

[14] Allison, *Sermon on the Mount*, 121, and Quarles, *Sermon on the Mount*, 192-3. Quarles argues that the *Kaddish* is more helpful for interpreting the first petition than the Old Testament examples. Quarles may be correct, but this would be the only example in the Lord's Prayer in which extracanonical literature is the best informant for understanding its petitions.

[15] See Davies and Allison, *Matthew 1-7*, 603.

[16] Nolland, *Gospel of Matthew*, 287. BDAG, 712, helpfully summarizes, "The period of our literature also sees—within as well as without the new community of believers—in the name something real, a piece of the very nature of the personality whom it designates, expressing the person's qualities and powers."

[17] Allison, *Sermon on the Mount*, 120.

[18] Noted by Nygaard, *Prayer in the Gospels*, 56. On Jesus and prayer, see Gupta, *Lord's Prayer*, 12-22.

[19] The parallels between the invocation and first petition are interesting. Allison, *Sermon on the Mount*, 120, rightly states, "The solemnity of this first request ensures that the intimacy conveyed by the

Gospel have several examples of calling God by different names. Specifically, in chs 5–7, Matthew uses the epithet "Father" almost exclusively (5:16, 45, 48; 6:1, 4, 6 [2x], 8, 9, 14, 15, 18 [2x], 26, 32; 7:11, 21).[20] Mowery explores how these epithets interact with the material in their respective chapters. He notes, "The Father is portrayed as an authoritative heavenly figure who knows what people need before they ask, expects people to do the divine will, promises forgiveness to those who forgive, and will reward the righteous."[21] This connection acknowledges the Old Testament emphasis of the inseparability of a name and the being to which it refers.[22]

The Temporality of the Name Petition

The primary focus in modern discussions of the first petition has been eschatology. Commentators typically assert that the petition refers exclusively to the future.[23] Evidence for this future reading includes the following: (1) the interpretation of the petition's passive verb, (2) the parallels with Ezek. 36:22-32, and (3) the first petition's relationship to the kingdom petition. The evidence is important for understanding the future aspect of the petition but does not exclude the present. We will discuss each of these arguments in turn before suggesting that the petition also has an ethical aspect in the next section.

The first petition, like the second and third, begins with an aorist verb (ἁγιασθήτω). The verb is typically understood as a divine passive, suggesting that God is the acting agent. God's name is already holy and therefore the request must go beyond the recognition of this holiness in the present time. Those favoring an eschatological future reading of the first petition argue that God's name is properly revered when he brings about the end of time and manifests his holy name on earth as in heaven.[24] This reading also equates the first petition with the second petition for the coming kingdom, which we will discuss below.

The second argument for an eschatological future reading is the parallel of Ezek. 36:22-32. Raymond Brown has argued that this is the clearest Old Testament parallel to the first petition.[25] The passage recounts a time when God's name had been profaned among the nations. Instead of defending God's name, the Israelites mimic the pagan nations, profaning the Name through their behavior. It is against this backdrop that

---

address 'Father' will not degenerate into presumptuous familiarity." It is interesting though that in earlier work, Davies and Allison are clear that the first petition needs to be read as independent of the invocation. Davies and Allison, *Matthew 1–7*, 602–3, states, "That there is a connection between hallowing God's name and the address, 'Father,' is doubtful."

[20] See Chapter 4 on the Invocation.
[21] Mowery, "Lord to Father," 654–5. Mowery anticipates the counterargument that chs 8–28 may change these associations between epithets and themes. He illustrates that chs 8–28 only strengthen and confirm the patterns introduced in Matthew 1–7.
[22] See also Gupta, *Lord's Prayer*, 60–3.
[23] See, for instance, Lohmeyer, *Lord's Prayer*, 17–33; Brown, "Pater Noster as an Eschatological Prayer," 175–208; and Heinz Schürmann, *Praying with Christ: The "Our Father" for Today* (New York: Herder & Herder, 1972).
[24] It is often argued that Jesus's ministry and teaching were eschatological, making the first petition a suitable complement to Jesus's already-end-times emphases.
[25] Brown, "Pater Noster as Eschatological Prayer," 186–7.

the Lord declares, "Therefore say to the house of Israel, 'Thus says the Lord God: It is not for your sake, O house of Israel, that I am about to act, but for the sake of my holy name (אִם־לְשֵׁם־קָדְשִׁי)) which you have profaned (חִלַּלְתֶּם) among the nations to which you came'" (v. 22). Interpreters will point to Israel's inability as moral agents to bring the proper reverence to God's name. It is only God who is worthy of restoring the holiness that is due.[26] The passage continues with a description of God bringing Israel together from among the nations and giving them their own land (Ezek. 36:24).[27] Brant Pitre has recently argued that the context of Ezekiel 36 presents a striking vision of the coming age. With parallels to the first petition, the request becomes a prayer for a "New Exodus." Pitre's arguments are convincing concerning the first petition but not conclusive. As we will argue in the next section, Ezekiel 36 also refers to the activity of Israel in the hallowing of God's name.

The last piece of evidence for an eschatological reading is the first petition's relationship with the kingdom petition. The structure of the Lord's Prayer suggests that the two petitions should be read together. Both petitions have the exact same word count and word order. As we have argued in Chapter 3, the first and second petitions are concentrically parallel to the sixth and seventh petitions. The first and second petitions are "positive" requests for God's name and kingdom, and are balanced by the "negative" emphases of temptation and evil one in the final petitions.[28] The second petition is primarily a future-oriented request, suggesting that the first petition should also be understood as primarily future-oriented.

The Ethics of the Name Petition

Despite the previous arguments for an eschatological future reading, it would be unwise to conclude a completely future-oriented interpretation of the first petition. The first petition also has a present/ethical dimension. In addition to references to the future, Ezek. 36:22–32 explains the hallowing of God's name by way of human beings.[29] In Ezek. 36:23, God declares that he will display his holiness through the lives of his people. It states, "I will sanctify my great name, which has been profaned among the nations, and which you have profaned among them; and the nations shall know that I am the Lord, says the Lord God, when through you [Israel] I display my holiness before their eyes." Other, often overlooked, texts also refer to humans hallowing God's name. These references include Lev. 20:3, 22:32; and Amos 2:7. Particularly interesting is Exod. 20:7 and Isaiah 29.[30] As noted above, Exod. 20:7 instructs its hearers to avoid using the Lord's name in vain. Israelites can profane God's name through their actions and, conversely, "hallow" God's name through keeping his commandments. This ethical concern is made more explicit in Isa. 29:23 LXX: "For when he sees his

---

[26] Similar passages include Ezek. 39:7, 25; Pss. 106:47, 145:21; and 1 Chron. 16:35.
[27] Pitre, "Lord's Prayer and the New Exodus," 78–81.
[28] See also Lohmeyer, *Lord's Prayer*, 26.
[29] Gerald Friedlander, *The Jewish Sources of the Sermon on the Mount* (London: Routledge, 1911), 164–5, has argued that the entire Prayer is derived from this chapter.
[30] Luz, *Matthew 1–7*, 317, similarly agrees with the connection of the first petition and keeping the third commandment.

children, the work of my hands, in his midst, they will sanctify my name; they will sanctify the Holy One of Jacob, and will stand in awe of the God of Israel" (ἀλλ᾽ ὅταν ἴδωσιν τὰ τέκνα αὐτῶν τὰ ἔργα μου δι᾽ ἐμὲ ἁγιάσουσιν τὸ ὄνομά μου καὶ ἁγιάσουσιν τὸν ἅγιον Ιακωβ καὶ τὸν θεὸν τοῦ Ισραηλ φοβηθήσονται). The children of God here are the ones directly responsible for hallowing God's name as they live according to God's commands.

The literature from the Second Temple period echoes the Old Testament emphasis on both God and man being involved in the hallowing of God's name. The primary text for comparison in this regard is the opening lines of the *Kaddish*. Commentators often note its similarities with the Lord's Prayer.[31] First, both prayers are short prayers that were used both privately and publicly. Second, though opinions vary, there is considerable evidence that both prayers are from the first century.[32] Third, both prayers begin with petitions for the hallowing of God's name and link hallowing with requests for the kingdom. Because it is assumed that the *Kaddish* is eschatological in its focus, it is often argued that the Lord's Prayer must also be interpreted similarly, completely ignoring the dimension of man as an acting agent.

The liturgical reading of the *Kaddish* is between the *Amidah* and the *Shema* (Deut. 6:4-6). As Gibson states, "The *Shema* both calls the people of Israel to love God with their whole of heart, soul, and mind, and warns them sternly against 'forgetting' their covenant obligations to God, refusing to trust in him and his ways, and putting him to the test."[33] This conclusion is corroborated by John Nolland as he argues that the first petition closely parallels 1 En. 61:12 ("All who sleep not above in heaven shall bless Him: All the holy ones who are in heaven shall bless Him. And all the elect who dwell in the garden of life: And every spirit of light who is able to bless, and glorify, and extol, and hallow Thy blessed name, and all flesh shall beyond measure glorify and bless Thy name forever and ever.").[34] First Enoch emphasizes that hallowing God's name is an ethical exercise connected to works of justice and wise utterances (see 1 En. 61:7-9).[35] We agree with Gibson and Nolland but do not intend to completely shun the future elements of God's kingdom found in the *Kaddish*.

When we move to the Rabbinic material, the emphasis upon man's involvement in hallowing God's name becomes the norm. Specifically, obedience to the *Torah* becomes the means through which one properly hallows God's name. This connection is illustrated in *b. Yebam.* 79a: "'The fathers shall not be put to death for the children.' R. Hiyya b. Abba replied in the name of R. Johanan: 'It is better that a letter be rooted out of the *Torah* than that the divine name shall be publicly profaned.'" Reverence for

---

[31] Davies and Allison, *Matthew 1–7*, 595-6.
[32] Davies and Allison, *Matthew 1–7*, 603; Guelich, *Sermon on the Mount*, 309-10; Keener, *Gospel of Matthew*, 220; and Nolland, *Gospel of Matthew*, 287.
[33] Gibson, *Disciples' Prayer*, 108.
[34] Nolland, *Gospel of Matthew*, 286, argues that the *Kaddish* does not refer to the future.
[35] Although the Qumran parallels are not as numerous as the Old Testament and Second Temple literature, there is still evidence of prayers being offered to God in which the petitioner requests the holiness of God's name. 11QPs[a] states: "My soul cried out to extol your Name (שמכה להלל)." The Hebrew word להלל used here means to bring praise or worship. The phrase evokes the petitioner's desire that God's name is given proper reverence.

God's name and keeping the commandments is also mentioned in *b. Ber.* 40b.[36] In this passage, obedience and hallowing are almost synonymous. God's name is also often connected with the concept of the kingdom in Rabbinic literature. Consider the saying of *Seder Rabbah Amram* 1 (9a): "Make your name unique in your world; make your reign unique in your world."

Conclusion

From our analysis, we conclude that for Matthew the first petition is primarily concerned with the proper reverence of God's name. The petition is future-oriented, as it is structurally parallel to the second petition, but also a prayer related to the present as a longing for God to be properly worshipped. The reference to God's name is not simply something that God is called but, rather, refers to his presence. In this regard, the petition requests that the pray-er may follow God's commandments and resist representing the Name in ways that would be profane (see esp. Exod. 20:7).

"Hallowed Be Your Name" in the Sermon on the Mount

In the previous section, we argued that the first petition is primarily concerned with the holiness and proper reverence of God's Name. As Wenham notes, the Lord's Prayer then begins on a "high starting point."[37] The hallowing of God's name will take place not only in the eschatological future but also in the ongoing *Torah* obedience of God's people. We will argue that three passages in the Sermon on the Mount have shared themes with the first petition. The passages are Mt. 5:13-16; 5:33-37; and 7:21-23. Each passage refers to the name of God and parallels the themes argued above. It is interesting to note that these passages have other parallels to the invocation and petitions of the Lord's Prayer. We will note these textual connections below.

Matthew 5:13-16

As we have discussed in Chapter 4, Mt. 5:13-16 presents the twin metaphors of salt and light. The metaphors explain the identity (salt) and influence (light) of Jesus's disciples. The passage (Mt. 5:13-16) forms the "conclusion" to Jesus's introduction to the Sermon on the Mount (Mt. 5:3-16) and partners with vv. 17-20 to introduce Jesus's teaching on the Mosaic law (Mt. 5:21-48). Matthew 5:13-16 also parallels many of the ideas present in Mt. 7:13-27 (see esp. Mt. 7:21-23 below). Verse 16 states, "In the same way, let your light shine before others, so that they many see your good works and give glory to your Father in heaven." The phrase "give glory" (δοξάσωσιν) is an aorist active verb which refers to magnifying God. In v. 16, God is referred to as the "Father in heaven." As the verse and its context makes clear (Mt. 5:3-48), being "light" consists of the discipleship

---

[36] For it has been taught: I have not transgressed any of Thy commandments, neither have I forgotten. This means: "I have not transgressed" so as not to bless Thee, "neither have I forgotten" to mention Thy name therein. Of sovereignty, however, there is no mention here. R. Johanan, however, reads: "Neither have I forgotten" to mention Thy name and Thy sovereignty therein.

[37] Wenham, "Sevenfold Form of the Lord's Prayer," 380.

outlined by the Sermon, and as a result, the disciple "magnifies" the name of the Father in heaven.[38]

The thematic parallels between v. 16 and the first petition are threefold. First, both passages emphasize the proper reverence of God. The concept of "giving glory" to God is closely related to the instruction in the first petition (see Jn 12:28) to "hallow" God's name. This parallelism is evidenced by the close connection of the terms in passages such as Lev. 10:3 LXX ("This is what the Lord meant when he said, 'Through those who are near me I will show myself holy [ἁγιασθήσομαι], and before all the people I will be glorified [δοξασθήσομαι]'") and Isa. 6:3 LXX ("Holy, holy, holy [ἅγιος] is the Lord of hosts; the whole earth is full of his glory [δόξης]"). Second, both passages emphasize that the work of the petitioner/disciple is for the proper reverence of the "Father in heaven." As we argued above, the "Name of you" refers to the invocation. Similarly, Mt. 5:16 teaches that the work of the disciples is for the purpose of giving glory to the Father. Third, both passages emphasize the work of petitioners/disciples in the process of making God's name holy on earth. The teaching in v. 16 uses the metaphor of "shining light" to picture the influence of the disciples on earth. As we discussed in Chapter 4, Jesus's metaphor concerns the good works of the disciples in performing God's commands, as outlined in the verses that follow (Mt. 5:21-48).

Matthew 5:33-37

Matthew 5:33-37 records Jesus's teaching on taking oaths. Unlike the other "antitheses," the teaching here does not begin with a direct quotation of the Old Testament. As Charles Quarles notes, "This seems to be a rabbinic paraphrase of texts like Lev. 19:12; Num. 30:3; and Deut. 23:21-23."[39] Leviticus 19:12 LXX states, "And you shall not swear falsely by my name, profaning the name of your God: I am the Lord." Jesus's teaching presents the rabbinic paraphrase as, "You shall not swear falsely, but carry out the vows you have made to the Lord" (Mt. 5:33). The first clause gives the prohibition, while the second clause states the principle to follow. The NRSV translates ὅρκος in v. 33 as "vows," but the more literal translation is "oaths." The reference to "oaths" suggests that promises are being made to individuals or things. This misplaced allegiance is confirmed in the next few verses in which Jesus refers to different bases for these prohibited oaths. Jesus's prohibition to avoid swearing (vv. 34-35) includes oaths made to heaven, earth, Jerusalem, and one's own head.[40]

A helpful parallel to Mt. 5:33-37 is Mt. 23:16-22, in which the subject of oaths is taken up. In this passage, Jesus rebukes those who only observe certain types of oaths.

---

[38] Quarles, *Sermon on the Mount*, 193, states, "Jesus' ministry resulted in God's being glorified (9:8; 15:31). The lives of His disciples must pursue this same goal."

[39] Quarles, *Sermon on the Mount*, 136.

[40] The text reads in full:

> Again, you have heard that it was said to those of ancient times, "You shall not swear falsely, but carry out the vows you have made to the Lord." But I say to you, Do not swear at all, either by heaven, for it is the throne of God, or by the earth, for it is his footstool, or by Jerusalem, for it is the city of the great King. And do not swear by your head, for you cannot make one hair white or black. Let your word be "Yes, Yes" or "No, No"; anything more than this comes from the evil one.

The rabbis had developed a system of oaths in which one could avoid the obligation of truthfulness if the oath was sworn to something other than the Lord. First-century Jews viewed dishonesty toward the name of the Lord as a violation of the third commandment and ultimately as blasphemy (Exod. 20:7). To avoid this blasphemy, substitutions were created to allow leeway in oath-taking. This parallel helpfully explains Jesus's emphasis in Mt. 5:33-37. In these verses, Jesus is forbidding oaths that are used to avoid the obligation of truthfulness by swearing on people and things.[41] Jesus's teaching in Mt. 23:16-22 emphasizes the value of honesty without exception. Matthew 5:37 similarly states, "Let your word be 'Yes, Yes' or 'No, No'; anything more than this comes from evil."[42]

When understood in its context, Mt. 5:33-37 contains two thematic parallels with the first petition. First, Mt. 5:33-37 implies that oaths taken in the name of the Lord (or by substitution), which are mixed with dishonesty, are in violation of the third commandment (see Exod. 20:7). These types of oaths profane the name of God, paralleling the first petition's importance on properly revering the Name. Second, the teaching on dishonesty may be seen as reflecting the ethical emphasis of the first petition. Matthew 5:33-37 is clear that followers of Jesus must display honesty in their dealings. By maintaining an ethic of integrity, a disciple is hallowing the name of God. This parallel is less striking than Mt. 5:16 but still refers to properly hallowing the name of God.

Matthew 7:21-23

Perhaps the clearest parallel to the first petition is Mt. 7:21-23. As we have discussed elsewhere, Mt. 7:21-23 has several parallels to the Lord's Prayer.[43] These parallels include references to the Father in heaven, the kingdom, the will, evil, and several shared themes. In v. 22, Jesus recounts the questions that wicked disciples will ask at the final judgment. These "workers of lawlessness" (οἱ ἐργαζόμενοι τὴν ἀνομίαν) will say, "Lord, Lord, did we not prophesy in your name, and cast out demons in your name, and do many deeds of power in your name?" Jesus proclaims that they are not true disciples but workers of evil.

Matthew 7:21-23 contains three parallels to the first petition. First, the teaching in Mt. 7:21-23 contains three references to God's name. The verses directly address the "Father in heaven," and the dual references, "Lord, Lord" (vv. 22-23), as well as the thrice-repeated "in your name" in v. 22.[44] Second, the teaching in Mt. 7:21-23 contrasts the work of those who profane the Name and those who bring proper reverence to God's name.[45] False disciples declare "Lord, Lord" but are called "workers of lawlessness." By

---

[41] For an explanation of the oaths that were binding and nonbinding, see Quarles, *Sermon on the Mount*, 139–43. Also, McKnight, *Sermon on the Mount*, 113–5.
[42] For an explanation of "evil" in this passage and its relationship to the Lord's Prayer, see Chapter 4.
[43] See Chapters 4 and 5.
[44] Pennington, *Sermon and Human Flourishing*, 275, fn.13, gives the phrase prominence in his own translation to show its importance. Thus, Pennington's translation reads: "Lord, Lord, *in your name* we prophesied, and *in your name* we cast out demons, and *in your name* we produced many miracle, didn't we?" Emphasis mine.
[45] This parallel assumes that in this eschatological setting, Jesus's name and God's name are the same.

way of comparison, true disciples perform the same actions but do so properly in the name of the Lord. It is reasonable to assume that those who do the will of the Father in heaven "sanctify" the name. Third, Mt. 7:21-23 overlaps with the eschatological and ethical aspects of the first petition. The will of God (v. 21) performed on earth is a testament of those who look toward the consummation of earth. Until then, those who are identified by the name of God will prophesy, cast out demons, and perform deeds of power for the glory of God.

Name Conclusion

In the previous sections, we have examined the meaning of the first petition. This petition is primarily concerned with the holiness and proper reverence of God's name. The name refers to the very character of God and is properly hallowed when not only the kingdom finally comes but also through the ongoing work of his disciples. We have examined those instances in the Sermon on the Mount that mention names of God and share themes with the first petition. We have shown that the Lord's Prayer and Sermon on the Mount should be read together considering these textual connections. When read in this manner, "hallowing God's name" includes being salt and light (Mt. 5:13-16), a commitment to truth-telling (Mt. 5:33-37), and performing the will of the Father in heaven (Mt. 7:21-23).

Sixth Petition: "Lead Us Not into Temptation"

We conclude our examination of the Lord's Prayer with the petition to avoid "trials/temptations." The sixth petition is the first of the Prayer's requests which is negative in connotation. As stated above, the sixth petition lacks extensive parallels with the Sermon on the Mount but can be broadly paralleled to several passages. In the following sections, we will seek to establish these textual connections by exploring the meaning of the sixth petition within Matthew's cultural milieu. This analysis will establish the basis for thematic parallels with passages in the Sermon on the Mount. As we will show, the meaning of the sixth petition is associated with several themes present in the Sermon on the Mount, creating the possibility of various parallels. Therefore, we will focus on those parallels with the Sermon on the Mount that have been previously unexamined—Mt. 5:27-30 concerning adultery and Mt. 7:6 concerning holy things/dogs.

The Meaning of "Lead Us Not into Temptation"

Like the first and second petitions, the sixth petition (καὶ μὴ εἰσενέγκῃς ἡμᾶς εἰς πειρασμόν) is not distinctive in its wording. The petition is in verbatim agreement with both the Lukan and *Didache* versions of the Lord's Prayer. Yet, in the Matthean version of the Lord's Prayer, the sixth petition is followed by the seventh petition, likely indicating Matthew's understanding of the type of "trials/temptation" in view here.[46]

---

[46] We have argued similarly concerning the kingdom petition that the addition of the will petition. For an examination of the seventh petition, see Chapter 4.

This section will explore the meaning of the sixth petition by defining its keywords and its relationship to the seventh petition. We will begin with the meaning of "do not enter into" (μὴ εἰσενέγκῃς ἡμᾶς) before exploring the theological issues surrounding the translation of πειρασμός. We conclude that for Matthew, the sixth petition is primarily a request to be spared "trials/temptations" authored by the evil one (seventh petition).[47] In cases where these trials/temptations come, the petitioner prays to escape these moments for fear of apostasy (see Lk. 8:13/Mt. 13:20-21). The context of prayer shows the frailty of the petitioner as he or she seeks God before the "trial/temptation" comes (i.e., the sixth petition) and then in the midst of evil appeals to God for rescue (i.e., the seventh petition).

"Lead Us Not into"

The sixth petition begins with the request to avoid "entering" or "being brought into" πειρασμός. The verb (μὴ εἰσενέγκῃς) is the aorist subjunctive of εἰσφέρω followed by the preposition εἰς. The verb is not commonly used in Matthew but appears in other places in the New Testament. Within the New Testament, the verb has two connotations. The first meaning refers to "being brought into" a specific place. In Lk. 5:18-19, some disciples are said to "bring in" a man confined to a cot. Similarly, 1 Tim. 6:7 refers to what we have "brought" into this world. Paul responds that we have "brought" nothing into this place.[48] The other connotation refers to "being brought" into an event or area. This connotation is much broader than the first. Consider the message of Acts 17:20: "For you bring (εἰσφέρεις) some strange things to our ears. We wish to know therefore what these things mean."[49] Paul brings the message of Jesus to the "ears" of the Athenians. In the case of the sixth petition, Jesus appears to be using the second connotation, referring to one being brought into the realm of "trial/temptation" or before the enticement of the evil one (see Mt. 6:13b).

Πειρασμός

The second key term in the sixth petition is πειρασμός. The precise meaning of πειρασμός is difficult to determine, with various commentators disagreeing on its temporality, its proper connotation, and its relationship to the seventh petition.[50] Is

---

[47] This interpretation does not eliminate all aspects of the future. Of course, resisting temptation in the present is a picture of final resistance in the eschatological future. See Chapter 2 on presuppositions and scope. Additionally, there are those who will argue that the sixth petition refers not to the petitioner being tempted, but, rather, the petitioner is putting God to the test by a lack of trust. For a fuller explanation of this position, cf. Gibson, *Disciples' Prayer*, 135–60; this distinction between being tested and testing God is not important for the present book.

[48] Also, LXX of Gen. 43:18, Exod. 23:19, and Num. 31:54. For an excellent discussion, see Fitzmyer, "Lead Us Not into Temptation," 259–60.

[49] This translation is from the ESV. The ESV captures the meaning of εἰσφέρω better than the NRSV used throughout the book.

[50] Another important question concerning the temptation petition is the source or author of the temptation. While this distinction is important for broader theological discussions (i.e., theodicy), we will reserve our comments to the questions of temporality, connotation, and relationship with the

πειρασμός ever-present or referring to the eschatological future? Should the πειρασμός be considered negative or positive and what type of πειρασμός? What is the relationship of the sixth and seventh petitions and its consequences for the meaning of petition? The proper sense of a word is normally determined by the context in which it is found, but Matthew's only immediate clue is the addition of the seventh petition. Often, one must wrestle with each question in turn to give clues to the next.[51] We will begin with the temporal reference in the sixth petition before considering the connotation/translation of πειρασμός and the implications of the seventh petition.

The Temporality of πειρασμός: The Eschatological Trial or Daily Temptation?

Not surprisingly, interpreters of the Lord's Prayer who lean toward an eschatological future interpretation of the entire prayer translate the sixth petition as a reference to the end times.[52] According to this view, the sixth petition should be rendered as "Do not lead us into the final test," that is, the "Great Tribulation" (Mt. 24:21, 29; Rev. 7:14). The clearest piece of evidence for this interpretation of the Lord's Prayer is the parallel in Rev. 3:10 ("Because you have kept my word of patient endurance, I will keep you from the hour of trial [πειρασμοῦ] that is coming on the whole world to test [πειράσαι] the inhabitants of the earth").

This explanation of πειρασμός is reasonable but ignores several clues within the Matthean version of the Lord's Prayer. Both Rev. 3:10 and the sixth petition share references to πειρασμός, but the context of Revelation has an end-times emphasis.[53] The end-times emphasis is not immediately evident in the petitions that precede and follow in the Lord's Prayer. We have argued elsewhere that the focus of the temporality (eschatological future/present) switches to the daily tasks of kingdom living in the fourth petition (i.e., prayers for daily food). The wording of the forgiveness petition is stylistically linked to the fourth petition to similarly emphasize the present.[54] Appeal to the seventh petition does not strengthen the case for an end-times reading, since interpreting it that way is often based on the sixth petition. It is also interesting that the reference to πειρασμός in the sixth petition lacks the definite article, which one would expect if the reference were to a specific time of testing.[55]

seventh petition. The parallels we will seek to establish between the Sermon and the sixth petition are not dependent upon an answer to this question and therefore do warrant a thorough discussion. For a fuller discussion, see the different aspects highlighted by C. F. D. Moule, "Unresolved Problem in the Temptation Clause in the Lord's Prayer," *RTR* 33 (1974): 75; Pennington, *Sermon and Human Flourishing*, 227, fn.45; Allison, *Sermon on the Mount*, 130; Betz, *Sermon on the Mount*, 407.

[51] Crump, *Knocking on Heaven's Door*, 151–5, lists at least seven different options for understanding the various combinations of these issues.

[52] Among others, see Pitre, "Lord's Prayer and the New Exodus," 91, and Brown, "Pater Noster as an Eschatological Prayer," 205. Davies and Allison, *Matthew 1–7*, 130, see the sixth petition referring primarily to the future but hint that it may include a present dimension as well.

[53] Crump, *Knocking on Heaven's Door*, 154. Luz, *Matthew 1–7*, 322, notes that apart from Rev. 3:10, "Almost everything speaks against this view. Neither in Jewish apocalypticism nor in the New Testament is [πειρασμός] an apocalyptic technical term."

[54] Nolland, *Gospel of Matthew*, 290, who notes, "The verb and object of verses 11 and 12a are probably interchanged to tie the two petitions together in a chiastic manner." This stylistic change places the forgiveness petition alongside the requests for "daily" bread.

[55] Nolland, *Gospel of Matthew*, 292. Contra Davies and Allison, *Matthew 1–7*, 613.

Πειρασμός as Character Development or Destruction?

In the previous section, we argued that πειρασμός refers to daily temptation. When referring to the present, the Greek word πειρασμός can be understood in three different ways. First, the Greek term can refer to "trials/temptations," in which one is drawn to do evil. This interpretation has a primarily negative connotation. The key example of "trials/temptations" with a negative connotation is Gen. 3:1-9. In these verses, Adam and Eve were presented with a "temptation." Satan tempts Adam and Eve with the opportunity to be like God.[56] This "trial/temptation" ended with Adam and Eve succumbing to Satan's lies and initiating the tragic fall of humanity. As Seesemann notes, "In so doing [humankind] rebels against God's commandment, transgresses it, and thus becomes guilty. From the time of the fall . . . obedience to God is subject to constant threat through trial, whether it be that God tests and proves [the disciple] or that the adversary (Satan) is at work."[57]

Second, the term can refer to a test which ultimately proves one's good character. This definition has a more positive sense which refers to ongoing tests as a means of growing disciples. Instances of this type of testing are found in Gen. 22:1-19. In Gen. 22:1-19, Abraham is commanded by God to sacrifice his son. Abraham faithfully obeyed God and passed the test. In so doing, Abraham became the exemplar of obedient faith to God (see *Sir.* 44:20; Heb. 11:17-19).

Third, πειρασμός can have the role of a tutor, instructing a disciple in righteousness. Similar to the second option, this meaning also has a positive connotation. The evidence for this connotation of πειρασμός is primarily found in the Second Temple literature among the Wisdom books.[58] Commentators will often note the close connection of the teachings of *Sirach* and *Wisdom* to the sixth petition.

> *Sirach* 2:1, 6: My child, when you come to serve the Lord, prepare yourself for testing (πειρασμόν). Trust in him, and he will help you; make your ways straight and hope in him.
>
> *Sirach* 4:17: For at first, she will walk with them on tortuous paths; she will bring fear and dread upon them and will torment them by her discipline until she trusts them, and she will test (πειράσει) them with her ordinances.
>
> *Wisdom* 3:5: Having been disciplined a little, they will receive great good, because God tested (ἐπείρασεν) them and found them worthy of himself.
>
> *Wisdom* 11:9: For when they were tried (ἐπειράσθησαν), though they were being disciplined in mercy, they learned how the ungodly were tormented when judged in wrath.

---

[56] Although the specific wording of "temptation" is not used in this passage, Adam and Eve are subjected to "temptation" from the Serpent.

[57] H. Seesemann, "πειρασμός," in *TDNT*, vol. 6, ed.G. Kittel and G. Friedrich, trans. G. W. Bromiley (Grand Rapids: Eerdmans, 1964–76), 24.

[58] The Qumran literature does not explicitly refer to temptation but describes situations where temptation is most likely present. Because of the lack of clear verbal parallels with the sixth petition in the Qumran literature, we will reserve our studies to those examples of Second Temple literature that explicitly mention πειρασμός and its cognates.

In each of these instances, the πειρασμός is for the purpose of instruction in moral goodness. The negative connotation of falling to temptation is almost completely absent in these passages, and πειρασμός appears to be desirable for the purpose of edification.[59] God is the agent of testing in these passages and uses these tests to perfect his followers.

The New Testament continues with the diverse meanings of πειρασμός found in the Old Testament and Second Temple Literature. Πειρασμός, which "proves one's character," is found in passages such as 1 Pet. 1:6 ("In this you rejoice, even if now for a little while you have had to suffer various trials") and 4:12 ("Beloved, do not be surprised at the fiery ordeal that is taking place among you to test you, as though something strange were happening to you").[60] First Peter is addressed to those scattered abroad (i.e., Diaspora Jews) and encourages Christians to consider tests as a way to grow in faith. The pedagogical function of πειρασμός is found in passages such as Jas 1:2 ("My brothers and sisters, whenever you face trials of any kind, consider it nothing but joy") and 1:12 ("Blessed is anyone who endures temptation. Such a one has stood the test and will receive the crown of life that the Lord has promised to those who love him"). These verses are part of James's theme of "trial/test" as a tool for instruction. The examples in 1 Peter and James are similar in content but influenced by their respective contexts. In both cases, the πειρασμός is mainly seen as having a positive connotation. Yet, when it comes to Matthew, the consistent usage of πειρασμός is the negative connotation.[61] Two passages that are important for understanding the Matthean usage in general, and the sixth petition in particular are Mt. 4:1-10 (see Heb. 4:15) and Mt. 26:41 (see Mk 14:38; Lk. 22:40, 46).

Matthew 4:1-10
Matthew 4:1-10 records Jesus's temptation in the wilderness. The passage begins, "Then Jesus was led up by the Spirit into the wilderness to be tempted (πειρασθῆναι) by the devil" (Mt. 4:1). In what follows, Jesus is faced with three temptations. In the first temptation, Jesus is tempted with the allure of bread (Mt. 4:2-4). Having fasted for forty days and nights, Jesus responds that man cannot live by bread alone but must "devour" first the word of God. The second temptation is the allure of safety. Jesus is led to the pinnacle of the temple. Upon arrival, the devil instructs Jesus to throw himself to the ground and allow his angels to catch him before he hits (Mt. 4:5-7). Jesus responds that the devil is not permitted to tempt God (οὐκ ἐκπειράσεις κύριον τὸν θεόν σου). The verb ἐκπειράζω is closely related to πειραζω and relates to temptation. The third temptation concerns the promise of the kingdoms of the world (Mt. 4:8-10). On top of a mountain, the devil displays the kingdoms of earth and promises to give them to Jesus if he bows down in worship. Jesus responds that God alone is to be worshipped (Mt. 4:10).

---

[59] See Seesemann, "πειρασμός," in TDNT, vol. 6, 26.
[60] See also Rev. 2:10.
[61] Quarles, *Sermon on the Mount*, 216, notes that in Matthew's Gospel, πειρασμός and the related verb πειράζω are consistently used in a negative sense (4:1, 3; 16:1; 19:3; 22:18, 25; 26:41).

Matthew 4:1-10 discusses several themes which parallel the Lord's Prayer (i.e., the kingdom, bread, temptations, and the evil one).[62] Although the primary focus of the narratives is the content of each temptation and Jesus's responses, it is obvious that the trial/temptation is overtly negative and used as an attempted disruption of Jesus completing God's will.

Matthew 26:41

Matthew 26:41 is part of Jesus's prayers in the Garden of Gethsemane.[63] In this narrative (Mt. 26:36-46), Jesus retreats with some of his disciples to seek God the night before his crucifixion. While Jesus is praying for the strength to endure his upcoming death, he asks his disciples to stay away and also pray. He leaves the disciples on three separate occasions and upon returning between his prayers, he finds that the disciples are sleeping. During his second return, Jesus remarks (Mt. 26:41), "Stay awake and pray that you may not come into the time of trial (πειρασμόν); the spirit indeed is willing, but the flesh is weak."

Like Mt. 4:1-10, Mt. 26:41 and its context has several connections to the Lord's Prayer. Allison helpfully shows the verbal agreement:[64]

The Lord's Prayer	*Jesus in Gethsemane*
"Our Father"	"My Father"
"Your will be done"	"Your will be done"
"do not bring us to the time of πειρασμός"	"Pray that you not come to the times of πειρασμός"

Especially interesting in this case is the paralleled prayers concerning the will of God (Mt. 26:42/6:10) and the avoidance of temptation (Mt. 26:41/6:13). The thrust of the request in the garden is that Jesus would not succumb to the temptation of forsaking God's will. What is sure in these parallels is that the πειρασμός in view has a primarily negative connotation. On the one hand, Jesus goes on to successfully complete God's will. On the other hand, the disciples fail in their assigned task.

It is important to note from these parallels that Jesus is not being spared from πειρασμός, as people often assume the sixth petition requests. In fact, Jesus is already in the midst of "trials/temptations" in the Garden of Gethsemane.[65] The prayer in Gethsemane and arguably in the Lord's Prayer is an admission of frailty ("the spirit is indeed willing, but the flesh is weak"). Each prayer then asks to not be led into a moment of falling away but realizes the inevitability of trials. Within the context of prayer, those

---

[62] These connections have been explored in Chapter 4 concerning Mt. 4:1-10 and the evil one, and will be discussed later in this chapter concerning Mt. 4:1-10 and bread.
[63] Paul S. Minear, "But Whose Prayer Is It?," *Worship* 76 (2002), 328, calls the prayers in Gethsemane the "original *Lord's* Prayer." Emphasis his.
[64] Allison, *Sermon on the Mount*, 119.
[65] Moule, "Unresolved Problem," 75, states, "And the Lord's own prayer in Gethsemane is: 'take this cup away from me. Yet not what I will, but what thou wilt.' Admittedly, Jesus has not escaped testing: he is actually in it at the time."

who pray, humbly admit their own weaknesses. The question remains though, what type of "trial/temptation" is in view in the sixth petition? We have partially answered this question with Mt. 4:1-10 and 26:41, but to answer this question more fully, we will consider the implications of Matthew's addition of the seventh petition.

The Sixth and Seventh Petitions

Unlike the Lukan version of the Lord's Prayer, Matthew has provided an additional petition that gives insight into his understanding of πειρασμός.

Sixth petition: καὶ μὴ εἰσενέγκῃς ἡμᾶς εἰς πειρασμόν
Seventh petition: ἀλλὰ ῥῦσαι ἡμᾶς ἀπὸ τοῦ πονηροῦ

Structurally, the seventh petition provides a positive counterpart ("deliver us") to the negative connotation of the sixth petition ("lead us not into"). The seventh petition also gives an explanation of the source of πειρασμός. Luz correctly notes that the evil petition "intensifies and generalizes" the sixth petition.[66] The sixth petition is intensified because the evil one is immediately present as the source of "trials/temptations." The sixth petition is generalized because the seventh petition presupposes that *every* disciple will have to endure these trials.[67] In other words, while the sixth petition prays to completely avoid trials and temptations, the seventh petition acknowledges already being present in the trials and temptations.

With the seventh petition in mind then, we might ask, are there other places where the evil one "tests/tries" disciples? Within Matthew's Gospel, the only other mention of the evil one is Matthew 13. In this chapter, Matthew groups several of Jesus's parables together along with their explanations. The parables are centered around the kingdom of heaven, an equally important theme in both the Lord's Prayer and Sermon on the Mount.[68] In vv. 19–21, Jesus explains an earlier parable concerning a sower and his seed,

> When anyone hears the word of the kingdom and does not understand it, the evil one (ὁ πονηρὸς) comes and snatches away what is sown in the heart; this is what was sown on the path. As for what was sown on rocky ground, this is the one who hears the word and immediately receives it with joy; yet such a person has

---

[66] Luz, *Matthew 1–7*, 323.
[67] See *Sir.* 2:1 ("My child, when you come to serve the Lord, prepare yourself for testing [πειρασμόν]."); *Sir.* 33:1 ("No evil will befall the one who fears the Lord, but in trials such a one will be rescued again and again."); Acts 20:19 ("serving the Lord with all humility and with tears, enduring the trials that came to me through the plots of the Jews."); 2 Pet. 2:9 ("then the Lord knows how to rescue the godly from trial, and to keep the unrighteous under punishment until the day of judgment."). Each of these references sees the inevitability of trials and temptations for Christians. Also, *b. Ber.* 60b: "Bring me not into the power of temptation." *b. Sanh.* 107a. See *Ex. Rab.* 31, *b. Menah.* 99b. 11QPs 24:11: "Do not bring me into situations that are too hard for me." Paul provides encouragement for those within testing/temptations, "No temptation (πειρασμὸς) has overtaken you except what is common to mankind. And God is faithful; he will not let you be tempted (πειρασθῆναι) beyond what you can bear. But when you are tempted (πειρασμῷ), he will also provide a way out so that you can endure it" (1 Cor. 10:13).
[68] We have argued for this importance in Chapter 5.

no root, but endures only for a while, and when trouble (θλίψεως) or persecution (διωγμοῦ) arises on account of the word, that person immediately falls away (σκανδαλίζεται).[69]

Jesus explains that there will be those who hear the words concerning the kingdom and fall away when the evil one comes (v. 19). The Lukan parallel (Lk. 8:11-15) to this explained parable (Mt. 13:18-23) makes the connection between Mt. 13:19-21 and the sixth petition even more explicit. Luke 8:13 states, "The ones on the rock are those who, when they hear the word, receive it with joy. But these have no root; they believe only for a while and in a time of *temptation* (πειρασμοῦ) fall away." Luke describes the apostasy of some who had believed in the context of a trials and temptations (πειρασμός).[70]

Returning back to the Gethsemane narrative (Mt. 26:36-46), it appears that Jesus may be echoing Mt. 13:19-21 when he encourages his disciples to stay awake. Jesus realizes that his own flesh is weak and the will of God is at stake (see Lk. 21:36).[71] He does not want his disciples to succumb to disbelief by failing to perform the will of God.[72] Read together, then, the temptations of the sixth petition describe those temptations authored by the evil one which causes one to fall away or desert the faith.

Conclusion

In this section, we have argued that the sixth petition is not referring to temptations that edify or prove one's character but rather to trials and temptations that the evil one uses to destroy disciples (see Mt. 6:13b). The Sermon assumes that its adherents will be persecuted for righteousness' sake (Mt. 5:10-12). As Jesus withstood the trial to disavow God's will (Mt. 4:1–10; 26:41), so his disciples, despite their human frailty, must also withstand their various trials (see Lk. 21:36).

"Lead Us Not into Temptation" in the Sermon on the Mount

In the previous section, we have argued that the sixth petition concerns requests to avoid trials or temptations where one might fall away. Temptations of this sort are throughout the Sermon. They include most of the ethical exhortations: using insults (Mt. 5:11-12), divorce (Mt. 5:31-32), retaliation (Mt. 5:38-42), hating your enemies

---

[69] The wording of these verses is reminiscent of the testing and tribulations which Jesus promises in the Sermon on the Mount. The words include διωγμός and σκανδαλίζω. Διωγμός is used in the *macarism*, when Jesus declares blessings on those who are "persecuted" for righteousness' sake (Mt. 5:11-12). Σκανδαλίζω is used in the section concerning the temptations of the right eye and right hand (Mt. 5:29-30). These parallels suggest that persecution and lust are means of great temptation and can cause disciples to fall away. As we will argue below regarding Mt. 5:27-30, such is the need for the sixth petition.
[70] Also Mt. 24:10: "Then many will fall away, and they will betray one another and hate one another."
[71] Luke 21:36 states, "Be alert at all times, praying that you may have the strength to escape all these things that will take place, and to stand before the Son of Man."
[72] It is interesting that in the narrative preceding the Garden of Gethsemane (Mt. 26:31-35), Jesus foretells of the disciples falling away (σκανδαλισθήσεσθε, lit. "become deserters") and Peter's threefold denial.

(Mt. 5:43-47), displaying righteousness for others' approval (Mt. 6:1-18), fixating on earthly possessions instead of heavenly rewards (Mt. 6:19-21), the seduction of wealth (Mt. 6:22-24), doubting God's provision (Mt. 6:25-34), and unfair judgment of others (Mt. 7:1-5). Because we have discussed these passages in other sections, we will not elaborate on their textual connections with the sixth petition. In this section, we will specifically detail the teachings in Mt. 5:27-30 and 7:6, as they have not been discussed in previous chapters.

Matthew 5:27-30

In Mt. 5:27-30, Jesus addresses the topic of adultery and the disposition of the heart. As with the other teachings in Jesus's instruction on the Mosaic law (Mt. 5:21-48), the passage begins with the reiteration of a Mosaic law ("You shall not commit adultery [μοιχεύσεις]") followed by Jesus's explanation. The specific law appears to be a combination of the seventh commandment (i.e., prohibiting adultery [μοιχεύω]) and tenth commandment (prohibiting the desire/coveting [ἐπιθυμέω] of another's wife [Exod. 20:13, 17 LXX]).[73] Jesus quotes the seventh commandment ("You have heard that it was said"), while his explanation ("everyone who looks at a woman with lust [ἐπι θυμῆσαι] has already committed adultery with her in his heart") of the law parallels the tenth commandment with the repetition of "desire" (ἐπιθυμέω). The Greek indicates that the object of desire is another's wife (ὁ βλέπων γυναῖκα πρὸς τὸ ἐπιθυμῆσαι). Jesus's explanation stretches beyond the prohibition of adultery to even a lustful look. As Quarles notes, the "teaching urges disciples to guard their eyes and hearts carefully from lust, fantasizing, and any other thought or act that might lead to acts of sexual sin."[74] Jesus continues with instruction to expunge one's "right eye" and cut off one's "right hand" if they cause stumbling (vv. 29–30). Jesus does not appear to encourage self-mutilation, but one must be careful not to rid the teaching of its severity.[75] The teaching links adultery with the condition of the heart and makes it clear that one must cut out those things that cause one's heart to succumb to sin.[76] The basis for Jesus's analogy is that it is better to lose a body part than gain that which leads to eternal punishment (i.e., "whole body to go into hell").[77] If a disciple does not put these things to death, they will succumb to their sinful desires.

The parallels between the sixth petition and the teaching on adultery are twofold. First, both petition and vv. 29-30 have negative connotations. The petition requests that temptation be avoided ("lead us not into") so that the disciple will not be overcome. Similarly, Jesus's teaching in vv. 29-30 speaks of the "eye" and "hand" as agents of destruction when used for adultery and lust. This observation leads to the second

---

[73] Quarles, *Sermon on the Mount*, 118.
[74] Quarles, *Sermon on the Mount*, 119.
[75] Nolland, *Gospel of Matthew*, 239–40, makes a similar point.
[76] See also the teaching in Mt. 18:7-20. This section of ch. 18 repeats the instruction of expunging the "eye" and cutting off the "hand" but in the context of church discipline. Matthew 5:27-30 does not appear to have church discipline in view, as the context is examining adultery.
[77] Paul similarly echoes this instruction for believers to put to death "fornication, impurity, passion, [and] evil desire" (Col. 3:5; see also 1 Cor. 5:6–13).

parallel. Both petition and passage refer to temptations that prey on human frailty. The sixth petition is an admission of frailty, while Mt. 5:29-30 describes the right eye and right hand as something that causes one to sin (σκανδαλίζω).[78] The metaphor evokes the idea of the lustful hand and eye as deadly to the rest of the body and bringing about the body's destruction ("thrown into hell"). Jesus's answer to these impending dangers is that they must be "cut off."

Matthew 7:6

Commentators will often note that Mt. 7:6 is the most difficult verse to understand in Matthew's Sermon on the Mount, if not the entire Gospel.[79] Before examining these difficulties and how scholars have explained the verse, we will argue what we know. First, the verse is structured chiastically:[80]

> Do not give what is *holy* to *dogs*.
>   Do not throw your *pearls* before *swine*,
>   They (the *swine*) will trample them under foot
> And (the *dogs*) turn to attack you.

This chiastic structure equates dogs and swine, holy things and pearls. In both cases, the unclean animal (i.e., dogs/swine) ravages the good thing (holy things/pearls/people). The force of the verbs is one of destruction (καταπατέω/ῥήγνυμι). Second, the logion in Mt. 7:6 does not automatically fit its context. The verse arguably has connections with both Mt. 7:1-5 on judging and Mt. 7:7-11 on prayer, but not an overwhelming amount of evidence argues for one over the other.[81]

Five interpretations have dominated the discussions concerning Mt. 7:6. Interpreters have attempted to be sensitive to the metaphors, while recognizing that their referents are varied in parallel literature. This section will not attempt to be exhaustive but will address those interpretations that have carried support in modern interpretations. Although the meaning remains difficult, there is no evidence to suggest Matthew's first readers were unaware of its meaning.

1) Some commentators suggest an Aramaic substratum of v. 6 and mistranslations on the part of Matthew.[82] In this instance, the reference "τὸ ἅγιον" is a mistranslation from the Aramaic word for "rings." Since "holy" and "rings" share the same consonants in Aramaic (קדש), Matthew misunderstood the saying's true meaning. His intention then was to evoke Prov. 11:22 ("Like a gold ring in a pig's snout is a beautiful woman without good sense"). Numerous exegetes have used this approach to make various assertions. The most popular

---

[78] See also Mt. 13:21, which we have argued links to the sixth petition.
[79] Pennington, *Sermon and Human Flourishing*, 254.
[80] See McKnight, *Sermon on the Mount*, 237.
[81] See Bornkamm, "Der Aufbau der Bergpredigt," 428–9.
[82] Most recently, S. Llewelyn, "Matt. 7:6a: Mistranslation or Interpretation," *NovT* 31.2 (1989): 76–103, argues that the change is intentional.

is to assert that this mistranslation has resulted in a saying in Matthew's Gospel that is now inaccessible to the modern interpreter.[83] While these suggestions are interesting, they are unlikely. If Matthew was intentional in including such a phrase that is unattested elsewhere (something he most likely did with care), why would he record it in a haphazard way (misspelling/mistranslations) that allows for such confusion?[84] It is also difficult to understand which words may underlie the extant Greek translation we have. Retro-translations of this sort are at best conjectural and more likely answers are available.

2) A very early reception of Mt. 7:6 is the writer of the *Didache*. The *Didache* applies the metaphors to the *Eucharist*. *Didache* 9:5 states, "Let no one eat or drink of your *Eucharist* save those who have been baptized in the name of the Lord, since the Lord has said, "Do not give what is holy to the dogs (Μὴ δῶτε τὸ ἅγιον τοῖς κυσὶν)."[85] The message in the *Didache* is quite clear—the table's elements ("what is holy") have no place among those who are "outsiders."[86] While it is generally helpful to consider parallel accounts such as the *Didache*, the *Didache's* appropriation of this verse is something completely foreign to the Matthean context. If Matthew intended for the logion to refer to the *Eucharist*, he has not made that readily available in the context of his teaching on judging (Mt. 7:1-5) or persistent prayer (Mt. 7:7-11).

3) Dale Allison has argued that the immediate context is the clearest indicator of the verse's meaning.[87] He links the teaching in Mt. 7:6 to 7:1-5.[88] He argues,

> Matt. 7:1–5 has commanded that there be not too much severity. Matt. 7:6 follows up by saying that there should not be too much laxity. That is, the text anticipates a problem and searches for a balance, for moral symmetry. The principles in 7:1–5 are not to be abused. They do not eliminate the use of critical faculties when it comes to sacred concerns.[89]

Allison's approach is commendable, at the very least, for paying attention to the Matthean context. Yet, his links to the previous passage are based on thematic

---

[83] Betz, *Sermon on the Mount*, 499, states, "The SM seems to have given the saying a special application, which, however, is *withheld from us*. The original hearers or readers of the SM knew what the terms meant." Emphasis mine.

[84] It is also important to note that the concept of pigs "trampling" and dogs "ravaging" produces a more sensible parallel than pearls in a pig's snout and a ring in a dog's nose. See Gundry, *Matthew*, 123. Bornkamm, "Der Aufbau der Bergpredigt," 428, fn.10, says that this translation would malign the Greek, or in his words, make the phrase "nonsensical" ("unsinnig").

[85] See Huub van de Sandt, "'Do Not Give What Is Holy to the Dogs' (Did 9:5D and Matt 7:6A); The Eucharistic Food of the Didache in Its Jewish Purity Setting," *VC* 56 (2002), 223–46.

[86] Gundry, *Matthew*, 122, does not fully affirm the exclusion of "outsiders" from the table but similarly argues that there are "outsiders" who are disrupting the fellowship.

[87] Allison, *Sermon on the Mount*, 154.

[88] So also, Thomas J. Bennett, "Matthew 7:6—A New Interpretation," *WTJ* 49 (1987): 371-86. He not only thinks the verses are linked but also v. 6 reiterates the exact point of Mt. 7:1-5. Bennett, "Matthew 7:6," 384–5, states, "'Do not give dogs what is holy; and do not throw your pearls before swine'=Do not judge; 'lest they trample them underfoot and turn to attack you'=lest you be judge."

[89] Allison, *Sermon on the Mount*, 155.

correlations without concern for the grammatical arrangement of Mt. 7:1-11. In vv. 1-2, Matthew has the subject of the verbs as plural. The verb tense changes to singular in vv. 3-5. Interestingly, Mt. 7:6 switches back to the plural subject—a switch that continues in vv. 7-11. The switch between vv. 3-5 and v. 6 create grammatical dissonance between the two topics.[90] This switch will be examined in more detail below.

4) In his *Hermeneia* commentary on Matthew's Gospel, Ulrich Luz has argued that the meaning of the passage cannot be known. He states, "This logion is a puzzle. Even its symbolic meaning is uncertain; its application and its sense in the Matthean context are a complete mystery."[91] Luz reasons that the logion may have been understood in its original context and even by its original readers, but Matthew has disconnected it from its original setting and not integrated into his own context. Therefore, its meaning is lost to the modern reader. Luz conjectures, "What is this verse meant to convey today?" He comments, "My advice is radical: one should not use it as a biblical word."[92] While Luz is typically a careful interpreter, in this case he may be too careful. It does not follow that Matthew would make the Sermon intelligible to disciples (Mt. 5:1-2) and the crowds (Mt. 7:28–8:1) but intend for the future readers to be in the dark.[93]

5) Donald Hagner argues that "what is holy" and "pearls" are references to the gospel of the kingdom.[94] Evidence for this translation is found in Mt. 13:45-46 where the kingdom is described as a hidden treasure and a costly *pearl*.[95] According to Hagner, the "pigs" are unclean animals in the Jewish religion and "dogs" were often used to refer to Gentiles in a derogatory fashion.[96] Therefore, the logion refers to prohibiting the spread of the gospel to the Gentiles.[97] This interpretation would accord with Jesus's other teachings in Mt. 10:5 and 15:24-26 about taking the word to the Jews first. Hagner is careful not to push the application too far because Jesus expects the gospel to go to Gentiles eventually. Hagner also prefaces his argument with the possibility of the Jews regarding the gospel as foolishness. Hagner thinks it is best to see the logion as referring

---

[90] For an alternative view which sees the changes as indicative of Mt. 7:6 belonging with 7:1-5, see Pennington, *Sermon and Human Flourishing*, 259, fn.15.

[91] Luz, *Matthew 1–7*, 354.

[92] Luz, *Matthew 1–7*, 356.

[93] See Richard Bauckham, ed., *Gospel for All Christians: Rethinking the Gospel Audiences*, New Testament Studies (Grand Rapids: Eerdmans, 1997), argues that the Gospels were not only written for their respective communities but also for future readers.

[94] Hagner, *Matthew 1–13*, 171. The original meaning of "what is holy" would have been rooted in the Old Testament depiction of food offered in sacrifices (Exod. 29:33; Lev. 2:3; 22:10-16; Num. 18:8-9; see also *Gos. Thom.* saying 93).

[95] Emphasis mine to illustrate lexical parallel. See also Pennington, *Sermon and Human Flourishing*, 261, fn.22.

[96] Hagner, *Matthew 1–13*, 171. See also *1 Enoch* 89.

[97] Similarly, Hermann von Lipps, "Schweine füttert man, Hunde nicht—ein Versuch, das Rätsel von Matthäus 7:6 zu lösen," *ZNW* 79 (1988): 165–85, argues that the metaphors are Hellenistic and refer more loosely to wrongly causing harm to others and being punished. This interpretation works with the range of the metaphors but does not properly take into account the Jewish context of the metaphors.

to withholding the gospel from "all who are unreceptive."[98] A similar idea is found in Heb. 10:29 where apostate Christians trample that which is holy.

Hagner's reading of this logion is understandable given the parallels within Matthew's own Gospel and other New Testament evidence concerning the care in which one distributes the gospel. While Hagner's final conclusion appears to be correct, especially concerning the identification of the holy things and pearls, the transition from Gentiles to a more general audience (i.e., non-Jews and apostates) is unnecessary. Several arguments suggest that the "dogs" and "pigs" unambiguously refer to those who are hostile to the gospel, whether obstinate hearers, false prophets, or apostates. First, if Matthew had intended for such a difficult verse to be understood in light of Gentile exclusion, why would he have placed it between teachings on unfair judging (Mt. 7:1-5) and prayer (Mt. 7:7-11)?[99] Second, the references to "Gentiles" in Matthew's Gospel are not used with the same negative rhetorical force, as we find in Mt. 7:6. In Matthew's Gospel, the term often refers less to ethnic Gentiles, and more to "non-disciples." In Mt. 18:17, there are Jews (specifically, Pharisees) who are called "Gentiles," a derogatory means to refer to their behavior as pagans. Further, the exclusion of ethnic Gentiles is not in keeping with Matthew's overall message (see Mt. 15:21-28; Mt. 28:19-20).[100] As Gundry states, then, "Among Jesus' disciples, who are the new people of God, 'Gentiles' can lose the meaning of 'non-Jews' and take the meaning of 'non-disciples' (see Matt. 5:47; 6:7, 32; 18:17; Luke 12:30)." Third, several passages use similar metaphors and connotations found in Mt. 7:6 to refer to scorners of the gospel. Psalm 22:16 ("For dogs are all around me; a company of evildoers encircles me. My hands and feet have shrivelled") describes those who are hostile to believers in God. The word used to describe these people, πονηρεύομαι (Ps. 21:17 LXX), is reminiscent of the seventh petition. In conclusion, the saying warns against forfeiting the words of the kingdom to those who are hostile to its message, whether obstinate hearers, false prophets, or apostates. Yet, even with this tentative definition, the question remains, why has Matthew inserted this verse in its present context? And, how does the context of ch. 7 affect the meaning of v. 6?

As we stated above, Mt. 7:6 does not neatly fit with its surrounding context. Most commentators have preferred to see v. 6 alongside Mt. 7:1-5, as we illustrated with Dale Allison's proposal. Günther Bornkamm and, more recently, Glen Stassen have argued that the best reading of Mt. 7:6 is alongside 7:7-11. In Bornkamm's proposal, the second half of the Sermon on the Mount (Mt. 6:19–7:6) follows the order of the petitions until Mt. 7:7-11.[101] At 7:7-11, Matthew forms an *inclusio* with the Lord's Prayer itself. Bornkamm assigns Mt. 7:1-5 to the forgiveness petition, and rightfully as we

---

[98] Hagner, *Matthew 1–13*, 172.
[99] Also, Keener, *Gospel of Matthew*, 242. Additionally, the Sermon on the Mount, in which Mt. 7:6 is found, is presented to not only disciples but also the crowds (Mt. 7:28–8:1). It is reasonable to assume that non-Jews would have been among these crowds.
[100] See Luz, *Matthew 1–7*, 355. It is also noteworthy that several non-Jews are mentioned in the genealogy of Jesus, see Mt. 1:1-17. These references appear to create an *inclusio* around the entirety of Matthew's Gospel.
[101] See Chapter 3 for a fuller explanation. Bornkamm, "Der Aufbau der Bergpredigt," 419–32.

have argued in Chapter 5. But, with only one verse left before the *inclusio*, Bornkamm sees Mt. 7:6 as a parallel to the sixth and seventh petitions. This observation shows the split between vv. 1-5 and v. 6.

Stassen follows Bornkamm's work with his own proposal, seeking to strengthen Bornkamm's initial ideas. Stassen begins his analysis of the Sermon on the Mount with an argument for a triadic shape in each section of the Sermon on the Mount. These triads consist of a "traditional teaching," "vicious cycle," and "transforming initiative."[102] These are classified as follows:[103]

a) The *Traditional Righteousness* is presented as coming from Jewish tradition. It occurs first in a triad and does not begin with a particle. Its main verb is usually a future indicative or a subjunctive with an imperatival function, as is typical in Matthew for many citations of Old Testament commands; its mood apparently varies with the received tradition.

b) The *Vicious Cycle plus Judgment* is presented as Jesus's teaching, with authority. It diagnoses a practice and says it leads to judgment. Its main verb is a participle, infinitive, subjunctive, or indicative but not an imperative. It begins with "but," "for," "lest," or "therefore" (δέ, οὖν, Διὰ τοῦτο, μήποτε), or a negative such as μή or οὐκ, and often includes λέγω ὑμῖν ("I say to you").

c) The *Transforming Initiative* is also presented as Jesus's teaching, with authority. Its main verb is a positive imperative—an initiative—not a negative prohibition, calling for a practice of deliverance from the vicious cycle and to participation in the reign of God. It usually begins with δέ and ends with a supporting explanation: that is, "he may deliver you to the judge."

Stassen sees fourteen such triads that occupy the main section of the Sermon, 5:21–7:12.[104] They are as follows:[105]

1. On being reconciled (5:21-26: 21, 22, 23-26)
2. On removing the practice that leads to lust (5:27-30: 27, 28, 29-30)
3. On divorce (5:31-32: 31, 32a-b [no Transforming Initiative])
4. On telling the truth (5:33-37: 33, 34-36, 37)
5. Transforming initiatives of peacemaking (5:38-42: 38, 39a, 39b-42)
6. Love your enemy (5:43-48: 43, 44-45, 46-47, 48 [summary])
   [Introduction to next section: 6:1]
7. Almsgiving (6:52-4: 2a, 2b, 3-4)
8. Prayer (6:5-6: 5a, 5b, 6)
9. Prayer (6:7-15: 7a, 7b-8, 9-15)

---

[102] Stassen, "Fourteen Triads," 268.
[103] Stassen, "Fourteen Triads," 275.
[104] Stassen does not deal with the sections of the Sermon outside of Mt. 5:21–7:12.
[105] See Johan C. Thom, "Dyads, Triads, and Other Compositional Beasts in the Sermon on the Mount (Matthew 5–7)" in *The New Testament Interpreted: Essays in Honour of Bernard C. Lategan*, ed. Cilliers Breytenbach, Johan C. Thom, and Jeremy Punt (Leiden: Brill, 2006), 294. In the parentheses, the verses represent the triadic structure as presented by Stassen.

10. Fasting (6:16-18: 16a, 16b, 17-18)
11. Storing treasures (6:19-23: 19a, 19b, 20-23)
12. Serve first God's reign and justice (6:24-34: 24ab, 24c-25, 26-34)
13. Judge not, but take the log out of your own eye (7:1-5: 1, 2-4, 5)
14. Place your trust not in gentile dogs but in our Father God (7:6-12: 6a, 6b, 7-12)

In the last triad, Stassen argues that Mt. 7:6 functions as the "traditional teaching" (6a) and "vicious cycle" (6b), followed by the "transforming initiative" in Mt. 7:7-11. The traditional teaching is "do not give holy things to dogs or cast pearls before swine." The vicious cycle is that the holy things and pearls will be torn to pieces and trampled underfoot (see Mt. 5:13). Matthew 7:7-11 provides the alternative to these evil practices. Stassen defines the transforming initiative in Mt. 7:7-11: "give your trust, your loyalty, and your prayers, to your Father in Heaven."[106] If Mt. 7:6 is the opposite of 7:7-11, its intended meaning is "do not give your trust and loyalty to the dogs and pigs instead of to God."[107]

Stassen's position has many commendable elements but overlooks some additional parallels between Mt. 7:6 and 7:11.[108] In addition to the consistency of the plural verbs mentioned above, the connection of Mt. 7:6 to 7:7-11 provides a contrast between good and evil, which has been characteristic of Matthew's last section of the Sermon's body to this point (Mt. 6:19–7:5). Second, the contrasts in Matthew's last section are characterized by their heavenly and earthly dimensions (i.e., heavenly/earthly treasures; sound/evil eye; God/mammon; kingdom and righteousness/earthly worries of food, drink, and clothing). The metaphors of Mt. 7:6 present things of earth as contrasts to the heavenly emphasis of 7:7-11 (i.e., Father in heaven).[109] In light of our above discussion and this consideration of the relationship between Mt. 7:6 and 7-11, we are now more prepared to provide an interpretation of Mt. 7:6. The verse is referring to how one shares ("gives") the gospel. One must be careful to avoid those who are obstinate to its message. The evil one empowers false teachers and apostates to reject the message of the kingdom. On the other hand, God "gives" to those who are receptive (Mt. 7:7-11). As Keener summarizes, "One should discerningly continue to

---

[106] Stassen, "Fourteen Triads," 290.
[107] Stassen, "Fourteen Triads," 290.
[108] Stassen's proposal is careful and well documented but is not without fault. One major concern of Stassen's work is his dismissal of dyads. He is quick to point out that the use of dyads is atypical for the Gospel of Matthew. Arguably, one of the major themes in the entirety of the Gospel is the dyad of heaven and earth. Matthew is also very keen to use the literary device of comparisons (a dyadic structure). Before getting to the Sermon, Matthew compares Jesus with John the Baptist and Moses. In the Sermon, the disciples of Jesus are compared to the scribes and Pharisees. After the Sermon, Jesus is compared to his own disciples, Jonah, Solomon, and the temple. A complete reading of the Sermon reveals that there are two groups of people hearing Jesus's teachings, the disciples and the crowds. The first major section of the Sermon is filled with dyads: two sets of four beatitudes and the twin metaphors of salt and light. Also, the Sermon ends with various comparisons: the wide gate versus the narrow gate, good fruit versus bad fruit, and rocky foundations versus sandy foundations. Though these sections fall outside of Stassen's exegesis, they are still vital parts of the Sermon's message.
[109] Stassen, "Fourteen Triads," 294, notes this consistent theme but misses the contrasting themes of heaven and earth as part of the glue holding the section (Mt. 6:19–7:11) together.

offer wisdom or the gift of the kingdom (see Matt. 13:45–46) only to those willing to receive what one offers, just as God does (7:7–11)."[110]

If Mt. 7:6 is read alongside the prayer motif of 7:7-11, the first parallel with the sixth petition is established. The sixth petition and Mt. 7:6 share an emphasis on prayer. Second, both petition and Mt. 7:6 are negative in their connotations. The sixth petition requests to avoid trials and temptations that may cause one to succumb to apostasy. The teaching in Mt. 7:6 instructs disciples to avoid giving the words of the kingdom to false teachers and apostates. Third, both passages share an element of human frailty. The sixth petition is spoken by someone who realizes his own weakness in light of temptations from the evil one. Matthew 7:6 expresses vulnerability in that the rejection of "what is holy" can lead to harm. In conclusion, the ambiguity of Mt. 7:6 leaves the parallel with the sixth petition difficult to establish with certainty, but the discussion above is at least possible.

Temptation Petition Conclusion

In the previous sections, we have attempted to define the sixth petition by examining its place in Matthew's cultural milieu and its relationship with the seventh petition. We have argued that the sixth petition is primarily a request to avoid trials and temptations authored by the evil one. The petition is a request to avoid moments of apostasy and an admission of human frailty and weakness. Although these types of temptations underlie most of the Sermon's teaching, we have focused on those passages that have been previously undiscussed.[111] Throughout this book, we have attempted to show that the Lord's Prayer and the Sermon on the Mount should be read together. Although these parallels are looser than previous parallels, the arguments are at least plausible. When read in this manner, the temptation petition requests that disciples avoid sexual temptation, which can lead to destruction (Mt. 5:29-30), and the potential harm caused by those who reject the gospel (Mt. 7:6).

Chapter Conclusion

In these remaining petitions, the parallels are looser but still important. Hallowing the Name entails doing good works before men (Mt. 5:16, 7:21-23). These works bring glory to the Father in heaven and help bring about the kingdom of heaven to earth. Specifically, disciples will be honest (Mt. 5:33-37) and become "workers of God's laws" (Mt. 7:21-23). The temptation petition requests the avoidance of exerting ruthless power (Mt. 5:11-12, also 5:5), retaliation (Mt. 5:38-42), hate of enemies (Mt. 5:43-47), righteousness for man's approval (Mt. 6:1-18), the allure of earthly treasures (Mt.

---

[110] Keener, *Gospel of Matthew*, 244.
[111] Examples of other passages read in light of the sixth petition include: a prayer to embrace meekness (Mt. 5:11-12, see also 5:5), avoid retaliation (Mt. 5:38-42), love your enemies (Mt. 5:43-47), display righteousness for God's approval (Mt. 6:1-18), rejoice in heavenly rewards instead of earthly possessions (Mt. 6:19-21), be content (Mt. 6:24), trust God's provision (Mt. 6:25-34), and avoid judging others (Mt. 7:1-5, see also 7:12).

6:19-21), greed (Mt. 6:24), comfort from food/drink/clothes (Mt. 6:25-34), and unfair judgment (Mt. 7:1-5, see also 7:12). More specifically in this chapter, we have argued for parallels between Mt. 5:27-30 and Matt. 7:6. The temptation petition would then include the avoidance of the allure of lust (Mt. 5:27-30) and the destruction by those who oppose the gospel (Mt. 7:6).

7

Conclusion

The Sermon's Prayer, Word and Deed/Hearers and Doers, and Points for Further Research

Matthew 6:9a: Οὕτως οὖν προσεύχεσθε ὑμεῖς

This book has set about the task of examining the relationship of the Lord's Prayer and the Sermon on the Mount in Matthew's Gospel. We have suggested that these texts should be read together, as the Lord's Prayer is central to the Sermon on the Mount. We have interacted with Dale C. Allison, Hans Dieter Betz, Mary Hinkle, Walter Grundmann, Günther Bornkamm, Ulrich Luz, and Jonathan Pennington, who have all noted the centrality of the Lord's Prayer. Despite their attempts, each scholar has missed key indicators of Matthew's intratextuality. The result is a neglect of structural, lexical, and thematic parallels between the two texts, and as a result, a lack of precision in defining the centrality of the Lord's Prayer within Matthew's chosen context. It is the contention of this book that the centrality of the Lord's Prayer is defined by (1) the structure of the Sermon on the Mount, and (2) the lexical and thematic parallels with various passages throughout the Sermon on the Mount. We have suggested that it is likely that Matthew noted similarities between the Lord's Prayer and the Sermon on the Mount from the traditions he received, leading him to establish connections between the two texts. Matthew then edited parts of the Sermon, and the Prayer itself, with a desire to increase the parallelism structurally, lexically, and thematically. The importance of prayer in the Sermon on the Mount is marked by not only the centrality of the Lord's Prayer but also the instruction to "ask, seek, and knock" at the end of the Sermon's body (Mt. 7:7-11). The Sermon's body then comes to a formidable end with a reemphasizing of prayer (Mt. 7:7-11) and a summation of "greater righteousness," the Golden Rule (Mt. 7:12).

In addition to bringing clarity to the Prayer's centrality, we have also attempted to determine Matthew's purpose in making the Prayer central to the Sermon on the Mount. We have argued that the purpose of the Prayer's location in the center of the Sermon is to clarify what the answer to the petitions might look like in the life of the disciple of Jesus. In turn, this prayer to the Father is key to committing to and living by the Sermon's mandated kingdom righteousness.

To achieve this study, we have implemented an eclectic method, incorporating insights from historical and literary methods of exegesis. The approach throughout this book has been to blend the best insights of redaction criticism, which considers antecedent texts, and rhetorical criticism, which focuses on the final form of a text. This blending of methodological considerations takes into account the final form (rhetorical criticism) of the text, the distinctive features (redaction criticism) of the text, and related compositions (i.e., Jewish parallels) to the text. The benefit of this approach is that it takes into account the final shape of Matthew's editing (i.e., structure and literary conventions), the distinctive elements within the Matthean Prayer and Sermon (i.e., Mattheanisms), and the insights from comparing similar types of literature (i.e., Matthew's cultural milieu).

After detailing our thesis, surveying those who have noted the centrality of the Prayer, and explaining our methodology, we began with an analysis of the relationship of the Lord's Prayer and the Sermon on the Mount by noting the Sermon's structure. We argued that the Sermon is arranged concentrically using *inclusios* to bring the reader's attention to its centerpiece, the Lord's Prayer (Chapter 3). The Lord's Prayer is also concentrically structured, suggesting that Matthew may have noted the structural similarity and/or enhanced the structural parallels for the sake of consistency. The next section of the book examined three different sets of petitions (Chapters 4 through 6). In Chapter 4, we began with those petitions that are most likely to be Matthean by comparing Matthew and Luke's respective versions of the Lord's Prayer. Those petitions, which are only in Matthew's Gospel are the invocation, the will petition, and the evil petition. Interestingly, the wording of these petitions is prominent within chs 5–7, as opposed to the rest of Matthew's Gospel. This clustering of references signals that the references should be read together. Further, we argued that these established lexical parallels were reinforced by shared themes.

In Chapter 5, we examined the kingdom, bread, and forgiveness petitions. These petitions are found in the Lukan version of the Lord's Prayer but have slightly distinctive elements that affect how they are understood. We additionally analyzed the petitions in light of Matthew's cultural milieu to establish a basis for thematic parallels. After examining these distinctive elements and the meaning of the petition, we considered the lexical and thematic parallels with various Sermon passages.

In Chapter 6, we concluded our investigation with the Name and temptation petitions. These petitions are not distinctive in comparison with Luke and, interestingly, do not possess lexical parallels with the Sermon. Yet, each petition is thematically related to passages throughout the Sermon. In sum, those petitions that were arguably more Matthean and had distinctive elements, as defined by their wording and prominence, displayed stronger parallels with the Sermon and more numerous parallels. On the other hand, those petitions that were verbatim with Luke displayed less substantive parallels. It is also interesting to note that several Sermon passages had parallels with the same petition. These observations are to be expected if Matthew was noting parallels between the texts and increasing those parallels.

We now hope to show that our understanding of the dynamics of reading this Matthean masterpiece changes, when our conclusions are taken into account. As Jesus began to teach the Lord's Prayer, he commended his disciples to "pray then in this way." In light of the findings of this book, we will offer three insights from the Prayer's centrality on how to "pray then in this way."

The "Sermon's" Prayer

Throughout the history of studies on the Lord's Prayer, commentators have often debated what to call the prayer. The most obvious and enduring names for the prayer have been the "Lord's Prayer" and the "Our Father" (*Pater Noster*, or *Vater Unser*). These names, of course, have to do with the one who taught the prayer and its first words.[1] Recently, the traditional name for the prayer has been challenged by Jeffrey Gibson. This is not the first time someone has challenged the prayer's name, but Gibson has argued most persuasively. Gibson reasons that despite the source of the Lord's Prayer and its first words, its intended audience is the disciples of Jesus and its purpose is to instruct them.[2] His book is aptly titled *The Disciples' Prayer: The Prayer Jesus Taught in Its Historical Setting* to reflect his concerns that the prayer's focus should be on its recipients.

It has been the contention of this book that the Lord's Prayer is central to the Sermon on the Mount in Matthew's Gospel. In light of these arguments, we propose that future studies of the Matthean Prayer and Matthean Sermon interpret these texts as they are presented in their final form. Yes, the prayer is the Lord's and disciples', but in its Matthean context, the prayer is central to the "Sermon." This centrality results in a certain reading of each petition and its Sermon parallels.[3]

When read in this manner, calling on "our Father in heaven" entails a commitment to Sermon living, for example, to prayer (Mt. 5:45; 6:6 [2x], 8, 14, 15, 26, 32; 7:11), good works and righteousness (Mt. 5:16, 48; 6:1, 4, 18 [2x]; 7:21), and being part of the family of God (Mt. 5:9, 21-26).

"Hallowing God's name" includes being salt and light (Mt. 5:13-16), a commitment to truth-telling (Mt. 5:33-37), and performing the will of the Father in heaven (Mt. 7:21-23).

Praying "your kingdom come" implies embodying the kingdom ethics of the *macarisms* (Mt. 5:3-10), fulfilling the law and prophets (Mt. 5:17-20), seeking the kingdom and righteousness (Mt. 6:33), and performing the will of God (Mt. 7:21-23). The request may also imply a desire to avoid the easy way of life that leads to destruction (Mt. 7:13-14).

The will petition is a request to embody the *macarisms* (Mt. 5:3-12), to be salt and light (Mt. 5:13-16), to live according to God's laws (Mt. 5:17-20), to speak truthfully

---

[1] For convention's sake, we have continually referred to the text under examination as the Lord's Prayer.
[2] Gibson, *Disciples' Prayer*, 5–8.
[3] We will discuss this combining of words below.

(Mt. 5:33-37), to love enemies and emulate the perfection of the Father (Mt. 5:45, 48), to practice righteousness by storing up heavenly treasure (Mt. 6:1, 19-21, 22-24), to seek the kingdom among earthly desires (Mt. 6:25-33 [esp. v. 33]), to do good to others (Mt. 7:12), and rightfully to confess "Lord, Lord" (Mt. 7:21).

The bread petition is a request and affirmation of fully trusting that God will provide daily sustenance (Mt. 6:25-34; 7:7-11) but not at the expense of God's kingdom and righteousness (Mt. 6:33). The request may also loosely parallel the instruction to the disciples to "hunger and thirst" after righteousness (Mt. 5:6), seek heavenly treasures above earthly treasures (Mt. 6:19-21), and worship God over wealth (Mt. 6:24).

The forgiveness petition is a commitment to repair broken relationships in the same manner God has restored a relationship with his disciples (Mt. 6:14-15). This triangular shape demands that petitioners will be merciful (Mt. 5:7; 6:14-15), seek reconciliation with others (Mt. 5:21-26), resist retaliation (Mt. 5:38-42), love and pray for enemies (Mt. 5:43-47), and avoid unnecessary judgment (Mt. 7:1-5).

The temptation petition reflects, among other things, the hope that disciples avoid sexual temptation that can lead to destruction (Mt. 5:27-30) and the potential harm caused by those who reject the gospel (Mt. 7:6).

The evil petition prays to avoid slander (Mt. 5:11), falsehood (Mt. 5:37), retaliation (Mt. 5:39), hating your enemy (Mt. 5:45), duplicitous desires (Mt. 6:23, "evil eyes"), doubting God's good gifts (Mt. 7:11), bearing bad fruit (Mt. 7:17-18), and being a worker of lawlessness (Mt. 7:23).

Word and Deed/Hearers and Doers

In the previous sections, we concluded by reiterating the reasons Matthew has made the Lord's Prayer central to the Sermon on the Mount and how this centrality changes our understanding of these two texts. On a broader level, the combination of Jesus's words concerning prayer (i.e., the Lord's Prayer) and teachings concerning discipleship (i.e., the Sermon on the Mount) reflects an important exegetical point regarding Christian praxis.[4] A petitioner comes to God offering thanks, lament, praise, and petition. Yet, Mt. 6:33 uses prayer language ("strive") alongside the goals of discipleship (i.e., "the kingdom and righteousness"). This point is also emphasized in both the conclusion to the Sermon's body (Mt. 7:12) and conclusion to the entire Sermon (Mt. 7:24-27).[5] Matthew 7:12 and 7:24-27 share an emphasis on hearing the word of God and doing it. The Golden Rule, as Mt. 7:12 is commonly known, commends the reciprocity of treating others based on the word of the "law and prophets." Matthew 7:24-27 tells the parable of two contrasting figures. The wise man hears the word of God and acts accordingly, while the foolish man ignores the word of God and perishes. Considering

---

[4] See for an extensive study of these concepts, Nygaard, *Prayer in the Gospels*. Also, I. Howard Marshall, "Jesus—Example and Teacher of Prayer in the Synoptic Gospels," in *Into God's Presence: Prayer and the New Testament*, ed. Richard N. Longenecker (Grand Rapids: Eerdmans, 2001), 113–31. Mattison, *Sermon and Moral Theology*.

[5] See also the *inclusio* of Mt. 4:23-25 and 9:35-38. Jesus's words in the Sermon on the Mount (chs 5–7) are followed by Jesus's healing ministry in chs 8–9.

the wider context of Matthew, Jesus is prescribing a prayer that is now read in a post-Easter context. This new context provides the life and example of Jesus as a means through which readers may understand the Lord's Prayer anew. Jesus was clearly in constant dialogue with the Father and included in this model prayer issues pertinent to his life (kingdom, forgiveness, resisting temptation, etc.). It is reasonable to assume that these issues in the prayer would have been the subject of Jesus's own prayer life (see Mt. 26:36-46). It is also reasonable to assume that if the prayer has an ethical thrust, Jesus "performed" the prayer perfectly. In this sense, the Matthean Jesus is the model petitioner giving a model prayer to live a model lifestyle of fulfilling "greater righteousness" (see Mt. 5:17-20).[6]

For Further Study

Because of the limiting nature of focused research, several aspects of the current project could not be explored. With the newest monographs and articles on the Lord's Prayer and the Sermon on the Mount, these omissions become more painfully obvious. We will briefly note three areas of further study.

In his newest book on the Sermon on the Mount, Jonathan Pennington has proposed a reading that situates Jesus's words in the "dual context of Jewish wisdom literature and the Greco-Roman virtue tradition."[7] Pennington argues that both of these traditions are concerned with the question of human flourishing and seeks to explain how the Sermon on the Mount answers this question. Pennington's new work brings up an important focus of the Sermon on the Mount and, consequently, the Lord's Prayer. His attention to the influence of Greco-Roman literature would be an additional component for further consideration, particularly as these sources of tradition affect the meaning of the petitions.[8] In our analysis, we have focused on Jewish parallels, because Matthew's Gospel is primarily a Jewish document written by a Jew *about* a Jew. It is yet to be seen what influence Pennington's work will have on subsequent scholarship of the Sermon as a whole, but undoubtedly, he moves forward Sermon studies as they relate to the cultural situatedness and cultural encyclopedia of the Sermon. His work and the present book may also contribute to scholarly interests in Matthew's social and ecclesiastical context.

Second, the emphasis of the current work has been the relationship of the Lord's Prayer and the Sermon on the Mount, specifically the centrality of the Prayer structurally, lexically, and thematically. We have argued that this specific prayer is influenced by its context in Matthew's Gospel and vice versa. This project was originally inspired by

---

[6] The only caveat to this statement is the prayer for forgiveness. Although Jesus would not have needed to pray for forgiveness, he nevertheless performed the petition in forgiving others.
[7] Pennington, *Sermon and Human Flourishing*, 1.
[8] This statement is not intended to suggest that Pennington is the only commentator to notice Greco-Roman parallels to the Prayer and the Sermon. Pennington uses these parallels as a means of examining the Sermon's message of human flourishing and studying the intertextuality of the Sermon. Commentators who have generally noted Greco-Roman parallels to the Prayer and the Sermon include Betz, *Sermon on the Mount*, Keener, *Gospel of Matthew*, and Talbert, *Sermon on the Mount*.

an examination of Jesus's cry from the cross in which he quotes a lament psalm (Ps. 22:1), "My God, my God, why have you forsaken me?" in the narrative concerning the crucifixion. It is evident that this prayer and its theology were thematically related to the narrative in which it was found (Mk 15:34; Mt. 27:46). As laments move from cries of dereliction (Ps. 22:1 states, "Why have you forsaken me?") to praise (Ps. 22:25 states, "From you comes my praise in the great congregation; my vows I will pay before those who fear him"), so the crucifixion depicts Jesus in incredible anguish but arising from death to glory. In other words, the ordering of the prayer parallels the progression of its narrative context. We wanted to pursue other prayers that may have these parallels with their context. Having completed this book, the questions now arise: Are there other prayers that have a context that influences how its petitions are understood and vice versa? Is there a holistic "ethic of prayer"? Should theologies of prayer include a performative/ethical component in their studies? The current study only contributes one example as part of answering these questions fully but suggests that further study is necessary.

Lastly, the present book has opened our eyes to the vast scope of material and meaning within the Sermon on the Mount. Even in light of the multitude of studies, Dale Allison's words still inspire. Allison, a Sermon expert in his own right, states, "It is my conviction that the discussion [concerning the Sermon on the Mount] has not yet run its course, that some interesting and important observations have been missed."[9] The present book has argued that one aspect which has been missed is the centrality of the Lord's Prayer. Yet, this aspect does not even begin to exhaust the Sermon's potential. Not to mention, one could substitute the "Lord's Prayer" into Allison's comment and safely be correct. Broadly speaking then, the Sermon and the Prayer are texts that guarantee a lifetime of further study. For, to truly understand the Lord's Prayer is to engage, in the words of Tertullian, "a summary of the whole gospel."[10]

---

[9] Allison, *Studies in Matthew*, 173.
[10] Similarly, Dietrich Bonhoeffer, *The Cost of Discipleship* (New York: Touchstone, 1995), 197, notes concerning the Sermon on the Mount, "The only proper response to this word which Jesus brings with him from eternity is simply to do it. Jesus has spoken: his is the word, ours the obedience." His words equally apply here.

Appendix A: The Lord's Prayer and Its "Centrality" within the Sermon on the Mount

	Invocation	1st Petition	2nd Petition	3rd Petition	4th Petition	5th Petition	6th Petition	7th Petition
	"Father in heaven" prominent in MG	Same as LLP	"Kingdom of heaven" prominent in MG	"Will be done"/"Heaven and earth" prominent in MG			Same as LLP	"Evil" prominent in MG
	Prominent in SM		Prominent in SM/ch. 13	"Heaven and earth" prominent in SM/ch. 16/chs 23–25		"Debt" language prominent in ch. 18		Prominent in SM/ch. 12
	Only in MLP	Verbatim	Verbatim	Only in MLP	Variations in MLP	Variations in MLP	Verbatim	Only in MLP

Textual Parallels between the Lord's Prayer and Sermon on the Mount

	Invocation	1st Petition	2nd Petition	3rd Petition	4th Petition	5th Petition	6th Petition	7th Petition
	"Father": 5:45, 48; 6:1, 4, 6 (2x), 8, 14-15, 16, 18 (2x), 26, 32; 7:11, 21	Name is inferred: 5:13-16, 33-37; 7:21-23	"kingdom": 5:3–10 (*inclusio*), 17-20; 6:33; 7:21-23	"will of God": 7:21; "righteousness": 5:6, 10, 17-20, 45, 48; 6:33; 7:12, 21; "Heaven and earth": 5:3-12, 13-16, 33-37; 6:1, 19-21, 22-24, 25-34	"Bread": 6:25-34; 7:7-11	Forgiveness/debt is inferred: 5:7, 21-26, 38-42, 43-47; 6:14-15; 7:1-5	Temptation is inferred: 5:11-12, **27-30**, 38-42, 43-47; 6:1-18, 19-21, 24, 25-34; 7:1-5; **7:6**	"Evil/Evil one": 5:11, 37, 39, 45; 6:23; 7:11, 17-18, 23

Looser Parallels between the Lord's Prayer and the Sermon on the Mount

	Invocation	1st Petition	2nd Petition	3rd Petition	4th Petition	5th Petition	6th Petition	7th Petition
	5:9, 21-26		7:13-14		5:6; 6:19-21, 24			

Shared Function (Lord's Prayer References within Prayer Material in the Sermon on the Mount)

5:45; 6:6ab, 8, 14-15, 26, 32; 7:11 (prayer motif)	6:33 (prayer motif)	6:33 mimics words and order of words in 6:7-11; 7:7-11	7:7-11 (prayer motif)

Shared Themes between the Lord's Prayer and the Sermon on the Mount

Invocation is relational, covenantal, communal, affirmation of God's sovereignty, commitment to do God's will	Eschatological Name, but ethical concerns	Eschatological future and present kingdom; kingdom of heaven contrasts with the kingdoms of earth; kingdom living includes keeping God's laws	Will of God is eschatological and ethical; will of God is synonymous with righteousness in MG; heavenly and earth will are contrasted	God is sovereign; His provision is steadfast and sufficient	Debts are financial and moral obligations; divine and interpersonal forgiveness are connected; petition is about broken relationships	Trials/temptations are to be avoided for fear of apostasy; these temptations are authored by the evil one	Evil one stands at odds with the Father; Prayers against evil are an affirmation of God's power over evil

Appendix B: Matthew and Luke's Sermons Compared

Matthew's SM	Mark	Luke's SP	Broad Outline
5:1-2		6:20a	Introduction
5:3-12		6:20b-23 (Woes: 24-26)	Beatitudes
5:3		6:20b	Poor
5:4		6:21b	Mourn
5:5			
5:6		6:21a (hunger)	Hunger
5:7		6:36 (being merciful)	Merciful
5:8			
5:9			
5:10			
5:11-12		6:22-23	Reviled Prophets
5:13-16			
5:13	9:49-50	14:34-35	
5:14			
5:15	4:21 (22-23)	8:16 (17-18), 11:33	
5:16			
5:17-20			
5:17			
5:18 (24:35)	13:31	16:17/21:33	
5:19			
5:20			
5:21-48			
5:21-24			
5:25-26		12:57-59	
5:27-28			
5:29-30 (18:8-9)	9:43-48		
5:31-32	10:11-12	16:18	

5:33-37 (Jas 5:12)			
5:38-42		6:29-30	On Retaliation
5:43-47		6:27-28, 32-35	Love Your Enemies
5:48		6:36	Imitating the Father
6:1-18			
6:1-4			
6:5-6			
6:7-8/14-15	11:25 (26)		
6:9-13		11:2-4	Lord's Prayer
6:16-18			
6:19–7:12			
6:19-21		12:33-34	
6:22-23		11:34-36	
6:24		16:13	
6:25-34		12:22-32	
7:1-5 (13:12)	4:24-25	6:37-42 (8:18)	On Judging
7:6			
7:7-11		11:9-13	
7:12		6:31	Golden Rule
7:13-27			
7:13-14		13:23-24	
7:15			
7:16-20 (12:33-35)		6:43-45	Fruits
7:21		6:46	"Lord, Lord"
7:22-23		13:25-27	
7:24-27		6:47-49	Two Builders
7:28–8:1			
7:28a		7:1	Conclusion
7:28b-29	1:22	4:32	
8:1			

Appendix C: Word Comparisons between Matthew and Luke's Sermons

Matthew 5–7	References Luke (Bold: Parallels outside of Ch. 6)	Words in Matthew Alone	Shared Vocabulary	Words in Luke Alone (Ch. 6)	Words in Luke Alone (outside of Ch. 6)
5:1-2	6:20a	20	4	7	
5:3-12	6:20b-23			Woes (24-26)	
5:3	6:20b	5	7	2	
5:4	6:21b	5	1	5	
5:5		8			
5:6	6:21a	4	3	3	
5:7		6			
5:8		10			
5:9		8			
5:10		12			
5:11-12	6:22-23	18	10	5	
5:13-16					
5:13	**14:34-35**	14	12		17
5:14		13			
5:15	**8:16 (11:33)**	15	5		16 (15)
5:16		23			
5:17-20					
5:17		15			
5:18	**16:17**	17	10		5
5:19		22			
5:20		23			
5:21-48					
5:21-24		95			
5:25-26	**12:57-59**	16	27		31
5:27-28		25			

5:29-30		65				
5:31-32	**16:18**	22	12		5	
5:33-37		82				
5:38-42	6:29-30	58	11	23		
5:43-47	6:27-28,32-35	76	20	87		
5:48	6:36	8	4	5		
6:1-18						
6:1		29				
6:2-4		64				
6:5-6		65				
6:7-8/14-15		32/30				
6:9-13	**11:2-4**	28	31		13	
6:16-18		63				
6:19–7:12						
6:19-21	**12:33-34**	31	18		18	
6:22-23	**11:34-36**	19	26		37	
6:24	**16:13**	0	27		1	
6:25-34	**22:22-32**	72	119		60	
7:1-5	6:37-42	24	59	48		
7.6		25				
7:7-11	**11:9-13**	23	51		24	
7:12	6:31	15	8	3		
7:13-27						
7:13-14	**13:23-24**	37	7		22	
7:15		16				
7:16-20	6:43-45	52	9	54		
7:21	6:46	23	2	9		
7:22-23	**13:25-27**	37	5		56	
7:24-27	6:47-49	61	29	54		
7::28–8:1						
7:28a	7:1	15	1	13		
7:28b-29	**4:32**	17	3		11	
8:1		10				

Bibliography

Abrahams, I. *Studies in Pharisaism and the Gospels*. 2nd ed. Cambridge: Cambridge University Press, 1924.

Albright, W. F., and C. S. Mann. *Matthew: Introduction, Translation and Notes*. AB. Garden City: Doubleday, 1971.

Alkier, Stefan. "From Text to Intertext: Intertextuality as a Paradigm for Reading Matthew." HTS 61.1-2 (2005): 1-18.

Allen, Willoughby C. *A Critical and Exegetical Commentary on the Gospel According to St. Matthew*. 3rd ed. ICC. Edinburgh: T&T Clark, 1993.

Allison, Dale C. "The Configuration of the Sermon on the Mount and Its Meaning." In *Studies in Matthew*, 173-216. Grand Rapids: Baker, 2005.

Allison, Dale C. *The New Moses: A Matthean Typology*. Minneapolis: Fortress, 1993.

Allison, Dale C. "The Sermon on the Mount: A Commentary on the Sermon on the Mount, Including the Sermon on the Plain: Matthew 5:3-7:27 and Luke 6:20-49: A Review." JBL 117 (1998): 136-8.

Allison, Dale C. *The Sermon on the Mount: Inspiring the Moral Imagination*. New York: Herder & Herder, 1999.

Allison, Dale C. "The Structure of the Sermon on the Mount." JBL 106 (1987): 423-45.

Allison, Dale C. *Studies in Matthew: Interpretations Past and Present*. Grand Rapids: Baker, 2005.

Anderson, Gary A. *Sin: A History*. New Haven: Yale University Press, 2009.

Aune, David E. *Jesus, Gospel Tradition and Paul in the Context of Jewish and Greco-Roman Antiquity*. Vol. 2. WUNT 303. Tübingen: Mohr Siebeck, 2013.

Argyle, A. W. *The Gospel According to Matthew*. CBC. Cambridge: Cambridge University Press, 1963.

Bacon, Benjamin. *Studies in Matthew*. London: Constable, 1930.

Bailey, James L., and Lyle Vander Broek. *Literary Forms in the New Testament: A Handbook*. Louisville: Westminster, 1992.

Bandstra, Andrew J. "The Original Form of the Lord's Prayer." CTJ 16 (1982): 88-97.

Barr, James. "'Abba' Isn't Daddy." JTS 39.1 (1988): 28-47.

Barth, Karl. *Prayer*. Louisville: WJK, 2002.

Bauckham, Richard. *Jesus and the Eyewitnesses: The Gospels as Eyewitness Testimony*. Grand Rapids: Eerdmans, 2006.

Bauckham, Richard. "Kingdom and Church According to Jesus and Paul." HBT 18.1 (1996): 1-26.

Bauckham, Richard, ed. *The Gospel for All Christians: Rethinking the Gospel Audiences*. New Testament Studies. Grand Rapids: Eerdmans, 1998.

Bauer, D. R., and M. A. Powell, eds. *Treasures Old and New: Contributions to Matthean Studies*. Atlanta: Scholars, 1996.

Bauman, Clarence. *The Sermon on the Mount: The Modern Quest for its Meaning*. Macon: Mercer University Press, 1985.

Baumgardt, David. "Kaddish and Lord's Prayer." JBQ 19.3 (1991): 164-9.

Beare, F. W. *The Gospel According to Matthew: A Commentary.* Oxford: Basil Blackwell, 1981.
Beasley-Murray, G. R. *Jesus and the Kingdom of God.* Grand Rapids: Eerdmans, 1986.
Bennett, Thomas J. "Matthew 7:6—A New Interpretation." WTJ 49 (1987): 371–86.
Betz, Hans Dieter. *Essays on the Sermon on the Mount.* Philadelphia: Fortress, 1985.
Betz, Hans Dieter. *Sermon on the Mount: A Commentary on the Sermon on the Mount, Including the Sermon on the Plain: Matthew 5:3–7:27 and Luke 6:20–49.* Hermeneia. Philadelphia: Fortress, 1995.
Bird, Michael F. *The Gospel of the Lord: How the Early Church Wrote the Story of Jesus.* Grand Rapids: Eerdmans, 2014.
Black, Matthew. "The Doxology to the Pater Noster with a Note on Matthew 6:13B." In *A Tribute to Geza Vermes: Essays on Jewish and Christian Literature and History*, 327–32. JSOTSupp 100. Edited by Philip R. Davies and R. T. White. Sheffield: JSOT, 1990.
Boda, Mark J. "Poethics? The Use of Biblical Hebrew Poetry in Ethical Reflection on the Old Testament." CBR 14.1 (2015): 45–61.
Bonhoeffer, Dietrich. *The Cost of Discipleship.* New York: Touchstone, 1995.
Bonnard, P. *L'Evangile selon Saint Matthieu.* 2nd ed. Neuchâtel: Delachaux et Niestlé, 1970.
Borg, Marcus J. *Jesus in Contemporary Scholarship.* Valley Forge: Trinity International, 1994.
Bornkamm, Günther. "Der Aufbau der Bergpredigt." NTS 24 (1978): 419–32.
Bornkamm, Günther, G. Barth, and H. J. Held. *Tradition and Interpretation in Matthew.* Philadelphia: Westminster, 1963.
Breck, John. *The Shape of Biblical Language: Chiasmus in the Scriptures and Beyond.* Crestwood: St. Vladimir's Seminary, 1994.
Brown, Raymond. "The Pater Noster as an Eschatological Prayer." TS 22.2 (1961): 175.
Bruner, F. D. *Matthew: A Commentary.* Vol. 1: The Christbook Matthew 1–12. Rev. ed. Grand Rapids: Eerdmans, 2004.
Byargeon, Rick W. "Echoes of Wisdom in the Lord's Prayer (Matt. 6:9–13)." JETS 41.3 (1998): 353–65.
Caird, G. B. *New Testament Theology.* Edited by L. D. Hurst. Oxford: Clarendon, 1995.
Carmignac, Jean. "*Recherches sur le 'Notre Père.*" Paris: Letouzey & Ané, 1969.
Carson, D. A. *Matthew 1–12.* EBC. Grand Rapids: Zondervan, 1995.
Carter, Warren. *Matthew: Storyteller, Interpreter, Evangelist.* Rev. ed. Peabody: Hendrickson, 2004.
Carter, Warren. *What Are They Saying about Matthew's Sermon on the Mount?* New York: Paulist, 1994.
Charlesworth, James H., ed. *The Old Testament Pseudepigrapha.* Vol. 2. Anchor Bible Reference Library. New York: Doubleday, 1985.
Charlesworth, James H., Mark Harding, and Mark Kiley, eds. *The Lord's Prayer and Other Prayer Texts from the Greco-Roman Era.* Valley Forge: Trinity International, 1994.
Chilton, Bruce. "God as 'Father' in the Targumim, in Non-Canonical Literatures of Early Judaism and Primitive Christianity, and in Matthew." In *The Pseudepigrapha and Early Biblical Interpretation*, 151–69. Edited by J. H. Charlesworth and C. A. Evans. Sheffield: JSOT, 1993.
Clark, David. *On Earth as in Heaven: The Lord's Prayer from Jewish Prayer to Christian Ritual.* Philadelphia: Fortress, 2017.
Collins, John J. *Daniel: A Commentary on the Book of Daniel.* Hermeneia. Minneapolis: Fortress, 1994.

Conzelmann, H. "φῶς." In *TDNT*, vol. 9, 310–58. 10 vols. Edited by G. Kittel and G. Friedrich. Translated by G. W. Bromiley. Grand Rapids: Eerdmans, 1964–76.

Crossan, John Dominic. *The Greatest Prayer: Rediscovering the Revolutionary Message of the Lord's Prayer*. New York: HarperCollins, 2010.

Crump, David. *Knocking on Heaven's Door: A New Testament Theology of Petitionary Prayer*. Grand Rapids: Baker, 2006.

Dalman, Gustaf. *The Words of Jesus*. Translated by D. M. Kay. Edinburgh: T&T Clark, 1902.

D'Angelo, Mary Rose. "*Abba* and 'Father': Imperial Theology and the Jesus Traditions." JBL 111.4 (1992): 611–30.

Davies, W. D. *The Setting of the Sermon on the Mount*. Cambridge: Cambridge University Press, 1964.

Davies, W. D., and Dale C. Allison. *A Critical and Exegetical Commentary on the Gospel According to Saint Matthew*. ICC. 3 vols. Edinburgh: T&T Clark, 1988–97.

DeJonge, M., and A. S. Van Der Woude. "11Q Melchizedek and the New Testament." NTS 12 (1965–6): 301–26.

Drake, Lyndon. "Did Jesus Oppose the *Prosbul* in the Forgiveness Petition of the Lord's Prayer." NovT 56 (2014): 233–44.

Draper, Jonathan A. "The Genesis and Narrative Thrust of the Paraenesis in the Sermon on the Mount." JSNT 75 (1999): 25–48.

Duling, Dennis C. "Kingdom of God/Kingdom of Heaven." In *Anchor Bible Dictionary*, vol. 4, 49–68. 6 vols. Edited by D. N. Freedman. New York: Doubleday, 1992.

Dumbrell, W. J. "The Logic of the Role of the Law in Matthew 5:1–20." NovT 23.1 (1981): 1–21.

Dunn, James D. G. *Jesus Remembered*. Christianity in the Making. Vol. 1. Grand Rapids: Eerdmans, 2003.

Dunn, James D. G. "Prayer." In *DJG*, 617–24. Edited by Joel B. Green, Scot McKnight, and I. Howard Marshall. Downers Grove: IVP, 1992.

Dupont, J. *Les Béatitudes*. Vol. 1. Paris: Gabalda, 1969.

Eubank, Nathan. "Storing Up Treasure with God in the Heavens: Celestial Investments in Matthew 6:1–21." CBQ 76 (2014): 77–92.

Eubank, Nathan. *Wages of Cross-Bearing and Debt of Sin: The Economy of Heaven in Matthew's Gospel*. Beihefte zur Zeitschrift für die neutestamentliche Wissenschaft 196. Berlin: De Gruyter, 2013.

Evans, Craig A. "Daniel in the New Testament: Visions of God's Kingdom." In *The Book of Daniel: Composition and Reception*, vol. 2, 490–527. Edited by John J. Collins and Peter W. Flint. Leiden: Brill, 2002.

Evans, Craig A. *Jesus and His Contemporaries: Comparative Studies*. Leiden: Brill, 2001.

Evans, Craig A. *Matthew*. NCBC. Cambridge: Cambridge University Press, 2012.

Fenton, J. C. "Inclusio and Chiasmus in Matthew." In *Studia Evangelica* 1. Edited by Kurt Aland, F. L. Cross, Jean Danielou, Harald Riesenfeld, and W. C. Unnik. Berlin: Akademie-Verlag, 1959.

Fenton, J. C. *Saint Matthew*. Pelican Gospel Commentary. Harmondsworth: Penguin, 1963.

Finkel, A. "The Prayer of Jesus in Matthew." In *Standing Before God: Studies on Prayer in Scriptures and in Tradition with Essays in Honor of John M. Oesterreicher*, 131–69. Edited by A. Finkel and L. Frizzell. New York: KTAV Publishing, 1981.

Fitzmyer, Joseph A. "And Lead Us Not into Temptation." *Bib* 84.2 (2003): 259–73.

Fitzmyer, Joseph A. "Further Light on Melchizedek from Qumran Cave 11." JBL 86 (1967): 25–41.
Flusser, David. "Psalms, Hymns, and Prayers." In *Jewish Writings of the Second Temple Period*, vol. 2, 551–77. Edited by Michael E. Stone. Philadelphia: Fortress, 1984.
Flusser, David. "Qumran and Jewish Apotropaic Prayers." IEJ 16 (1966): 194–205.
Foerster, Werner. "επιούσιος." In *TDNT*, vol. 2, 590–9. 10 vols. Edited by G. Kittel and G. Friedrich. Translated by G. W. Bromiley. Grand Rapids: Eerdmans, 1964–76.
Foster, Paul. *Community, Law, and Mission in Matthew's Gospel*. Wissenschaftliche Untersuchungen zum Neuen Testament 2. Reihe 177. Tübingen: Mohr Siebeck, 2004.
Foster, Robert. "Why on Earth Use 'Kingdom of Heaven'?: Matthew's Terminology Revisited." NTS 48.4 (2002): 487–99.
France, R. T. *Matthew: Evangelist & Teacher*. Downers Grove: IVP, 1998.
France, R. T. *The Gospel of Matthew*. NICNT. Grand Rapids: Eerdmans, 2007.
Friedlander, Gerald. *The Jewish Sources of the Sermon on the Mount*. London: Routledge, 1911.
Garland, David E. "The Lord's Prayer in the Gospel of Matthew." RevExp 89 (1992): 215–28.
Garland, David E. *Reading Matthew: A Literary and Theological Commentary*. Macon: Smyth & Helwys, 2001.
Garlington, Don. "'The Salt of the Earth' In Covenantal Perspective." JETS 54.4 (2011): 715–48.
Gerhardsson, Birger. "The Matthean Version of the Lord's Prayer (Matt. 6:9b–13): Some Observations." In *The New Testament Age: Essays in Honor of Bo Reicke*, vol. 1, 207–20. Mercer: Mercer University Press, 1984.
Gibson, Jeffrey B. "Matthew 6:9–13//Luke 11:2–4: An Eschatological Prayer?" BTB 31 (2001): 96–105.
Gibson, Jeffrey B. *The Disciples' Prayer: The Prayer Jesus Taught in Its Historical Setting*. Minneapolis: Fortress, 2015.
Goldin. J. "The Three Pillars of Simeon the Righteous." PAAJR 27 (1958): 43–56.
Goldingay, John. *Daniel*. WBC. Waco: Thomas Nelson, 1989.
Goodacre, Mark. *The Synoptic Problem: A Way through the Maze*. Understanding the Bible and Its World. London: T&T Clark, 2004.
Goshen-Gottstein, Alon. "God the Father in Rabbinic Judaism and Christianity: Transformed Background or Common Ground?" JEC 38.4 (2001): 470–504.
Goulder, M. D. "The Composition of the Lord's Prayer." JTS 14 (1963): 32–45.
Goulder, M. D. *Midrash and Lection in Matthew*. London: SPCK, 1974.
Green, H. Benedict. *Matthew, Poet of the Beatitudes*. JSNTSupp Series 203. Sheffield: Sheffield Academic, 2000.
Greenman, Jeffrey P., Timothy Larsen, and Stephen R. Spencer, eds. *The Sermon on the Mount through the Centuries: From the Early Church to John Paul II*. Grand Rapids: Brazos, 2007.
Grelot, Pierre. "L'arriere-Plan Arameen du 'Pater.'" Reveu Biblique 91.4 (1984): 531–556.
Grundmann, Walter. *Das Evangelium nach Matthäus*. 5th ed. THNT. Berlin: Evangelische Verlagsanstalt, 1981.
Guelich, Robert. *The Sermon on the Mount: A Foundation of Understanding*. Waco: Word, 1982.
Gundry, Robert H. *Matthew: A Commentary on His Handbook for a Mixed Church under Persecution*. 2nd ed. Grand Rapids: Eerdmans, 1982.

Gupta, Nijay K. *The Lord's Prayer*. Smyth & Helwys Bible Commentary Supp Series. Macon: Smyth & Helwys, 2017.
Gurtner, Daniel M., and John Nolland, eds. *Built Upon the Rock: Studies in the Gospel of Matthew*. Grand Rapids: Eerdmans, 2008.
Hagner, Donald A. *Matthew*. WBC. 2 vols. Dallas: Word, 1993-5.
Harder, G. "πονηρός, πονηρία." In *TDNT*, vol. 6, 546-62. 10 vols. Edited by G. Kittel and G. Friedrich. Translated by G. W. Bromiley. Grand Rapids: Eerdmans, 1964-76.
Hare, Douglas R. A. *Matthew*. Interpretation. Louisville: John Knox, 1993.
Harrington, D. J. The Gospel of Matthew. Sacra Pagina. Collegeville: Liturgical, 1991.
Hatina, Thomas R. "Intertextuality and Historical Criticism in New Testament Studies: Is There A Relationship?" BibInt 7.1 (1999): 28-43.
Hauck, F. "ὀφείλω." In *TDNT*, vol. 5, 562-3. 10 vols. Edited by G. Kittel and G. Friedrich. Translated by G. W. Bromiley. Grand Rapids: Eerdmans, 1964-76.
Hays, Richard B. *Echoes of Scripture in the Gospels*. Waco: Baylor, 2016.
Hays, Richard B. *Echoes of Scripture in the Letters of Paul*. New Haven: Yale University Press, 1989.
Heinemann, Joseph. "The Background of Jesus' Prayer in the Jewish Liturgical Tradition." In *The Lord's Prayer and Jewish Liturgy*, 81-9. Edited by J. J. Petuchowski and M. Brocke. New York: Seabury, 1978.
Heinemann, Joseph. *Prayer in the Talmud: Forms and Patterns*. Berlin: De Gruyter, 1977.
Hemer, Colin. "ἐπιούσιος." JSNT 22 (1984): 81-96.
Hendrickx, Herman. *The Sermon on the Mount*. Studies in the Synoptic Gospels. London: Georffrey Chapman, 1984.
Hill, David. "The Meaning of the Sermon on the Mount in Matthew's Gospel." IBS 6 (1984): 120-33.
Hinkle, Mary E. "The Lord's Prayer: Empowerment for Living the Sermon on the Mount." WW 22.1 (2002): 9-17.
Holmes, Michael, ed. *The Apostolic Fathers: Greek Texts and English Translations*. Grand Rapids: Baker, 2007.
Hood, Jason. *The Messiah, His Brothers, and the Nations: Matthew 1:1-17*. LNTS 441. London: T&T Clark, 2011.
Huizenga, Leroy A. "The Old Testament in the New, Intertextuality, and Allegory." JSNT 38.1 (2015): 17-35.
Instone-Brewer, David. *Prayer and Agriculture*. Vol. 1. TRENT. Grand Rapids: Eerdmans, 2004.
Jeremias, Joachim. *The Prayers of Jesus*. SBT 6. London: SCM, 1967.
Jeremias, Joachim. *The Sermon on the Mount*. London: Athlone, 1961.
Keener, Craig S. *A Commentary on the Gospel of Matthew: A Socio-Rhetorical Commentary*. Grand Rapids: Eerdmans, 1999.
Keener, Craig S. *The IVP Bible Background Commentary: New Testament*. 2nd ed. Downers Grove: IVP, 2014.
Kennedy, George A. *New Testament Interpretation through Rhetorical Criticism*. Chapel Hill: University of North Carolina Press, 1984.
Kiley, Mark. "The Lord's Prayer and Matthean Theology." In *The Lord's Prayer and Other Texts from the Greco-Roman Era*, 15-27. Edited by James H. Charlesworth, Mark Harding, and Mark Kiley. Valley Forge: Trinity International, 1994.
Kingsbury, Jack. *Matthew as Story*. 2nd ed. Minneapolis: Fortress, 1988.
Kingsbury, Jack.*Matthew: Structure, Christology, Kingdom*. London: SPCK, 19750.

Kingsbury, Jack. *Parables of Jesus in Matthew 13: A Study in Redaction Criticism.* London: SPCK, 1977.
Kingsbury, Jack. "The Place, Structure, and Meaning of the Sermon on the Mount within Matthew," Int 41 (1987): 131–43.
Kistemaker, Simon J. "The Lord's Prayer in the First Century." JETS 21.4 (1978): 323–8.
Knowles, Michael. *Jeremiah in Matthew's Gospel: The Rejected Profit Motif in Matthean Redaction.* JSNTSupp Series 68. Sheffield: Sheffield Academic, 1993.
Kürzinger, Josef. "Zur Komposition der Bergpredigt nach Matthäus." *Bib* 40 (1959): 569–89.
Kuhn, Karl Georg. *Achtzehngebet und Vaterunser und der Reim.* Wissenschaftliche Untersuchungen zum Neuen Testament. Tübingen: Verlag J.C.B. Mohr, 1950.
Lachs, Samuel T. "On Matthew 6:12." NovT 17.1 (1975), 6–8.
Lachs, Samuel T. *A Rabbinic Commentary on the New Testament: The Gospels of Matthew, Mark, and Luke.* Hoboken: KTAV, 1987.
Ladd, George E. *The Gospel of the Kingdom: Popular Expositions on the Kingdom of God.* Grand Rapids: Eerdmans, 1959.
Lambrecht, Jan. *The Sermon on the Mount: Proclamation and Exhortation.* GNS 14. Wilmington: Glazier, 1985.
Leonard, Jeffrey. "Identifying Inner-Biblical Allusions: Psalm 78 as a Test Case." JBL 127.2 (2008): 241–6.
Lightfoot, J. B. *On a Fresh Revision of the English New Testament.* 2nd ed. London: Macmillan, 1872.
Lischer, Richard. "The Sermon on the Mount as Radical Pastoral Care." Int 41 (1987): 157–69.
Llewelyn, Stephen. "Mt. 7:6A: Mistranslation or Interpretation?" NovT 31.2 (1989): 97–103.
Lochman, Jan Milič. *The Lord's Prayer.* Translated by Geoffrey W. Bromiley. Grand Rapids: Eerdmans, 1990.
Lohmeyer, Ernst. *The Lord's Prayer.* London: Collins, 2005.
Lund, Nils W. *Chiasmus in the New Testament: A Study in the Form and Function of Chiastic Structures.* Peabody: Hendrickson, 1970.
Lunde, Jonathan. "Heaven and Hell." In *DJG,* 307–12. Edited by Joel B. Green, Scot McKnight, and I. Howard Marshall. Downers Grove: IVP, 1992.
Lundbom, Jack R. *Jesus' Sermon on the Mount: Mandating a Better Righteousness.* Minneapolis: Fortress, 2015.
Luz, Ulrich. *Matthew 1–7: A Commentary.* Hermeneia. Minneapolis: Fortress, 2007.
Luz, Ulrich. "Intertexts in the Gospel of Matthew." HTR 97.2 (2004): 119–37.
Luz, Ulrich. *The Theology of Matthew.* New Testament Theology. Cambridge: Cambridge University Press, 1995.
Luz, Ulrich. *The Theology of the Gospel of Matthew.* Translated by J. Bradford Robinson. Cambridge: Cambridge University Press, 1995.
Luz, Ulrich. "Vaterunser I. Neues Testament." TRE 34 (2002): 504–12.
Manson, T. W. "The Lord's Prayer." BJRL 38 (1955/56): 436–88.
Marshall, I. Howard. "Jesus—Example and Teacher of Prayer in the Synoptic Gospels." In *Into God's Presence: Prayer and the New Testament,* 113–31. Edited by Richard N. Longenecker. Grand Rapids: Eerdmans, 2001.
Martin, Michael Wade. "Poetry of the Lord's Prayer." JBL 134.2 (2015): 365.
Martínez, F. Garcia. "4Q 'Amram B 1, 14: Melki-resha or Melki-sedeq?" RevQ 12.45 (1985): 114.

Martinez, F. G., and E. J. C. Tigchelaar, eds. *The Dead Sea Scrolls: Study Edition*. Vols. 1–2. Brill: Leiden, 1997–9.
Matson, Mark A. "Luke's Rewriting of the Sermon on the Mount." In *Questioning Q: A Multidimensional Critique*, 43–70. Edited by Mark Goodacre and Nicholas Perrin. Downers Grove: IVP, 2004.
Mattison, William C. *The Sermon on the Mount and Moral Theology: A Virtue Perspective*. Cambridge: Cambridge University Press, 2017.
Mauser, Ulrich W. "'Heaven' in the World View of the New Testament." HBT 9.2 (1987): 31–51.
McArthur, Harvey K. *Understanding the Sermon on the Mount*. London: Epworth, 1960.
McEleney, Neil J. "The Principles of the Sermon on the Mount." CBQ 41 (1979): 552–70.
McKnight, Scot. *A New Vision for Israel: The Teachings of Jesus in National Context*. Grand Rapids: Eerdmans, 1999.
McKnight, Scot. *Sermon on the Mount*. The Story of God Bible Commentary. Grand Rapids: Zondervan, 2013.
McNamara, Martin. *Targum and Testament-Aramaic Paraphrases of the Hebrew Bible: A Light on the New Testament*. Grand Rapids: Eerdmans, 1972.
M'Neile, A. H. *The Gospel According to St. Matthew*. London: Macmillan, 1957.
Meier, John P. *A Marginal Jew: Rethinking the Historical Jesus*. Vols. 1–2. New York: Doubleday, 1994.
Meier, J. P. *Matthew*. NTM 3. Dublin: Veritas Publications, 1984.
Menken, M. J. J. *Matthew's Bible: The Old Testament Text of the Evangelist*. BETL 173. Leuven: Leuven University Press, 2004.
Metzger, Bruce M. "How Many Times does 'epiousios' Occur Outside the Lord's Prayer?" ExpTim 69 (1957): 52–4.
Metzler, Norman. "The Lord's Prayer: Second Thoughts on the First Petition." In *Authentication the Words of Jesus*. NT Tools and Studies, 187–202. Edited by Bruce Chilton and Craig Evans. Leiden: Brill, 1999.
Meynet, Roland. "La composition du Notre Père." Liturgie 119 (2002): 158–91.
Meynet, Roland. *Rhetorical Analysis: An Introduction to Biblical Rhetoric*. JSNTSupp Series 256. Sheffield: Sheffield Academic, 1998.
Migliore, Daniel L., ed. *The Lord's Prayer: Perspectives for Reclaiming Christian Prayer*. Grand Rapids: Eerdmans, 1993.
Milton, A. Edward. "'Deliver Us from the Evil Imagination': Matt. 6:13B in Light of the Jewish Doctrine of the Yêser Hârâ." RelStTh 13 (1995): 52–67.
Minear, Paul S. "But Whose Prayer Is It?" Worship 76 (2002): 324–38.
Minear, Paul S. "The Salt of the Earth." Int 51 (1997): 31–41.
Montefiore, C. G. *Rabbinic Literature and Gospel Teachings*. London: Macmillan, 1930.
Moore, G.F. *Judaism in the First Centuries of the Christian Era the Age of the Tannaim*. Vols. 1–5. Cambridge: Harvard University Press, 1966.
Morris, Leon. *The Gospel According to Matthew*. PNTC. Grand Rapids: Eerdmans, 1992.
Moule, C. F. D. "An Unsolved Problem in the Temptation Clause in the Lord's Prayer." RTR 33 (1974): 65–76.
Mounce, William D. *The Analytical Lexicon to the Greek New Testament*. Zondervan Greek Reference Series. Grand Rapids: Zondervan, 1993.
Mounce, William D. *The Morphology of Biblical Greek*. Grand Rapids: Zondervan, 1994.
Mowery, Robert L. "From Lord to Father in Matthew 1–7." CBQ 59.4 (1997): 642–56.
Muilenburg, James. "Form Criticism and Beyond." JBL 88.1 (1969): 1–18.

Nel, Marius J. "The Forgiveness of Debt in Matthew 6:12, 14–15." Neot 47.1 (2013): 87–106.
Neusner, Jacob. "The Kingdom of Heaven in Kindred Systems, Judaic and Christian." BBR 15.2 (2005): 279–305.
Nijman, M., and K. A. Worp. "'ΕΠΙΟΥΣΙΟΣ' In a Documentary Papyrus?." NovT 41 (1999): 231–4.
Nolland, John. *The Gospel of Matthew: A Commentary on the Greek Text*. NIGTC. Grand Rapids: Eerdmans, 2005.
Nolland, John. *Luke*. WBC. Vols. 1–3. Dallas: Word, 1989–93.
Nygaard, Mathias. *Prayer in the Gospels: A Theological Exegesis of the Ideal Pray-er*. BibInt 114. Leiden: Brill, 2012.
Oakman, Douglas E. *Jesus, Debt, and the Lord's Prayer: First-Century Debt and Jesus' Intentions*. Eugene: Cascade, 2014.
Oakman, Douglas E. "The Lord's Prayer in Social Perspective." In *Jesus, Debt, and the Lord's Prayer: First-Century Debt and Jesus' Intentions*, 42–91. Eugene: Cascade, 2014.
O'Donovan, Oliver. "Prayer and Morality in the Sermon on the Mount." Studies in Christian Ethics 22.1 (2000): 21–33.
Olsthoorn, M. F. *The Jewish Background and the Synoptic Setting of Mt. 6:25–33 and Lk. 12:22–31*. SBFA 10. Jerusalem: Franciscan, 1975.
Pamment, Margaret. "The Kingdom of Heaven According to the First Gospel." NTS 27 (1981): 211–32.
Patte, Daniel. *The Gospel According to Matthew: A Structural Commentary of Mathew's Faith*. Philadelphia: Fortress, 1987.
Pennington, Jonathan. *Heaven and Earth in the Gospel of Matthew*. Grand Rapids: Baker, 2009.
Pennington, Jonathan. *The Sermon on the Mount and Human Flourishing: A Theological Commentary*. Grand Rapids: Baker, 2017.
Perrin, Norman. *Rediscovering the Teachings of Jesus*. New York: Harper & Row, 1967.
Perrin, Norman. "Eschatology and Hermeneutics: Reflections on Method in the Interpretation of the New Testament," JBL 93 (1974): 3–14.
Perry, Alfred M. "The Framework of the Sermon on the Mount." JBL 54.2 (1935): 103–15.
Petuchowski, Jakob J. *Understanding Jewish Prayer*. New York: KTAV, 1972.
Petuchowski, Jakob. J., and Michael Brocke, eds. *The Lord's Prayer and Jewish Liturgy*. New York: Seabury, 1978.
Pitre, Brant. "The Lord's Prayer and the New Exodus." Letter & Spirit 2 (2006): 69–96.
Plummer, Alfred. *An Exegetical Commentary on the Gospel According to St. Matthew*. London: Robert Scott, 1915.
Powell, M. A., ed. *Methods for Matthew*. Methods in Biblical Interpretation. Cambridge: Cambridge University Press, 2009.
Procksch, O. "Holiness." In *TDNT*, vol. 1, 88–97. 10 vols. Edited by G. Kittel and G. Friedrich. Translated by G. W. Bromiley. Grand Rapids: Eerdmans, 1964–76.
Przybylski, Benno. *Righteousness in Matthew and his World of Thought*. SNTS. Cambridge: Cambridge University Press, 1980.
Quarles, Charles. "The Blessings of the New Moses: An Examination of the Theological Purpose of the Matthean Beatitudes." JSHJ 13.2/3 (2015): 305–27.
Quarles, Charles. *Matthew*. EGGNT. Nashville: B&H, 2017.
Quarles, Charles. *Sermon on the Mount: Restoring Christ's Message to the Modern Church*. NAC Studies in Bible and Theology. Nashville: B&H Academic, 2011.
Riesner, Rainer. "Der Aufbau der Reden im Matthäus-Evangelium." TBei 9 (1978): 173–6.

Riesner, Rainer. "The Orality and Memory Hypothesis." In *The Synoptic Problem: Four Views*, 89–112. Edited by Stanley Porter and Bryan Dyer. Grand Rapids: Baker, 2016.

Rowland, Christopher. *Christian Origins: An Account of the Setting and Character of the Most Important Messianic Sect of Judaism*. London: SPCK, 1985.

Runge, Steve E. *Discourse Grammar of the Greek New Testament: A Practical Introduction for Teaching and Exegesis*. Peabody: Hendrickson, 2010.

Schnackenburg, Rudolf. *All Things Are Possible to Believers: Reflections on the Lord's Prayer and the Sermon on the Mount*. Translated by James S. Currie. Louisville: Westminster, 1995.

Schürmann, Heinz. *Praying with Christ: The "Our Father" for Today*. New York: Herder and Herder, 1972.

Schweizer, Eduard. *The Good News According to Matthew*. Atlanta: John Knox, 1977.

Schuller, Eileen M. "The Psalm of 4Q372 1 Within the Context of Second Temple Prayer." CBQ 54 (1992): 67–79.

Seesemann, H. "πειρασμός." In *TDNT*, vol. 6, 24–36. 10 vols. Edited by G. Kittel and G. Friedrich. Translated by G. W. Bromiley. Grand Rapids: Eerdmans, 1964–76.

Stanton, Graham N. *A Gospel for a New People: Studies in Matthew*. Edinburgh: T&T Clark, 1992.

Stassen, Glen H. "The Fourteen Triads of the Sermon on the Mount (5:21–7:12)." JBL 122.2 (2003): 267–308.

Stassen, Glen, and David P. Gushee. *Kingdom Ethics: Following Jesus in Contemporary Context*. Downers Grove: IVP, 2003.

Stendahl, Krister. "Prayer and Forgiveness." SEÅ 22 (1957): 75–86.

Stevenson, Kenneth. *The Lord's Prayer: A Text in Transition*. Philadelphia: Fortress, 2004.

Strack, Hermann L., and Paul Billerbeck. *Kommentar zum Neuen Testament*. Vol. 1: Das Evangelium Nach Matthäus. München: C.H. Beck'sche Verlagsbuchhandlung, 1922.

Strecker, Georg. *The Sermon on the Mount: An Exegetical Commentary*. Translated by O. C. Dean. Nashville: Abingdon, 1989.

Swetnam, James. "Hallowed Be Thy Name." *Bib* 52.4 (1972): 556–63.

Syreeni, Kari. "Between Heaven and Earth: On the Structure of Matthew's Symbolic Universe." JSNT 40 (1990): 3–13.

Syreeni, Kari. *The Making of the Sermon on the Mount: A Procedural Analysis of Matthew's Redactional Activity, Part I, Methodology and Compositional Analysis*. AASF. Dissertationes Humanarus Litterarum 44. Helsinki: Suomalainen Tiedeakatemia, 1987.

Talbert, Charles H. *Matthew*. Paideia. Grand Rapids: Baker, 2010.

Talbert, Charles H. *Reading the Sermon on the Mount: Character Formation and Decision Making in Matthew 5–7*. Grand Rapids: Baker Academic, 2006.

Tan, Randall K. J. "Recent Developments in Redaction Criticism: From Investigation of Textual Prehistory Back to Historical-Grammatical Exegesis?" JETS 44.4 (2001): 599–614.

Thom, Johan C. "Dyads, Triads, and Other Compositional Beasts in the Sermon on the Mount (Matthew 5–7)." In *The New Testament Interpreted: Essays in Honour of Bernard C. Lategan*, 291–308. Edited by Cilliers Breytenbach, Johan C. Thom, and Jeremy Punt. Leiden: Brill, 2006.

Thompson, Marianne M. *The Promise of the Father: Jesus and God in the New Testament*. Louisville: WJK, 2000.

Tuttle, Gary A. "Sermon on the Mount: Its Wisdom Affinities and their Relation to its Structure." JETS 20.3 (1977): 213–30.

Van Bruggen, Jacob. "The Lord's Prayer and Textual Criticism." CTJ 17 (1981): 78–87.

Van De Sandt, Huub. "'Do Not Give What Is Holy to the Dogs' (Did. 9:5D and Matt. 7:6A): The Eucharistic Food of the Didache in Its Jewish Purity Setting." VC 56 (2002): 223–46.
Van Tilborg, Sjef. "A Form-Criticism of the Lord's Prayer." NovT 14 (1972): 94–105.
Vermes, Geza. *Jesus and the World of Judaism*. Minneapolis: Fortress, 2003.
Vermes, Geza. *Jesus the Jew*. Philadelphia: Fortress, 1981.
Vledder, E.-J. "'Laat uw Naam geheiligd worden': Een uiting van eerbied aan God." HTR 67.1 (2011): 1–6.
Von Lipps, Hermann. "Schweine füttert man, Hunde nicht—ein Versuch, das Rätsel von Matthäus 7:6 zu lösen." ZNW 79 (1988): 165–85.
Walker, W. O. "The Lord's Prayer in Matthew and in John." NTS 28 (1982): 237–56.
Watson, Francis. *Gospel Writing: A Canonical Perspective*. Grand Rapids: Eerdmans, 2013.
Welch, John W., ed. *Chiasmus in Antiquity: Structures, Analyses, Exegesis*. Hildesheim: Gerstenberg, 1981.
Wenham, David. *From Good News to Gospels: What Did the First Christians Say About Jesus?* Grand Rapids: Eerdmans, 2018.
Wenham, David. *Paul: Follower of Jesus or Founder of Christianity?* Grand Rapids: Eerdmans, 1995.
Wenham, David. "Preaching the Sermon on the Mount." In *We Proclaim the Word of Life: Preaching the New Testament Today*, 73–86. Edited by Ian Paul and David Wenham. Nottingham: IVP, 2013.
Wenham, David. "The Kingdom of God and Daniel." ExpTim 98.5 (1987): 132–4.
Wenham, David. "The Sevenfold Form of the Lord's Prayer in Matthew's Gospel." ExpTim 121 (2010): 379–82.
White, Aaron, David Wenham, and Craig A. Evans, eds. *The Earliest Perceptions of Jesus in Context: Essays in Honour of John Nolland*. LNTS. London: Bloomsbury, 2018.
Williams, James G. "Paraenesis, Excess, and Ethics: Matthew's Rhetoric in the Sermon on the Mount." Semeia 50 (1990): 163–87.
Willis, Wendell, ed. *The Kingdom of God in 20th-Century Interpretation*. Peabody: Hendrickson, 1987.
Willitts, Joel. *Matthew's Messianic Shepherd-King: In Search of "The Lost Sheep of the House of Israel."* Beiherfte Zur Zeitschrift Für Die Neutestamentliche Wissenschaft. Berlin: Walter de Gruyter, 2007.
Willitts, Joel. "Presuppositions and Procedures in the Study of the 'Historical Jesus': Or, Why I Decided Not to Be A 'Historical Jesus' Scholar." JSHJ 3.1 (2005): 61–108.
Wright, N. T. *Jesus and the Victory of God*. COQG 2. Minneapolis: Fortress, 1996.
Wright, N. T. *Matthew for Everyone: Chapter 1–15*. New Testament for Everyone. Louisville: WJKP, 2004.
Wright, N. T. *The Lord and His Prayer*. London: SPCK, 1996.
Wright, N. T. "The Lord's Prayer as a Paradigm of Christian Prayer." In *Into God's Presence: Prayer in the New Testament*, 132–54. Edited by Richard N. Longenecker. Grand Rapids: Eerdmans, 2001.
Wright, N. T. *The New Testament and the People of God*. COQG 2. Minneapolis: Fortress, 1992.
Yamauchi, Edwin M. "The 'Daily Bread' Motif in Antiquity." WTJ 28 (1966):145–56.
Young, Brad. *The Jewish Background to the Lord's Prayer*. Austin: Center for Judaic-Christian Studies, 1984.

Index of Primary Sources

Genesis
  1:1   73
  3:1-9   189
  12   72
  22:1-19   189
  22:16-18   108
  43:18   187

Exodus
  3:13-14   179
  16   147
  16:1-36   146
  16:11-12   146
  20:7   177, 181, 183, 185
  20:13   194
  23:19   187
  29:33   197

Leviticus
  2:3   197
  10:3   184
  18:21   177
  19:12   177, 184
  19:22   184
  20:3   177, 181
  21:6   177
  22:2   177
  22:10-16   197
  22:32   177
  25   162
  25:8-17   162
  262:19   73

Numbers
  18:8-9   197
  30:3   184
  31:54   187

Deuteronomy
  4:19   73
  6:4-6   182
  15   162
  15:1-11   162
  15:2   161
  16-18   168
  23:10   113–14
  23:21-23   184
  27-30   138
  32:6   72
  33:13   73

Joshua
  10:11   73

1 Samuel
  16:7   77

2 Samuel
  13:22   113, 115

2 Kings
  17:16   73

1 Chronicles
  16:31   73
  16:33   131
  16:35   181
  28:5-7   131
  29   73
  29:10   72

2 Chronicles
  19:5-10   168

Esther
  4:8   114

Index of Primary Sources

Job
- 1:1 — 113–14
- 1:8 — 113–14

Psalms
- 2 — 134
- 6:5 — 108
- 7:2 — 108
- 16:13 — 108, 113–16, 118
- 18:49 — 178
- 21:17 — 198
- 21:21 — 113–14
- 22:1 — 71, 208
- 22:8 — 108
- 22:16 — 198
- 22:25 — 208
- 37:11 — 97
- 38:9 — 113–15, 121
- 40:8 — 91
- 42:1 — 113–14, 117–18
- 68:5-6 — 72
- 74:7 — 177
- 78:9 — 113–14, 116
- 79:9 — 116
- 89:20-29 — 72
- 106:47 — 181
- 119:2 — 113–14, 118
- 139:2 — 113–14
- 145:21 — 181

Proverbs
- 11:22 — 195
- 30 — 178
- 30:7-9 — 146, 177
- 30:8-9 — 146

Isaiah
- 6:3 — 184
- 13:6 — 131
- 14:19 — 134
- 23:17 — 134
- 24:2 — 161
- 24:21-23 — 129
- 24:23 — 131
- 26:21 — 131
- 29 — 181
- 29:18 — 130
- 29:23 — 181
- 35:5-6 — 130
- 37:16 — 134
- 41:21 — 129
- 52:7 — 128
- 57:15 — 72
- 61 — 161
- 61:1 — 138
- 61:10-11 — 117
- 63:10-17 — 19
- 63:16 — 72, 113–14, 116
- 64:8 — 72
- 65:25 — 120

Jeremiah
- 15:4 — 134
- 29:18 — 134
- 31:9 — 72
- 34:16 — 177
- 44:17-23 — 73
- 50:41 — 134

Ezekiel
- 20:33 — 129
- 36 — 181
- 36:20 — 177
- 36:22-32 — 180
- 36:23 — 181
- 36:24 — 181
- 39:7 — 177, 181
- 43:7-8 — 177

Daniel
- 2-7 — 74, 129, 133–6
- 2:10 — 134
- 2:18 — 134
- 2:19 — 134
- 2:28 — 134
- 2:44 — 134
- 3:1-18 — 134
- 3:26 — 134
- 3:28 — 134
- 4:1-3 — 135
- 4-5 — 135
- 4:10-11 — 135
- 4:13-17 — 135
- 4:15-17 — 135
- 4:25-27 — 135
- 4:28-33 — 135
- 4:37 — 135

6:7-8	134	4:1	190
6:7	135	4:1-4	147
6:10-18	134	4:1-10	112, 145–6, 190–2
6:22	135		
6:26	135	4:2-4	190
7:1-8	134	4:5-7	190
7:7-8	13	4:8	126
7:9	134	4:8-10	190
7:13-14	73, 131	4:10	109, 190
7:13	134	4:17	125, 128
7:22	134	4:17-11:1	31
7:23	134	4:23	125, 128
7:25	134	5-7	1, 24, 49, 107, 123, 175, 212–15
Joel			
2:1	131	5	71
		5:1	24, 55
Amos		5:1-2	11–12, 16, 24, 31, 36–7, 41, 54, 56
2:7	177, 181		
8:11	93		
		5:1-48	11
Micah		5:1-6:18	54
1:3	131	5:1-8:1	23
4	127	5:2-7:27	36
4:1-8	129–30	5:3	98, 125
4:6	127	5:3-10	40–3, 56, 93, 137, 161, 173, 205
4:8	19, 126, 128–9, 131		
4:10	127	5:3-12	16, 34, 36, 89, 92, 96–8, 133, 205
4:11	127		
		5:3-16	11–12, 31–2, 56
Zephaniah		5:3-7:12	11
3:3	120	5:3-7:27	56
3:15	129, 131	5:5	98, 201
		5:6	85, 92, 97–8, 136, 148, 154, 206
Zechariah			
14:1	131		
14:9	128–9, 131		
		5:7	167, 157, 168, 173, 206
Malachi			
2:10	72	5:9	75–6, 84–5, 99, 205
4:5	131		
		5:10	92, 94, 117, 125
Matthew		5:10-12	117
1-4	130	5:10-16	94–5
3:2	125	5:11	107, 117, 206
3:15	92	5:11-12	8, 10, 43, 56, 78, 108, 193, 201
3:16-17	77		
4	62	5:11-16	40–1, 56

5:12	117	5:33-37	10, 51, 100, 117, 177, 184–5, 201, 205–6
5:13	22, 37, 98–9		
5:13-16	33–4, 38, 44, 56–7, 83, 88–9, 95–6, 98–9, 183, 205		
		5:34-35	88–9, 95–6
		5:34-37	8–9
		5:35	129
5:13-7:12	36	5:37	10, 107, 109–11, 117–18, 185, 206
5:14	22, 98		
5:16	8–9, 32, 75–6, 82–3, 85, 88, 94–5, 177–8, 180, 184, 201, 205		
		5:38-42	51, 157, 170, 173, 193, 201, 206
		5:38-48	16
5:17	57	5:39	8, 10, 107, 118, 206
5:17-19	9, 40, 42–3		
5:17-20	12, 34, 37–8, 42, 57, 83, 92, 99, 102, 138–9, 173, 205, 207	5:39-42	108, 171
		5:42	8–9
		5:43-47	51, 101, 171, 173, 194, 201, 206
5:17-45	31		
5:17-48	11, 32, 37, 44–5, 54, 98	5:44	7, 8–9, 118
		5:45	10, 75–6, 78–9, 81, 83, 85, 89, 96, 101, 107, 109–10, 118–19, 180, 205–6
5:18	88–9, 92, 95, 100		
5:18-19	100		
5:19	125		
5:20	31, 34, 41, 43, 89, 92, 96, 100–1, 125	5:46-48	33
		5:47-58	41
		5:47-48	41
5:21	51	5:48	8–9, 60, 75–6, 82–3, 85, 96, 101–2, 180, 205–6
5:21-26	51, 75–76, 84–5, 157, 168–9, 205–6		
5:21-47	41	6	71
5:21-48	6, 12, 34, 51–3, 55, 57, 59–60, 83, 130, 184	6:1	40–1, 75–6, 84–5, 88, 92, 94–6, 102–3, 155, 180, 205–6
5:21-7:11	51	6:1-6	7, 12, 51
5:21-7:12	34, 199	6:1-7:11	34
5:22-24	8–9	6:1-18	6, 7, 31–2, 34, 37, 39, 44, 46, 76–8, 84, 154, 194, 201
5:23-24	167		
5:23-25	85		
5:26	169		
5:27-30	51, 186, 193–4, 202, 206	6:1-21	88–9, 95
5:29-30	193, 195	6:2-18	35, 41, 6, 841
5:31-32	51, 193	6:2-4	1, 6
5:33	51	6:4	75–6, 84–5, 180, 205

6:5	84, 140	6:19-7:11	11–12, 34, 36–7, 46, 49, 51–3
6:5-6	1, 5, 60, 77, 91		
6:5-8	29, 139	6:19-7:12	13, 31, 39, 54–5, 59–61
6:5-15	6, 46, 60, 78, 91		
6:6	75–6, 78–9, 81, 84–5, 180, 205	6:19-7:23	11
		6:19-7:27	44
6:7	105	6:19-21	8–9, 40–1, 47, 58, 96, 102–4, 148, 155, 173, 194, 206
6:7-8	12, 51, 60, 78, 91, 151		
6:7-11	151		
6:7-13	6	6:19-7:23	107
6:7-15	6, 7, 11, 44, 46	6:22-23	37, 59, 108, 119
6:8	35, 71, 75–6, 78–9, 81, 84–5, 180, 205	6:22-24	104, 194, 206
		6:22-34	155
		6:22-7:12	41–3, 46
6:9	1, 68, 76, 139–40, 180, 203	6:23	10, 119, 206
		6:24	17, 37, 59, 148, 155–6, 173, 202, 206
6:9-10	11, 133		
6:9-13	1, 7, 11, 65, 123, 140, 175		
		6:24-35	44, 59
		6:24–7:11	38
6:9-15	1, 35	6:25-32	78
6:10	35, 85, 94, 125–6, 139–40, 154, 165	6:25-33	38, 88, 95, 104, 206
6:11	47, 87, 143, 153–4, 156	6:25-34	8–9, 11, 19, 35, 47, 52, 58–9, 78, 89, 96, 139, 145, 148–9, 152, 155, 173, 194, 201–2
6:12	47, 60, 157–9, 165, 171		
6:13	47, 109–11, 118, 140, 171, 187		
		6:26	75–6, 78–9, 81, 85, 180, 205
6:14	75, 78–9, 85, 157, 180, 205		
6:14-15	6, 12, 19, 51, 60, 76, 78, 81, 84, 161, 165–8, 173, 206	6:26-30	96
		6:30	144, 152–3
		6:31	150
		6:31-34	143, 149, 151
		6:32	75–6, 78–9, 81, 85, 140, 180, 205
6:15	76, 78–9, 81, 85, 180, 205		
6:16	84	6:33	4, 59, 78, 92, 105, 126, 136, 139–140, 149, 156, 173, 205–6
6:16-18	1, 7, 12, 51		
6:18	39, 75–6, 84–5, 180, 205		
6:19	38	6:34	38, 151
6:19-20	35	7	35
6:19-23	44	7:1-2	37, 39–40
6:19-24	11–12, 35, 46–7, 52, 58	7:1-5	12, 17, 35, 47–8, 59, 157, 171–3, 194–6, 198, 202, 206
6:19-34	11, 32, 47, 51–2, 58		

7:1-6	11, 45, 48	7:24-27	17, 34, 206
7:1-11	51–2, 197	7:28	17, 24, 55
7:1-12	32, 59	7:28-29	41
7:3-5	37	7:28-8:1	12, 31, 36–7, 24, 54–6
7:5	45		
7:6	11, 35, 37, 45–8, 59, 186, 195–202, 206	8:1	55
		8:8	179
		8:11	125
7:6-10	110	8:12	126
7:7	45, 139	8:20	133
7:7-11	2, 7, 11, 35, 38, 46, 59, 79, 82, 108, 145, 149, 153–4, 173, 195–6, 198, 200, 203	8:25	179
		9:4	109
		9:13	167
		9:27	167
		9:35	125, 128
		10:5	197
7:7-12	11, 44–5, 58	10:7	125
7:8	154	10:22	117, 179
7:9	153	10:31	75
7:11	8–10, 35, 75–6, 78–9, 85, 119–20, 153, 180, 205–6	10:32-33	75, 88, 95
		10:33-34	88, 95
		11:11	125
		11:12	125
7:12	12, 17, 34–5, 49, 57, 60, 96, 105, 202–3, 206	11:23	88, 95
		11:25	69, 88, 95
		11:25-26	71
7:13-14	34, 56, 121, 141–2, 173, 205	12:7	167
		12:8	133
7:13-20	41, 43, 56	12:21	179
7:13-23	11, 34	12:25	126
7:13-27	12, 31–2, 34, 36, 45–6, 56–7, 183	12:26	109, 126
		12:28	18–19, 126, 133
7:15-20	56	12:33-37	136
7:15-23	34	12:34-35	110, 117
7:16-20	17	12:34	109
7:17	109–10	12:35	108–9, 111
7:17-18	10, 120, 206	12:38-42	133
7:18	109–10	12:39	109–10
7:19	120	12:45	109–10
7:21	8–10, 17, 74–6, 82, 85, 91, 94–5, 106, 125, 141, 180, 205–6	12:50	74, 83, 86, 91, 136
		13	192
		13:11	125
7:21-23	56, 130, 140, 173, 177, 185–6, 205	13:18-23	193
		13:19	109, 111, 121, 125, 136
7:21-27	41, 43, 57	13:19-21	193
7:22	106, 179	13:20-21	187
7:23	10, 121, 206	13:22-23	136

13:23	136	18:17	198
13:24	125	18:18	88, 95
13:31	125	18:18-19	89
13:33	125	18:19	75
13:37	133	18:20	84, 179
13:38	109, 111, 121, 125	18:21-22	164
		18:23	125
13:41	121, 126	18:23-35	81, 158–60, 164, 166, 168, 172
13:41-42	133		
13:43	126	18:24	159
13:44	125	18:28	159
13:45	125	18:30	159
13:45-46	197	18:32	109, 159
13:49	109	18:33	164, 167
13:51-52	1	18:34	159
13:52	125	18:35	75, 165
14:30	179	19:12	125
15:13	75	19:14	125, 133
15:19	109	19:16-30	141
15:21-28	198	19:19	88, 95
15:22	167, 179	19:23	125, 141
15:24-26	197	19:24	125, 141
15:25	179	19:29	179
16	71	20:1	125
16:4	108	20:14	163
16:8	152	20:15	109, 119
16:17	76	20:17-19	133
16:17-19	88–9, 95	20:21	126
16:19	88, 95, 125	20:30-31	167
16:23	109	20:30-33	179
16:27-28	133	21:9	179
16:28	126	21:25-26	88, 95
17:15	167, 179	21:31	86–7, 91–3, 126, 133
17:25-18:1	88, 95		
18	71, 87, 164–5, 170, 172	21:32	92
		21:43	136
18:1	125	22:2	125
18:3	125	22:10	109
18:4	125	22:18	109
18:5	179	23:9	74, 88, 95
18:6-9	87, 164	23:13	89, 125
18:6-14	136	23:14	89
18:7-20	194	23:15	89
18:10-14	164–5	23:16	89, 159
18:11	133	23:16-22	184–5
18:14	83, 86–7, 91, 164	23:16-23	159
		23:18	159
18:15-20	87	23:23	89
18:15-22	164	23:25	89

23:27	89	6:23	126
23:28	121	8:33	109
23:31	167	8:34	143
23:39	179	9:1	126
24:5	179	9:43-48	212
24:7	126	9:47	126
24:9	179	9:49-50	22, 212
24:10	193	9:50	98
24:12	121	10:11-12	212
24:14	125, 128	10:14	126
24:15-16	133	10:15	126
24:21	188	10:23	126
24:30	88–9, 95, 133	10:24	126
24:35	88–9, 95	10:25	126
25:1	125	11:10	126
25:31-32	133	11:18	143
25:31-46	136, 167	11:22-26	166
25:34	126	11:25	69, 166, 169, 213
26:29	126		
26:31-35	193	11:26	213
26:36-46	191, 193, 207	12:34	126
26:32	91	13:8	126
26:39	87, 91	13:26	88
26:41	87, 190–2	13:27	88
26:42	83, 86–7, 91, 106, 191	13:31	88, 212
		14:25	126
26:46	128	14:36	86–7
26:64	133	14:38	190
27:43	108	15:34	71, 208
27:46	208	15:43	126
28:16-20	179		
28:18	88, 95	Luke	
28:19	179	1:33	126
28:19-20	198	1:35	79
		1:49	178
Mark		1:66	158
1:13	109	1:74	108
1:15	126, 128, 139	2:37	143
1:22	213	3:19	108
3:23	109	3:22	79
3:24	126	4:2	109
3:26	109	4:3	109
3:35	86	4:6	109
4:11	126	4:13	109
4:15	109	4:18-19	130
4:21	22, 99, 212	4:25	88
4:24-25	213	4:43	126, 139
4:26	126	5:8	119
4:30	126	5:18-19	187

5:30	119	10:9	126
5:37	110	10:11	126
5:45	110	10:18	109
6:13	110	10:21	88
6:20	16, 126	11:1	1
6:20-26	89	11:1-13	1, 11, 78
6:20-23	16, 34	11:2	68, 125-6, 151
6:20-49	1, 18, 31-4, 60, 212-15	11:2-4	1, 6, 18, 46, 60, 65, 123-4, 175, 204
6:21	97		
6:27-28	118	11:3	143, 145
6:27-36	16	11:4	156-8, 167
6:27-42	34	11:9-13	79
6:31	17	11:13	21, 69, 79-80, 108
6:32	119, 158		
6:32-35	118	11:17	126
6:33	119, 158	11:18	109
6:34	119	11:20	126
6:35	79, 108	11:26	108-9
6:36	80, 83, 166	11:29	108-9
6:37-42	17	11:33	22, 99
6:45	108-9, 111, 120	11:34	108
6:43-45	17, 34, 120-1	11:39	108
6:46	17, 106, 140	12	151
6:47-49	34, 17	12:22-34	150
6:49	106	12:24	80
7:1	17	12:28	152
7:8	158	12:30-32	150
7:17	110	12:30	151, 198
7:18	110	12:31	126, 151
7:21	108	12:32	79-80, 126
7:28	126	12:47	86
7:30	92	12:51	88
7:34	119	12:56	88
7:37	119	13:2	119
7:39	119	13:16	109
8:1	126	13:18	126
8:2	108	13:20	126
8:10	126	13:25-27	121, 140
8:11-15	193	13:27	121
8:12	109	13:28	126
8:13	187, 193	13:29	126
8:16	22, 99	14:15	126
9:2	126	14:34	99
9:11	126	14:34-35	22, 98
9:23	140	14:35	99
9:27	126	15:1	119
9:60	126	15:2	119
9:62	126	15:7	119

15:10	119	12:32	83
16:5	159	17:11	179
16:7	159	17:15	111, 118
16:13	17	22:42	87
16:17	88		
16:19	143	Acts	
16:16	126	2:33	80
17:10	159	2:46-47	143
17:20	126	3:2	143
17:21	126	4:23-31	79
18:13	114, 119	7:26	145
18:16	126	10:47	158
18:17	126	11:17	158
18:24	126	13:33	158
18:25	126	16:5	143
18:29	126	16:11	145
19:7	119	17:11	143
19:11	126	17:20	187
19:22	108	17:28	158
19:38	126	19:9	143
19:47	143	20:15	145
21:10	126	20:19	192
21:27	88	20:29	120
21:31	126	21:26	145
21:33	88	22:5	158
21:36	193	25:10	158
22:3	109		
22:16	126	Romans	
22:18	126	3:10	112, 188
22:29	126	9:17	179
22:30	126	12:9	111
22:31	109	14:17	133
22:37	158	15:9	178
22:40	190		
22:41-44	71	1 Corinthians	
22:42	86–7	4:20	133
22:46	190	16:22	19
22:53	143		
22:59	158	2 Corinthians	
23:25	86	11:20	118
23:34	71		
23:42	126	Galatians	
23:51	126	1:4	111
24:7	119		
24:41	143	Ephesians	
		1:7	167
John		6:16	111
11:41-42	71		
12:28	178–9, 184		

Philippians		1 Macc.	74, 159
2:9	179	3 Macc.	72
		PsSol.	113–16, 118, 120–1
Colossians			
1:13-14	133	Sir.	72, 113, 114, 165, 189, 192 n.67
3:5	194		
4:11	133		
		Tob,.	114
1 Thessalonians		Wis.	72
5:15	118		
		Other Early Jewish and Christian Literature	
1 Timothy		Gen. Rab.	162
6:7	187	Ex. Rab.	162, 192 n.67
		Pesiq. R.	162
2 Timothy		Tg. Isa.	115, 132 n.41
4:18	111, 113, 115–16	Tg. Mic.	132
		Tg. Neof. Ex.	162
		Tg. OnkE.	162
Hebrews		Tg. Zech.	132 n. 41
2:17	167	B. Bat.	116 n.191
4:15	190	y. Ber.	132 n.41
10:29	198	b. ʿAbod. Zar.	74 n.35
11:17-19	189	b. Ber.	115, 132 n.41, 183, 192 n.67
13:15	178		
		b. Hag.	116 n.191
James		b. Menah.	192 n.67
1:2	190	b. Ned.	100 n.141
5:12	212	b. Sanh.	74 n.35, 93 n.107, 192 n.67
1 Peter			
1:6	190	b. Taʾan.	73 n.29, 75 n.37
		b. Yebam.	182
2 Peter		t. Ned.	100 n.141
2:9	192	m. ʾAbot	39, 74 n.35
		m. Ber.	136 n.64
1 John		m. Cant. R.	132 n.41
1:5	119	m. Kil.	74 n.35
2:13	111	m. Ned.	100 n.141
		m. Sanh.	100 n.141
Revelation		m. Šebu	100 n.141
2:10	190	m. Sotah.	74 n.35
3:10	19, 112, 188	m. Taʾan.	75 n.37
22:20	131–2	m. Yoma.	74 n.35, 131, 163
Pseudepigrapha/Apocrypha		Josephus	72
Apoc. Bar.	132	Did.	3, 16 n.7, 67 n.9, 116 n.94, 144 n.94, 157 n.135, 186, 196
Add. Est.	116 n.193		
As. Mos.	132 n.41		
1 En.	95 n.117, 182, 197 n.96		
		Gos. Thom.	197 n.94

Dead Sea Scrolls

1QH	72
4Q 'Amram B	115 n.188
4QLevi b	115
4Q280	115 n.189
4Q372	72
4Q544	115 n.188
11QMelchizedek	162
11QPs	115, 182 n.35, 192 n.67
CD	161

Index of Authors

Abraham, I. 165 n.170
Albright, W. F. and Mann, C. S. 29 n.2
Allen, Willoughby C. 29 n.2
Allison, Dale C. 3 n.7, 5, 6, 8, 10, 12 n.47, 24 n.47, 28, 36–40, 47 n.61, 48 n.63, 54, 55, 59, 60 n.96, 81, 98, 103 n.154, 120, 179, 188 n.50, 191, 196, 198, 203, 208
Anderson, Gary A. 161
Argyle, A. W. 29 n.2
Aune, David E. 18 n.16, 157 n.134

Bacon, Benjamin 31 n.6
Bailey, James L. and Lyle Vander Broek 40
Bandstra, Andrew J. 107 n.162
Barr, James 71 n.20
Barth, Karl 73
Bauckham, Richard 16 n.5, 136, 197 n.93
Bauman, Clarence 3 n.7
Baumgardt, David 130 n.30
Beare, F. W. 30 n.2
Beasley-Murray, G. R. 18 n.18, 127 n.15, 133 n.47
Bennett, Thomas J. 196 n.88
Betz, Hans Dieter 6, 7, 8, 9, 16 n.7, 23 n.41, 30 n.4, 58–9, 77 n.44, 107, 137, 159 n.141, 159 n.143, 161 n.148, 163, 188 n.50, 196 n.83, 203, 207 n.8
Bird, Michael F. 128 n.19
Black, Matthew 107 n.162, 115 n.187
Boda, Mark J. 25 n.50
Bonhoeffer, Dietrich 208 n.10
Borg, Marcus J. 127 n.14
Bornkamm, Günther 4, 5, 6, 10–12, 20, 21 n.32, 35, 36, 43–9, 54, 107, 121, 195 n.81, 196 n.84, 198–9, 203
Breck, John 40 n.41
Brown, Raymond 18–19, 90, 144 n.97, 180, 188 n.52
Bruner, F. D. 30 n.4
Byargeon, Rick W. 178 n.11

Caird, G. B. 131
Carson, D. A. 98 n.129
Carter, Warren 17 n.14, 37 n.30, 38, 51
Charlesworth, James H. 5 n.11, 25 n.53, 72 n.26, 75 n.37
Chilton, Bruce 72 n.26, 176 n.5
Clark, David 3 n.7
Collins, John J. 134
Conzelmann, H. 98 n.134
Crossan, John Dominic 130 n.27
Crump, David 16 n.7, 19, 20 n.26, 188 n.51, 188 n.53

D'Angelo, Mary Rose 71 n.20
Davies, W. D. 39
Davies, W. D. and Allison, D. C. 18 n.18, 18 n.20, 19 n.24, 68 n.10, 71 n.22, 91, 92 n.102, 93 n.107, 93 n.109, 102 n.148, 102 n.149, 105 n.158, 111 n.173, 131 n.40, 148 n.108, 155, 159 n.142, 163 n.166, 164, 166, 167, 168 n.182, 170 n.191, 170 n.192, 176 n.6, 179 n.15, 180 n.19, 182 n.31, 182 n.32, 188 n.52, 188 n.55
DeJonge, M. and Van Der Woude, A. S. 162 n.156
Drake, Lyndon 161 n.150
Draper, Jonathan 49 n.64
Duling, Dennis C. 125 n.4, 129 n.20
Dumbrell, W. J. 94 n.113
Dunn, James D. G. 16 n.7, 127 n.15, 129 n.20, 129 n.24
Dupont, J. 30 n.2

Eubank, Nathan 103 n.153, 156 n.132
Evans, Craig A. 4 n.10, 25 n.52, 30 n.2, 38 n.31, 72 n.26, 176 n.5

Fenton, J. C. 102 n.149, 103
Finkel, A. 16 n.6
Fitzmyer, Joseph A. 162 n.158, 187 n.48

Flusser, David 25 n.51, 115 n.190
Foerster, Werner 144 n.96
Foster, Paul 94 n.114
Foster, Robert 126 n.6
France, R. T. 1–2, 13 n.50, 22 n.38, 30 n.2, 43 n.49, 56 n.80, 58, 78 n.49, 92 n.102, 138 n.70, 167 n.179, 169 n.189
Friedlander, Gerald 181 n.29

Garland, David 6, 7, 30 n.2, 145 n.146, 146 n.104, 155, 167
Garlington, Don 9 n.136
Gerhardsson, Birger 4 n.10, 112 n.182, 130 n.29
Gibson, Jeffrey B. 18 n.17, 130–3, 182, 187 n.47, 205
Goldin, J. 39 n.37
Goldingay, John 134
Goodacre, Mark 16 n.2, 16 n.3, 21 n.33
Goshen-Gottstein, Alon 72 n.24
Goulder, M. D. 4 n.10, 43 n.52
Green, H. Benedict 38 n.31, 43 n.52
Greenman, Jeffrey P. 3 n.7
Grundmann, Walter 6, 10–11, 43–9, 54, 120 n.209, 137 n.66, 203
Guelich, Robert 6, 10–11, 17 n.9, 30, 32 n.11, 33–6, 43–9, 54, 79 n.50, 81, 84, 91 n.91, 92 n.99, 99 n.103, 97 n.122, 102 n.150, 105 n.158, 111 n.173, 136, 143, 152 n.117, 172 n.198, 182 n.32
Gundry, Robert H. 4 n.10, 19 n.21, 21 n.34, 75 n.39, 92 n.100, 98 n.131, 102 n.149, 111 n.173, 119, 120, 138 n.72, 139 n.75, 142, 163 n.166, 164 n.168, 196 n.84, 196 n.86, 198
Gupta, Nijay K. 25 n.53, 179 n.18, 180 n.22
Gurtner, Daniel M. 92 n.99

Hagner, Donald 1, 42 n.48, 56 n.82, 57 n.87, 58 n.90, 74, 83, 92 n.99, 98 n.133, 98 n.135, 118, 156, 169, 197, 198
Harder, G. 114 n.184
Hare, Douglas R. A. 30 n.2
Harrington, D. J. 30 n.2
Hatina, Thomas R. 20 n.31
Hauck, F. 160 n.145
Hays, Richard B. 24–7, 163 n.161
Heinemann, Joseph 4 n.10, 16 n.6

Hemer, Colin 142, 145, 151 n.114
Hendrickx, Herman 30 n.2
Hill, David 30 n.3
Hinkle, Mary 5, 6, 7, 8–10, 203
Holmes, Michael 116 n.194
Hood, Jason 20, 23 n.45
Huizenga, Leroy A. 25 n.49

Instone-Brewer, David 25 n.52

Jeremias, Joachim 4 n.10, 17, 18 n.18, 25 n.54, 37 n.30, 69 n.14, 71 n.20, 72, 75 n.37

Keener, Craig S. 4 n.10, 19 n.21, 30 n.4, 71, 92 n.102, 102 n.149, 111 n.173, 143, 154 n.125, 162 n.160, 169, 172, 182 n.32, 198 n.99, 200, 207 n.8
Kennedy, George A. 23 n.41, 30 n.4
Kiley, Mark 5, 6, 10–11, 75 n.37, 107, 121, 126 n.10, 141, 164 n.169, 165 n.169
Kingsbury, Jack 5, 6, 10, 30–3, 36, 54
Kistemaker, Simon J. 3 n.7
Knowles, Michael 20 n.28
Kürzinger, Josef 12 n.48

Lachs, Samuel T. 116 n.191
Ladd, George E. 17, 133 n.45
Lambrecht, J. 6, 10, 11, 12 n.47, 48 n.62, 172 n.198
Leonard, Jeffrey 26
Lightfoot, J. B. 145
Lischer, Richard 17 n.14
Llewelyn, Stephen 195 n.82
Lochman, Jan Milič 5 n.10
Lohmeyer, Ernst 5, 62 n.102, 111–12, 180 n.23, 181 n.28
Lundbom, Jack R. 103 n.153, 104 n.156, 155 n.130
Lund, Nils W. 40 n.41
Lunde, Jonathan 74 n.34
Luz, Ulrich 3 n.7, 6, 10, 12–14, 19, 22 n.36, 24 n.47, 25 n.50, 39, 43 n.53, 49–53, 55, 57 n.83, 57 n.86, 58, 61 n.100. 67, 71 n.22, 78 n.47, 98 n.130, 102 n.147, 111 n.179, 116 n.195, 144 n.95, 152 n.115, 163 n.162, 165, 166 n.172, 168 n.184, 177 n.7, 181 n.30, 188 n.53, 192, 197, 198 n.100, 203

Manson, T. W. 5 n.10
Marshall, I. Howard 19 n.21, 20 n.30, 74 n.34, 206 n.4
Martin, Michael Wade 144 n.90
Martínez, F. Garcia 115 n.188, 161 n.154
Matson, Mark A. 16 n.2
Mattison, William C. 5 n.11, 6, 17 n.14, 206 n.4
Mauser, Ulrich W. 74 n.32
McArthur, Harvey K. 3 n.7
McEleney, Neil J. 30 n.3
McKnight, Scot 19 n.21, 20 n.30, 74 n.34, 99 n.138, 102 n.145, 125 n.3, 133 n.45, 171 n.197, 177, 185 n.41, 195 n.80
McNamara, Martin 162
Meier, John 6, 10–11, 18 n.18, 30 n.2, 46 n.59, 129 n.23
Menken, M. J. J. 25 n.52
Metzger, Bruce M. 142 n.83
Metzler, Norman 176 n.5
Migliore, Daniel L. 3 n.7, 25 n.53
Milton, A. Edward 116 n.191
Minear, Paul S. 99 n.136, 191 n.63
Montefiore, C. G. 25 n.52
Morris, Leon 72
Moule, C. F. D. 188 n.50, 191 n.65
Mounce, William D. 163
Mowery, Robert L. 70 n.17, 82 n.60, 87 n.76, 179, 180
Muilenburg, James 22–4, 27

Nel, Marius J. 161 n.150
Neusner, Jacob 125 n.5
Nijman, M. and Worp, K. A. 142 n.83
Nolland, John 5 n.10, 19 n.21, 22 n.36, 30 n.2, 38 n.31, 62 n.104, 66 n.2, 71 n.22, 80 n.53, 90 n.88, 91 n.92, 92 n.99, 97 n.122, 105 n.158, 132, 144, 160, 161 n.150, 167, 169 n.187, 176 n.6, 179 n.116, 182, 188 n.54, 188 n.55, 194 n.75
Nygaard, Mathias 17 n.14, 179 n.18, 206 n.4

Oakman, Douglas E. 130 n.27, 161 n.148
O'Donovan, Oliver 5 n.11, 6, 7
Olsthoorn, M. F. 149

Pamment, Margaret 125 n.5
Patte, Daniel 6, 40–3, 49, 54, 55

Pennington, Jonathan 4 n.8, 6, 12, 14, 56 n.81, 62 n.104, 69, 73 n.31, 74 n.33, 74 n.35, 77 n.44, 77 n.45, 81 n.57, 88, 95, 96 n.119, 96 n.121, 97 n.123, 98 n.127, 102 n.149, 103, 133, 134, 136 n.61, 136 n.64, 138 n.71, 85 n.44, 188 n.50, 195 n.79, 197 n.90, 197 n.95, 203, 207
Perrin, Norman 127, 128 n.16
Perry, Alfred M. 60
Petuchowski, Jakob J. 4 n.10, 73 n.29
Pitre, Brant 18 n.18, 126 n.11, 127 n.12, 129 n.24, 130, 131, 132, 162 n.158, 181, 188 n.52
Plummer, Alfred 30 n.2
Procksch, O. 177 n.10
Przybylski, Benno 87 n.75m, 92 n.105, 93–5, 103

Quarles, Charles 5, 6, 49 n.64, 83, 91 n.94, 97 n.126, 98 n.132, 99, 100–1, 105, 112, 129 n.24, 132 n.44, 133, 138 n.72, 158 n.138, 163 n.166, 168, 171, 179 n.14, 184–5, 190 n.61, 194

Riesner, Rainer 12 n.48, 16 n.4
Rowland, Christopher 39 n.39
Runge, Steve E. 77 n.44

Schnackenburg, Rudolf 6, 10–11, 46 n.59
Schürmann, Heinz 180 n.23
Schweizer, E. 10–11
Seesemann, H. 189, 190 n.59
Stanton, Graham 1, 8 n.23, 22, 52 n.72, 58 n.89, 85, 97 n.124, 97 n.125
Stassen, Glen 36 n.26, 38, 99 n.137, 198–200
Stendahl, Krister 167 n.179
Stevenson, Kenneth 3 n.7
Strack, Hermann L. and Paul Billerbeck 25 n.52
Strecker, Georg 30 n.2
Swetnam, James 176 n.4, 176 n.5
Syreeni, Kari 89 n.83, 92 n.104, 96

Talbert, Charles 32 n.9, 32 n.10, 207 n.8
Tan, Randall K. J. 20 n.31
Thom, Johan C. 199 n.105
Tuttle, Gary A. 30 n.4

Van Bruggen, Jacob 107 n.162
Van De Sandt, Huub 196 n.85
Van Tilborg, Sjef 5 n.10
Vermes, Geza 73 n.29, 75 n.37, 107 n.162
Vledder, E.-J. 176 n.5
Von Lipps, Hermann 197 n.97

Walker, W. O. 111 n.177
Watson, Francis 13 n.53, 16 n.3
Welch, John W. 40 n.41
Wenham, David 16 n.4, 26, 38, 62, 92 n.101, 93, 111 n.177, 112, 133, 161, 178 n.13, 183

White, Aaron, Wenham, David and Evans, Craig A. 38 n.31, 107 n.162
Williams, James G. 8 n.23
Willis, Wendell 133 n.50
Willitts, Joel 2022 n.37, 24
Wright, N. T. 18 n.18, 67, 85, 128 n.15

Yamauchi, Edwin M. 145 n.102, 146 n.104, 148, 152
Young, Brad 91, 92 n.97, 158, 161